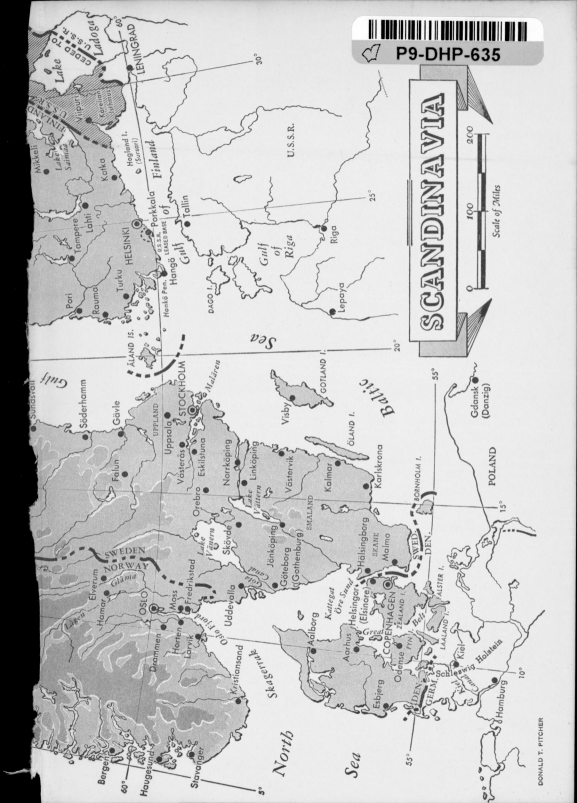

SCANDINAVIA

Scale of Miles

100   200

DONALD T. PITCHER

The Challenge of Scandinavia

NORWAY, SWEDEN, DENMARK
AND FINLAND IN
OUR TIME

By William L. Shirer

Novels

THE TRAITOR

STRANGER COME HOME

Nonfiction

BERLIN DIARY

END OF A BERLIN DIARY

MIDCENTURY JOURNEY

THE CHALLENGE OF SCANDINAVIA:
NORWAY, SWEDEN, DENMARK AND FINLAND IN OUR TIME

WILLIAM L. SHIRER

The Challenge of Scandinavia

NORWAY, SWEDEN, DENMARK
AND FINLAND IN OUR TIME

BOSTON · *Little, Brown and Company* · TORONTO

Fourth Printing

*Published simultaneously in Canada
by Little, Brown & Company (Canada) Limited*

PRINTED IN THE UNITED STATES OF AMERICA

To the Northern Peoples —

with Admiration

The world looks with admiration . . . to Scandinavia where . . . countries, without sacrificing their sovereignty, live united in their thought, in their economic practice and in their healthy way of life. From such fountains new and brighter opportunities may come to all mankind.

—Winston Churchill

In his message accepting the 1953 Nobel Prize for Literature

Contents

The Challenge of Scandinavia

NORWAY, SWEDEN, DENMARK
AND FINLAND IN
OUR TIME

CHAPTER I

Journey to the North

Between the wars, when a reporter in Europe was kept busy chronicling the frenzied peace, one heard of a bold and imaginative attempt by the Scandinavians — a pragmatic people, by all accounts — to build a genuinely democratic society which, by its own freely expressed will, offered to all its citizens a fair measure of personal security, well-being and an opportunity to lead a decent and even a creative life.

Americans who had visited the northern region of Europe called it the "Middle Way" — a way of life which had rejected the strait jacket of Communist tyranny on the one hand, and unbridled private enterprise on the other.

Some, such as Marquis Childs, the distinguished columnist, liked what they saw. Others — some businessmen, for example — were not so enthusiastic. They saw the northern countries being engulfed by "creeping socialism" and facing ruin from too much social welfare.

Someday I wanted to see for myself, but the opportunity did not come for a long time. To my editors back home, in the Twenties and Thirties, the northern countries were not big news. They were too quiet, too peaceful, too orderly, too fond of minding their own business. We correspondents were kept busy in the more troubled regions, which provided the headlines. We hustled from one crisis to another that led inexorably toward war.

The war that began in the autumn of 1939 engulfed all of neutral, peaceful Scandinavia except Sweden, cutting it off from an Allied correspondent. For years we had but scant news of what was really going on in occupied Denmark and Norway and in war-torn Finland. What exactly, I wondered, was the impact of the varying fortunes of war and occupation and resistance on these countries?

Recently, thanks to some free time, the interest of my publisher and the generous co-operation of the four countries themselves, I was finally able to journey to Norway, Sweden, Denmark and Finland,[1] seek answers to my questions and gather impressions and material for this report.

Some Initial, General Observations

I did not find in the North the Utopia so often depicted by a number of American and English writers. Likable as the Scandinavians are, and intelligent and warm and friendly and perceptive and tolerant and civilized, they turned out to be just as humanly fallible as other peoples I have known, including my own, involved in some of the same messes brought about by the same mistakes that are common to all modern societies, including those of the English-speaking world. This, of course, was no surprise. It would have been astonishing had it been otherwise.

Life in the northern countries is not a bed of roses. Men and women work hard for a modest living. The resources of the land, by our standards, are meager. The farmer in most parts of Norway, Sweden and Finland must struggle relentlessly with a rocky and not very fertile soil on an all too small plot, and in most instances he survives only because his wife and his sons and daughters also toil in the fields and in the barns and because his shrewdly operated co-ops — and often his government — insure him fair prices for what he buys and sells. In Denmark the farmer has a richer soil and a kinder climate and the most ingenious set of agricultural co-ops in the world, but his prosperity depends largely on prices set by British government officials in London, who arrange for the purchase of most of his product and who, he often complains, drive a hard and sometimes cruel bargain.

Economically all the four countries of the North are somewhat in

---

[1] Though Finland is not usually regarded as a Scandinavian state, I have included it in this study. Racially, of course, the Finns are a people quite apart from the Swedes, Norwegians and Danes; and the Finnish language is utterly different from that of the other three countries; it springs from quite other roots. However, Finland was a part of Sweden for six centuries, and from that connection and from its geographical position, it has much in common with the three other northern countries. It has the same devotion to democracy, its state church too is Lutheran, and the rise of the Labor party, the co-operative movement, social welfare, adult education, has been somewhat similar to that in Sweden, Norway and Denmark. Also, its story fascinated me and needed telling, I think, in any report such as this.

the position of Great Britain; they must export or expire. And this creates dire problems for Scandinavian businessmen, farmers and workers, who are never for a moment unaware that their well-being depends not so much on their own skills and creativeness as on the blind, unreasonable uncertainties of a world market over whose changing prices and demands they have little or no influence.

It is these uncertainties, which became acute with the establishment of modern industry, that have led in the North to the creation of "the welfare state." Until relatively recently the Scandinavian countries — even Norway, where only 3 per cent of the soil is tillable — were largely agricultural. Standards of living were necessarily low, but the family, functioning as a closely knit economic-social unit, did enjoy a good measure of security. The industrial revolution in the North, as elsewhere, raised the standard of living to heights undreamed of a century ago. But the Scandinavians believe that a price was paid for increasing prosperity that was unnecessarily high. This was the rapidly mounting insecurity of the individual; not only of the industrial worker, who suffered periodically from unemployment or whose living was destroyed through injury, illness or old age, but of almost everyone else in society — the farmer, the salaried man, the lawyer and doctor, the shipper, the seaman, the small businessman — whose well-being depended on the fickle ups-and-downs of national and world commerce.

This increase of personal insecurity, of course, has been common to all industrialized nations, and each in its own way, depending on its national background, character, political evolution and resources, has tried to meet the challenge. There is little doubt that the Scandinavians have gone further to meet it than any other peoples of the West.

The fabric of social welfare, however, is no longer an issue in Norway, Denmark and Sweden. While its vast extension in the last two decades is due largely to the efforts of Labor or Labor-dominated governments, the framework was established by Conservative or Liberal-Conservative governments before the rise of the Socialist parties.[2] There are still bitter debates in the press and parliaments

---

[2] As is the custom in Scandinavia, the terms "Labor," "Social-Democrat" and "Socialist" are used interchangeably in this book, to denote the party of the Left, which is dominant in Norway, Sweden and Denmark and the largest, by one Parliamentary vote, in Finland. In all four countries the party is similar to the Labor party of Great Britain and is, of course, violently anticommunist.

over details concerning the pace and the scope of new social welfare legislation. But on the desirability or the necessity of the basic program there is general agreement. Today social expenditures of the state, voted usually by large parliamentary majorities, amount to some 10 per cent of the net national incomes in Norway, Denmark, Sweden and Finland.

The Scandinavians do not delude themselves that they are getting something for nothing. They are much too hard-headed for that. They have simply decided — as it was explained to me time and again — that it is worth 10 per cent of their collective income to have the community — and not charity — see to it that everyone has a decent minimum standard of living and is protected against the disasters and disabilities which economic misfortune and other hazards of mortal life often threaten to inflict.

On the whole, labor and management appear to get along better in the North — with the possible exception of Finland — than in any other region I have known. This is due, as we shall see, to a number of developments, including mutual respect and mutual good will achieved after a half-century of often bitter conflict, the high degree of responsible, democratic organization on both sides, and the power of the Labor Courts to settle irrevocably disputes over the interpretation of collective agreements.

No one can tarry in the northern countries very long without becoming aware of the impressive part which the co-operative movements play in the lives of the people. They are much more than a form of economy. They have become a sort of way of life for millions of people, giving them not only a sense of participation in a powerful economic enterprise, but determining where and how and for how much they buy and sell and what they eat and wear, how they furnish their homes, manage their farms, and even what they read.

The number of co-ops in the four northern countries runs into the thousands. Roughly they may be divided into consumer and agricultural production co-operatives, but in my peregrinations I ran into wholesale co-ops, laundry co-ops, housing co-ops, co-operative burial societies, mortgage societies, credit and insurance societies, co-operative banks, oil companies, bakeries, mills, fisheries, publishing houses, travel agencies, film companies and, to top them all, in Sweden, a co-operative society to help rescue co-operative societies which have fallen into financial difficulties.

It is an impressive movement, but it has not replaced private enterprise in Scandinavia by any means. And unlike social welfare, it is completely independent of the state.

The northern countries, let me repeat, are neither Utopias nor social paradises. Not one of the hundreds of Norwegians, Finns, Swedes and Danes I visited with ever claimed that they were. Indeed in some cases I heard earnest people bemoaning, just as they do at home, the state of many things, including some of the very social problems that a social welfare state might have been expected to solve. Mass neurosis, they said, and crime and insanity, were ever on the increase; and in Denmark an eminent educator informed me that 85 per cent of the inmates of prisons there came from broken homes and that divorces had increased from 500 a year in 1900 to 7000 in 1950, though the population had only doubled — so that today one out of five Danish marriages ends in divorce.

And yet, as we shall see in some detail in the ensuing pages that take us to each of the four countries in turn, the northern peoples have succeeded in building a society that is indeed enviable. They are few in numbers and they are a homogeneous people and 97 per cent of them belong to the same Church, the Lutheran. But perhaps citizens of more populous lands which are not so homogeneous nor so free of religious differences but which may be richer and more powerful can learn a little from observing them. For it seemed to me that, by trial and error, by the exercise of intelligence, tolerance, perseverance and good will, they had managed to erect as genuine a democracy as there is on earth, not only a political democracy but a social and, in part, an economic democracy and that while it had not solved all its problems, and never would, it offered its members without exception a fair opportunity to live a life of some meaning both in and beyond the daily toil for a living, relieving them of some of the needless wear and tear and fear that saps the human spirit in so many other countries.

There was a leveling, to be sure, but it was a leveling upward and to the vast majority it seemed tolerably equitable. One could say of its results what the great Poet-Bishop N. F. S. Grundtvig, whose burning spirit rescued Denmark from national disintegration only a century ago, said of the Danes: "Few have too much and still fewer too little."

A Capsule of Geography

Even if you arrive in the late spring, as I did, after the snows have melted and the early flowers have burst into bloom, you quickly become aware of how far north the Scandinavian peoples dwell. It is not the cold but the light which tells. From the middle of May until the middle of August a soft twilight lingers throughout the short night in Oslo, Stockholm and Helsinki, and during the summer the street lights are not turned on in the Finnish capital. Farther north, above the Arctic Circle, the sun never sets for several weeks. This is the vaunted land of the midnight sun, one of Scandinavia's chief tourist attractions. At the North Cape, in Norway, the sun remains above the horizon continuously from May 22 to July 29.

The winters, conversely, are plunged into darkness most of the day; even in the southern regions there are only six hours of daylight in midwinter. Coming to Oslo in the spring I found the Norwegians in the midst of an annual rejoicing that marked their emergence from the long winter's hibernation, as they called it; and it was only then that I began to grasp the reason for the passion of these northern peoples for the sun — a passion which, before June is out, drives them en masse out of the cities and the towns to the countryside, the beaches and mountains, where they can drench themselves until mid-September in the light and the warmth of the solar rays.

It is the angle of the sun which reminds you that Scandinavia lies close to the cold top of the Northern Hemisphere. A glance at an ordinary globe, rather than at a Mercator projection map, will indicate just how close it is. Oslo, Stockholm and Helsinki, all of which are situated in the southern parts of their respective lands, lie astride the 60th parallel, which, running westward, touches the southern tip of Greenland, the northern corner of Labrador, continuing on through the middle of Hudson Bay and across the frozen wastes of northern Canada to Alaska well north of Sitka and Juneau. One third of Norway and Finland and a fifth of Sweden, all dotted with thriving towns, factories and mines, lie above the Arctic Circle.

No other extensive, civilized society thrives elsewhere at such a northerly latitude. How then can the Scandinavians prosper there? The answer lies in what meteorologists call the strangest weather anomaly on the surface of the globe.

It is the Gulf Stream, and the winds which blow its warmth east-ward, which make the Scandinavian peninsula and Finland habitable, bringing a relatively temperate climate and a rainfall adequate enough to make the soil sprout with the greenest of stable crops. Without this phenomenon most of Norway, Sweden and Finland would be an arctic wasteland, similar to Greenland, Labrador and northern Canada, and there would be no Scandinavian people to write of, except perhaps the few Lapps who still follow their reindeer herds in the Far North.

As it is, you can travel 350 miles north of the Arctic Circle to Tromsö, in Norway, and there find winter temperatures averaging well above freezing (37 degrees) with a comfortable summer average of a little over 50 degrees and with spring flowers beginning to bloom in February, which is weeks before there is the faintest sign of them in Oslo, a thousand miles to the south.

There are no railroads or highways north to Tromsö; you can get there only by boat (or lately, by plane) reminding you that it is the sea that has largely shaped the growth of the Scandinavian lands, unifying each of them and bringing them all together and turning their faces southward and westward across the waters. The sea is the main link of commerce in Norway and Denmark and between the four northern lands and between them and the outside world. In Norway, indeed, it is the rugged land which divides, making one re-gion inaccessible by rail or by car to the other; it is the sea which unites.

The northerly position of Scandinavia had one fortunate advan-tage for its peoples for about a thousand years. They lay just off the main lanes over which the continuing wars of Europe were fought. Sweden, it is true, sent its armies and navies south to battle and con-quer across the Baltic and in Russia. Denmark once saw its capital bombarded by a British fleet and also became involved in war with rapacious Prussia, which coveted and eventually grabbed southern Jutland. But on the whole (except when they were fighting each other) and especially after the Napoleonic wars (when they had ceased their fraternal wars), the Scandinavian countries were left in peace, managing successfully even to remain neutral and unravaged in the First World War. But the Second World War enveloped all of them except Sweden. And the shifting of world power out of Europe after the war into the hands of two non-European nations, Russia and the United States, involved even neutrality-obsessed Sweden. This development, coupled with the advent of the long-range bomber, the jet plane and the atom and hydrogen bomb, and the strides made in polar flying, had a staggering consequence and one which, I found, weighs heavily on the minds of the northern peoples today.

Geography, they were forced to learn, is not an abstraction, not something absolute, merely to be noted and measured on a map. It always bears a relationship with people, politics and technology. The revolution in politics and technology since 1945, they saw, brought about a revolution in Scandinavian geography!

Today, they realize, they no longer lie outside the main highways of war. They find themselves right in the middle of what is perhaps the main thoroughfare in any future conflict. They lie directly on the air route between Russia and the United States. But that is not all. Their once peaceful lands have suddenly become also the crucial northern flank in the struggle between the Soviet Union and the West.

A Dream of Scandinavian Union

They remain, as they almost always have, un-united. For a thousand years the idea of Scandinavian union has preoccupied the minds of these people, but except for a brief period at the turn of the fourteenth century it has remained but a dream. In 1397 the great Danish Queen Margaret succeeded at a meeting in Kalmar in uniting Norway, Sweden and Denmark under one crown. But the union was short-lived. Sweden soon broke away and by 1523 the union was formally at an end. Denmark and Norway remained united under a Danish monarch for four centuries — until 1814, when the great powers which had defeated Napoleon severed their ties and joined Norway — without consulting her — in an unhappy union with Sweden, which the Norwegians managed to terminate only in 1905.

Norway's restoration as a completely sovereign nation, after four hundred years of existence as little more than a Danish province and of a further hundred years as an unequal partner under the Swedish crown, is thus a development of our own century. The last king whom

Norway could call its own, Haakon VI, died in 1380. The country had to wait exactly five and a quarter centuries before it could pick his successor, a Danish prince, who was elected by popular vote to the throne in 1905 and who, not illogically, assumed the name of Haakon VII. He is the only king modern, independent Norway has had, and he had reigned nearly fifty years when I came to Oslo.

Finland's sovereign independence is of course of even a more recent date. For some six centuries, until 1809, Finland belonged to Sweden. Then Russia absorbed it as a Grand Duchy. Taking advantage of the Bolshevik Revolution, Finland declared its independence in 1917; resolved first, in 1918, to set up a monarchy with a German prince on the throne — a Hohenzollern if possible, though at the end it settled for a prince of Hesse whom the Diet actually elected as king — and finally, in 1919, established the present Republic. Finland is thus the only one of the northern countries which is not a monarchy — a condition it owes not to any original decision on its own part but to the march of history: the demise of the Hohenzollern Empire, which prompted Prince Friedrich Karl of Hesse not to accept the throne which the Diet in Helsinki offered him on October 9, 1918, by a vote of 75 to 25. The overthrow of the monarchy in Berlin, a month later, made German princes as a whole less desirable than they had been and the practical Finns lost no time in deciding on a president instead of a king.

Since the beginning of the century, then, Norway, Denmark and Sweden have gone their separate national ways, as has Finland since the end of the First World War. Yet the three Scandinavian monarchies have much in common, and their bonds with Finland are close, as they demonstrated by their aid to the Finns during the Winter War with Russia toward the close of 1939.

The Bonds that Unite

To begin with, the Danes, Norwegians and Swedes are drawn together by linguistic ties. A Dane and a Norwegian have no difficulty in understanding each other's language, which for centuries, insofar as they were written, were practically the same. With a little effort both can understand a Swede, and vice versa. None of the three can comprehend a Finn, whose language is utterly different, unless he belongs to the 10 per cent of the population of Finland which clings to Swedish as its native tongue.

Another factor that links the Scandinavian monarchies is the blood relationship between the three royal families, King Haakon VII of Norway was the younger brother of the late King Christian X of Denmark, their reigns paralleling for thirty-five years. Their mother was the daughter of Charles XV of Sweden. Later there were further royal ties between the three houses. Frederick IX, King of Denmark since 1947, married Princess Ingrid, daughter of the present King Gustav VI Adolph of Sweden. Crown Prince Olaf of Norway was married to the late Princess Martha, a niece of the late King Gustav V of Sweden. Thus Gustav V, at the time of his death in 1950, was grandfather of the Danish queen and uncle of the crown princess of Norway. One is tempted to say that the three royal houses of Scandinavia comprise one great happy, hard-working family.

The days of the nobility are not what they used to be in Scandinavia. The fiercely democratic and somewhat egalitarian Norwegians will have nought of the titled folk. In 1821, the Norwegian Storting (Parliament) abolished all titles and the privileges that went with them. In Denmark, I found some two hundred families still listed as titled nobility; but Article 83 of the new Constitution of 1953 states bluntly that "all privileges attached by legislation to nobility, title or rank are abolished." Furthermore, Article 84 stipulates that "no fief, entail, entailed estate or other family estate shall be established in the future" — a deathblow to the old way of life of the nobility. About all they have left is their titles — and their memories.

In Sweden, too, the privileges of some one thousand titled families have been abrogated despite a provision in the Constitution saying their rights could not be taken away from them without their consent. However, they have made little fuss about it and in Sweden a title still carries considerable social importance.

The northern countries have had another common experience, and it is one which links them to America. This was the wave of emigration to the United States, with consequences momentous not only for America but for Scandinavia. No less than two and a half million Scandinavians — including a million Swedes, three quarters of a million Norwegians — emigrated to our shores in the hundred-year period between 1825 and 1925, and it is estimated today that ten million Americans are wholly or in part of Scandinavian descent.

The northern countries, by the middle of the nineteenth century, were faced with a disastrous loss of their population to the New World. Not a little of the social transformation in Scandinavia sprang from an effort to cope with that problem. Many of the economic and political reforms — especially the establishment of democratic, parliamentary government — were hastened by the flood of propaganda which flowed back across the Atlantic from the sturdy Scandinavian pioneers in the New World. I can recall scarcely a town or a village that I visited in Norway, Denmark, Sweden and Finland where I did not meet at least one family which heard regularly from its relatives in America.

Today the Scandinavian emigration has virtually ceased. The northern peoples like what they have now, and prefer to remain at home. But the effects of their mass migration to the New World in the nineteenth century will continue to be felt for generations — on both sides of the Atlantic.

With such a community of experience, geography, tradition, culture, religion and (Finland excepted) language, it was natural that the Scandinavian peoples should take easily to co-operation between their respective societies. They have an expression for it, *nordisk samarbejde*, which means, roughly, "Scandinavian teamwork." And though, as we shall see in these pages, it has foundered when confronted with most of the vital issues of the twentieth century, Scandinavians point with pride to a number of accomplishments that have helped, they feel, to bring them ever closer together.

Not long ago the delegates of Denmark, Iceland, Norway and Sweden to the Council of Europe thought so well of them that they prepared a special report for that eminent European debating society. They found many facts to relate. There was the establishment of the Scandinavian Parliamentary Council, made up of members of the various national assemblies, who consort annually to consider legislation of common interest. There was the joint juridical agency set up to ponder bringing the laws of the northern lands closer together, and in this much progress has been made. Steps were taken to improve co-operation in the social field, and one result was that the far-reaching social security benefits were made available to citizens of one country residing in another. The co-operative societies of the four countries set up a joint purchasing agency abroad. The national airlines of Denmark, Norway and Sweden were merged into the Scandinavian Airlines System, which has now become one of the giant carriers of the world, plying commercial air routes over the five continents and pioneering a regular service over the polar regions from the northern capitals to Los Angeles and Tokyo.

Scandinavian co-operation has eliminated the necessity of passports for its citizens traveling between the four countries. It has brought about dozens of common cultural projects fathered by the Norden societies, the Scandinavian Art Union, the Scandinavian Cultural Commission and a host of other groups. It has even given birth to a Scandinavian language committee whose task it is to seek to curb the mounting differences between the three Norse tongues.

But it is on the big issues of economics and politics that the efforts toward Scandinavian co-operation have foundered. In 1950 the Joint Scandinavian Committee for Economic Co-operation tried to lay the foundation for a customs union but soon abandoned the task. The vital economic interests of the various northern countries were simply too conflicting and competitive.

However, they were taken up again in 1954 by a new body which promises to be by far the most important organization for Scandinavian co-operation. This is the Nordic Council, which held its first meeting in Copenhagen on February 13, 1954. It is composed of sixteen members each from Norway, Sweden and Denmark, and five from Iceland, the representatives being selected by their respective parliaments. The statutes provide that the members must represent all shades of political opinion and that the four governments may appoint cabinet ministers to sit in the Council, though the latter have no vote. Thus in the meeting at Oslo, in the summer of 1954, seven cabinet ministers, 24 former cabinet ministers, as well as 53 members of Parliament attended.

The Nordic Council is not a Scandinavian parliament. Its great weakness is that its decisions do not bind the individual governments. Its task is to discuss questions of common interest and to make proposals to the governments. The latter can also submit problems to the Council for its advice.

In the summer meeting of 1954 the council did try to come to grips with the problem of a Scandinavian customs union, and even Norway, which because of its relative industrial weakness had no enthusiasm for such proposals, indicated that it might be willing to share in a tentative first step to lower or abolish customs on chemical and textile goods. The council has also given consideration to such matters as a Nordic Post, Telegraph and Telephone Union, a tunnel under or a bridge over the sound between Denmark and Sweden, and the establishment of lines which would bring some of Norway's hydroelectric power through Sweden to Denmark.

The statutes of the Nordic Council expressly leave a place open to Finland. But because of fear of Russian displeasure, the Finnish government so far has contented itself with merely sending an observer to the council's meetings.

The most spectacular and far-reaching postwar failure of Scandinavian co-operation came in the political field — specifically, on the issue of neutrality and common defense — though not before one last mighty effort was made in 1949 which promised, for a few exciting weeks, to bring the Norwegians, Swedes and Danes closer to voluntary union than they had been since the days of Queen Margaret's Kalmar Union in the fourteenth century.

I found some persons in the North, chiefly in Sweden, who thought that the three Scandinavian nations might have succeeded in their aim, which was to establish their own defensive union, had the United States, for its own good reasons, not interfered in the negotiations, much to the dismay of the Swedes but to the eventual benefit, it must be added, of the North Atlantic community, including Norway and Denmark.

Our timely and effective intervention in Scandinavian affairs on this occasion had been preceded by an interesting incident which was not made known to the public on either side of the Atlantic. Shortly after the Soviet-backed Communist *coup* in Czechoslovakia in February of 1948, the Department of Defense in Washington received intelligence that the Soviet Union intended to invade Norway over their common frontier in the far north. The information was promptly passed along to the Norwegian government, which became greatly alarmed — especially in view of what had just happened in Prague.

Later it was ascertained in Washington that the intelligence was faulty and that, in fact, the Kremlin did not contemplate an attack on Norway. The Norwegian government was so informed, but it had been given a bad scare. Years later I found more than one highly placed official in Oslo who, in looking back, wondered if the United States had not exaggerated the Soviet threat for its own good purposes. So far as I can ascertain, the Pentagon at first fully believed its faulty Intelligence and was considerably alarmed. In fact, it was one of the reasons, I am told, for President Truman's urgent request in the spring of 1948 for a drastic increase in the size of American armed forces.[3]

To understand the next step, which before the year was over involved considerable American pressure to get the Scandinavian governments to abandon the idea of a neutral defense alliance and instead to join the proposed North Atlantic Pact for mutual defense against Russia, we must go back a bit and get clear what a devastating blow was dealt to the historic conception of Scandinavian unity and neutrality by the fortunes of the Second World War.

Neutrality, War, Occupation and Lost Illusions

For more than a century after the Scandinavians had untangled themselves from both sides of the Napoleonic alliances in 1814 neutrality appeared to be the best policy for a people, few in numbers, who had finally renounced their ancient holdings in northern Germany and along the rest of the southern Baltic shore. Henceforth they would mind their own business, cultivate their own gardens and resolutely stay out of the quarrels of the Big Powers.

This seemingly sensible idea actually worked. Though subject to many pressures and temptations, the Scandinavians — with the Dan-

[3] It now seems probable that the Soviet government itself planted the false tip about a Russian attack on Norway in order to distract American attention from Greece, where a Communist revolt threatened the independence of that country. Incidentally, in answer to my inquiry, the State Department denies any knowledge whatsoever of the incident, though I am told on good authority that General Marshall, then Secretary of State, was fully aware of it. At any rate, it was confirmed to me by unimpeachable sources in the Norwegian government and by a trustworthy private source in Washington. In 1951 the Foreign Policy Association published a brief report on it, which, so far as I know, was never denied by the State Department.

ish exception already noted — managed to stay out of Europe's continual conflicts.

The war of 1914-1918 put a tremendous strain on their neutrality. Both sides threatened and cajoled them. But they survived as neutrals. And despite blockades and the sinking of their merchant ships — Norway lost a greater proportion of her shipping than Britain — they made a great deal of money out of trading with both belligerents. Also their common experience, as neutrals in a world war that raged all around them, drew them closer together than at any time in a century.

The very success of neutrality contained, however, the seeds of a dangerous illusion that was to prove disastrous to all of the four nations except Sweden when the next war came. This illusion was that if you were a small country and wished to be neutral, and behaved neutrally, you could remain neutral. There was a corollary: that a neutral nation, since it would have nothing to do with war, did not have to arm for war.

It all sounded perfectly logical and reasonable. But there was a flaw in it. The northern countries had reckoned without Hitler — and without Stalin.

The war that Hitler launched in the autumn of 1939 engulfed peaceful, unarmed, neutral Scandinavia; brought ruin, devastation and disillusionment to the peoples of three of the four northern nations, shattering not only their economic life and their illusions but the very basis of their political position in the world.

Each of the four lands fared differently. Sweden alone escaped invasion and occupation, but the price she paid for a devious neutrality left scars not only on her national conscience but on her relations with Denmark and Norway which may not be healed for a generation. Denmark, which in the fateful spring of 1940 had only 14,000 men under arms out of a population of four million — and most of them green recruits — succumbed to the treacherous Nazi invasion in one day almost without firing a shot. Norway, after recovering from the initial shock of the German blow and the treason of Quisling, fought back against the invaders, holding out longer that disastrous spring than did Belgium, Holland or even France. To Finland the war brought tragedy and heartbreaking confusion. Finland was first attacked by Russia, then joined the Germans in the 1941 Nazi onslaught on the Soviet Union, made peace with Moscow in

1944, and the last year of the war fought a bitter campaign against the Germans which left the whole northern third of the country an utter wasteland — a tangled ordeal which, capped as it was by severe peace terms, probably would have destroyed a less doughty people.

The war demolished the ancient basis of Scandinavian unity. Norway and Denmark emerged as Allied powers, official members of the victorious coalition. Moreover both countries had learned, at dreadful cost, certain lessons. One was that there was no longer any security in neutrality; a second was that they could hope to survive only by permanently allying themselves with the West.

Sweden's experience did not serve to teach her those lessons, though some Swedes — a small minority — believed their nation might easily have learned them from the tragic fate of their blood brethren in Norway and Denmark. Good fortune and an armed neutrality which favored first Germany, when she was winning, and then the Allies, when they began to triumph, had spared her the horrors visited upon all her neighbors in the North during the second war. Sweden today remains determined to trust to her luck, and to continue to try to remain outside the conflicts of the Great Powers. The overwhelming majority of Swedes, regardless of party, support this policy, though they realize, not without misgivings, that it has isolated them from Norway and Denmark on the most vital issue of the day: the survival of Scandinavian society in a world divided into two hostile, clashing camps.

Finland has isolated herself too from her northern friends and neighbors, but this is due not at all to her own wishes but to the demands of Russia. Saddled with heavy war reparations by the Soviet Union, she has been fully occupied in trying to pay them and with remaining relatively free and independent of her giant, rapacious neighbor, which has quashed the independence of every other country bordering it in Eastern Europe. Finland finished paying reparations — some $570,000,000 — right on time, at the end of 1952, but that did not bring her complete freedom to do what she pleases. She must tread a wary path. She is restricted by the terms of both the peace treaty and the "Agreement of Friendship, Co-operation and Mutual Assistance," as it is called, which Russia forced on her in 1948. For the moment Finland simply dares not draw too close to her Scandinavian friends for fear of an unpleasant, and perhaps disastrous, Russian reaction to such a move.

A few days after New Year's in 1949 Sweden made a bold attempt to bring the three Scandinavian monarchies together in a defensive alliance. She offered to amend her age-old policy of national neutrality and join Norway and Denmark in a pact for mutual defense. She stipulated only that this military alliance be based on strict neutrality, with no entangling alliances with outside powers.

Such an arrangement might well have saved Denmark and Norway from German aggression in 1940. Hitler might have hesitated to overrun them if he had known that he would have to take on a fairly well-armed Sweden too.

But in 1949 the Swedish offer was too late, and it was too little. It was the Norwegians, and especially their brilliant and astute foreign minister, Halvard M. Lange, who had emerged but four years before from a German concentration camp where he had learned to look at the world with a certain realism, who realized this most acutely. The Norwegians were all for a Scandinavian defense alliance, but they insisted that it be linked to a North Atlantic security system backed by the United States. The three little Nordic countries, the Norwegians argued, were simply not strong enough to defend themselves, even if they stood together. They numbered only fourteen millions. What could they do against a Russia of one hundred and eighty millions? It was simply a pipe dream to imagine that they could hope to survive without the backing of the big Western powers, above all of America.

If the argument seemed unanswerable it must be said in all fairness that the Swedes marshaled some potent points of their own to try to confute it. I was to listen to them by the hour from some of the highest civilian and military authorities[4] when I got to Stockholm. In brief, they were these:

Naturally Sweden's sympathies lie with the West, to which, like Denmark and Norway, she is bound by strong economic, cultural and spiritual ties. But the three Scandinavian countries happen to be situated close to a suspicious and not very friendly Russia. They

[4] I should prefer to be more specific. But in order to gather worthwhile, first-hand material for this book and not just collect well-meaning but meaningless formal statements, I assured all informants in Scandinavia — kings, cabinet ministers, permanent officials, generals, diplomats and business, farmer and labor leaders, etc. — with whom I talked that I would not identify them with what they said unless they gave specific permission. This is the only way I know to induce statesmen, generals and the others to talk frankly and informatively.

could therefore best promote peace, while saving their skins, by staying out of the East-West cold war and making themselves militarily strong enough to discourage both a Soviet attack and Western pressure for bases against Russia. They could thus contribute toward peace by becoming a bridge, a mediatory link, between the Soviet Union and the Western powers. This bridge, if well defended by their combined efforts, would be one less potential area of conflict between the Big Powers.

Anyway, the Swedes said, there is little possibility of a Western alliance, even if we joined it, getting adequate military aid to us in time, if we were attacked by Russia. Do not American strategists talk of *withdrawing* from the Elbe to the Rhine to the Meuse and eventually behind the Pyrenees? Isn't that why they are courting Fascist Franco? By joining this American-dominated coalition, and giving it air and naval bases on our territory, we provoke Russia. Then we are left helpless if Russia reacts and attacks. It would be wiser to depend on our own united strength. It may not be great, but it is considerable — enough, we think, to deter the Russians.

There was another argument which the Swedes made a great deal of and which I also heard echoed in Helsinki. If they were to join NATO and allow it to set up air and naval bases in Sweden, the Russians might well feel justified in retaliating by occupying bases in Finland next door to Sweden. (Moscow could probably justify such a move juridically by the terms of the Russo-Finnish Mutual Aid Treaty of 1948). This, said the Swedes, would not only mean the tragic end of Finland as a relatively independent nation, but it would be a catastrophe for Sweden. For Sweden's considerable defensive power against Russia is postulated on one condition: that she have time — at least nine days — to mobilize her citizen army of some half a million men. She cannot keep such a large force permanently under arms. For a nation so small to attempt to do so would bankrupt her. As long as the Soviet armies are kept *beyond* the frontiers of Finland, Sweden believes she would have time to mobilize against a Russian attack. Were the Red armies to take up a position in Finland on Sweden's very frontier, or across the narrow Gulf of Bothnia, she would have no time to put herself in a state of defense, and would be left in a hopeless plight.

The Norwegians and Danes listened to these arguments. The Norwegians were not much impressed. The Danes were not unimpressed, but they were sorely troubled. They were in the middle. Of the three countries, Denmark was in the weakest position. She lacked Sweden's military capacity and Norway's strategic position behind rugged mountains and a broad sea. Russia, with air, naval and land bases in Germany but a few flying minutes away, could overwhelm her in a day or two, as Germany had done in 1940. Much more than Norway, which faces West toward Britain and America, she welcomed Sweden's proffered aid. But by itself, she reluctantly realized, it would not be enough. Perhaps Western help could never arrive in time, as the Swedes suggested. But it was the only hope there was. If Denmark were a member of the North Atlantic Defense Community and an attack on her was considered, as it would have to be, as an attack on all the Atlantic nations, including the United States, then that fact might deter Russia from giving in as easily as Hitler had to the temptation of invading her. This was a straw to grasp.

Toward the end of 1948 the State Department informally approached Norway and Denmark, telling them of the progress the seven North Atlantic states had been making toward founding a defense community and inviting them to participate in further negotiations as charter members. The reaction was immediate. At Norway's request the prime ministers, foreign ministers and defense ministers of the three Scandinavian states hastily met at Karlstad, in southwestern Sweden, on January 5-6, 1949. At this meeting Sweden sprang its proposal for a neutral Scandinavian military bloc. On one important point the Swedes played into American hands. Though Sweden has a surprisingly large armament industry for a nation of seven millions, it was obvious that she could not supply sufficient arms for all three nations. She suggested therefore that the United States be approached to see if American arms could be procured on reasonable conditions. Whereupon the Karlstad meeting adjourned, to be reconvened in Copenhagen on January 22.

Before it could reopen, Washington jumped in to try to break it up. On January 14 a spokesman of the State Department made a statement which must have sounded innocuous enough to most Americans. He announced that American military supplies would have to go, in the first place, to countries which joined with the United States in collective security agreements. The meaning was not lost on Scandinavian ears. Just to make sure that it wasn't, the American Ambassadors in Oslo, Stockholm and Copenhagen called at the respective foreign offices and repeated it. It was thus made clear to the Scandinavians that if they wanted American arms they would have to join our side.

Then Russia intervened. It addressed a strong diplomatic note to Norway inquiring as to Norway's intentions and reminding her that she had a common frontier with the Soviet Union. The Russians asked Norway two pointed questions: did it intend to join the North Atlantic Pact, which Moscow contended was aggressively directed against Russia? And if Norway did intend to join the pact, did it contemplate making bases on its territory available to foreign (that is, Atlantic) powers?

In the meantime the ministers of the three Scandinavian countries resumed their talks at Copenhagen on January 22. This time they were accompanied by members of the parliamentary affairs committees of their respective states. Sweden stuck to its insistence that the Scandinavian alliance must be strictly neutral. Norway insisted that it be linked to the North Atlantic security system. Unhappy Denmark tried to think of a compromise. All three countries, between which there was so much in common, hesitated publicly to confess failure. It would be, they realized, a heavy blow to the age-old efforts of Scandinavians to draw together. They agreed to make one final attempt to reach agreement at a meeting in Oslo a week later.

They duly met in the Norwegian capital, but after two more days of fruitless discussions, could agree only to formally registering their disagreement. Gustav Rasmussen, the then Foreign Minister of Denmark, called January 30, 1949, a dark day in the history of the North. The project of a Scandinavian neutral defense union was dead. It is not likely to be resurrected in this century.

The decision once made, Norway and Denmark lost no time in sending their foreign ministers to Washington to discuss adhering to the North Atlantic Pact. The Norwegians answered the first Russian protest and soon received a second one rejecting Norway's answer, again denouncing the Atlantic Alliance and ending by offering Norway a nonaggression treaty with the Soviet Union!

The Norwegians had not been frightened by Moscow's blunt notes of protest. But the offer of a nonaggression pact was something else. Had not Stalin, like Hitler, been in the habit of making nonaggression treaties with nations just before he overran them? Nonaggression pacts had not stood in the way of Stalin's invading Finland, Poland and the

Baltic states. Moscow's nonaggression treaty with Finland in 1948 had reduced that little country's independence and made her uneasy of the future. Was Norway to be treated similarly? All Scandinavia was worried.

The Norwegians perhaps least of all. At any rate, in due time they answered Moscow, politely but firmly rejecting the offer of a nonaggression pact on the ground that the United Nations charter, which both nations had signed as wartime Allies at San Francisco, obligated all members to desist from aggression. Late in March the parliaments of Denmark and Norway approved by overwhelming majorities adherence to the North Atlantic Pact. On April 4 their ambassadors joined with the other representatives of the North Atlantic Community as original signatories of the treaty.

Norway and Denmark had gone with the West. Sweden had gone alone.

In answering the first Russian note of protest Norway had given a considered and careful answer to the Russian inquiry as to whether the Norwegians would permit foreign powers to occupy bases on her soil: "The Norwegian government will never join in any agreement with other states that contains obligations for Norway to open bases for the military forces of foreign powers *as long as Norway is not attacked or subjected to threats of attacks.*"

The assurance had consequences. The problem of NATO bases was to raise a serious domestic political issue in both Norway and Denmark, and cause a good deal of friction and misunderstanding between them and NATO, and between them and the base-hungry United States. We were to build great NATO air bases in both countries but we were not allowed to man them. Yet the last five words of the Norwegian statement offered an out — as we shall see.

Scandinavia and the United States

The ties between Scandinavia and the U.S.A. are many, and today they are more important to both communities than ever before.

Culturally the influence of both worlds on each other — above and beyond the direct contacts of millions of immigrants and their descendants with their home countries — has been considerable. One thinks of what Ibsen and Strindberg did for our theater and of the stimulation in literature of Knut Hamsun, Sigrid Undset and Selma Lagerlöf, and of how much Sibelius has added to our store of great modern symphonies. And is not Hans Christian Andersen still eagerly read by children in every home in America? Is not the explosive Sören Kierkegaard regarded by young American writers as the father of present-day existentialism? Did not a Swede, Gunnar Myrdal, give us by far the most exhaustive study ever made of the American Negro problem in his monumental book, *An American Dilemma?*

The Scandinavians read American authors too. I sat up many a night in Oslo, Stockholm, Helsinki and Copenhagen listening to Scandinavians speak passionately and well of Hemingway, Faulkner, Steinbeck, Dos Passos, Sinclair Lewis, Upton Sinclair, Jack London and Mark Twain. Their books are on display in every bookstore, in the original and in translation. Even our Broadway plays are popular in the northern capitals. No Ibsen play happened to be on the boards while I was in Oslo, but Clare Boothe Luce's *The Women* and John O'Hara's *Pal Joey* were sell-outs. O'Neill's plays have long been part of the standard drama repertory in the North, and more recently the works of Elmer Rice, Maxwell Anderson, Robert Sherwood, Lillian Hellman, Tennessee Williams and Arthur Miller have been added. American movies, American comics, American jazz, have had more of an influence on Scandinavian youths than their elders — and some Americans — approve of. The American libraries maintained by the State Department are crowded with eager readers.

There is a vast exchange of students and scholars, of labor leaders, industrialists and engineers. Oslo University has an American Institute and a special summer school for American students. A half-million dollars a year is allotted to Finnish youth for study and training in the United States, thanks to a law passed by the 81st Congress which stipulated that all remaining payments on Finland's First World War debt be set aside for this purpose. Grants from the State Department, the Fullbright Fund, the American-Scandinavian Foundation, and other public and private American sources have enabled hundreds of leaders of public opinion in Scandinavia — educators, editors, writers, artists, politicians, union officials and businessmen — to come to the United States, with no strings attached, to study our techniques and our ways and to see for themselves that life in America is somewhat different than is usually depicted in Hollywood movies, newspaper comics and Communist propaganda.

Conversely, the northern lands are jammed each summer not only by Yankee tourists, whose dollars help balance national budgets, but by less conspicuous Americans who have come over to study the Scandinavian systems of social security, co-ops, public housing, labor relations, forestry, temperance, education and a host of other subjects wherein they think they have something to learn.

There is a lively exchange of goods too. Norway, Sweden and Denmark buy more per capita from the United States than Britain and France — some $16.75 annually per head against $13.25 for Britain and $8.70 for France. In 1952 the three countries, whose total population is only 14 million, absorbed $252,000,000 of American exports.

If today the Scandinavians feel that perhaps they have a lesson or two in the workings of political and social democracy to impart to America, it used to be the other way around. The influence of the American Revolution, of the Declaration of Independence and the Constitution, and of the writings of Franklin, Benjamin Rush and Jefferson was a profound one in helping to liberate the northern countries from centuries of absolutism and in encouraging them to set up representative government. The Norwegian Constitution, adopted in 1814 at Eidsvold, owed much to the study of the American federal and various state constitutions. In fact, one draft of it copied, literally, Article XXX of the Massachusetts State Constitution concerning the separation of powers.

Even the American temperance movement exercised a powerful influence on Scandinavia, where excessive drinking had become a major social problem in the early part of the nineteenth century. American temperance leaders journeyed to Norway, Sweden and Denmark to preach the gospel of abstinence from alcoholic beverages, and temperance societies — still active today — sprang up everywhere. Finland and Norway emulated the example of the United States in adopting National Prohibition after the First World War. Today drinking in the northern countries is possible, but it is not easy to indulge in, being generally discouraged either by deliberately high taxes or by complex regulations — or by both. An American visitor is impressed by the success of the Scandinavians in almost stamping out drunken driving by the simple expedient of imposing automatic jail sentences of at least three weeks on anyone caught driving after imbibing more than one cocktail or its equivalent in alcoholic content.

A further bond between the two worlds was established by American Marshall Plan aid, which helped Norway and Denmark, ravaged and plundered by the occupying Germans, to get back on their feet after the last war.

Finally, though we may say that Scandinavia, especially Norway and Denmark, is largely dependent upon America for the military protection it needs to survive, we must also say that the northern countries have now become of immense strategic value to the United States. They constitute the northern section of the wall in Europe which we hope will hold back Russian expansion toward the West. They guard the approaches to the Arctic seas over which Soviet air and naval power might break out into the North Atlantic and reach our American shores. They stand astride the shortest air route between the Soviet Union and the great cities and industrial concentrations of the United States.

Were this northern bastion of the free world to crumble, either from internal causes or from attack from without, the consequences to America — and of course to Western Europe — would be grievous and might prove disastrous. Thus American security and survival are tied in our century for the first time with the security and survival of Scandinavia.

The long dark shadow of the Russian bear which hangs ominously over the northern countries reminds you that the Scandinavians are closer to danger than are we. Stockholm and Oslo are less than an hour's flying time from the nearest Soviet jet-bomber bases. Copenhagen and Helsinki are but minutes away.

The Kremlin maintains an incessant diplomatic pressure on Denmark and Norway, castigating them for their alliance with the West, suggesting to Norway that Russia share in the "defense" of Spitsbergen on the edge of the Polar Sea, angrily protesting to Denmark, through Poland, when the Danes are tardy in returning Polish MIG-15's which land on Danish soil, and seizing Danish and Swedish fishing smacks along the southern and eastern shores of the Baltic. Unarmed Swedish military planes are shot down over the Baltic by Soviet fighters; Swedish patrol boats are fired upon. In Stockholm, Swedes speak resentfully of the "gray war" in the Baltic. In Helsinki the Finns are aware that the big guns from the Russian-leased military base at Porkkala, fourteen miles southwest of the Finnish capital, could obliterate them in the twinkle of an eye.

Yet there is no hysteria in Scandinavia about Russia and the Russians. There is none either over Communism, though in all the four countries the Communists have an organized open movement which is strong enough to elect a few members (in Finland, more than a few) to Parliament. There is Soviet espionage too, carried out both by Russians and their Scandinavian stooges. And while this inspires increasing vigilance it does not arouse hysteria. Instead of being unduly worried about Communism in their own lands, the Scandinavians are proud that it has failed utterly to appeal to their people. They have a robust confidence in the strength and worth of their democratic societies. They will tell you they see no need for loyalty oaths or tests, and they have none, though they are realistic enough to keep Communists out of sensitive posts in government. Witch hunts are unknown — except insofar as one reads about them in the history books or in current newspaper dispatches from both sides of the iron curtain.

Fear there is of Soviet Russia. Fear and mistrust. But these deep feelings are kept under control. The Scandinavians remind you that they have lived next door to the Russians for a long time — in peace and war. They think they know a little about them. And their knowledge is not built on illusions. This millenium-old experience teaches them to be on the alert, to become as strong as possible, to avoid appeasement but not give-and-take. It does not lead them to believe inexorably that they are doomed. The Russians, they will tell you, have always been difficult. Difficult and sometimes dangerous. Today they are both. This is a serious matter — to be treated seriously by sane and sober men.

With this modicum of background, let us turn now to each of the four northern countries in turn.

The first is Norway.

CHAPTER II

Norway

ON THE evening of April 5, 1940, the German Minister in Oslo, Dr. Kurt Bräuer, gave a gala private showing at his legation of a gruesome Nazi film depicting the savage destruction inflicted on Poland by the Wehrmacht during the previous autumn. Among Dr. Bräuer's guests were several members of the Norwegian government. They listened in silence to a German narrator in the film exulting over the horrors of the war for the Poles and commenting that "for this they could thank their English and French friends."

Earlier on that same day Dr. Halvdan Koht, the Norwegian Foreign Minister, and Colonel Birger Ljungberg, the Minister for Defense, had received alarming Intelligence reports from Berlin. They were not the first of the kind by any means, but they were the most specific and the most frightening. They spoke of the imminent possibility of German landings on the coast of southern Norway. The two ministers, however, were skeptical. They thought the warnings were exaggerated and therefore decided to keep them secret so as not to alarm the public. The next day, in fact, Dr. Koht in a speech to the Storting dwelt on what seemed a more pressing problem: the British violations of Norwegian neutrality along the west coast.

Three days later, on April 9, the Germans struck with savage ferocity and without warning. Until that disastrous dawn Norway had been at peace for one hundred and twenty-six years.

For the last thirty-five of those years, ever since it had broken away from Sweden in 1905, elected its own king and re-established its complete sovereignty, Norway had been engaged in building up a new and peaceful democratic nation of an admirable kind.

Slightly larger in area than the British Isles or Italy, lined with high, rugged mountains and cut by deep fjords that combined to give it some of the most magnificent scenery on earth, Norway had a population of just three million. This was about the right number if all were to prosper, for over half the land was covered by bare mountains, a fourth by dense forests, and only 3 per cent could be cultivated. Some food had to be imported but the forests were a source of wealth and so was the sea.

From the woods of conifers and birch came a yearly cutting of some ten million cubic yards, and timber products accounted for 21 per cent of Norway's exports. Production of paper and pulp alone came to $70,000,000 a year. The annual catch by Norwegian fishermen was the biggest in Europe and this did not include the whaling industry, which was the largest in the world. The sea too gave the Norwegians an opportunity to exploit their seafaring genius in building up the fourth largest merchant fleet in the world — some 2,000 ships totaling 5,000,000 tons. Income from shipping alone balanced the import surplus of $100,000,000 a year and thereby kept Norway's economy on an even keel.

The towering mountains provided more than beautiful scenery. They contained valuable ores, of which iron and pyrites were the most important. Norway was the largest producer in the world of sulphur pyrites. But, above all, the mountains were a source of hydroelectric power. Norway's water power resources were the largest in Europe, being calculated at 120 billion KWH per annum,[1] of which only 14 per cent was harnessed when the long era of peace came to an abrupt end.

The mountains also divided the land, and the great distances added to the remoteness of one part from another. From the south of Norway to the north it is eleven hundred miles, nearly half as far as New York is from San Francisco. Towns on the south coast are nearer to Rome than they are to the Norwegian North Cape. No roads or railways ran the entire length of land. To go by rail from Oslo, or from Bergen and Trondheim, to Narvik one had to travel by way of Sweden and then cross back on the iron-ore line from Kiruna to Narvik.

Space and mountains, and fjords, which made deep indentations on the west coast of from 50 to 100 miles, combined for centuries to

[1] A figure considerably higher than the hydroelectric production in the United States in 1953.

keep many Norwegian communities isolated into more or less self-contained, self-supporting units. But about the middle of the nineteenth century, with the advent of steamships and railroads, this isolation began to be broken. Fast steamers began to link up the towns on the long coast line that stretched for 2100 miles and, if the fjords and bays are counted, came to 12,000 miles. By 1909 the Bergen-Christiania (as Oslo was then called) railroad had been completed over the mountains connecting the chief port in the West with the capital. Motor highways began to stretch out from Christiania northwards. By 1939 Norway had 2500 miles of railroad, constructed at great cost over some of the most difficult terrain in the world, and some 12,500 miles of main highways. Despite the engineering difficulties and the great expense, the country had finally solved its immense communications problem. By steamer, by train and truck and bus, and by plane, all of Norway's far-flung communities had finally been linked together.

On the whole these communities were small, but they were numerous. Some 2,000,000 persons lived in rural areas, the other million in cities and towns. Roughly 37 per cent of them were engaged in agriculture, forestry and fishing, 27 per cent in mining and manufacture, 20 per cent in shipping, commerce and transportation, and the rest in professions and various other occupations. It was a healthy balance. Per capita income in 1929, to take a normal year between the wars, was $249. This wasn't as much as in the United States ($701) or Great Britain ($426) but it equaled that of the French and was far higher than the Italian. It made for a decent, modest living.

And it was enhanced by the benefits to all citizens of a comprehensive social welfare system. By 1909 compulsory health, accident and unemployment insurance for workers was on the statute books. In 1936 old age insurance had been introduced. By the time Hitler struck, Norway had one of the most advanced social security systems in the world.

In the meantime the Norwegians went ahead in the first heady days of their newly won national sovereignty to widen the basis of their democracy. Already in 1898, seven years before the breaking of the union with Sweden, the property tax for voters was dropped in favor of universal suffrage for men. Then the women were gradually brought in. In 1901 they were given the vote in municipal elections, subject to a small property qualification. In 1907 women thus qualified won the right to vote in national elections, making Norway the first sovereign country in Europe to give the vote to women. In 1913, on the eve of the First World War, all property qualifications were abolished and universal suffrage for men and women was adopted. Long before their sisters in America were allowed to participate in politics, Norwegian women were getting into it up to their necks.

For reasons which will be sought later, the Norwegians after the First World War gravitated toward the Labor party. The elections of 1933 established it as the largest political party in the country and since 1935 it has held the reins of government, even though until 1945 it lacked a clear majority in the Storting. The elections of 1945, 1949 and 1953 gave it an absolute majority in Parliament and confirmed its hold on the government. Thus Norway has experienced the longest continuous Labor rule of any country in the world and is the only one of the Scandinavian countries where the Socialists enjoy an absolute parliamentary majority.

Though Lutheranism was established by law as the "public religion of the nation," and the Lutheran Church was made the State Church of Norway, and 97 per cent of the population nominally belonged to it, complete freedom of religion was guaranteed except for one provision in the Eidsvold Constitution of 1814 which emphatically declared that Jesuits would not be tolerated.[2]

For a country whose population was only a million and a half midway through the nineteenth century, and only a little over two million in 1900, the intellectual, literary and artistic life of Norway in the century before Hitler's legions came was remarkable. In fact, the creativeness of such a tiny segment of the human race — smaller than that which dwelt in Chicago — was quite phenomenal.

Out of it came the impressive figures of Henrik Ibsen and of Björnstjerne Björnson in the drama, of Edvard Grieg in music and, a little earlier, of Henrik Wergeland, who is regarded in Norway as the greatest lyrical genius of the nation and who, though he died in 1845 when he was only 37, is generally credited with having contributed more than any other through his poems, dramas, essays and historical works, to the great literary and artistic renaissance which followed. Moreover Wergeland's stirring sense of history and his eloquent pleas for freedom and democracy exercised a profound influence on the po-

[2] An amendment to the Constitution, introduced in Parliament in 1954, promised to abolish the prohibition against the Jesuits in the near future.

litical development of the country. As one eminent Norwegian critic has written: "Wergeland intervened decisively in Norway's history." One might add that so did Björnson and Ibsen, and a host of lesser authors, through their passionate interest in the social and political problems of the day. In no other country, perhaps, have writers exercised such a decisive influence in these fields. No wonder that for the last century, at least, in Norway, an author has become a highly respected and influential (though often controversial) member of the community.

Norway's literary revival continued right down to the Second World War in the persons of two giants of contemporary literature: Knut Hamsun and Sigrid Undset. Hamsun in his old age was to deteriorate into an enthusiast for Nazism and to be regarded by most of his fellow countrymen during the occupation as a traitor, but even this appalling lapse could not wipe out the memory of his genius in the earlier novels *Hunger, Pan* and *Growth of the Soil* — in which with moving style, an exuberant vitality, a deep passion and an almost mystic grandeur he glorified man's eternal struggle with the land, the sea and society.

After the first war Hamsun was overshadowed by Sigrid Undset, who had made her early reputation in novels and stories dealing with the problems of the middle class and of women. A historian of immense learning, she turned later to the historical novel and in *Kristin Lavransdatter* and *The Master of Hestviken* she delved back to the fourteenth century for the material for novels which have been hailed around the world as masterpieces of modern literature. They won for her, as the earlier works had won for Hamsun, the Nobel Prize. In contrast to Hamsun, she played a noble role in the last war.

In painting and sculpture too this sparsely populated country in the Far North made notable contributions. Here too there were two artists who towered above all the rest, Edvard Munch in painting and Gustav Vigeland in sculpture. Born in the 1860's, both lived to midway through the second war, and left behind a large body of work which placed them among the few geniuses of modern European art. I found in postwar Norway a tendency among the artists and critics to disparage the work of Vigeland, but surely Frogner Park on the outskirts of Oslo, into which he fitted literally hundreds of sculptured figures in a harmonious whole, is a testimony to a staggering imagination and an original and daring art. The park itself is unique in the world, being the only one, I believe, in which one artist conceived the landscape and the design and then proceeded to fill it and people it exclusively with the structures and figures of his own creation. I had seen Meštrović achieve a harmony of architecture and sculpture in the exquisite little church at Civtat on the Dalmatian coast. But Vigeland created a whole park. It occupied him for forty years and it is a commentary on the artistic bent of the Norwegians that the people of Oslo and the municipal government cheerfully raised millions of crowns to see the great sculptor through his titanic task. They might skimp on money for arms, but they were prodigal when it came to art.

The tragedy of Norway — as it turned out — was that she did skimp on arms. After more than a century without war, pacifism had become deeply rooted in the Norwegian people and it was especially strong in the Labor party, which had taken over the government in 1935. For years after the First World War Norway, like the other Scandinavian countries, put her trust in the League of Nations as the preserver of peace. But when France and Britain declined to carry out League sanctions against Italy after Mussolini's invasion of Ethiopia, and when this failure was followed by other examples of the League's impotence to halt totalitarian aggression, Norway began to think of its own long-neglected defenses. They were practically nonexistent. The army, in spite of an age-old system of annual conscription, was little more than a token force. In 1940 it numbered 9000 men. The navy consisted of 57 small, obsolete ships. The air force had fewer than 100 antiquated planes.

Finally awakened to the danger of Nazi Germany, the Labor government, with the support of all parties, embarked on a modest program of rearmament. Annual expenditures for defense rose from $9,000,000 in 1935 to $12,000,000 in 1938, and in March of the latter year a special loan of $13,000,000 was applied to strengthening national defense. Planes and ships and guns were ordered from abroad.

But the awakening in Norway, as in so many other places, came too late. And it was only a partial awakening. The military command indeed seemed to be as irresolute as the parliament and people. On the eve of Hitler's treacherous attack the army remained unmobilized and the easily mined approaches through the narrow fjords to Oslo, Bergen, Trondheim and the other principal cities remained unmined. Had Norway mobilized its trained reserve of 200,000 men and mined the fjords and fully manned the forts and taken more seriously the warnings of what the Germans were up to, history might have taken another turning on that fateful morning of April 9, 1940.

A Treacherous Attack

The day of April 8 was nerve-racking enough for the harassed Norwegian authorities. Early in the morning the Allied governments had announced the mining of Norwegian territorial waters in three places as a first step in halting the shipment of iron ore from Narvik to Germany. However justifiable from the Allied standpoint, the measure was a flagrant violation of Norway's neutral rights and the Norwegian government was understandably angry. It immediately drew up a strong protest to Britain, demanding that the British Navy remove the mines and threatening to remove them itself unless prompt action was taken. The dread possibility of armed conflict between these two friendly nations suddenly arose and made the Norwegians, whose sympathies were entirely with the British, heartsick. But not for long.

Early that afternoon the evening papers appeared on the streets with a sensational report that a British submarine off the southern coast of Norway had sunk a German transport, the *Rio de Janeiro*, bound for Bergen. Hundreds of bodies of German soldiers were reported being washed ashore but some Germans managed to reach land alive. They told of being on their way to Bergen to protect it against the British.

If this was alarming news, worse was soon to follow. A message arrived in Oslo from the Norwegian Legation in London relaying a report from the British Admiralty that German naval forces had been sighted steaming north to Narvik and might reach the port by midnight. In Oslo Parliament met in secret session and the government, at 9:15 P.M., decided to order partial mobilization in the vulnerable coastal areas. It also gave authority to the navy to mine the Oslo Fjord. But even these half-measures were too late.

At 11:23 P.M. came the news that the fortifications in Oslo Fjord, which guarded the sea approach to the capital, were under fire. Shortly after midnight the sirens sounded an air-raid alarm in Oslo, but most people thought it was merely a practice alarm. Late strollers were amused at circulars being handed out in the streets in which a discredited, disgruntled politician, Major Vidkun Quisling, proclaimed that Norway was at the dawn of a new day.

Prime Minister Johan Nygaardsvold convoked the Cabinet at 1:30 A.M. on April 9. By that early hour the situation had become disastrous beyond belief. Within a few hours — the cabinet members learned, to their consternation — the Germans had succeeded in occupying every important Norwegian city on the west and south coasts: Narvik, Trondheim, Bergen, Stavanger, and Kristiansand. They had taken all the important airfields. And they were pounding at the gates of the capital — the gunfire could be heard in the cabinet room.

As the stunned members of the government discussed desperately what, if anything, could be done, the German Minister appeared at the Foreign Office at 4 A.M. and presented a written ultimatum of nineteen typewritten pages demanding immediate surrender but insisting that the Germans had arrived as friends to protect Norway against an Anglo-French attack. Dr. Bräuer, who had entertained several of the cabinet members so charmingly a few evenings before with his obscene film of what Nazi savagery had done to Poland, demanded an immediate reply.

He got it. The Norwegian government unanimously rejected the German ultimatum.

Someone in the dazed government had the presence of mind to order a special train to be made ready. At 9:30 A.M., the King, his royal family, the members of the government and of the Storting, hastily departed on it for Hamar, a railroad junction eighty miles to the north. At about the same hour twenty trucks loaded with the gold of the Bank of Norway and three trucks carrying the most secret papers of the Foreign Office also headed north. The getaway was just in time and it decisively thwarted the well-made plans of Hitler to capture the King and the government and the members of Parliament as well as all the gold he could lay his hands on.

But the escape was made possible only by the heroic action of a handful of Norwegian sailors and soldiers who held up a powerful German fleet sailing up Oslo Fjord to the capital, delaying it for several hours and inflicting heavy damage on it.

The German plan had been for the ten-thousand-ton cruiser *Bluecher* to dock in Oslo during the night and disembark its large staff of Gestapo officials and civil administrators, who were to take over communication and administration centers and seize the King, the government and the members of Parliament. All through the chilly night a gay welcoming party from the German Legation, which was joined at intervals by the busy Dr. Bräuer, stood at the dock awaiting the ship. They waited in vain. The *Bluecher* never arrived.

The big cruiser was part of a formidable force consisting of the pocket battleship *Deutschland,* two other cruisers, the *Emden* and *Brummer,* and numerous transports, destroyers and smaller craft. It had entered Oslo Fjord early in the evening, but at Horten, a Norwegian naval base, had encountered difficulties. There the *Olav Trygvesson,* a minelayer, sank a German transport and a destroyer and badly damaged the *Emden.* Further up the fjord, where it narrows to but a few miles in width, stood the old fortress of Oskarsborg. Here more trouble developed. Torpedoes and shells from the fort sank the *Bluecher* with the loss of 1,600 men, including all the Gestapo and administrative officials who were to take over the task of occupation. Their carefully worked out plans went down with them. It took the German fleet until nearly noon to reduce Oskarsborg, and by that time the Norwegian King and government had slipped safely out of reach. German airborne troops did not reach Oslo until 2 P.M.

With the capital and all the important coastal cities in their hands, the Germans now tried to persuade the King and government to surrender. The situation of the Norwegians seemed hopeless. The Danes had already capitulated. It was obvious that the Swedes were not going to help. Prime Minister Chamberlain offered British aid, but what good would it be now?

On the afternoon of April 9 the Storting convened in Hamar. Of the 150 members only five were absent. Nygaardsvold, the Socialist prime minister, tried to resign so that an all-party government might be formed. But on the urgence of C. J. Hambro, leader of the Conservative party and president of the Storting — a man who played a heroic role at this juncture — the Assembly unanimously insisted that the Labor government remain in power and that three opposition members be added to the Cabinet as ministers without portfolio. At 7:30 that evening the parliamentary session was interrupted by the news that German forces were approaching Hamar. The members fled to Elverum, a few miles to the east toward the Swedish border.

It was at this little town in the hills that a momentous decision was taken the next day. It was there, and in the neighboring village of Nybergsund on April 10, that King Haakon VII showed a mettle that confounded Hitler, rallied the Norwegian government and people and assured for himself a place of great honor in the history of this brave little country.

In the morning the Storting had reassembled at Elverum. On the motion of Hambro, who foresaw that it might soon be impossible for the Parliament to function freely, the Storting unanimously voted the government full powers to act for the nation until the Assembly could meet again. It was agreed that such authority was to be valid even if the King and government were forced to leave Norwegian soil. Thus was laid the legal base for the continuance of the Norwegian government in exile.

But the inimitable German envoy, Dr. Bräuer, like his Fuehrer in Berlin, still did not comprehend Norwegian character. He insisted on an audience with the King. After considerable reluctance, Haakon agreed to receive the minister in the presence of his foreign minister, Dr. Koht. To this stipulation Dr. Bräuer objected. It was necessary, he said, for him to see the King alone. Haakon finally consented to this. The audience took place at 3 P.M. and lasted for ten minutes. The German diplomat alternately flattered and tried to intimidate the King. He told of the high respect in which the Norwegian monarch was held by Hitler and the German people. Then he underlined the grave responsibility which would be the King's if Norwegian youth were to be slaughtered in a useless war. Haakon, a modest man but not a weak one, patiently explained to the German that in Norway the King did not make political decisions. Under the Constitution, that was the exclusive business of the government.

Dr. Koht then joined the two in time to hear the German minister demand that the King appoint a Quisling government. This the King flatly refused even to consider. And with that the astonished Nazi diplomat was dismissed.

Later that day in a small inn in the village of Nybergsund, near Elverum, the King made a historic personal decision. It was a declaration to his government assembled with him as the Council of State and constitutes one of the most courageous and eloquent utterances of the war.

I am deeply affected by the responsibility laid on me if the German demand is rejected. The responsibility for the calamities that will befall people and country is indeed so grave that I dread to take it. It rests with the government to decide, but my position is clear.

For my part I cannot accept the German demands. It would conflict with all that I have considered to be my duty as King of Norway since I came to this country nearly 35 years ago . . .

I have desired to create a constitutional kingdom in loyalty to the people whose invitation I accepted in 1905. I *cannot* depart from that course. I do not want this to be decisive for the government. I do not want the decision of the government to be influenced by or based upon this statement. But I have carefully examined my mind and my position, and I find that I *cannot* appoint Quisling Prime Minister, a man in whom I know that neither our people as a whole nor its representatives — the Storting — have any confidence at all.

If therefore the government should decide to accept the German demands — and I fully understand the reasons in favor of it, considering the impending danger of war in which so many young Norwegians will have to give their lives — if so, abdication will be the only course open to me. I have come to this conclusion after grave struggles and self-examination. I have wanted to impart this to you that you may be clear about my position, but I ask you not to take it as an attempt to commit the government to a certain policy.

I do not want my view, which I have been unable to withhold from you, to be decisive for the government. It must make up its mind without regard to my personal opinion. But I believe I am right in giving the government a clear statement as to how I look at the matter.

Thirteen years later in Oslo when I expressed my feelings at so eloquent, courageous and self-effacing an utterance and my wonder that the King had found the time and the composure to compose it — for he and the government members had been without sleep for forty-eight hours and had been hounded from one place to another by the advancing Germans — he smiled modestly and said:

"I'm afraid there was no time to think of eloquence. My thoughts however were clear. I had made up my mind as to the course I would take. So it was just a matter of saying as simply and as briefly as I could what I thought."

The words were preserved by one of the ministers present, who noted them down as they were spoken.

King Haakon also told me that before the war he had kept a copy of *Mein Kampf* on his desk and had given strict orders to his secretary that it should never be removed.

"I read it, and reread it, and marked many passages," he smiled. Then in a more serious vein he added:

"There was one passage above all that struck me in *Mein Kampf*. It was the one in which Hitler said that no nation which would not fight in self-defense was worthy of survival. That piece clung to my mind, especially in the confusing days just after the Germans came. For I was convinced that if we did not resist the Germans, we well might be destroyed as a people and nation."

That night, from a nearby local radio station, the only means of communication to the outside world available, the Norwegian government broadcast its decision not to accept the German demands and called upon the people to resist the invaders. The King associated himself with the appeal. But the Nazi conquerors could not quite bring themselves to believe that the Norwegians meant what they said. Two more attempts were made to dissuade the King. On the morning of April 11, an emissary of Quisling, a Captain Irgens, arrived to urge the King to return to the capital. He promised that Quisling would serve him loyally. His proposal was dismissed with silent contempt.

In the afternoon a message came from the insistent Dr. Bräuer, requesting a further audience with the King to talk over "certain proposals." This time Dr. Koht, after consulting the King, replied that if the German minister had certain proposals he could communicate them to him, as foreign minister.

The German reaction to this rebuff was immediate and in character. They had failed, first to capture the King and the members of the government and then to persuade them to surrender. Now the Germans tried to kill them. Late on the eleventh, the Luftwaffe was sent out to give the village of Nybergsund the full treatment. The Nazi flyers demolished it with explosive and incendiary bombs and then machine-gunned those who tried to escape the burning ruins. The Germans apparently believed at first they had succeeded in massacring the King and the members of the government. The diary of a German airman, later captured in northern Norway, had this entry for April 11: *Nybergsund. Oslo Regierung. Alles vernichtet.* ("Oslo government. Completely wiped out.")

But it had not been wiped out. The sixty-eight-year-old King, along with his ministers and the villagers, had taken refuge in the nearby woods. The inhabitants of Nybergsund still tell of the King sitting with them in the snow trying to console them while they watched the German barbarians reducing their modest cottages and possessions to ashes.

Haakon and his ministers now made their way — a step ahead of the advancing Germans — up the Gudbrands Valley and, on April 23, reached Molde on the Romsdals Fjord. On the twenty-ninth the Luftwaffe, still intent on killing the defiant Norwegian leaders, severely bombed the town. That evening, while Molde was going up in flames, the King, the Crown Prince and the government ministers went aboard the British cruiser *Glasgow*, which took them far north to Tromsö, where on May Day the provisional capital was set up.

By this time the southern half of Norway had been irretrievably lost. The British and French had made a desperate effort to help the Norwegians stem the tide by trying to recapture the vitally important city of Trondheim. But it was too little and too late. On April 15 some 8000 British and French troops, without artillery or antiaircraft support, were landed at Namsos, north of Trondheim; and on the seventeenth, three British battalions were disembarked at Åndalsnes, south of Trondheim. But the drive on the city failed and, by the end of the month, the Anglo-French command announced to the discouraged Norwegians that it had been ordered to withdraw. On the first of May, the Norwegian forces in the south formally capitulated.

In the north around Narvik, the great port from which Swedish iron was shipped to Germany, the fighting continued for another month. Narvik had been treacherously surrendered to the Germans on April 9 by the Norwegian commander, Colonel Konrad Sundlo, a friend of Quisling, though not before Norway's two largest warships, the *Eidsvold* and the *Norge*, each of about four thousand tons, had gone down fighting with the loss of three hundred men — almost their entire crews. But soon afterward two British naval attacks wiped out the German naval force there, and on May 28 a sizable army of Norwegian, British, French and Polish troops recaptured the city. It seemed probable that the Norwegians, with Allied help, would be able to hold the northern third of the country indefinitely, not only depriving Germany of the iron ore which came out of Narvik, but forcing the Germans to maintain considerable forces in central Norway. For a few heady days it appeared that for the first time Hitler had been stopped. He had failed to conquer all of Norway. A free government at Tromsö still ruled over a vast area in the North.

But this happy situation was not to last. Already disaster had struck the Allies in the Low Countries and in France. The British and French needed every ship, soldier, gun and plane they could muster at home. An immediate Allied withdrawal from northern Norway was ordered. The Norwegians, left alone, were forced to capitulate, and on June 7 the King, the Crown Prince and the members of the government boarded the British cruiser *Devonshire* at Tromsö and departed for London and five years of bitter exile.

Treason, Oppression and Resistance

Meanwhile in Oslo a weird figure, who was to make his name a new synonym in all languages for a traitor, was striving to take over the government and to curry the favor of his Nazi German masters with whom he had long intrigued.

Major Vidkun Abraham Lauritz Quisling had begun his career honorably enough. Born in 1887 of peasant stock, he had graduated first in his class at the Norwegian Military Academy and while still in his twenties had been sent to Petrograd as military attaché. For his services in looking after British interests after diplomatic relations were broken with the Bolshevik government, Great Britain awarded him the C.B.E. In Russia his brilliance and knowledge of Russian had attracted the attention of Fridtjof Nansen, Norway's great explorer and humanitarian, whose assistant in Russian war relief he became.

The success of the Communists in Russia impressed the young Quisling, and when he returned to Norway he offered his services to the Labor party, which at that time was a member of the Comintern.

He suggested that his experiences in Russia and on the Norwegian General Staff fitted him to establish a "Red Guard" in Norway. The Labor party was suspicious of him and of his project, and turned him down.

He soon veered to the opposite extreme, violently denouncing the Laborites and becoming interested in the budding Nazi movement in Germany. But it was not until he was named Minister of Defense in a Peasant party government in 1931 that he attracted national attention. In this post he proved not only a failure but, what was worse for him, a joke. One incident made him the laughingstock of the nation. On an evening in February 1932, he called the police to his home and announced that he had been attacked in his office that afternoon by unknown assailants who threw pepper in his eyes and knocked him senseless. The police offered a large award for information leading to the arrest of the thugs but none was ever discovered. And since no one else in the Ministry of Defense had noticed the assailants, the public concluded that the "attack" was a figment of the minister's imagination.

In February, 1933, the Peasant government was defeated and Quisling ceased to be Minister of Defense. Hitler's taking over power in Berlin a month before had kindled a great fire in Quisling's breast, and in May he launched his Norwegian brand of the Nazi party, the *Nasjonal Samling,* appropriating Hitler's ideology and tactics, even to having a herd of storm troopers whom he called the *Hird.*

Nasjonal Samling did not thrive in the fertile democratic soil of Norway. In the fall elections of 1933, it polled but 2 per cent of the votes; in 1936 but 1.83 per cent. In neither case was that enough, even in a proportional system of election, to send a single representative to Parliament. Defeated at the polls, Quisling turned to Germany for support. The war afforded him his opportunity.

It was not until the Nuremberg trial, after the war, brought to light the secret German documents that we were able to ascertain the extent of Quisling's treason. Apparently the unsuspecting Norwegian government had no inkling of it at the time. From the Nuremberg papers it is clear that Quisling, more enthusiastic about a German occupation of Norway than were the Germans themselves at first, spent half a year trying to interest Berlin in the project.

In the beginning Hitler was cool. It took some time before Alfred Rosenberg, who directed part of the Nazi foreign network, and Grand

Admiral Raeder, succeeded in inducing the Fuehrer to see Quisling. Finally a meeting was arranged on December 16, 1939, and a second one two days later. Quisling tried to convince Hitler that the British intended to occupy Norway with the secret assent of the Norwegian government and that Germany must beat Britain to the punch. To accomplish this, Quisling emphasized, he was in a position to render valuable support. In fact, he already had a plan.

The secret papers of Rosenberg and Admiral Raeder reveal what it was. Quisling and his aides, reinforced by a few specially trained German Nazi agents, would seize power in Oslo and then call upon the Germans for military aid which, in fact, would already be on the way. (This was the pattern that had worked so well in Vienna in 1938.)

Hitler and his military advisers obviously had little confidence in Quisling's ability even to grab control for a few hours. They eventually decided to conquer Norway outright. But there is no doubt that Quisling was a party to the German plans. Rosenberg records that toward the end of March 1940 he received an urgent message from Quisling saying that "any further delay would mean a grave risk." The German response was to send a General Staff officer to confer secretly with Quisling in Copenhagen at the beginning of April. On April 4, when the first German ships were putting out for northern Norway, General Jodl noted in his diary: "Piepenbrock, chief of Military Intelligence I, returns with good results from the talks with Quisling in Copenhagen."

So it was not surprising that in Oslo, on the fateful evening of April 8, Quisling moved from his apartment to the centrally located Hotel Continental, where he set up headquarters and sent out his storm troopers to distribute handbills calling on the government to resign, demanding power for his "Nasjonal Samling" and assuring the populace, as we have seen, that Norway stood at the dawn of a new day.

The following evening, after German troops had occupied the capital, Quisling stormed into the Oslo radio station, and, taking to the air, proclaimed himself head of the government, canceled all mobilization orders and commanded all Norwegian resistance to the Germans to cease. If this precise moment was one of national shame for the Norwegian people it also turned out to be a blessing in disguise. For it instantly aroused a public which had been stunned by the unexpected German onslaught. Treason was something the mass of the people understood and execrated. It was the treason of Quisling which first shocked the Norwegian people into a resistance which was to grow to formidable proportions in the ensuing brutal years. Even many of Quisling's closest followers deserted him that evening when they saw what he was really up to.

He was allowed to be up to it, to begin with, for just six days. Then the Germans, astonished at the paucity of his supporters and at his unpopularity and incompetence, dismissed him and requested the Supreme Court to appoint an administrative council of seven leading citizens to try to restore some semblance of order. The council had no legal title or political standing and was, in fact, approved by the King as a stopgap measure.

On April 24, Hitler appointed Josef Terboven, a tough young Nazi *Gauleiter*, to be Reich commissar for Norway. This youthful thug, aided by the Gestapo, immediately set to work to "co-ordinate" Norway.

Hitler had not forgiven Haakon VII for defying him and then slipping beyond his grasp, and so one of his first orders to Terboven was to force the Norwegian Parliament to depose the King once and for all. Paal Berg, the venerable but scrappy Chief Justice of the Supreme Court, who was later to become the Chief of the Home Front (the underground) — a secret revealed only at the war's end — declared that any such step would be unconstitutional, but the Germans were not interested in his juridical arguments. They sent an ultimatum to the Presidential Board of the Storting, stating that unless it got rid of the King all Norwegians of military age would be shipped off to concentration camps in Germany. The Norwegian parliamentarians weakened. The alternative to capitulation seemed hideous. Besides, far stronger countries were giving in to Hitler at this very moment. The King of the Belgians had just surrendered to him. France had just collapsed and the venerable Marshal Pétain had offered Hitler his collaboration. A weakening of the Norwegians was at least understandable. On June 27 the Presidential Board gave in to the Germans and wrote King Haakon asking him to abdicate. In a dignified reply pointing out that the parliamentarians had acted under compulsion and in an unconstitutional way, the King politely declined the request.

In September the Germans made one last attempt to force the Storting to depose the King. This time it flatly refused. The Nazi attempt to induce Norway to take its place in Hitler's New Order by constitutional action had failed. On September 25, Terboven himself decreed that "the Norwegian Royal Family had forfeited their right to return." He also dissolved the democratic political parties and appointed a state council of Quislingites in which Quisling's name was conspicuously absent. From now on Norway was to be ruled with an iron hand by the Germans as a conquered province.

Gradually the Norwegians began to organize resistance to that rule both in the open and underground. The principal institutions of the country set an example to the people by declining to become Nazified or "co-ordinated" and by stubbornly refusing to compromise their principles. In December 1940, the Chief Justice and the fifteen judges of the Supreme Court resigned rather than comply with the German commissar's orders. The Church showed great courage from the beginning. Pastoral letters, issued in spite of Nazi bans, protested against Nazi barbarity. After Germany attacked Russia all but 27 of the 1100 pastors refused to sign an appeal for Norwegian volunteers to join the "crusade against Bolshevism." In February 1942 all the bishops and deans, led by the ranking primate, Dr. Eivind Berggrav, Bishop of Oslo, resigned their offices in protest against Nazi persecution, and on Easter Sunday that year all the clergymen, except for a handful of Quislingites, followed suit. Bishop Berggrav and many other leaders of the Church were arrested and sent to concentration camp, where several of them were tortured.

The professors, teachers and students showed equal courage. At Oslo University all but two of the 90 members of the faculty declared their anti-Nazism. The rector of the university, Professor Didrik Arup Seip, and a good part of his faculty, were arrested and carted off to concentration camp. Some 650 students were transported to camps in Germany. Of Norway's 14,000 public school teachers, 12,000 refused in written statements to participate in a forced program to Nazify education. The Germans arrested 1300 of them and packed them off like cattle to the arctic port of Kirkenes near the Soviet frontier. There they were housed in filthy, overcrowded bar-

racks with Russian prisoners of war and put to work as slave laborers.

The trade-union movement was very strong in a Norway that had
had a Labor government for five years, and the Germans set about
immediately to smash it. On September 10, 1941, over a thousand
union leaders were arrested and two of the most popular of them
condemned to death and shot. But an underground free trade-union
movement continued throughout the war.

The Norwegian underground, known as the Home Front, was
divided into a military and a civil section. The first, "Milord," gradually built up a secret army that numbered 47,000 men at the war's
end. In close contact with the High Command in London, which
flew in both arms and specially trained commandos, its task was to
carry out sabotage, provide intelligence to the Allies, prepare for
guerrilla war and eventually either join in driving the Germans out
or take over immediate control should the Germans surrender.

The civil section of the Home Front was concerned mainly with
maintaining the morale of the people, keeping them informed of
what was going on outside and inside Norway, and sabotaging German efforts to recruit man power and increase industrial production.
Eventually some three hundred underground publications with a total
circulation of a quarter of a million supplied the people with the
foreign and domestic news denied them by the heavily censored press
and by the German action in confiscating all radio sets and imposing
the death penalty on anyone caught listening to a broadcast from
London.

To participate in the resistance movement was not child's play, as
the Norwegians soon learned. In order to stamp it out the Gestapo
instituted a reign of terror. It carried out 336 executions, many
of them of completely innocent but prominent persons who were
shot as hostages or as mere warnings. In all, 40,000 Norwegians were
arrested during the occupation and imprisoned, of whom 2000 died
from maltreatment (torture), starvation and illness. When I got to
Norway I met few persons prominent in public life, in government,
in business, in labor, in the university, in the arts, who were not
"graduates" — as they said — of Sachsenhausen concentration camp
in Germany, or the Grini concentration camp in Norway. This cir-

cumstance may explain why the Norwegians do not completely share the current illusions about the Germans so prevalent in certain other Allied lands.

In the meantime, the Norwegian government in London was organizing a considerable contribution to the Allied war effort. It possessed one tremendous weapon of war desperately needed by the hard-pressed Allies: a merchant fleet of more than 1000 ships totaling 4,000,000 tons, and manned by 25,000 seamen, which had not fallen into Germany's hands. It was immediately pressed into service in the war against Hitler. At the peak of the battle of the Atlantic nearly half of all the precious oil arriving in Great Britain came in Norwegian tankers. "Norwegian tankers," said one British minister in 1942, "are to the battle of the Atlantic what the Spitfires were to the battle of Britain." And Admiral Land, chairman of the U.S. Maritime Commission, declared that the Norwegian merchant fleet was worth a million soldiers to the Allies.

Moreover this fleet enabled the Norwegian government-in-exile to pay its own way. "Nortraship," as the organization which controlled the ships was called, became the world's largest shipping enterprise, with fifty branch offices all over the world, and brought in a gross profit of over half a billion dollars.

From its headquarters in London the Norwegian government also organized new armed forces. Flyers were trained in "Little Norway," a camp near Toronto. Special commando and sabotage detachments were formed in Britain and parachuted into Norway. Among their accomplishments was the blowing up of the sole industrial plant in the world producing heavy water, which the Germans were using in their efforts to develop an atomic bomb. A new navy of 57 ships was built up which succeeded in sinking or damaging 153 enemy vessels. The valiant little Norwegian air force, which included two squadrons of Spitfires, was credited with destroying or damaging 445 German planes and 18 submarines. As the war neared an end Norway had an armed force of 76,300 men — 15,000 in Britain, 47,000 in Norway and 14,300 (police troops) in Sweden.

In February, 1942, the Germans had made Quisling Prime Minister, but all the traitor's efforts to Nazify his people broke down against the stubborn resistance of 98 per cent of the populace who refused to have anything to do with him. The real ruling power of course remained with the Germans. Late in January, 1945, as Germany began to crumble before the Allied attacks from the West and East, Hitler received Quisling at his headquarters and promised to restore Norway's freedom and independence as soon as victory was won. But news of this did nothing to enhance Quisling's reputation at home. The ridiculous man apparently believed to the very last that he could head a transition government that would "save the country from civil war."

On May 8, 1945, following the German capitulation in the West, the Reich forces in Norway surrendered. Terboven, General Rediess, the sadistic head of the S.S., and Jonas Lie, his Norwegian counterpart, committed suicide and Quisling and his "ministers" gave themselves up and were imprisoned. On June 7, five years to the day after he had been forced to leave his native soil, King Haakon VII returned to Oslo in triumph and was accorded a wildly enthusiastic welcome by a deliriously happy population.

The Germans were defeated, Quisling was in jail.[3] The hateful occupation was over. Norway was free. But devastated and plundered, it faced a Herculean task of reconstruction and readjustment to a strange new world that bore little resemblance to the one that had gone down in 1940 — except that it seemed full of uncertainties.

The Miracle of Reconstruction

When the summer's celebration of liberation was over, the Norwegians settled down to start rebuilding what the war had destroyed. The extent of that destruction was appalling. The northern part of Norway, an area as large as Belgium and the Netherlands combined, had been laid waste by the Germans in their retreat before the Russians who had come in from the Petsamo region. All the towns, harbors, mines, factories, bridges, homes and livestock in the region had been completely destroyed. During five years of war half of the Nor-

---

[3] He was given an exhaustive and eminently fair trial, found guilty of treason and sentenced to death on September 17, and after the Supreme Court had rejected his appeal on October 13, executed on October 24.

Knut Hamsun fared better. Treason charges against him were dropped on the grounds of his old age and senility, and he was merely tried for "profiting from the Nazi regime" and fined $85,000, a sum which the Supreme Court later reduced to $65,000. He died on February 19, 1952, at the age of ninety-three.

wegian merchant fleet had been sunk. Stocks of goods were exhausted. Germany had milked the country dry, drawing some three billion dollars from the Bank of Norway to finance the occupation expenses. All in all the war had cost Norway some 20 per cent of its national wealth, or the equivalent of three years of national income. It was a staggering blow and it was made worse by the fact that the only means by which Norway could exist — the export industries — shipping, fisheries, mines and manufacturing — had been shattered. Moreover Norway's markets and sources of imports in Germany and the rest of Europe were in shambles at the war's end.

Victory and restored freedom were sweet. But the prospect for decent survival seemed dark indeed.

The response of the Norwegian people to this predicament was characteristic of them. They at once embarked on a bold program of rebuilding which called for, above all, severe austerity and hard work. If the economy was to be restored, immense sums had to be poured into capital investment. Consumption had to be held to a bare minimum so that more money could be spent to buy ships, machines and building material. Large surpluses of imports had to be risked to augment investments.

Here the wartime unity of the people helped to carry Norway through. Labor unions gave a no-strike pledge so that there should be no costly work-stoppages. Businessmen and financiers went along with a system of strict government controls of every aspect of commerce. The people put up with high taxes and drastic rationing. For the next few years they cheerfully accepted a continuance of the Spartan life which they had been forced to endure during the war. Even politics was largely postponed. All parties supported the Labor government's basic national program of reconstruction.

Its initial achievements were prodigious. Within a year industrial production was back at prewar levels. By the end of 1948 it stood at 125 (1938 equaled 100). At least one half of the entire reconstruction job had been completed. The merchant fleet had been brought up to its prewar tonnage, giving the little country again the third largest merchant marine in the world.

But there were difficulties and they were increasing. Norway, like other countries, was slowed down by the "recession" in 1947. An abnormal drought that year reduced agricultural output and curtailed the supply of hydroelectric power. To pay for the heavy excess of imports over exports, which was necessary to continue the reconstruction program on schedule, Norway had to borrow sizable sums. Some one hundred million dollars was borrowed from the United States and another forty million from Canada and Sweden. By the fall of 1947, it became evident that Norway would not be able to obtain the additional credits she needed. Brakes had to be immediately applied to the whole recovery program. Inports were cut down, and consumption. This was a severe blow to recovery, and for the people it spelled a hardship in the sinking standard of living that in many ways was worse than during the years of the occupation. Worst of all it dimmed the prospects for the future for which such heavy sacrifices by all citizens had been made.

In 1948, in the nick of time, as Erik Brofoss, the brilliant Minister of Commerce put it, there came aid from the United States under the aegis of the Marshall Plan. It was like manna falling from the heavens. It had not been expected. No other country in the world had ever made outright gifts to another.

For Norway the Marshall Plan and subsequent forms of American aid meant that it could continue and even speed up its planned reconstruction. It meant that the harsh rationing could be eased and eventually — by 1952 — largely abandoned. Already in 1949 — after four years of deprivation that had followed the five grim war years — Norwegians began to get more to eat and the diet was healthier. Also they were able to make a modest start in replenishing their depleted wardrobes. American aid to other countries in Europe also stimulated Norwegian trade with the continent. Finally, by contributing to Norway's economic recovery, it later put the country in a position where it could afford to rearm against the Russian threat on a scale not dreamed of in the dreamy days before 1940.

No American meandering about Norway and Denmark in recent years could fail to feel a certain pride on hearing from the people of these lands what Marshall Plan aid had done for them. Here was a generous and solid contribution to their welfare that in the end, I think, outweighed their later misgivings over the quality of our leadership of the free world.

It would be easy, of course, to exaggerate the benefits of our aid. It did not, by itself, save Norway and the other countries which received it. It did furnish the additional margin which, coupled with hard work and sacrifice, enabled them to get fully back on their feet. For Norway, it made up 10 per cent of her war losses. It provided 18 per cent of her net investments. Up until 1953, when it virtually ended, it amounted for Norway to $458,500,000, of which 10 per cent was in repayable loans.

With this help and their own further efforts the Norwegians were able in a short time to accomplish what European and American observers have called a "miracle of reconstruction." Taking 100 as the index of 1938, industrial production at the beginning of 1953 stood at 149, agricultural output at 117. The merchant fleet had a tonnage of over six million tons — 27 per cent more than before the war. The North was rebuilt. Hydroelectric power was increased 50 per cent. Real wages were 16 per cent higher than before the war, and there was no unemployment.

These are dry figures and facts. But they measure the magnitude of a very real triumph of the Norwegian people, the results of which were apparent when I reached Norway. In eight years of sacrifice and toil the country had, with American help, recovered from the worst disaster in its history. Taken into account with other developments which we shall shortly cover, life for Norwegians had become, as they said, full of promise again.

Behind the reconstruction lay a philosophy. It was one that was, and is, constantly debated in Norway but which has become increasingly dominant in a country ruled for more than two decades by a powerful Labor party. It was best articulated for me in a long and exhaustive talk with Erik Brofoss, the then Minister of Commerce, who later became President of the Bank of Norway, and expanded by notes which he gave me.

Brofoss is a controversial figure in Norway today. The Labor government regards him as one of its most brilliant men. He strikes you at once as a highly intelligent, dynamic, energetic fellow who has mastered all the intricacies of modern economics and who will battle fanatically for his interpretation of them. He is personable, and has a passionate concern for the welfare of the common people. Business leaders did not conceal from me their admiration for his brilliance and his capacity to get things done. But they made no bones either about their resentment of what they considered his aggressiveness toward businessmen, his scorn of untrammeled private enterprise and his burning zeal for state planning and for government restrictions on every phase of commerce.

Brofoss readily admits that political and social as well as economic considerations determined the Labor government's program of reconstruction. "Fascism, Nazism and also Communism," he argues, "were the offspring of the frustration and despondency which were the results of the mass unemployment and economic stagnation caused by the deflationary policy of the 1920's and the 1930's. Full employment was therefore essential to the preservation of democracy, and it became the cornerstone of Labor policy. Equally important was a policy of 'fair shares,' that is, of a more even distribution of income.

"When we embarked on our recovery program, the government felt that it could not rely upon the market mechanism, partly because the monetary system was dislocated but also because the experience of the interwar period had shown the imperfections of the principles of *laissez faire* in attaining full employment and the full utilization of available resources. Therefore, we decided, it should be the responsibility of the elected constitutional bodies, the Storting and the Cabinet, to take an active part in achieving full employment and the utilization of resources through a planned economy, having powers to stimulate, control and direct a mixed economy of private and public enterprise."

That was the basis, and it was part of what Brofoss glowingly speaks about as the working out of economic and social democracy, which he regards as being as important as political democracy.

"The Labor party," he told me, "considers it essential to develop an economic democracy. Our views of that are based upon what can be called the 'social concept of capital.' The owner of a private enterprise does not merely exercise exclusive private legal rights and does not administrate his private property only. He is entrusted with the management of the productive capital of our society, upon which economic progress, social prosperity and the economic future of the workers depend. We think that democracy is something more than political democracy with a right to vote. It should also include the recognition of the workers as partakers in the organization of economic life."

I had a question, but he anticipated it.

"All right, you ask — but what will happen to initiative when management no longer is an exclusive right of the owner?

"My answer is this: It is right to stress the importance of initiative, but we believe it to be beside the point to consider *only* the initiative demonstrated by the owners of industrial enterprises. The decisive point is the initiative, the will to work and the will to make a contribution demonstrated by the tens of thousands who produce the goods. To achieve this end we must find ways to appeal to and catch the imagination of the common man. He must feel himself responsible."

Were not such policies leading to the nationalization of private industry?

The Norwegian Minister of Commerce did not think so.

"The Labor party does not believe that all private enterprise should be nationalized. We would support co-operatives rather than nationalization. In general, the Labor party thinks that control and direction are more essential than nationalization. . . .

"As for our program of 'fair shares' for all," Brofoss added, "that does not mean a mechanical equality for all men, but rather a recognition that deviation from equality requires in all cases a particular justification on grounds either of social need or of effort."

All this constituted a view that I was to hear echoed by Labor party leaders in all of the northern states. And being in the saddle, except in Finland and for a short period (1950–1953) in Denmark, they were in a position to translate their ideas into action.

The Conservatives seemed impotent. They were not silent. They still controlled most of the press, though not any of the radio, which was run on nonpartisan lines by the state. They still had sizable groups in Parliament, whose leaders were indeed vocal in their protests against the way things were going.

In Oslo, I attended a debate in the Storting on a drastic new law to set up governmental machinery for permanent price controls. The Conservative press had been outraged by the proposal, now that Norway was back on its feet, and its sentiments were being purveyed to the Assembly by the Conservative members. One shouted that the new legislation would undermine the state based on law. All the familiar objections to a permanently directed economy were aired. But the Labor majority passed the bill, and in the elections which shortly followed — in the fall of 1953 — it was returned to office by the electorate.

The point was that Labor had the political power. This enabled it to accumulate economic and social power too. It was true — and it should be emphasized — that private enterprise, despite the flourishing of the co-ops and the nationalization of public utilities, communications and some few industries and some trade, (mostly nationalized by Conservative governments before the advent of Labor), still owned most of the business undertakings in Norway. But it was held strictly accountable to a Socialist government, which controlled it with an eagle and sometimes suspicious eye.

The common people had achieved at the polling booth, where they had the most votes, the right to rule the country through their own party. They were using their newly-won authority — as they believed the upper classes had in the years before — to get a good deal of what they wanted. Such is the "revolution" — as some regard it — in Norway, and, to a slightly less extent, in Sweden and Denmark. It has been carried out bloodlessly, legally, democratically. It is far from finished, and could be reversed by the same method which brought it about: the vote of the people.

If the Norwegian Labor government believes in a planned economy at home directed by the state, it is all for free trade among the nations. Because it must export to live, Norway's prosperity depends largely on the state of the world market, and the postwar restrictions on international commerce and the fall of world prices beginning in 1952 have hit it badly. In the first quarter of 1953 alone sinking world prices cost Norway two hundred million dollars and produced a serious trade deficit for the year. World prices and foreign restrictions on imports of goods are factors which, of course, are beyond the control of the Norwegian Labor government. There is nothing it can do about them and this impotency sometimes, I found, weighs heavily upon its leaders. Brofoss, who calls free trade "an international division of labor," reminded me that Norway has no restrictions on 83 per cent of its imports from Marshall Plan countries; and he, like all other Scandinavian ministers, economists and businessmen I was to see, finds it difficult to understand why the United States, which professes to believe so strongly in the free market, puts so many difficulties through high tariffs and import quotas on the buying of Norwegian and other foreign goods.

The principal immediate economic objectives of the Labor government, besides maintaining full employment, and ensuring an equitable distribution of the available supply of goods and services, are to achieve a balance of trade at a high level and to obtain additional capital to increase production, above all, by developing its great potential of hydroelectric power. Exports and imports were balanced in 1951 and 1952 and then became unbalanced due to world conditions. As to the last objective, savings through austerity, loans and Marshall Plan aid together produced sufficient capital to enable Norway to carry out a higher rate of investment than any other country in the world — some 35 per cent of the national product — enough to more than restore the economy shattered by the war.

But foreign private capital, Brofoss told me, is shy of Norway, especially since the threat of Russian aggression became acute in 1948. He cited the example of two of the world's biggest electrical companies which became interested after the war in investing in Norway's water power development. They withdrew in 1948 after the Communist coup in Czechoslovakia, and the rumors of a coming Soviet attack on Norway. Investment in Norway, they said, had become too risky.

The Way Norwegians Live

Until comparatively recently the Norwegians had lived for centuries mainly from farming, fishing and sailing. Many of them still do.

Although only 3 per cent of the land is cultivable, some one-quarter of the population is engaged in agriculture. Their 345,000 farms are small. About half of them average only four tillable acres and the other half about 18 acres. In the entire country there are only 37 farms of 250 acres or more. Yet these sparse holdings supply 70 per cent of the agricultural produce required by the nation and furnish almost all of the meat, eggs and milk consumed in the country. Since the war mechanization, although not always suitable to the small rocky fields, has helped increase production and make up for the loss of man power. The number of tractors in 1954 was 22,000 compared to 4000 in 1945. Combines were unknown in Norway before the war, but in 1954 there were 2000 of them in use, almost all of them in pools.

A typical farm in Norway lies at the foot of a mountain. On 18 cultivated acres the proprietor — and 90 per cent of the farmers own their land — and his family maintain a horse or two, 8 cows, 10 sheep and goats, 2 pigs and 15 hens. The buildings are grouped around a courtyard, so that the family and its animals live in close proximity.

In the summer the livestock, the womenfolk and the children, like as not, move up to a mountain pasture, a *seter*, where the farmer has grazing rights and where a small cottage houses the ladies, young and old, who look after the animals.

On the whole, the Norwegian farmers look prosperous. This may be due partly to the fact that in most cases they enjoy a subsidiary income. If a man's farm is near the sea, as many are, he is a part-time fisherman. If his holdings border the forests, as many do, he becomes a woodsman in the winter months. The probability is that a chunk of the nearby forest belongs to him, as the farmers own, individually, 70 per cent of the Norwegian timber land. Since it amounts to a total of 19,000,000 acres — one of the biggest wooded tracts in Europe — it is obviously a considerable source of profit to a man who on his tiny plot keeps only a few cows, sheep and goats, but who possesses a hundred acres or so of woods.

Finally, the farmers in Norway are highly organized in producers' and purchasing co-operatives, receive support and encouragement from the government, and the more prosperous ones even have their own political party to make their views known in Parliament.

But agriculture has long ceased to be the principal source of production in Norway. In 1953 mining and manufacturing ranked far ahead of all other enterprises, followed — in the order of the amount of money earned — by shipping, agriculture, building, forestry, fisheries, electric power and whaling.

Wood products, especially pulp, paper and paper products, constitute the leading export commodity, followed by iron, steel and non-ferrous metal goods, fish, and oil and fat products which come largely from whaling.

Actually Norway's chief export, in terms of money earned abroad, is shipping, which in 1952 and 1953 brought in annual sums — almost all in badly needed foreign exchange — equal to half of all the other exports put together. One cannot dwell in this seafaring land for long without becoming aware of the importance of shipping and the allied enterprises of fishing and whaling in the life of the nation and the people. They are the foundation of the country's high standard of living.

I spent a morning chewing the fat with the shipping magnates of Oslo. They are an energetic and resourceful lot of fierce free-enterprisers, the last of the Viking adventurers, as some of the Labor party planners call them. The shipowners had plenty of gripes against the Socialist government, and they were not backward in venting them. While they agreed with the basic policy of the government immediately after the war in restricting consumption to the bare minimum so that as much as possible of the national income and foreign exchange reserves could be devoted to investment in capital goods, above all in new ships, they complained vociferously against the way the government had treated them. In the first place, they said, the shipowners themselves privately financed the purchase of every single ton of the 3½ million tons of new shipping, 90 per cent of which had to be bought from foreign shipyards and paid for in foreign currency.

"Didn't the government help you with subsidies?" I asked one old gentleman.

"On the contrary! We subsidized the government. And still do. Through tremendous taxes!" he replied.

Aside from high taxes, the shipowners' chief complaint was the familiar one of government interference in their business — which, as one explained, was risky enough without such hazards. There was time-wasting bureaucratic red tape, they said. There were rigid restrictions in the granting of licenses for placing contracts abroad for new ships. What seemed to burn these gentlemen above all was that between 1948 and 1950 the government forbade their ordering any new ships at all from foreign yards even though they had private means of financing such purchases.

Nevertheless it must be said that they did not do badly. On May 8, 1945, the merchant fleet, halved by sinkings during the war, was down to 2,700,000 tons. By 1948 it had risen to four million tons and by 1954 to six and a half million tons, or somewhat larger than it had been at the outbreak of the war. Only the United States and Great Britain outranked Norway in this field.

Today the Norwegian merchant fleet sails the seven seas and only 15 per cent of its vessels ever touch at home ports. The rest, including 95 per cent of the tankers, which comprise over half the fleet, voyage year after year exclusively between foreign harbors. More and more the Norwegians are concentrating on the lucrative oil trade. Three quarters of the contracts for new vessels are for tankers.

The Norwegian shipping moguls have one gripe against the outside world. Too many countries, including America, they complained to me, insist on too much of their goods being carried in their own ships, and these restrictions make it difficult for the Norwegians, who have comparatively little trade of their own, to stay in business.

"Don't forget," one shipowner said, "that our merchant marine played a decisive part in the Allied victory in the last war. Now we've joined NATO. In any future emergency a highly developed and experienced transport fleet such as ours could play a vital role for the Western world — that is, if you don't stifle us first by your restrictions." Like the Labor government, which so aggravates them, the Norwegian shipowners are fanatic believers in free world trade. They too call it the ideal international division of labor.

The smell of fish often permeates the air along the waterfront of the innumerable and picturesque harbor towns that lie on Norway's fjord-indented mountainous west coast. Fishing has become Big Business, though today most of the fishermen own — either outright or through co-ops — their own boats and gear. In 1952 and 1953 the annual catch in Norway amounted to a million and a half tons of fish and was worth a hundred million dollars. These yearly figures represent quite a lot of food and money for a country whose population is less than half that of New York City. The Norwegians don't eat all the fish they catch. They devour a lot, but most of it is sold abroad, constituting the country's third biggest export.

In Bergen, the chief port on the west coast, I picked up a good deal of lore from the hardy fishermen and others. I learned that commercial fishing had become not only Big Business but a science. A century of remarkable research has produced an amazing amount of scientific information about the habitat of fish, their biology, their migrations and their life cycle.

The fruitful areas of the sea are the shallow-water regions, and not only Norway's broken coast line and multitude of fjords and islands provide these but also the great belts of banks which lie off its shores in the North Sea, the Norwegian Sea and the Barents Sea far to the north above the Arctic Circle. It is in these places that the sea bed provides a prolific plant and animal life to which vast shoals of fish are drawn in search of food and suitable locations to spawn.

Light and temperature and sea currents are important factors too. As the warm Gulf Stream approaches Europe, it splits into several branches. One flows northward along the coast of Norway to the Barents Sea. Another turns north towards Bear Island and Spitsbergen and on into the Polar Sea. But from the polar regions come counter cold-water currents flowing southward along the bottom of the sea. A third current of water of low saline content sweeps in from the Baltic so that along the Norwegian fishing banks there is a stratification of water in three layers, of various temperatures and salt content. The changes in the composition and position of these water strata, the periodic variations in temperature and the strength of the sun determine the growth of marine food supplies, and therefore the amount of fish which are sustained by them.

Herring and cod form 90 per cent of the Norwegian catch. The herring is a pelagic fish. Its home is in the great open sea. With the coming of winter it moves to the Norwegian coast to spawn. It is this part of its life cycle which forms the basis of the great winter herring catches from January to April. When the eggs are fructified, they sink to the bottom, often covering the sea bed so thickly that only the top layer hatches. The lower ones die from stifling. Great quantities of herring larvae are carried out to sea by the current. Others develop along the coast where the fish remain from three to five years. Those which are not caught move out to sea, remaining there until they are from four to seven years old — when they complete the cycle by returning to the coast to spawn. For centuries the Norwegian fishermen wondered what became of the great herring shoals outside of the spawning season. Not long ago it was discovered that many of them migrated to the vicinity of Iceland. Then in the summer of 1950 the Norwegian oceanic exploration ship *G.O. Sars* found large bodies of them summering in the open sea between Iceland and Jan Mayen Island in the North Atlantic. That autumn and winter the vessel, by means of the asdic and echo-sounder, was able to follow the herring back to their winter spawning on the Norwegian coast. The result of this discovery is that the Norwegians now fish for herring during the summer off Iceland and greatly enhance their annual catch.

As all fishermen know, there are good years and bad years. But by studying old records the Norwegians have been able to discover a striking pattern in herring fishing. From 1500 to 1847, they found, there were just four good periods when herring showed up on the coast in great numbers. Fortunately each period lasted a long time: from 50 to 80 years. The Norwegians say they are now in one of the good stretches. It began in 1885 and thus has been going on for 68 years.

Is the good cycle ending? The Norwegians don't know.

The cod, second in value in the Norwegian catch, is also pretty well known by now. Its local home is in the chilly Barents Sea north of Norway. It does not become sexually mature until it is from six to fifteen years old, after which it becomes *skrei*, as the Norwegians call it, and moves south to Norway's coast to spawn. For some reason not known, most of the cod make their way to one spot. This is the West or Vest Fjord, between the Lofoten Islands and the mainland. Once a year, in February and March, the annual Lofoten cod fishery takes place. It is a great event and has been for centuries, for in a few weeks it brings in more than half the cod caught in Norway. In an average recent year, 20,000 fishermen in 4000 boats took part in the Lofoten fishery. On a typical day, working in the lee of the snow-covered mountains of the islands, they put out 70,000 nets, five million line hooks and 14,000 hand lines. In 1947, which was a good year, they landed 38 million cod (145,000 tons) which through their own co-operative sales organization they sold for $10,000,000. On the other hand, 1953 and 1954 were disastrous years, the Lafoten catch sinking to all-time lows — one-third of the 1947 yield. The fishermen were so badly hit that the Storting had to vote a half-million dollars to provide most of them with other work.

In fishing, as in so many other fields, the Norwegians who do the actual work have combined, with the encouragement of the government, to see that they receive the full fruits of their labor. Between the wars, and especially in the 1920's, the fisher folk barely eked out a living. Prices fluctuated, but at a low level, and the fisherman did not always feel that he got his rightful share. The solution was sought in the establishment of fishermen's co-operative societies for the firsthand sale of fish. The Labor government[4] helped out by pushing through Parliament in 1938 the "Raw Fish Act," which prohibited the sale, processing or export of fish unless it was pur-

---

[4] To emphasize the importance it wished to give to fishing, the government established a Ministry of Fisheries after the last war. It also maintains a Directorate of Fisheries, and a Fisheries Research Institute at Bergen.

chased through a recognized fishermen's organization. Today the co-ops handle almost all the firsthand sales of fish.

There are some small companies which specialize mostly in deep-sea fishing with large steam and motor vessels, and they pay their men a percentage of the catch. But most of the 70,000 men who engage in fishing as their sole occupation own their own boats and tackle. To buy and operate some 12,000 decked vessels and thousands more of open boats takes capital — and here the government has stepped in to help by setting up the State Fishermen's Bank, which grants loans on easy terms.

Thus most Norwegian fishermen are independent operators — capitalists, if you like — not wage earners. They work for themselves and at their own risk, which is considerable to their lives, as well as — since there are bad years — to their pocketbooks. They form a sturdy group of individualists who have learned by experience the benefits of co-operation. Courageous, rugged and enterprising, they form one of the bulwarks of the Norwegian nation today.

Modern whaling dates from 1868 when a Norwegian, Svend Foyn, invented the shell harpoon. Until then the whale hunters had been unable to catch and secure the baleen type of whale, which was speedier in its movements than other whales and unfortunately sank when killed. Foyn's invention solved that problem and a great number of blue whales began to be caught in northern waters. Too many, in fact. For along about the turn of the century the stocks of whales in the Arctic Ocean became so slender that whaling hardly paid for itself. It was then that the whalers turned to the virgin waters of the Antarctic. In 1905 Chr. Christensen of the town of Sandefjord, which is now the international headquarters of the whaling industry, sent out the first floating factory ship to the Antarctic.

This invention enabled a ship to do the processing of whale into oil, which formerly had to be done at land stations to which the giant fish were hauled by the catching ships. It marked a revolution in whaling, which soon became Big Business.

The Norwegians, who continued to perfect the floating factory ship until by the 1920's it had become a giant vessel of as much as 25,000 tons, equipped with hauling slipways, giant rotary pressure boilers and much other ingenious gear, walked off with the bulk of this big business. In 1925 they took 61 per cent of the 14,000 whales landed in the Antarctic. In 1930 they brought in 63 per cent of the 40,000 whales caught. Of a world production of some 3½ million barrels of whale oil processed that year, the Norwegians accounted for 2¼ millions. But it was soon realized that more whales were being caught than were being spawned — the female of the species bears only one calf every two or three years — and that unless there was an international limitation agreement the Antarctic would soon be as scarce of whales as the Arctic — and for the same reason. The Japanese, who had entered the business in 1934, refused to be bound by an international agreement and the Germans, who came in two years later, also balked at first. However, the Second World War came to the rescue of the whales. Very little hunting was done and, as the Norwegians put it, the whales got a well deserved rest. In 1944 the Allies made an agreement to restrict the catch after the war to 16,000 blue whale units annually — an accord which is still observed. Most of the Norwegian whaling fleet was sunk during the last war, but was rebuilt up to ten giant floating factories and 131 catching ships. In 1950 the Norwegians processed 175,000 tons of whale oil valued at some $60,000,000. In 1953 Norway's share of the international pool was reduced and receipts fell off, though they were still sizable.

The Bureau of International Whaling Statistics of Sandefjord in Norway is a mine of information about the business. It swims with figures, such as this: since modern whaling began in 1868, until 1949, a total of 1,059,520 whales had been bagged in all the oceans, and 673,471 of them came from the Antarctic. That's quite a bit of big fish; and the Norwegians speared most of it.

Shipping, fishing and whaling, however, occupy only 8 per cent of some one and a half million persons gainfully employed. Mining and manufacturing employ one third, who produce nearly two billion dollars' worth of goods a year, or about one half of the national product, the leading industries being iron and steel, chemical and electric-chemical, wood and wood-products and pulp, cellulose and paper.

Such, then, in brief, is the economic basis of the Norwegian nation and people. But there is a great deal more to the story of how these people live.

Social Welfare and Social Security

The first thing that strikes an American in Norway — and indeed in the other Scandinavian lands as well — is that social welfare, including "socialized medicine," are no longer controversial public issues. This was illustrated in Norway as the country girded for the difficult task of reconstruction in 1945 immediately after the liberation.

A joint declaration of all the political parties stated: "Social legislation will be developed with a view to rendering public relief services superfluous. The social insurance schemes will be co-ordinated so as to constitute a universal social security system covering sickness, disablement, unemployment and old age. The problem of family allowances will be subjected to renewed consideration."

The task, now envisaged under what the government calls the "New Universal Social Security Plan for Norway," is far from finished. Chiefly for financial reasons its objectives can only be fully achieved by stages over a period of years. But a good start has been made — indeed it began around the turn of the century — and the accomplishments are sufficient to attract our notice. On the whole, the security offered by the state against unemployment, disablement and old age is similar to that which many Americans receive, under our various federal and state schemes. It is in health insurance and in family and child welfare that Norway (as well as Denmark and Sweden) has gone much further.

No man, woman or child in Norway lacks adequate medical and hospital care because he — or she — cannot afford it. No family in Norway faces the disaster of wiping out its life savings and going broke, or even going into debt, whenever a catastrophic siege of illness afflicts its members.[5] Illness is no longer even an economic hardship. These dread consequences have been rendered impossible by what the American Medical Association calls "socialized medicine" and what the Scandinavians call simply "health insurance."

[5] According to a survey conducted by the National Opinion Research Center under a grant from the Health Information Foundation and published in the *New York Times* on January 24, 1954, illness in the United States puts 8,000,000 families, or 16 per cent of the country's total, into debt each year for medical, hospital and dental services. In July, 1953, that debt amounted to $1,100,000,000. Voluntary health insurance covered but 15 per cent of the total cost of illness.

In Norway, I found, it works as follows:

Membership in the health insurance scheme is compulsory for all wage earners. Voluntary members are also admitted to health insurance irrespective of their income or financial status and subject only to their being in good health. The husband or wife of the insured person is also fully covered, as are dependent children under sixteen and parents staying with and supported by the insured person. If one is prevented by ill health from being voluntarily insured, he may insure his dependents.

According to the latest available figures, 85 per cent of the population, which numbers 3,375,000, is covered by the health insurance scheme, either compulsorily or voluntarily.

Health insurance gives them two distinct kinds of benefits:

1. Medical assistance, hospital and maternity-home treatment, transportation to and from hospitals, and funeral allowances.
2. Sickness benefits, family benefits and lying-in money, to compensate for unemployment during illness.

Originally medical treatment in Norway under the insurance system was granted absolutely free regardless of the expense. But this plan was abandoned in 1925 in favor of one based on the refund principle. It varies in different districts. In the cities the health insurance office pays the doctor directly according to the insurance rates for fees. But this does not cover the full fee charged each individual by doctors. The patient must himself pay the doctor the difference. In the smaller localities the patient pays the doctor his full fee and later, on presentation of the doctor's receipt, is refunded the insurance fee by the agency's office. In general, the insurance fund rate covers at least 65 per cent of the doctor's bill.

Thus in Norway, unlike in Britain and certain other countries, medical treatment is not absolutely free. From my talks in Oslo with doctors and government medical authorities I gathered that one reason for this was that it prevented abuses of the social insurance system. People are not likely to run to the doctor and take his valuable time on the slightest pretext — or on no pretext at all — if they have to pay at least part of his fee. Dr. Karl Evang, the dynamic Director General of Public Health in Norway, told me he did not like to contemplate a system whereby the care of disease should become entirely the responsibility of society. The individual, he thought, should have some responsibility too.

Be that as it may, the government's new universal social security plan does contemplate completely free medical treatment in the near future.

Incidentally, the Norwegian health insurance system provides that *all patients may consult doctors of their choice.* In Oslo, as well as in Stockholm and Copenhagen, one medical authority after another expressed to me his private resentment that this aspect of Scandinavian "socialized medicine" had been misrepresented by certain medical circles in America.

If doctors' care is not yet completely free in Norway, hospital care is. The only condition is that the patient must go to a "public" hospital — that is, one maintained by the state or the municipality. But since almost all of the hospitals in Norway are "public" by this definition, no handicap results from this stipulation. In the great public hospitals patients are given the accommodation they *need* and not necessarily that which they are willing to pay for. Private wards for those who can pay for them do not exist in Norway's public hospitals, but single and double rooms are available for patients who need them for medical reasons.

Medicines are not free under the Norwegian system. Dr. Evang has some very strong opinions on the subject. "Until more rational forms for production, distribution, advertising and control of drugs have been found," he told me, "and as long as the public is still partly under the strong influence of magic and emotional thinking and superstition regarding the effect of medicines, it seems to me to be the wisest procedure to limit free drugs under the sick insurance scheme (outside of the hospital, of course) to those which are of vital importance."

So in Norway the health insurance scheme provides free hospitalization, including surgery, and at least 65 per cent of the doctor's bill. There are numerous other benefits such as assistance by a licensed midwife and lying-in money for a period of twelve weeks — six weeks before and after a woman's confinement. All these provisions of the sick insurance plan take a load off the family budget and thereby ease one source of family worries. But what about the loss of income while one is ill and unable to work? This is considered too.

In such a case the Health Insurance office pays the member a so-called sick benefit. The sum depends upon the wage or salary of the person but in general it amounts to 60 per cent of one's average earnings. In addition to this, the patient receives what is called a "breadwinner's supplement." The rate for this is two crowns (30 cents) per day for the first dependent — wife or child — and one crown per day for each of the other dependents. In no case must the two benefits exceed 90 per cent of the patient's wage. What if the employer continues to pay the wage or salary of the sick person? In that case the employer is entitled to the employee's pecuniary sick benefit — either by direct payment from the employee or by deductions from his wages or salary.

One other detail. During a period of hospital treatment no pecuniary sick benefit is paid, but if the patient has dependents he receives family compensation at the rate of two-thirds of the pecuniary sick benefit for the first dependent, two crowns a day for the second dependent, and one crown a day for each of the others. If the patient dies the insurance fund chips in thirty dollars toward his funeral expenses.

In sum, a sick Norwegian breadwinner receives not only compensation for all of his hospital and two thirds of his doctor's bill; he is paid up to 90 per cent of his earnings lost by absence from his work.

Now, what does he pay in return for all this?

State health insurance premiums, unlike those of private insurance companies, are based not on the amount of benefits but on one's income. They vary from 8 cents a week in the lowest wage-salary group to 70 cents a week in the highest, with voluntary members paying about 25 per cent more than that, according to their income. But the employer, the municipality, and the state chip in too. The employer must pay a weekly sum equal to 45 per cent of the member's premium, the local authority must pay an amount equal to 25 per cent, and the state 20 per cent. Thus the member's premium is nearly doubled from other sources.

Unlike most other national health insurance systems, which are supported largely from general taxation, the Norwegian scheme pays for itself. The premiums are based on actuarial principles so calculated as to make the system self-supporting, though, of course, the share of the municipalities and of the state in the premium payments must come out of taxation.

In 1951, for example, expenditures on health insurance were $42,-500,000 and receipts from premiums $44,600,000, giving the insurance agency a surplus of a little over $2,000,000. Since then receipts and expenditures have generally balanced.

Dr. Karl Evang, M.D., F.R.S.M. Hon., F.A.P.H.A. (to give him a few of his titles), is Director General of Public Health in Norway and, as such, is not directly concerned with the Norwegian Health Insurance System. However, when I first arrived in Oslo nearly everyone advised me that he was the man to see about it. A restless, energetic, brilliant man of medicine, he is considered one of the world's authorities on public health and sick insurance. In 1949, for instance, he was called in by the United States Military Government in Germany to advise it about reviving the German Public Health Administration and the German Sickness Insurance System, which had fallen into slothful ways after the war. Like Erik Brofoss, Dr. Evang is one of the bright lights of the Labor movement — though often, I was told, at odds with the hierarchy of the party, against whom he frequently rebels. However, in Norway permanent government officials, high and low, are not at the mercy of politicians or witch hunters, and Dr. Evang does not have to worry about his job. He is free to apply his intelligence and his fierce energy to what interests him most: all aspects of public and private medicine.

I spent several hours with him gathering not only the facts of the health insurance scheme but a glimpse of the philosophy behind it, which I had often heard so maligned at home.

"I believe," he said, "that the medical treatment of the individual is today at a transition-stage between being the sole responsibility of the patient and the doctor, and the responsibility of society. The medical profession itself is gradually becoming convinced by its own experience that doctors under sickness insurance systems may be offered satisfactory working conditions and, above all, that the insurance of the patient's health also means insurance of the doctor's income. In countries where the medical profession has violently opposed the insurance schemes, the result has invariably been that doctors have partly missed the opportunity to influence the development themselves, and consequently such insurance has been organized without their co-operation and without that technical guidance which would have been a benefit both to the patient and the doctor. I believe very strongly that in the final analysis medical activities can only be controlled by men with medical knowledge — that is, by the doctors themselves."

"In my country," I interrupted, "many doctors seem to think that compulsory national health insurance will lower standards of medical care, discourage initiative in research and thus prevent progress."

"On the contrary!" Dr. Evang exclaimed. "The tremendous strides forward in medical research in the last decades have taken place simultaneously with development of sickness insurance in one country after another. It has been proved beyond doubt that the quality of medical care need not suffer under such systems. On the contrary, in many countries such as ours the high standard, especially of curative medicine, would be unthinkable without sickness insurance. Even in those countries where the medical profession still resists the introduction of national sick insurance, the understanding is growing that at least hospital medicine needs a sound and lasting financial basis which can most easily be offered through a health insurance system.

"Even in your own country," Dr. Evang smiled, "rich though it is, aren't your hospitals having great difficulty in making both ends meet?"

As to the absolute need of a national health insurance scheme, there was not a cloud of doubt in Dr. Evang's mind.

"To my mind," he asserted, "it has become a necessity and a condition for nationwide medical care. The overwhelming majority of any country's population does not have the financial reserves to go through an extended period of illness without great worry and a burden which should not be added to that of a sick individual. To a great many people it simply means economic disaster. Such a situation, it seems to me, is untenable. And sickness insurance makes it impossible."

The doctor had one parting shot. "Remember," he said, "no country, so far as I know, has ever introduced sickness insurance on a considerable scale, and then dropped it. The scheme soon becomes deeply rooted in the people. There is no way back."

Of special interest is the Norwegian program which goes under the general heading of Family and Child Welfare. Developments in this field were first spurred by the alarming decline of the birthrate which set in after the First World War, and by the growing strain of social life in an increasingly industrialized society, especially in the larger towns. Moreover the more recent war and occupation added to the complications and difficulties of family life and placed new burdens on the young. Since the war the acute shortage of housing and the shifting of families to new places of employment have augmented the problem. It would be wrong, I think, to say that the Scandinavians have attempted in their social legislation in this field merely to reward childbearing. As the Norwegians explained to me, they have simply tried to provide for a normal birth rate, which they have now achieved, and then have sought to reduce the economic burden resting upon families with children and to make life a little easier for young mothers and more promising for the younger generation.

Family and Child Welfare development is still, as they say in Oslo, in the melting-pot stage. But since the war much progress has been made. One thing the Norwegians, like the Danes and Swedes, are rather fierce about in these matters. Family and Child Welfare, they say, should not be left to private charity. Primarily, they are sure, it is the concern of the community — the municipality and the nation.

The first move in this field was to provide a family allowance. By Act of Parliament every family receives an annual gift from the state of $35.00 for the second child and $48.50 for each additional one. Typical of the Norwegian concern that those sums should not be frittered away (say, by a father blowing it on drinks) is a proviso in the law stipulating that the money be paid preferably to the mother unless there is reason to believe that the mother will misuse it, in which case it may be paid to the father or to another person who can be counted upon to use it for the benefit of the children. Today more than 400,000 children receive this allowance at a cost of some $12,000,000 a year to the state and $2,000,000 to the municipalities. The Norwegians calculate that this state aid, in addition to special tax reductions, defrays about one third of the cost of a family having three children.

What about unwed mothers and their illegitimate children? An average of about 4000 children, or about 6 per cent of the total, are born out of wedlock annually in Norway and the state has gone to interesting lengths to see that they are not penalized in society. There is a law, for example, which assures them complete equality of status with legitimate children in regard to their legal family relationship to the father, entitling them to the father's surname irrespective of how he feels about it. Such children also are guaranteed equal rights of inheritance from the father with children born in wedlock. The only condition is that a child's claim to paternity be reasonably established. Norwegian law is quite ingenious in trying to determine this, and sets up a legal procedure to solve the problem — one of the oldest and most difficult in all history.

It works like this. The mother must state to the authorities the name of the man whom she believes to be the father. Her declaration is submitted to the county governor, who then serves a writ on the gentleman concerned, granting him a period of four weeks in which to take legal action should he deny paternity. Should he take to the courts, the law prescribes that he must be the plaintiff and the mother the defendant. It is the job of the judge to make sure that all relevant evidence is at hand when the court sits. The case is then decided, so far as is humanly possible, on the evidence thus presented.

If the alleged father does not take court action, he is automatically deemed to be the father. All recognized fathers of children born out of wedlock must assume economic and moral responsibility for the children's upbringing to the age of sixteen.

Among the further practical measures taken by the Norwegian state and municipalities for the welfare of mothers and children is the operation by the state and towns of 800 "control centers" to examine and take care of expectant mothers and later their children. All examinations are made by doctors assisted by trained nurses, and are given free. Then there are mothers' milk depots, as they are called, where mothers who have more milk than their children need, give it for the use of sick and prematurely born babies. There are mental hygiene clinics for small children. And there are what is called "maternal hygiene centers," private undertakings subsidized by the authorities, which, I was told in Oslo, give instructions in sexual hygiene and the use of contraceptives, in the health control of pregnant women and babies, and so on.

Midwifery is organized by the state. Midwives must have their professional diploma after graduation from a special public training school, after which they are licensed by the government to practice and assigned to districts just like other state health authorities. They are paid by the state and the municipalities.

What about the poor housewife? In Norway, I found, the all-embracing state is even giving her some attention. There is a project called: "Measures to Lighten Women's Work in the Home." It is concerned principally with mothers who are employed outside or who are ill. Among other things, a "housewife relief service" has been organized which provides professional workers, trained not only in domestic duties but in nutrition, hygiene, psychology of children, etc., to help out in the home when the mother is away or sick. Domestic service, always more prevalent in Europe than in America, is being made more attractive. Domestic servants, under a new law, work only a ten-hour day, including breaks for meals; they must be paid for overtime, receive suitable time off during the week and are entitled to an annual vacation of three weeks with full pay.

Vacations for housewives are encouraged too. Various private organizations devote themselves to this objective and are helped by the public authorities. Free vacations are now given to thousands of housewives and their children annually at special seashore and mountain camps. As one woman in Oslo told me, it is getting to be "almost fun" to be a housewife.

I should say that today in Norway, as in the other northern countries, the entire population gets a good annual vacation. In fact, from the end of June until September there is such an exodus from the cities that they are virtually given over to the foreign tourists. This is due, to a large extent, to the law that gives all wage and salaried employees a three weeks' annual vacation with pay. Almost every worker I talked to in Scandinavia had a little family cabin by the seaside or up in the mountains.

Among the innumerable other measures taken for the welfare of children there remain three which interested me particularly. Norwegian health authorities, like those elsewhere, have long believed that much of the illness in the country was due to bad teeth and that this could be largely remedied by proper dental care for children. A law passed in 1949 provides free dental treatment to all children up to eighteen years of age. (Eventually it is planned to include dental service for the entire population in the national health insurance scheme.) Parents of modest income who had had to expend considerable sums on dentists' bills for their youngsters, or who had simply been forced to see their children's teeth deteriorate because they could not afford proper dental care, were understandably appreciative of this boon.

For years in Europe I had heard of the importance of the "Oslo breakfast" to school children in numerous countries where it had been introduced, but had never understood what it was. In Oslo, it was easy to find out. The "Oslo breakfast" is the brain child of the late Prof. Carl Schiötz of Oslo University. Years ago he became convinced that children of school age, especially those in the younger groups, were not getting either at home or at school a proper diet at the very period in life when it was most necessary to build up the rapidly growing body. The first free school meals — offered to the poorer children in the form of hot lunches consisting of soup, cooked meat or fish and vegetables — did not provide, he felt, what was necessary. Dr. Schiötz, after much experimenting, decided that if there was to be a free meal in the schools it should be breakfast and that it should be rich in vitamins and minerals as well as proteins. He therefore developed the following menu, which soon became known as the "Oslo breakfast": a pint of milk; three sandwiches (one of hardtack to stimulate the teeth and gums, and two of whole-grain bread) spread with cheese, smoked herring, jam, and margarine or cod-liver paste; a raw carrot; and either half an orange or apple or one tomato or one-third of a pound of raw rutabaga. A simple fare, but it makes a sound meal to start the day. These free school breakfasts cost the city of Oslo $350,000 a year and this sum is considered by everyone I met there an excellent investment.

During my sojourn in Norway I was constantly surprised at the range of imagination of public-spirited Norwegians; there seems to be almost nothing that they forget or neglect. In their solicitude for child welfare, for example, they have even taken up, with their usual practical sense, the matter of what they call "right toys" for the young.

Shortly after the last war numerous parents, psychologists, nursery teachers and government officials became convinced that too many of the toys on sale in shops were "unsatisfactory." Too many of them dealt with soldiers, tanks, guns, war planes; others were just plain stupid. But the Norwegians didn't merely talk and deplore; they acted. They formed a company called "Right Toys, Ltd." (A/S Riktige Leker) to produce and market toys, children's books, furniture, and so forth. It is a commercial company, though in 1948 the Ministry of Social Affairs became a stockholder and granted certain financial support. The sale of toys today is under the management of a teacher, and there is an advisory committee to the company consist-

ing of two psychologists, two teachers and an official from the
Ministry. Right Toys, Ltd. is today a going concern.

I do not mean to give the impression that social welfare in Norway
is entirely the business of the democratic national state. In the first
place, a great deal of it is financed and carried on by the municipalities. Because of the great size of the country and the relatively small
and scattered population, local government assumes a more important role in Norway than in other northern countries and it is deeply
ingrained in these rather fiercely independent and individualistic people.

Voluntary organizations also play a significant part in social welfare. Norwegians, like Americans, are great organizers. The number
of their voluntary organizations seems endless. The four biggest
and most important groups are the Red Cross, the Norwegian People's Relief Association, the National Antituberculosis Association for
Public Health and the Norwegian Women's Health Association. They
all do an immense amount of good work. And so do countless others.
Among those I encountered were: the Norwegian National Child Welfare Council, which is the nucleus of 30 other voluntary organizations; the Norwegian Housewives Association; the National Council
of Women; the White Ribbon — which, as I was told, works for
women exposed to moral dangers; the Norwegian Blue Cross, which
labors in the field of alcoholics; and scores of organizations devoted
to the blind, the crippled, the deaf and dumb, the homeless, and
others. In Oslo I found over two hundred organizations working for
social welfare alone. All of these private groups in Norway supplement the work of the welfare state.

Social welfare, then, largely organized by the state and municipalities and financed from taxation and obligatory contributions by individuals and employers, but supplemented by the work of myriad
private and voluntary organizations, is deeply embedded in the life
and thought of the Norwegian people today. There are very few of
them who would prefer to go back to the old days of rugged individualism and of mere charity for the poor. If social welfare, along
with high, graduated taxation which pays for much of it, has brought
a tremendous leveling in the standard of living, as it has, the vast
majority of people think that is all to the good. Most of them, of

course, have profited by it; but it appeals to their sense of fairness too.

The term "social welfare state" does not frighten them as it does some people elsewhere, especially in the lands where social welfare has not progressed very far. The term does not for them connote anything decadent or dangerous or "radical," or a thing to be ashamed of and apologize for. The welfare state has not, they are sure, made them lazy and indolent; it has not stifled their initiative or their lust for life, as some feared. Today the Norwegians believe they are probably working harder than ever before and certainly they are producing more. They feel that their lives have become richer — in numerous and sometimes subtle ways. Freed from so many of the worries that have warped the mind and soul in the industrial age, the fear of unemployment, of the disaster of illness and accident, of the uncertainty of old age when personal earnings cease, they can turn the energies and the creativeness with which man is naturally endowed beyond the necessities of mere physical survival toward higher and more worthwhile horizons.

One evening in Oslo I was a guest at a small private dinner at which were present an eminent statesman, the president of a bank, a leading lawyer and a ranking permanent official of government. During the course of an excellent repast we drank, I suppose, one cocktail, a couple of glasses of wine and, as the talk continued long after midnight, a brandy or two. When we broke up the banker offered to drive me to my hotel in his car. But just as we were preparing to step into it, he hesitated and then said something which surprised me.

"No," he said. "It would be against the law."

"Against the law?" I asked, wondering what he could possibly mean.

"Yes, we have had a couple of drinks. That's one too many for me to be legally entitled to drive this car."

He hailed a taxi.

It was in this way that I first became acquainted with the strictly enforced and severe temperance laws of Norway, which I later found to be similar all over Scandinavia.

The statutes against drunken driving are only a small part of them, but they are illustrative of the measures to check excessive (and in most places in Norway even modest) drinking and its consequences.

Anyone caught driving a car with more than 0.05 of 1 per cent of alcohol in his blood gets an automatic jail sentence of three weeks, no matter who he is, Norwegian or foreigner, rich or poor, eminent or unknown, and whether he causes any mishap or not. You learn quickly how much drinking it takes to get 0.05 of 1 per cent of alcohol in your blood: one ordinary drink of spirits (a cocktail, a whisky, an aquavit) plus one glass of light beer. If you indulge in more than that of an evening, you drive at your own peril. Most don't.

Norway eventually abandoned Prohibition for the same reasons we did: the curse of the bootleggers and illicit distillers, and the general flouting of the law which outweighed whatever advantages it may have had. A temporary Prohibition promulgated by the government during the First World War had been made permanent in 1919 by a popular vote of 487,999 to 304,207. But aside from the abuses at home, Norway ran into further difficulties with the wine-producing countries of France, Spain and Portugal, which refused to buy fish from the Norwegians unless they could sell them their wines in return. In a referendum in 1926, the Norwegians abandoned Prohibition by a vote of 531,084 to 423,031, and thereafter a rather complicated system was set up providing for local option, a government monopoly of the production and sale of wine and spirits and various other measures which have combined to make the people of Norway, who a century ago were considered a race of hard drinkers, one of the soberest peoples in Europe. The annual consumption, in terms of undiluted spirits, amounts to only two quarts per head.

Wines and spirits are taxed out of the reach of many people. A bottle of imported brandy or whisky costs ten dollars; even local aquavit, brewed from potatoes and wood, costs three dollars a bottle. Indeed the state receives so much revenue from its liquor monopoly, the *Vinmonopolet*, that in 1949 it amounted to one sixth of the budget.

In the second place, local option and a national law prohibiting the sale of spirits in towns of four thousand or less, regardless of the wish of the inhabitants, has made of most of Norway a dry area. Out of 744 municipalities, only 20 qualify as places where hard liquor may be bought, only 10 qualify as places where it may be served, and of these latter only 6 permit it. I found that most villages didn't even permit the serving of wine and beer. Even where drinks may be sold, the hours are strictly limited from 3 P.M. to 11:45 P.M. and no spirits may be served on Sundays or holidays.

Also, to curb alcoholism there is a State Sobriety Council of five members appointed by the government, the chairman of which is an eminent psychiatrist; and, more important, there are local Sobriety Councils which, by act of Parliament, have been given almost absolute powers to control drunks and drunkenness.

These bodies, which have been set up in almost all communities, have the legal right to summon — by force, if necessary — an inebriate and look into every aspect of his case. If he is spending, as is likely, too much on drink, the Sobriety Committee can attach his wages or other income and turn it over to his wife or some other responsible person. The employer is legally bound to comply with the committee's decision.

Furthermore these Sobriety Committees have the power to commit a drunk to a sanatorium for a period of up to two years, regardless of whether he agrees to it or not. If he objects, however, he may appeal to the Supreme Court against the verdict. If he goes to an institution he must pay his own expenses, though recently the National Health Insurance office, which regards alcoholism as an illness, agreed to pay part of his costs.

Drunkenness, of course, has not been abolished in Norway but it is being reduced. Arrests for drunkenness — and I got the impression in Norway that the police tended to arrest an inebriate on sight, regardless of whether or not he is disturbing the peace — have been halved since 1923.

Housing, too, is regarded in Norway as an integral part of social welfare. Actually it only became a problem in 1930, when the mass migration which had carried 840,000 Norwegians[6] to the New World in the previous 80 years came to a stop and it was discovered that a good many new homes would have to be built for a naturally increasing population that was beginning to stay put. Then came the Second World War which not only halted housing construction for five years but destroyed 22,000 dwellings. The result for Norway was a housing shortage so severe that not even a valiant and ingen-

[6] This figure represents more than half the population of 1850, and nearly one-third that of 1930.

ious united effort on the part of private enterprise, the state and
the co-operative societies has been able to meet the demand, nor will
it possibly be able to catch up with it for at least twenty years. The
need is too great; the supply of capital, materials and labor too small.
This is true despite the fact that more housing is being built today
in Norway than ever before — at a rate comparable with that in a
much wealthier United States.

One rainy day in the spring I traipsed through ankle-deep mud
looking at the new housing developments in Oslo and listening to
builders and other housing experts explain their accomplishments
and their problems. Assuming, as the Norwegians did, that every
family in the realm ought to have a dwelling of its own, the shortage
of accommodation at the end of the war in 1945 was 110,000 dwellings. In 1950, despite five years of prodigious building, the shortage
was 123,000 dwellings. Only in the years since then has building
begun to gain on requirements. It wasn't only the war and the
termination of emigration which made the demand for new housing
so great: from 1940 to 1947, marriages in Norway increased by 30
per cent over the previous seven years; not unreasonably, the newly-
weds wanted homes of their own.

The state did not go into the building business, as some of the
Socialists desired. What it did was to decide how much of the available supply of capital could be invested in housing, to whom the
building materials on hand would be allocated and, most important,
to establish or encourage means by which modest-income families
could finance the acquisition of new homes and apartments. The actual building was left in the hands of private construction firms,
which in Norway are extremely small and are usually owned by
craftsmen who take part in the work. The government also provided
architectural guidance. It established certain new standards such as
bathrooms, electrical heating, garbage-disposal units, light and airy
rooms; and, to help the builders get the most out of their scarce
materials, had architects draw up plans for various standard-type
houses. It also laid down regulations for town and country planning.

But financing was the main contribution of the government. In
1946 the Storting unanimously approved the setting up of the National Housing Bank of Norway, and empowered it to offer cheap
long-term loans and subsidies to prospective home buyers. The objective, as defined by Parliament, was to secure Norwegians a rea-

sonable housing standard at what it called "socially justifiable rent."
Loans and subsidies were to be calculated according to a person's
means, and the regulations aimed at rents not exceeding 20 per cent
of an average income for a family dwelling of three rooms, kitchen
and bath.

Loans from the Housing Bank were permitted up to 80-85 per cent
of the ratable value of the house, the government's view being that
the owner ought to put up some capital himself. The loans run for
75 years for small wooden houses, and 100 years for buildings made
of brick and concrete, and carry 2½ per cent interest — a rate guaranteed unalterable for fifteen years. Such cheap terms, the authorities
calculate, make up for about half of the rise in building costs since
the war. But they realized that the gap between present high costs
and ratable value based on socially justifiable rents was still considerable. To fill that gap they offered a subsidy. It takes two forms:
interest rebates on loans for families with two or more children, and
an outright contribution from the Housing Bank varying from $700
to $1200, according to the amount of floor space. Thus, on an
average, 60 per cent of the costs of a new family home are covered
by a loan, 20 per cent by a subsidy and 20 per cent by an owner's
own capital. Altogether, about three fourths of all housing in Norway today is financed by the State through the Housing Bank or
the Small Holders' Bank. The latter was set up by the government 50
years ago to deal largely with rural housing. It handles about one third
of the loans on new dwellings.

How does this work out in terms of rent actually paid? And here,
following Norwegian practice, we must include as "rent" sums paid
annually by the vast majority for amortization and interest on loans
for homes they own, plus expenditures for heating, water, insurance
and upkeep. In one-family houses, the average yearly rent on this basis
varies from $228 to $242 in the towns and $100 to $114 in the rural
districts. Rates in two-family houses are roughly one-fifth less. Thus
rents in Norway are considerably cheaper than in America. But of
course, individual incomes are also lower. The important factor here is
the relation between earning and rent. About three quarters of the
people in Norway spend less than 20 per cent of their income for
rent. Industrial workers spend 15 per cent, and those with two or
more children — recipients of special rebates — about 12 per cent.

You cannot get this state financial help unless the plans for your new house are approved by the Housing Directorate. This condition was introduced in order to put a stop to badly designed or jerry-built housing and to make sure that new homeowners benefited from all the recent improvements in architecture and construction. Twenty-seven district architects have been appointed to pass on all housing plans before the Housing Bank agrees to finance them. They also make architectural suggestions to buyers and contractors and furnish blue-prints for some 100 varieties of standardized houses. The Housing Directorate has done a great deal not only to improve building prac-tices but to make for more spacious, practical, healthy and attractive homes. It also controls the volume of building and the allocation of construction materials.

The landlord who builds for private profit has become practically extinct in Norway — a relic of bygone days. The little fellow, with the state help which we have just described, builds for himself if he wants a one-family house. If he lives in a city where land is scarce and expensive — and Oslo and Bergen are about the only such ones in Nor-way — he becomes a co-operative owner of a flat in a huge apartment building or in a long row of two and four-family houses. All sizable housing developments that call for large buildings are today built by the nonprofit co-operatives.

In Norway there are two kinds. Most of them are simply old-fashioned joint-stock companies formed by individuals for the specific purpose of financing the building of an apartment house in which they will own their own flat. As long as no one makes a private profit out of the venture, the Housing Bank will grant such enterprises even higher loans than are given to individuals. When the building is com-pleted, maintenance is carried out co-operatively and the members have no further interest in new building.

To correct that situation and to stimulate new construction, another type of co-operative has evolved whose principal interest is in continuous new building. Its chief example in Norway is the Oslo Housing and Savings Society, known as OBOS. The young architect from the Oslo City Hall, who one morning led me enthusiastically through a huge building project which was just being completed in the suburb of Lambertseter, kept constantly referring in glowing terms to OBOS.

The idea for OBOS came from Sweden, where HSB (the Tenants' Savings and Building Society) had pioneered in co-operative housing.

OBOS began operations in Oslo in 1934, and since the war has built one-half of all the new housing in the capital. All prospective tenants are gathered in the OBOS "parent" society. This is essentially a planning and executive body, with a trained technical staff which launches new projects, procures sites, engages private contractors and architects, arranges the financing, administers the work of building and takes over the management of the completed buildings. However, the parent society is not actually the owner of the buildings. For each single project a "daughter" society is organized co-operatively consisting of the prospective tenants. This subsidiary society is the real owner of the project. It is legally and financially separate from the parent co-op, and it is run by its own board elected from the member tenants. The parent society of OBOS has an elaborate democratic structure, the supreme authority being the General Assembly made up of a representative from every fifty members. In order to ensure that the parent body keeps its attention focused on new building, OBOS has a strict rule that the majority of representatives in the Assembly must come from those who are still on the waiting list for new flats.

The OBOS project I visited in Lambertseter was near enough completion so that one could get a good idea of what this co-operative enterprise attempts to do. What it had built was a modern self-contained neighborhood accommodating 10,000 persons in various three- and four-story apartment buildings containing a total of 3200 flats. The buildings themselves were of simple, modern design and built of plaster over brick. They were substantial-looking, but not particularly beautiful. The apartments varied from one to four rooms, the majority containing three rooms, kitchen and bath. The rooms were fairly large (the living rooms averaged 215 square feet) and very light and airy. All were heated by electricity, and a coal-wood stove was provided for each living room for use in extremely cold weather. Each apartment had one storeroom in the attic and a second one in the basement. A washing machine and drying room was available in each block, as was a garbage disposal machine. There were to be, I was told, day nurseries and kindergartens where wives who worked outside could leave their youngsters during the day at an extra cost of from three to four dollars a month, depending on their income. The municipality was building public schools, and consumers' co-ops as well as private retail stores were setting up shop in the neighborhood to cater to the 10,000 new residents.

Now what did it cost to live in this co-operative community? To get a flat — when your turn came (there are thousands of families on the waiting list) — you made a down payment for a three-room apartment of from $340 to $700 and your monthly rent, excluding heating, came to from $18 to $21. The down payment, you might say, was for stock in the co-op and the rent was a form of dues. If you sell your flat (stock) you get your down payment back, but you must make the sale through the co-op board — a rule which prevents an owner from making a profit, which is a mortal sin among co-op people.

We shall leave to our visit to Sweden, Finland and Denmark a comprehensive survey of the general co-operative movement, which, so far as Scandinavia is concerned, has reached its most advanced state in those countries. But no picture of Norway is complete without at least mention of the role co-ops play in the economic and social life of a large slice of its people.

Here, as in the other northern countries and indeed throughout the world, the ideas and the practices of the consumers' co-ops derive from "The Equitable Society of Rochedale Pioneers," which set up the first tiny co-operative store in the grim industrial town of Rochedale in northern England on a cold December day of 1844, and thus set off, as the co-op champions say, "a revolution in a grocery shop." The Rochedale principles, still adhered to in the co-operative movement, were few and simple. The first and cardinal one was to supply consumer goods for use and not for profit. To achieve this, the co-operative society was to eliminate the middleman, and eventually even the private manufacturer (by doing its own manufacturing); to sell at market prices, but return to individual members all profits in proportion to their purchases; to sell only for cash; and to stay out of politics.

You scarcely arrive in Oslo or Bergen or any other town or village in Norway before you become aware of something everyone refers to as NKL. This is the *Norges Kooperative Landsforening*, the National Co-operative Union of Norway, and it is the biggest wholesale and retail enterprise in the kingdom. It comprises 1084 consumers' societies, 51 purchasing (wholesale) societies, two bakers' societies, two insurance societies and a bank. NKL has 278,000 members, or, with their families, about one-fourth of the entire population. Its gross sales amount to $100,000,000 a year, of which some $3,000,000 is "profit," and most of which is refunded to members on their purchases.

Both the central body, NKL, and the local societies have numerous factories of their own, but not as many as they would like to have, because of government restrictions on new capital enterprises. As it is, NKL maintains plants which turn out shoes, leather goods, flour, chocolate, soap and cosmetics, tobacco, coffee, woolens, ready-made clothes, electric light bulbs and radios and other electronic products. The local co-ops, which in Norway really dominate the giant mother society, can buy their goods wherever they please and they also run more than 200 productive enterprises of their own, including 125 bakeries and 84 sausage factories.

The structure of NKL is about as democratic as the human mind can devise but is also organized to promote a standard of efficiency, management and promotion which puts it on a par with the best-run private enterprises. Personnel, and especially prospective managers, are given rigid training in a special NKL co-op school, and there is also a co-operative correspondence school which in 30 courses taken by 6000 students offers both theoretical and practical training to future leaders in the co-op movement.

The supreme authority in the NKL is exercised by the Congress, made up of representatives from local societies who meet every other year. The actual management is vested in a Board of Directors of seven members, six of whom are elected by the Congress, the seventh member being always the General Manager of the Wholesale Department. He and the Board Chairman and the General Secretary, the latter two elected by the Congress, are the top managers and receive a salary. In Norway, I was told, they are regarded as shrewd businessmen, but in addition are thoroughly imbued with the "co-operative idea."

"What about your advantage over private enterprise resulting from your not having to pay taxes?" I asked one co-op authority.

"The question is misleading," he said. "The consumers' co-ops do pay taxes — on their properties, on their income, and on their profits from sales to nonmembers." They were not obligated, he explained, to pay taxes on dividends to members based on their purchases, because these could not be considered "profits." This tax advantage, of course, is a sore point with private traders.

NKL is completely independent of the government, which it will fight as vigorously as private business when it thinks its interests are being jeopardized. When I was in Norway, NKL, which is politically neutral, had several gripes against the Labor government. It was battling against government quotas, which it argued did not take into consideration its increased membership, and which prevented it from procuring all the goods it needed. It was demanding that Parliament repeal the laws which restrict co-ops from having more than one shop open to the general public in each rural county or city municipality. In Oslo, for instance, there are 70 co-op stores, but only one of them can sell to nonmembers. Finally, though probably a majority of members of NKL vote Labor, they are firmly opposed to nationalization. They quite realize that nationalization would put them out of business.

The agricultural producing co-operative societies are a bigger business even than the consumers' co-ops, with three times as many societies (3,114), a larger membership (332,000) and a higher volume of gross sales (a billion crowns — $150,000,000) a year. The agricultural co-ops have worked wonders for the Norwegian farmer both in the marketing of his produce and in his purchases of fertilizer, fodder, seed and machinery. Unfortunately there is no space here to go into details, though I shall try to cover the subject with some thoroughness when we get to Denmark, where the farmer's co-ops are even more the backbone of the nation than in Norway. Suffice it to say here that the Norwegian farmer has banded together in various co-ops to market his milk, meat, eggs, cheese and butter, and to buy almost everything he needs. Membership is practically 100 per cent; and to a Norwegian on the land, farming today without co-ops would be unthinkable.

Labor and Management under Labor Government

Collective bargaining in Norway is largely the business of the labor and employers' federations, not of separate unions and individual managements. The high degree of centralization of both federations makes this possible and — in the opinion of both parties — desirable. Despite their centralized character Norwegian unions, it must be said at once, are strongly democratic. There are no dictatorial union bosses, no union presidents "elected" for life, and democratic union constitutions are respected and lived up to. Although in theory local disputes are handled by local unions and industry-wide disputes by the national unions, the Labor Federation actually exerts supreme authority in collective bargaining. It is the federation which controls the central strike fund — a position which gives it great power. No money is paid out of this fund unless the federation sanctions a strike. But under the new Constitution, adopted in 1949 by the Trades Union Congress which is the governing body of the federation, no collective agreement may be terminated, no wage demand raised or notice of strike given without the approval in advance of the Executive Council of the Labor Federation. This council, consisting of fifteen members elected by the congress, of whom four are full-time officials, is thus in a suitable position to negotiate or to control negotiations with the employers.

The employers also delegate negotiating authority to a degree unknown in the United States. In fact the Norwegian Employers' Association was formed in 1900 exclusively to deal collectively with labor problems. Every company which joins it — and today there are 7000 of them — pledges not to initiate or conduct negotiations with a union but to delegate this power to the central committee of the association or to the affiliate national association concerned. In other words, if you are an employer and a dispute with your workers over wages arises, you cannot negotiate a settlement yourself; you must leave that to your association. If it decides that a lockout or strike is called for, you must go along with that decision no matter how much you may be opposed to it personally. However, like your employees, you have the democratic right to vote by secret ballot to approve or reject any industry-wide agreement arrived at by the Labor and Employers' Associations.

This and other matters of concern between organized labor and organized management are laid down in the "Basic Agreement" entered into between the two federations in 1935 and renewed, with minor changes, in 1947, and 1951. These "basic agreements" are common to all the Scandinavian countries and constitute a solid foundation for the relations between labor and management. Its terms are automatically incorporated in every one of the 8000 collective agreements in force in Norway today. There are ten principal points in the Basic Agreement. They include recognition of the right of both sides to organize for collective bargaining; the selection, rights and duties of elected shop stewards; balloting on agreements; limitation of sympathetic strikes and lockouts to those which are approved by one or the other central federations and only after negotiation between them; and, most important, the establishment of procedures to settle grievances and disputes.

Section 10 of the Basic Agreement declares: "Disputes concerning the *interpretation* of collective agreements or claims based on collective agreements shall be settled by the Labor Court." This remarkable institution is one of the cornerstones of labor-management relations in Norway, as in all the other northern lands.

Resort to a Labor Court is not only dictated by the Basic Agreement; it has been a part of the law of the land in Norway since 1915. The statutes lay down two distinct kinds of labor disputes: first, those over "interests," such as wages, hours and conditions of labor — which are to be settled by collective bargaining or, as was stipulated during the immediate postwar years, by compulsory arbitration; second, those over *interpretation* of collective agreements, which must be submitted — if private negotiation or arbitration fails — to the Labor Court, whose decisions are final and binding. In Norway a strike over the interpretation of an agreement or against the findings of this court is prohibited.

The Labor Court consists of a chairman and two other members representing the public interest, two of whom must have the professional qualifications of a Supreme Court judge, two members nominated by the trade unions and two nominated by the employers' associations, all appointed by the government for terms of three years. Hearings are held in an informal and friendly manner and usually both sides to a dispute are represented by lawyers experienced in labor affairs.[7] Often if the chairman feels that an agreement can be reached without a formal judgment of the court, he will meet both parties privately in his chambers to seek an accord.

In each case a trade-union must be a party to the dispute. An individual, as such, cannot bring a case before the Court. This is be-

[7] Trygve Lie, the first secretary general of the UN, rose to prominence in Norway as counsel for the Trade-Union Federation.

cause the tribunal is set up to interpret collective agreements and also because its docket would be overwhelmed if it had to hear the multitude of petty complaints emanating from individual workers. Both the labor and employers' federations co-operate to prevent the docket from becoming cluttered with unimportant cases by sifting the complaints first themselves. The Employers' Association, for instance, receives as many as four thousand complaints a year from its members who want to resort to the Labor Court. It actually files no more than fifty or so in any one year. Also no party can bring a dispute before the court unless private negotiations have first taken place between the disputants and proved fruitless. All disputes must be submitted to the court by written petition. In other words, regular court procedure is followed and the decisions of the Labor Court set legal precedents in much the same way that those of the Supreme Court do in other matters.

At first, both workers and employers were skeptical of the Labor Court; but after nearly forty years of experience with it, both are today equally enthusiastic about its fairness and its effectiveness. Much of its success, no doubt, is due to Paal Berg, who headed it from 1916 to 1946. Not only did he make the Labor Court into a foundation of good labor-management relations and one of the most respected institutions in the country; but while doing so, he also served a term as Chief Justice of the Supreme Court and became the supreme head of the Norwegian secret underground resistance to the Germans. He is understandably a beloved and heroic figure in Norway today.

Political power for labor has forced the trade-unions to alter fundamentally their view of the very purpose and function of trade-unionism and to reconsider their traditional attitudes toward wages, strikes, collective bargaining and the whole position of labor organizations in an economy, a society and a state which they now dominate. With power has come responsibility. Quite naturally the Labor party leaders have been forced to view a great many problems in a different light than before. Yesterday a strike, for example, meant to them merely a form of pressure against a corporation to raise wages. Today they see a strike as an instrument which may seriously endanger the national economy which they are in the midst of reconstructing and trying to make prosper.

Konrad Nordahl, president of the Federation of Trade-Unions, a friendly, pipe-smoking and extremely able man, explained to me that the trade-union view depends upon the economic policy of the government.

"Today," he said, "there is a very close co-operation between the Labor Government and the trade-union movement on economic policy. Therefore the trade-unions approve of state intervention for the solution of disputes which otherwise would endanger the economic progress and reconstruction of the country."

The evolution in labor's attitude was put more succinctly in a workers' education pamphlet: "In a planned economy, where the labor movement has political leadership, it is unthinkable that wage disputes should lead to great conflicts between workers and employers, with the public a sort of unwilling middleman. . . . It is outmoded and uneconomic to demonstrate by wasting labor and stopping work. We must seek other and equally effective means of expressing our discontent, rather than have the production on which we ourselves are dependent reduced or halted entirely."[8]

Another workers' pamphlet comments: ". . . The strike represents a bygone point of view, a weapon belonging to a period when capitalists sat with complete power in the government, in municipalities and in the economy as a whole. Today a strike may result in greater harm to the labor movement . . . than to capitalists."[9]

Political responsibility for the nation's postwar reconstruction also taught labor a great deal about the relations between wages and prices. The rank and file in the unions did not take kindly to the wage-stops imposed immediately after the war and both the trade union federation and the labor government found it necessary to do some hurried educating in this field. It endeavored to show its followers that political power enabled labor to control prices and that real wages were much more enhanced by cheaper prices than by allowing runaway inflationary prices, to be followed by monetary wage increases. In 1947 the Trade-Union Federation found it necessary to issue the following proclamation to its members:

"We must realize that a general increase in current money wages cannot be accomplished without an increase in prices and a consequent increase in the cost of living. . . . To protect the position we

[8] Quoted by Walter Galenson in his excellent *Labor in Norway*.
[9] *Ibid.*

have achieved, safeguard the nation's economic independence and prevent the disasters of inflation, the main task of the trade-union movement today must be to co-operate in increasing production, and through sharpening of price control to force the cost of living down and thereby further raise the wage earner's living standard."

It is scarcely an exaggeration to say that it was the sense of responsibility illustrated by this statement of the unions' federation that enabled the Labor government to weather the rugged days immediately after the war and in the end achieve the "miracle of reconstruction."

Now, it is obvious to any objective observer that the working class in Norway has immensely benefited from Labor government and that the business class has suffered a severe curtailment of its traditional laissez-faire freedom and certainly of its profits. But it is also obvious that an irresponsible, all-powerful Labor government, devoted only to the immediate advantage of the workers, would have brought ruin to the nation. That it did not, that despite its class bias and its class doctrines it pulled Norway through one of the most difficult periods of its history, is due not a little to its consciousness of its responsibility to the country as a whole, with all its classes, which demanded as drastic sacrifices from labor as from other groups. Neutral diplomats in Oslo told me they doubted whether any middle-class government could have gotten away with the draconian lowering of living standards to the bare necessities of life which the Labor government imposed on the people from 1945 to 1948 in order to free capital, man power and available materials for the all-important task of rebuilding the nation's economy.

Political power has had a sobering influence too on the Norwegian Labor party, which is distinct from, but allied with, the unions. In the years immediately after the First World War it was further to the left than any of the other socialist parties in the Western European democracies. In fact it was the only such party to affiliate with Moscow's Comintern in 1921, an act of rashness which it repented in 1923 when the Kremlin's dictatorship became unbearable. But as late as 1925, two years after it had quitted the Comintern, it still declared itself to be a "communist party." [10]

[10] In Oslo Trygve Lie and Dr. Lange, the foreign minister, pointed out to me that in theory at least no member of the Norwegian government who was a mem-

The Norwegian Labor party had been founded in 1887, twelve years before the formation of the Trade-Union Federation, and at a time when Norway was still joined in union with Sweden. Most workers until then had supported the Liberal (*Venstre*) party, much as American labor later tended to back the Democratic party. But the more active trade-unionists came to the conclusion, as industrialization set in and the proletariat grew, that labor ought to have a party of its own. In its early days the party was rather reformist, stumping for the universal franchise, a progressive income tax and adequate labor legislation. The predominant influence on it came from the German Social-Democrats, though a Left Wing developed which drew some of its ideas from the American IWW. This latter development was due mainly to the zeal of Martin Tranmael, a fiery and controversial figure in the labor movement, who had lived for four years in the United States where he was a member of an AFL union and of the American Socialist party and an admirer of the IWW.

When Norway regained its complete independence in 1905, the Labor party began to rise. It had polled 23,000 votes in 1903. In 1906 it reached 43,000, and 128,500 in 1912. Its delegation of ten members in the Storting in 1906 increased to 23 in 1912.

As the great wave of revolution began to break over Europe in the closing months of the First World War its reverberation was felt in Norway where the so-called "Left Wing," led by Tranmael, gained control of the Labor party, by majority vote in the party congress. It was soon fired by Lenin's success in Russia. It called for socialization of industry, banks, transportation and trade, declared that revolution by, and dictatorship of, the working class was "absolutely necessary," authorized a general strike for political ends and resigned from the Socialist Second International, which had declined to go along with the Russian Bolsheviks.

But in joining the Third International, Norway's Labor party quickly ran into the difficulties which from 1921 onward have made it impossible for any democratically run group whose first allegiance is to its own country and people to get along with Moscow's tyrants.

---

ber of the Labor party before 1923, when it left the Comintern, can get a visa to the United States under the McCarran Act — a fact, I found, to be highly embarrassing to the American Embassy, especially since Norway has become a key nation in NATO.

A rude awakening was soon in store for the scrappy, independent Norwegian laborites. Moscow ordered them to accept and obey without question its commands. Once Tranmael committed the unforgivable crime of refusing to go to Moscow to submit to the Comintern's demands. Finally in 1923 Moscow sent an ultimatum to a special congress of the Norwegian Labor party insisting that the party fall into line with all Comintern decisions. This, by a vote of 169 to 103, the party declined to do, and it was promptly kicked out of the Third International. The minority of Laborites formed a purely Communist party. The orthodox Social Democrats had already split off in 1921. Thus, at the end of 1923, the Labor party was divided into three groups with the following representation in the Storting: Social Democrats 8, Communists 13, Labor party 15. But the elections of 1924 returned 24 Labor party members to Parliament, 8 Socialists and only 6 Communists. From then on the Communists were to be a negligible factor in politics and in the trade-unions. In 1927 the Socialists and the Laborites reunited, and in the elections of that year the new Labor party secured 62 seats, making it easily the largest party in Parliament.

The way was open for it to come to power. When the Storting met in 1928 the first Labor government in Norway's history was formed. It lasted only a month, but the taste of political power was sweet and in 1933 the Labor party, going all out on an election cry of "labor majority and labor government," just failed to win a clear parliamentary majority. In 1935 it again came to power and has remained there — since 1945, as we have seen, with an absolute majority in Parliament which it maintained in the elections of 1949 and 1953.

Why do so many Norwegians vote Labor? It was a question I put to many people of all classes and parties. There was not, of course, a common answer. The conservative groups thought the people had been misled. The Laborites thought the voting showed that the majority of Norwegians had confidence in them because they got things done, because they had successfully brought about the postwar reconstruction of the country and because they were establishing a more equitable society than ever before. My own feeling is that the Norwegian masses, like those in the other Scandinavian lands and in Britain, have discovered the "secret" of modern political power in a democracy: that those who work for wages and salaries always out-

number those who don't, and that if enough of them combine in one
political party, they can win a parliamentary majority and thus assume political rule.

Finally, to use an old cliché, nothing succeeds like success. The
Norwegian Labor party's continual victories have given it a tremendous momentum. It attracts the youth. It draws young intellectuals, anxious for a government career, to its ranks. It is compatible
to the mass of members in the various co-ops. Its zeal for temperance
has won it much "dry" support. Lately it has made headway among
the small farmers. I got the impression that a good part of the
younger generation of professional men, doctors, engineers, lawyers,
professors, teachers, tended to gravitate to the Labor party. And
finally, the organized workers and the co-operatively organized fishermen feel proud that the party, of which they are the backbone, today
rules the nation, and quite naturally they support it with enthusiasm
and devotion.

Legally and officially the Labor party and the Trade-Union Federation are quite independent of each other, though they work closely
together and about half of the party's quarter of a million members
are enrolled collectively through their local unions. However, a union
worker is perfectly free to join any party he wishes.

Some of the cohesion of the Labor movement in Norway is due, no
doubt, to the fact that it has a lively and comprehensive press of its
own. There is no question of a one-party press in Norway nor, as one
editor put it to me, of daily newspapers and the radio tending, because of dependence on advertising, to reflect the views of the business community. The radio, run by a public corporation set up by
the state, carries no sponsored programs and is politically neutral.

Almost all the country's 90 daily newspapers and 60 triweeklies are
affiliated with a political party. The Conservatives have the most, 50;
the Liberals, who slipped badly in the 1953 elections, 49; and Labor,
42. In Oslo the Labor paper, *Arbeiderbladet,* has the second-largest
morning circulation (63,000), though the Conservative *Aftenposten,*
with both morning and evening editions, tops all Norwegian dailies
with a combined circulation of 267,000, and the Liberal *Dagbladet,*
a somewhat sensational afternoon journal, circulates 82,000 copies
daily. The Labor press is usually owned by the local party organization,
not by the unions, though the latter sometimes offer financial aid.
Labor newspapers carry considerable advertising.

One must not get the impression from the foregoing pages that opposition to Labor rule in Norway is dead. It is very much alive, but it is also divided, and it is this division which makes it so impotent in contemporary politics. Actually in the fall elections of 1953, held under a new system which favored the smaller parties, the Conservatives increased their seats in the Storting from 23 to 27, the Christian Democrats from 9 to 14, the Agrarians from 12 to 14. Only the Liberals, once the strongest party in Norway, lost ground, dropping 6 of their 21 mandates. These parties are in more or less general agreement in opposing the rigid government controls of the nation's economy. But they seem unable to get together on a positive affirmative program that might capture the imagination and support of the majority of the electorate.

The Communists are not considered strong enough to worry either Labor or the Conservatives in Norway, though on this subject it might be said that the Norwegians worry less easily than some peoples in other lands where the Communists are even more politically impotent. In the first postwar elections in 1945, the Communists staged a comeback that did worry their opponents. They polled 12 per cent of the votes and elected 11 members to Parliament. Not only their active role in the wartime resistance gave them some popularity; the prestige of Russia, which had liberated northern Norway from the Germans, helped them too. But their subservience to Moscow hurt them with a people as fiercely independent as the Norwegians. In the 1948 elections their vote fell from 176,000 to 101,000, and due to the peculiar Norwegian electoral system they failed to win a single seat in the Storting. In 1953, their vote fell further to some 5 per cent of the total, but in accordance with the new electoral system they were awarded three seats in Parliament, where they once again enjoy a certain nuisance value, but little more.

Immediately after the war the Communists also made headway in the trade-unions, but their tactics in trying to sabotage the economic program of the Labor government by fermenting wildcat strikes soon lost them much of their support, while a firm hand by the noncommunist leaders of the national unions and of the Trade-Union Federation also blocked their progress. By the time of the 1949 Federation Congress they were able to elect only 13 out of 300 delegates to that body, and in the 1953 congress, their representation was reduced to 4 out of 302.

Without hysteria, witch hunts, or repression, the Norwegian workers and voters have found it easy to squelch Communism by simple, democratic means.

Some Capsule Notes on Other Aspects of Norwegian Life

Wages, salaries and prices in Norway are lower than in America, but taxes are much higher. Whereas an American breadwinner with a wife and two children pays no federal income tax on an annual income of $2,098 (15,000 crowns), his Norwegian counterpart pays $325 (2,327 crowns), or 15½ per cent of his income. The same American earning $2,797 (20,000 crowns) pays $24 a year, or less than 1 per cent. A Norwegian in that category pays $606 (4,335 crowns), or nearly 22 per cent of his income.[11]

What amounts to a tax on capital — a capital levy, to use a fighting term in America — has been a practice in Norway going back to 1911, long before Labor governments were even dreamed of. Both the state and municipality impose it in various forms. The latter assesses a flat rate of 0.4 per cent. The state capital tax is progressive, beginning at 0.25 per cent on assets between $3,000 and $6,000 and reaching a maximum of 1.75 per cent on capital amounting to $70,000 or more. Taxable capital is defined in Norway as the market value of all one's assets, minus debts. It includes not only such property as buildings and land, stocks and bonds and savings accounts, but even such things as furniture and clothing, if the tax collector estimates their value at more than $2500. Business enterprises and co-ops pay a tax on capital as well as on income. Since 1921 there has also been a state "emergency" tax on capital for both individuals and foreign companies ranging from 0.4 to 3 per cent on capital holdings over $18,000. So far as the revenue officials are concerned the "emergency" has never ceased to exist, nor the collection of taxes based on it.

But that is not the end of the capital levy in Norway. After the war Parliament decided to assess a single special levy on the increase of capital during the war, its feeling being that those who had profited by the German occupation owed it to the nation to cough up their gains to the state. Businessmen were allowed normal deprecia-

[11] Based on Marshall Plan studies. Municipal taxes are included in Norwegian calculations because they comprise at least half of an individual's tax on income.

tion allowances and could also write off sums devoted to investment in new plants; and increases in capital due to inheritance, gift or life insurance were exempted. This levy was very steep, beginning with 30 per cent on capital gains of $1,500 and mounting to 95 per cent on amounts over $10,000. In other words, all sizable accumulations of personal wealth during the Nazi occupation were wiped out.

The importance of the municipalities in a somewhat decentralized country such as Norway is reflected in taxes. The cities and towns impose an income tax that is only slightly graduated and averages 17 per cent of the individual's income. The state income tax is steeply graduated, starting with 2 per cent of an annual income of $1,000 (7,000 crowns), mounting to 30 per cent of an income around $3,000 (21,-000 crowns) a year and ending at 70 per cent on all incomes above $34,000 (240,000 crowns) a year. An Oslo merchant, groaning under the double tax burden of city and state, explained to me that the state kindly reduces its income tax assessment if a man's combined taxes come to over 90 per cent of his income. In theory, he said, no one must pay more than 90 per cent. But in practice, he maintained, in cases where a man's property is large in relation to his income, his combined taxes may well amount to more than his total income.

Finally, Norway has a whopping national sales tax of 10 per cent. This hits the modest-income groups much harder than the well-to-do, and to correct part of the inequality the Labor government, after the tax was raised from 6 per cent to 10 per cent in 1951, gave some tax relief to persons with low incomes and raised the children's allowances by 33 1/3 per cent.

So much for taxes, an unpleasant but important subject to every Norwegian I met.

What do Norwegians do when they are not busy earning a living? Well, a number of things. They go to church — 97 per cent of them to the same church, the Lutheran, which is the State Church, administered by the Storting and of which the King is the "supreme bishop." The State Church costs the people in taxes about $3,00,000 a year — a dollar apiece — and, as the official *Norway Year Book* puts it, "for this amount they get free services, baptism, confirmation, wedding ceremonies, funerals, etc." Incidentally, the clergymen are paid fixed salaries and old age pensions by the state, which makes them financially independent of their congregations. On the whole, I gathered, the pastors consider this state of affairs an advantage, though I found a good deal of feeling among them that the Church ought to become more independent of the state. The Church had a magnificent record in opposing the Nazi occupiers, and this did much to enhance its standing in the community. However, I did not find the churches in Norway overly crowded.

The places of sport were. Norwegians have a passion for sports, not only as onlookers but as participants. The national sport, of course, is skiing, and I don't recall meeting a single Norwegian, man or woman, from the age of five, when skis are first put on, to ninety who was not a skier.[12] The abundant hills and mountains and the prevalence of snow during the long winter and into the spring provide ideal conditions for skiing and the Norwegians make the most of them. The jumping championships at the Olympic ski-jump at Holmenkollen on the outskirts of Oslo on the first Sunday in March draw a bigger crowd than a baseball World Series at Yankee Stadium. At least 100,000 persons turn out for this annual event. Skiing in the high mountains goes right on into the summer. In Oslo I noticed a poster advertising the "Midsummer Ski Race — June 21" near Åndalsnes.

Football (soccer) is the most important summer game in Norway, as it is in all European countries. Incidentally, in Norway it is a prime source of revenue not only for sports in general but for science. Since Norwegians, like everyone else, will bet on football scores, the Storting after the war set up a public corporation called *Norsk Tipping,* which runs the national soccer-football betting pool. Half of the proceeds from ticket sales go to those who come closest to guessing weekly scores; the other half goes to sports and sciences, the latter getting two thirds of this revenue. In the last five years *Norsk Tipping* has been able to contribute $7,000,000 to scientific research and half that sum to a general sports fund administered by the State Sport Office and used to construct playgrounds, soccer fields, ski-jumps, gymnasiums, etc.

Like everything else in Norway, sports are highly organized. At

[12] The Norwegians have been skiing for a long time. A Swedish professor, Erik Granlund, has unearthed at Övrebö in Vest Agder a ski which he believes dates from the year 2000 B.C. This four-thousand-year-old ski, I was told, is as slender and streamlined and built for speed as today's skis designed for downhill racing.

the head of the pyramid is "Norway's Sport Association," comprising 2,500 sports clubs with a total membership of 350,000. The Labor government is extremely sports-minded, and after the war established a State Sports Office to encourage athletics and co-ordinate them. There are no professional sports in Norway.

The arts are also — if I may so put it — popular in Norway. Norwegians — and this is true of all the Scandinavian peoples, including first of all the Icelanders — buy a great many more books per capita than Americans. I found bookshops lively places of business and often crowded. Since most educated Norwegians read English there is a big sale of English and especially of American books and there is even a bigger one of translations issued by Norwegian publishers. Twice as many translations of foreign novels are published in Norway as Norwegian novels. In the first chapter of this book I have listed some of the American authors who enjoy great popularity in Norway. Often the books at the top of the best-seller lists in America enjoy the same position in Norway. This was true in recent years of such books as Robinson's *The Cardinal*, Forester's *Midshipman Hornblower*, Du Maurier's *My Cousin Rachel*, Salenko's *Désirée*, and Wouk's *The Caine Mutiny*.

Norway, of course, has a number of gifted writers of its own who, in the opinion not only of Norwegians but of some Americans in Oslo, are not as well known abroad as they should be. Their own public is terribly limited in size, since there are only a little more than three million Norwegians and four million Danes. (The Danes can read Norwegian with ease, but the Swedes have trouble.) I discussed this problem in Oslo with Francis Bull, an eminent literary critic, and with Sigurd Hoel, one of the best of the contemporary novelists, and I gathered that unless you are an Ibsen, a Knut Hamsun or a Sigrid Undset, there is little chance, barring an accident, of your works being translated abroad.

Obviously, with such a small public Norwegian authors find it difficult to live from their writing, and most of them, like their American brethren (whose potential reading public in English is seventy-five times as large), have to engage in other pursuits such as teaching, journalism, and publishing in order to earn a living. But the state steps in to give financial help to writers as well as to other artists. It awards them some fifty annual scholarships worth $26,000, and carries another 42 artists on its payroll as recipients of annual lifetime stipends totaling $40,000 a year. No strings, political or otherwise, are attached to these government grants. Ibsen received one for years despite the fact that many of his plays shocked the ruling circles. Finally, an Act of Parliament passed in 1947 stipulates that 5 per cent of all state grants toward the annual purchase of new books for public and school libraries must go to a special fund for the benefit of Norwegian authors.

The state and the municipalities also contribute generously to the theater, thus helping to make the Norwegian stage one of the finest in the Western world. They pay two million crowns ($288,000) apiece in annual subsidies to six theaters: three in Oslo, and one each in Trondheim, Bergen and Stavanger. Some playwrights and actors also receive yearly government stipends.

Further, the national government subsidizes a traveling theater known as *Riksteatret* which was set up by Parliamentary Act in 1948. A professional repertoire company, it brings good theater to the remotest villages and gives 600 performances a year. So anxious is the culture-conscious Storting to see that the good folk in the outlying districts of this far-flung country see the best in drama that it has passed a law stipulating that the six state-subsidized theaters also shall go on tour for the *Riksteater* and give not less than a total of 120 performances on the road annually. Probably no rural people in the world, including America, have seen as many fine stage plays professionally produced as have the Norwegians living in small towns. The Traveling Theater itself has shown them the best of Ibsen, Björnson, Chekhov, Holberg, Shaw, Synge. Incidentally I found in its repertoire for the past few seasons a number of popular American plays: O'Neill's *Anna Christie*, Wilder's *Our Town*, Miller's *Death of a Salesman*, Ardrey's *Thunder Rock* and Kanin's *Born Yesterday*.

Oslo itself, with less than half a million population, has six theaters, three of them purely commercial ventures, and in an average season they offer as many plays as New York's eight million inhabitants are shown. All of Norway's theaters have permanent repertoire companies with actors, directors and technicians employed on a twelve-month basis — with a two-month paid vacation. The greatest Norwegian drama house is the National Theater in Oslo, with its imposing structure at one end of the tree-studded thoroughfare Karl-Johans-Gate; in front of it stand the statues of Holberg, Ibsen and Björnson, the supreme triumvirate of Norway's playwrights. It has collected a brilliant company of players, including Per Aabel — who, besides being a talented dancer, painter, musician and linguist, is regarded in Europe as perhaps the finest comic actor in the world. One of the most interesting theaters in the capital is the Folk Theater, established by the joint effort of the Folk-Theater Society and the Trade-Unions, and presided over by Norway's most renowned director, Hans Jacob Nilsen, a noted actor himself.

If American movies dominate the screen in Norway, as they do, the popularity of contemporary American plays is no less significant. (Probably it is more significant.) Nearly every theater in Oslo was either performing an American piece or planning to when I was there. The New Theater (*Det Nye Teater*) was playing *Pal Joey* and getting ready Odets' *The Country Girl*. The National Theater was planning to do Miller's *The Crucible* and O'Neill's *Moon for the Misbegotten*. (New York had not yet seen the latter play.) The Norwegian Theater (*Det Norske Teatret*) was advertising Laurant's *Home of the Brave* and the program of the Central Theater included *South Pacific, Affairs of State* and *The Seven-Year Itch*.

At Oslo's Norwegian Theater, founded in 1912 as a state-subsidized house, you hear spoken a version of the language called "neo-Norwegian" (*nynorsk*) or *landsmål*, and thereby learn, if you haven't already, that this land of only a little over three million souls, perhaps the most homogeneous on earth, has two official languages, the other being *riksmål* or *bokmål* (book language), and that the conflict over their use is bitter, violent and confusing beyond comprehension for a foreigner, and has been for at least a century. One evening in Oslo, at the friendliest of banquets, a gentleman on my right, a distinguished newspaper editor, and a gentleman on my left, an equally distinguished broadcaster, got into such a battle over *landsmål* and *riksmål* that had I not stood between them they most certainly would have torn each other to shreds. From their violent tussle (it took place in neutral English) I got an insight into the epic Norwegian "language conflict" which has rocked the country since the middle of the nineteenth century.

Four centuries of being a mere province of Denmark resulted in the replacement of the old Norse tongue in Norway by what might be called a Danish-Norwegian language. The old Norwegian dialects continued to be spoken in the country districts, but the middle classes of the bigger towns took over the language of Copenhagen and it became not only official but the accepted written language of Norway. The Norwegians pronounced it somewhat differently than the Danes and always employed a number of old Norwegian words, but on the whole the two countries shared a common written language which Holberg, "the Voltaire of the North," as he is called, raised to literary heights in his great classical dramas. Holberg was a born Norwegian but lived and wrote in Copenhagen.

Shortly after 1814, when Norway was detached from Denmark and joined to Sweden, a reaction against Danish cultural influences set in among Norwegians. The more nationally minded conceived the idea of going back to the old Norsk language, which still survived, somewhat crudely, in the peasant dialects. Their champion was a self-educated peasant, Ivar Aasen (1814-1896), who despite his lack of formal learning became a prodigious scholar and at the mid-nineteenth century published two epochal books, a grammar and a dictionary of Norwegian folk-speech. His version of the language soon gained many followers and in 1885, by Act of Parliament, *landsmål*, or neo-Norwegian, as it came to be called, was declared one of the two official languages. Several provincial authors began to write in it, but to this day not a single newspaper in Norway has taken it up. Most of the writers, including Ibsen, refused to adopt it. Ibsen believed in a moderate norsification, but balked at trying to create a new language out of old dialects; and in *Peer Gynt* wrote a scathing satire of the *landsmål* fanatics in the character of Huhu, one of the inmates of his Cairo insane asylum, who was "a language-reformer from the coast of Malabar."

There were moderates who tried to bring the two languages together by making the spelling of *riksmål* (Danish-Norwegian) conform more with Norwegian pronunciation and by making written *landsmål* read more like *riksmål*. Reforms in this direction were made in 1907 and 1917, and in 1938 Parliament, after a committee of eminent scholars, teachers and authors had deliberated and fought for four years, passed a law laying down orthographic rules for both languages which served to narrow the gap between them. In fact some hailed the result as bringing forth at last a common Norwegian language, *samnorsk* ("same Norse"), but the majority thought the chief consequence was confusion worse confounded. The country's greatest poet, Arnulf Överland, was moved in 1940 to write a book: *Has Our Language Been Abolished?* He was almost afraid it had been. He wrote another in 1948, when Parliament again gave signs of trying to legislate on language matters. This was called *How Often Shall We Change Languages?* "This third language — *samnorsk* — has no literature," he wrote. "No one can speak it, and no one can write it; therefore children must learn it." For it had been introduced in the schools and had raised a storm of protest from parents.

In 1951 a bill was passed in the Storting to appoint still a new language commission to "further the mutual approach of the two languages." A fresh wave of angry protest swept the country. Students demonstrated, parents staged mass-meetings and formed a "National Committee for Parental Action against *Samnorsk*," authors set up a fighting *anti-samnorsk* organization, the newspapers fumed.

There we leave the matter, simmering still after a century of conflict. In the meantime unhappy students in the schools have to learn to read and write *both* languages, but must choose one as their chief language. They also have to learn English.

But on the place of art in the lives of people, there is no controversy in Norway. Ordinary folk not only buy books, they buy paintings; and the better-off buy sculpture. The shipowners buy a great many of both for their ships. The state and municipalities also are great purchasers of art works. All this helps to provide not only stimulation and encouragement but a decent living for artists, who are not neglected either by the housing authorities. The painters and sculptors of Oslo do not have to live in garrets or drafty ramshackle studios. The city and state have provided them with a modern artists' colony, a co-op venture, consisting of small rows of pleasant houses, each with a large studio, plenty of rooms for the children and all the modern gadgets. I spent a morning at this colony, built on the estate of Norway's most eminent painter, the late Edvard Munch, who had bequeathed the grounds and his paintings to the city of Oslo. I have never seen such well-housed painters and sculptors. Their dwellings were so constructed that the studio was separate from the other rooms, enabling the artist to labor without disturbance from the children, the houskeeping and the other distractions of family life.

Dr. Lange, the foreign minister, at the conclusion of a long discussion on world affairs, had said to me: "By the way, if you want to see what we're doing in modern art, go pay a visit to the new City Hall." I found every wall and nook crammed with the work of living Norwegian painters and sculptors, some of it quite original and striking — a fine example of the collaboration of artists with municipal authorities in achieving a building that is not only functional as the headquarters of city government but a work of art as well. Norwegians, both artists and laymen, disagree sharply on the merits of the architecture of the City Hall, which was formally opened in 1950 on the occasion of Oslo's nine hundredth birthday, and they hold various opinions as to its artistic embellishments. Originally, the Norwegian architects had planned the usual type of City Hall that you see all over northern Europe: a renaissance building built around a courtyard and topped by a high single tower — such as in Stockholm and Copenhagen. Gradually, as delays gave them more time to reflect on their plans, they abandoned the old idea and sought a more functional and modern-looking structure. Instead of the single tower, there are two multi-storied oblong structures, similar in shape to the U.N. Secretariat in New York, joined by a lower unit to make a whole. The facing is in red brick over steel and concrete. The lower center structure contains the reception and festival halls; the twin towers, as Norwegians insist on calling them, contain the offices. Located at the tip of Oslo Fjord on the site of the last of the old slums, which were torn down to make room for it, the City Hall is an imposing, pleasing structure that well expresses the character of the capital.

It is not a beautiful city, lacking the renaissance and eighteenth-century buildings that make Copenhagen and Stockholm so entrancing. But it exudes a charm, and the island-studded fjord, churned by ships plying to and from distant ports, and the surrounding pinewood hills, give Oslo a character that has its own beauty. Within its sprawling city limits there are still 500 farms with 2500 cows, 1500 horses, 3500 pigs, 20,000 hens, 200,000 fruit trees and half a million berry bushes — a charming contrast, I thought, to the miles of factories which make Oslo the principal industrial city of the realm.

The Lapps

What about the Lapps? In Norway I inquired. The Lapps are changing too, I was told, under the impact of twentieth-century civilization. These hardy, dark little people, apparently descendants of a Mongolian tribe which settled in the Arctic regions a thousand years before Christ, are giving up their ancient nomad habits, which means giving up their reindeer, and settling down. In Oslo it is said that the Lapp women are largely responsible for this. They are beginning to prefer life in a house — a heated house. But to herd reindeer successfully you have to wander all over the frozen North in search of pasture. There isn't enough of the proper kind — the animals feed off mosses and lichens mostly — near any one spot that one might call home. So Lapp husbands are selling off their reindeer and taking to farming and fishing. Only about 2000 out of the 20,000 Norwegian Lapps (the other 10,000 Lapps in the world belong, more or less, to Sweden and Finland) still follow their reindeer herds. One more primitive people is rapidly passing out of the nomad stage.

Norwegian Institutions

A word now on some of the Norwegian institutions which are pillars of the nation.

The Storting is a curious example of a single-chamber parliament which divides itself into two legislatures. After its election as one house, 38 of its 150 members are selected to constitute the *Lagting* and the remaining 112 members make up the *Odelsting*. All laws affecting or regulating the relations of citizens to each other or to the state must first be passed by the Odelsting and thereafter by the Lagting. In case of disagreement between the two houses, a plenary session of the whole Storting is called in which the issue must be decided by a two-thirds majority vote. All other legislation, such as that dealing with the budget, taxation, appropriations, and foreign policy, is the business of the whole Storting in plenary session.

Until recently the Constitution required that two thirds of the members of the Storting should come from the rural districts and one third from the towns and cities. This weighted the representation in favor of the country districts. A constitutional amendment dropped that system beginning with the 1953 elections, and no distinction is now made between the city and the rural areas. The new amendment also did away with the requirement that a member of Parliament must reside in the district which elects him. In no case does he run on his own, as does an aspirant for a seat in our Congress. His name appears on a party list of candidates. The total party vote in a district determines how many representatives from each party's lists are elected. In Norway you vote for the party, not for the individual candidate.

One feature of the Norwegian legal system deserves mention. No civil case may be referred to the courts until mediation has first been attempted before the so-called conciliation council (*forliksrådet*), which consists of three members elected for four years by the county or town council. Even if mediation fails the conciliation council may function as a court in cases considered too trivial to be taken up by the regular courts. This procedure has spared the ordinary courts in Norway a tremendous burden and incidentally saved petty litigants as well as the state much money in court costs. In an average year the conciliation councils handle 20,000 cases.

Norway is one of the few small countries in the world that has an atomic energy plant operating.[13] Its nuclear reactor is not large, and it is run for peaceful purposes only. Further, there is nothing secret about it. I, like hundreds of other visitors, was invited to look over every nook and cranny of the small atomic plant at Kjeller, near Oslo, where a joint Dutch-Norwegian state enterprise has operated a nuclear reactor since 1951. It produces radioactive isotypes for commercial sale — two thirds of which is exported — and also makes radioactive iodine. The director of the Kjeller Institute told me it was not interested in making bombs but was intensely interested in developing peaceful uses for atomic energy. The institute was working, he said, on a new heavy-water, natural-uranium reactor to develop 10,000 kilowatts of heat and 2,500 kilowatts of electricity. What the Norwegians would especially like to develop is an atomic engine for their merchant ships. For a country without oil or coal and yet with the world's third largest merchant fleet to maintain, such an invention would be a godsend. Plans to build prototypes for an

[13] Late in 1954 the completion of Sweden's first atomic reactor was announced in Stockholm. Containing three tons of uranium, moderated by heavy water, it developed a low effect of 100 kw. Plans were also made to build a 20,000 kw. reactor to yield plutonium for the production of energy. The initial reactor was built on the outskirts of Stockholm in an underground cavern hewn out of the rock under fifty feet of granite. Sweden has its own uranium oxide, extracted from shale deposits near Orebro, west of Stockholm.

atomic electric power plant and a uranium powered marine engine are under way.

This joint Dutch-Norwegian atomic project was made possible by the fact that Holland possessed some uranium and Norway was the world's greatest producer of heavy water, the latter being used as the moderator in the Kjeller reactor.

The Monarchy in a Labor-ruled Land

In Norway, as in other constitutional democracies, a king reigns but does not rule. Nevertheless King Haakon VII has played an important role in Norwegian affairs by the force of his personality and example. And his courageous stand during the war has made him the most popular of all Scandinavian monarchs.

In many ways, to start with, his position is quite unique. He is the first king the Norwegians have had of their own for half a millennium. He is, I believe, the only living king — and one of the very few in history — to be *elected* to his throne by secret ballot of all citizens entitled to vote in a national election.

This happened in 1905 when, after a quarrel with the Swedish King over Norway's right to have its own consular service, the Storting simply declared that the King had ceased to reign and that therefore the union with Sweden had ended. Immediately the Norwegian government started looking for a new king. It first offered the throne to a Bernadotte prince of the Swedish royal house, but received no response. Its eye then fell upon the thirty-three-year-old Prince Carl of Denmark, second son of King Frederick VIII, who was married to Princess Maud, the daughter of King Edward VII of England. Carl was favorable to an offer, but on condition that a referendum of the Norwegian people on his selection be held first. The Storting was opposed to a plebiscite on the grounds that Parliament had the full constitutional authority to choose a king. Carl's impulsive father-in-law, King Edward VII, urged him to proceed to Norway forthwith and become a king without waiting for an election. But here the resolute will when principles were involved which Carl was to show to such advantage later cropped out publicly for the first time. He would only accept the Norwegian throne if it were voted him by the Norwegian people. "Before I go to Norway," he told Fridtjof Nansen, the renowned explorer and diplomat, who headed the delegation that was dispatched to interest him in the job, "I want to know that the Norwegian people want me to come."

They voted on November 12 and 13, 1905, and the result was 259,563 to 69,264 for him, the negative ballots coming from a body of stalwart republicans who had nothing against Carl personally but who believed that Norway's experience with Danish and Swedish kings should lead it to trying a republic.

Thus Haakon VII, as these lines were being written in 1954, was the world's oldest living monarch and had reigned longer than any living king, and indeed had remained longer on a Norwegian throne than any of his predecessors going back to Harald I Fairhair in the ninth century. Queen Maud died in 1938 at the age of sixty-nine.

On August 3, 1952, the people of Norway joined in a nationwide celebration of the king's eightieth birthday. Among other things, they gave him, out of funds raised by popular subscription, in recognition of his wartime services, a gleaming white three-thousand-ton yacht, which rode at anchor just off the City Hall during my stay in Oslo.

He wears his eighty years well. When he received me in Oslo in June, 1953, he appeared hale and hearty, full of vigor and fairly bubbling with a sense of humor. Our talk covered in the short space of half an hour a wide variety of subjects — both light and heavy — in which he showed a profound grasp of world affairs and displayed a keen intelligence and — always — great wit.

He leads an unostentatious life. There is no nobility in Norway for a king to cavort with, as there is in Sweden and Denmark, and Haakon does little entertaining and goes out only infrequently and then mostly to official functions, festivals and concerts. In May, 1953, his granddaughter, the twenty-two-year-old Princess Ragnhild, elder daughter of Crown Prince Olaf, married a commoner, Erling Lorentzen, son of a shipowner. The gossip in Oslo was that the King did not entirely approve of the match, but if so he made no public display of such feelings. He decreed that she should retain her royal title, and gave a reception for the bridal couple in the palace to which four hundred guests were invited — the first glittering social gathering there that Oslo's citizens could remember. The palace, incidentally, is a simple but dignified edifice about the size of the White House in Washington, built in rather austere Renaissance style and lying in a small park at one end of the capital's main thoroughfare. The park is open to the public and the main path through it, along which the citizens tramp all day long, leads right under the palace windows.

Crown Princess Martha died on April 5, 1954, at the age of fifty-three. She had spent the war years, after Norway was overrun, in the United States at the invitation of President and Mrs. Roosevelt.

The two men the King sees most often are Oscar Torp, the Prime Minister,[14] and Halvard Lange, the Minister of Foreign Affairs. Both gentlemen typify the two quite different kinds of leaders who have come to the fore in the Labor party and in the Labor government. Torp, born in 1893, is a former electrician and the son of a worker. Dr. Lange, born in 1902 of an eminent father who was awarded the Nobel Peace Prize in 1921, is an academic intellectual, a teacher, a historian, a writer, a cosmopolitan who is as much at home in French or English or German as he is in his native Norwegian. Withal he has been identified all his life, as has Torp, with the Norwegian labor movement. At one time when he was working and studying in London, Lange became a member of the British Labour party.

It was Dr. Lange who, as we have seen in the first chapter, did more than anyone else, and in the face of tenacious Swedish opposition, to bring Norway and Denmark into NATO — a resolute and daring step which broke violently with the Scandinavian tradition of neutrality but which, on the other hand, faced realistically the new facts of the postwar world. We must now, in concluding this chapter, see why this step made Norway vastly more important to the United States than ever before.

Norway a Key to United States Defense in the North

A glance at the map gives the answer. The northern strip of Norway, from Kirkenes to Tromsö, lies athwart the sea and air lanes to and from northern Russia. If Soviet forces were to occupy this region either by land forces breaking across the 122-mile common border or by a naval-air strike designed to seize the ports and fjords, Russia

[14] In January, 1955, Oscar Torp was succeeded as Prime Minister by Einar Gerhardsen, leader of the Labor party and a former laborer and trade-union official. Gerhardsen had relinquished the premiership in 1951 to Torp.

would then be free to break out into the North Atlantic toward the United States. If she took this strip she could then easily occupy Spitsbergen, which lies halfway between northern Norway and the North Pole and only a few hundred miles from northeastern Greenland. By the terms of an international treaty, Norway is forbidden to fortify Spitsbergen.

These Arctic routes are the chief ones by which Russian bombers, laden with atom or hydrogen bombs, could directly reach the cities and industrial regions of the United States. They are the principal lanes which Soviet U-boats could use. If they can be blocked at their very beginning, that is, in northern Norway, American security is immeasurably enhanced.

Norway cannot block them alone. She has not the resources in man power or weapons or industrial strength. As a charter member of NATO, and through it allied to the United States, Norway is being helped to defend this vital area. But there are difficulties.

One is the question of allowing foreign (NATO) troops to help man Norway's widely scattered military bases which have been built largely with NATO (mostly American) aid. It was a burning domestic issue in Norway, as in Denmark, while I was there. No people likes foreign troops, even if they are friendly Allies, stationed on its soil, and the Norwegians are no exception.

But that is the least of the Norwegian government's difficulties. More serious is Russia's threatening attitude. We have seen (in the first chapter) that Moscow tried to frighten Norway out of joining the Atlantic Pact. After she had defied the Kremlin by joining NATO, Norway did give a written assurance to Russia that she would not open her military bases to foreign powers *as long as Norway is not attacked or subjected to threats of attacks.*

Those last five words give her an "out," but she is stubbornly determined to decide for herself when they do. So far, that time has not yet arrived.

From this fact arises a misunderstanding between Norway and NATO and between Norway and the United States. NATO would like to send in a small number of troops (preferably American) to help man the new bases in Norway. It would also like to station a few squadrons of jet fighters at these bases. And though Norway cannot possibly fully man the bases herself when they are completed shortly nor even man the necessary fighters, she thus far declines to let

NATO help her do it. On keeping foreign troops out, for the time being anyway, all political parties are in complete agreement.

In the meantime Norway is adding her own strenuous efforts to NATO and American aid in building up her defenses. A third of the national budget goes to defense — an increase of 740 per cent over 1938, which is the highest proportional increase of any NATO country in Europe. Conscription has been prolonged to sixteen months. The financial burden of drastically increased defense expenditures has forced Norway to curtail her economic reconstruction. Rearmament since 1951 has been given top priority. It has adversely affected the nation's balance of payments, and in the three-year period ending in 1954 raised her national debt by a further one hundred million dollars. Since all man power was gainfully employed, the increase in the armed forces has necessitated taking irreplaceable men from productive jobs in agriculture and industry, with a consequent lowering of national output.

Finally, in order to avoid a repetition of the catastrophe that occurred in 1940 when a handful of German airborne troops and another handful concealed in the holds of ships seized every important town and base in Norway in a few hours, the Norwegians are building up a Home Guard to supplement the conscript army. It is a voluntary body of 165,000 men — 10 per cent of the entire male population. The men keep their uniforms and arms at home and you can see them skirmishing over the hills and mountains on week ends and holidays.

Coming from all walks of life, and therefore truly representative of the Norwegian people, they think they have, all told, a pretty good country, and they are determined to see it defended better in the future than it was in the spring of 1940. This chapter has attempted to depict something of the Norway of which they are justly proud.

It is time now to cross the border to Sweden.

CHAPTER III
Sweden

STOCKHOLM was celebrating its seven hundredth anniversary when I arrived, reminding one that here was an ancient land which had survived the vicissitudes of many centuries to transform itself, in our time, into one of the most progressive and democratic nations on earth.

It was summer, and the good folk of what is surely the most beautiful city in the North were making merry. A hundred and fifty thousand of them jammed into the *Kungsträdgården*, a pleasant little park in the heart of the capital which had been laid out as a royal garden a century before Columbus, to watch King Gustav VI Adolf and Queen Louise inaugurate the birthday festivities. Below the park, in the little stream that connects Lake Malaren with an inlet of the Baltic, fishermen were raising and lowering their big round nets under the shadow of the flood-lit, baroque royal palace, and if you strolled down to the water's edge you could see not far off along the banks of the Malären the brightly illuminated dark red front of the City Hall with its great tower topped by three crowns, an edifice considered by many to be the finest piece of modern architecture in the North.

One summer night I drove out to Drottningholm Palace, and there in the Royal Dramatic Theater, which has been preserved — stage machinery and all — just as it was two centuries ago, saw a performance of an eighteenth-century pastoral play of Olof von Dalin which had been revived for the first time in two hundred years. Even the members of the orchestra were attired in rococo costumes and they were all bewigged. It was sheer escape into the past on a happy birthday occasion, but as you drove back to Stockholm in the eerie twilit summer night you passed great modern housing developments for the workers — the sight of which jerked your mind back to the present and the realization that this land, with all its royal trappings and its architectural reminders of a bygone rococo day, was, like Norway, dominated by the working class, which had replaced the king, the nobility and the upper middle classes, one after the other, as the real ruler of the nation.

The ancient fabric of Sweden still cropped up on the surface, here and there, especially during such a gala season. But it was a mere showpiece. It gave color and entertainment, and perhaps revived memories of former imperial splendor when Sweden was a great, conquering European power with mighty kings and renowned armies that once marched triumphantly across the plains of Europe and deep into the steppes of Russia. That Sweden was gone, beyond any Swede's desire of recall. The unfathomable course of history had reduced Sweden to a relatively small power and swept it off the main highway along which the European nations had continued their eternal struggles for supremacy in the last 140 years. Yet, left in peace, it had turned its energies to admirable purposes, transforming itself into a political and social democracy which today, in the opinion of not a few observers, is, in many respects, a model for the Western world.

Sweden is the largest, the heaviest-populated, the most industrialized of all the northern countries, and the only one of the four which, through luck and its own determination, was spared the agony of being involved in the past world war. Its armies have not been in combat for 140 years — since 1814, when the Napoleonic wars came to an end — and no enemy shell has fallen in Stockholm for nearly half a millennium though a Russian army got within 20 miles of the capital in 1719.

Sweden's contemporary story, like the character of its people, differs therefore from that of its northern neighbors. And yet there are many similarities, for in Sweden too labor has obtained political rule and the co-ops are strong and social welfare has been carried to lengths which Americans may not reach — or care to reach — in this century, if ever. Like the other Scandinavian lands, Sweden contributed an immense wave of emigration to the New World. By 1914 more than a million Swedes had settled in America so that today there are at least three million Americans of Swedish descent. In Sweden I got the impression from my own experience — and it was confirmed by learned historians — that every other family had one or more relatives in the "States."

In size, Sweden is the third largest country in Europe (excluding Russia), being surpassed only by France and Spain. It is about twice the size of Great Britain or Minnesota, and a comparable area in America would be the six New England states plus New York, Pennsylvania, New Jersey and Delaware. Its population of 7,200,000 equals that of Norway and Denmark combined, and is roughly that of Texas or Ohio. It stretches north and south for a thousand miles so that a city on its southern tip, such as Malmö, is nearer Rome than it is the northern border, which reaches 250 miles beyond the Arctic Circle. It is a land of lakes and mountains and forests, the great wooded tracts occupying more than half the area. About 10 per cent of the land is cultivated — enough to make Sweden self-supporting in food. Until toward the end of the nineteenth century farming occupied most of the population, but today less than a quarter of the people depend upon it for a living. Nearly half live from industry and two thirds of the population is now urban. But thanks to the tardiness of Swedish industrialization and its decentralization and — to an American — an amazing mental maturity that made them reluctant to let the machine become the master of men to the detriment of decent living, the Swedes were able to avoid those hideous sores which the early factory system made of so many cities in England and America, and to see to it that even in the centers of industry most people could live in decent, pleasant, airy, well-lit homes with space for trees, flowers, gardens and sport on which the sun could shine. I saw no slums in Sweden — or anywhere else in the North — though there was much overcrowding in the dwellings.

The Swedes have had a long and tortuous struggle to get where they are today. The privileged classes there, as elsewhere, clung tenaciously to their advantages and stubbornly resisted reform. All through the nineteenth century the rapid increase in population and the slow pace of industrialization created problems that seemed insoluble.

As recently as a hundred years ago Sweden was a poor country with poverty so widespread that one of its writers declared that poverty almost could be regarded as a national characteristic. The country's physical resources were simply inadequate to provide a living for a population which in the early 1800's began rapidly to multiply. Crop failures brought disaster and many died of famine. As late as the 1860's the records show sharp rises in the mortality rate in years of poor harvests.

One result of this condition was a mass exodus to America. Emigration had begun early in the century as a movement of those who sought political and religious freedom or opportunities for a better material life in the New World. But after the American Civil War tens of thousands of Swedes were driven to America out of sheer desperation. In 1887-1888 no less than 100,000 Swedes left for the United States and the total for the decade of the 1880's — a time of disastrous harvests in Sweden — was 347,000. Emigration to America, which at first had been regarded in Sweden as a desirable safety-valve, an easy means of siphoning off surplus population, had become by the turn of the century an alarming loss to the mother country. It was depopulating Sweden. In some sections nearly all the young men and women pulled out for America.

The Swedes, like the Norwegians, were attracted to the region just west of the Great Lakes, which in many ways resembled the land and the climate of the provinces they had forsaken. Frederika Bremer, the Swedish author and feminist, whose books on the New World became best-sellers around the midcentury, wrote back from one of her trips to the Midwest: "What a glorious new Scandinavia might not Minnesota become! Here the Swede would find his clear, romantic lakes, the plains of Skane, rich in grain, and the valleys of Norrland . . ." Half a century later it was evident that many of her fellow countrymen had responded to her words. One eighth of Minnesota's inhabitants were Swedish immigrants.

Two things happened to put a brake to emigration and eventually to halt it: industrialization and political and social reform. Industry created jobs — and wealth. The reforms, bringing political freedom and relative security for all, made life attractive enough for Swedes to prefer to stay put. In both cases American influence, exercised largely through the contacts which Swedish immigrants maintained with the old country, was considerable. It helped teach Sweden modern industrial and agricultural techniques; it kindled the insistence of the common people in Sweden for universal suffrage, complete representative government and social reform. Ironically, the influence of the

Swedish pioneers in America was at first (until about 1918) considered radical if not downright subversive by the ruling classes in Sweden. Now that labor has become the ruling class in Sweden, the tables are reversed. I have heard many a prosperous businessman of Swedish origin in my native Midwest lament the "creeping" socialism and the "welfare state" in "the old country." In Stockholm, I have heard Labor party leaders, taking time off from their job of running the state, express astonishment at America's conservatism and at American labor's failure to organize politically. In Scandinavian labor circles American trade-unions are considered somewhat "backward."

Politically, until well after the turn of the century, Sweden remained decidedly backward; there was no doubt about that. As late as 1905 only 8 per cent of the population was allowed to vote; in 1911 some 19 per cent became eligible. It was not until directly after the First World War, under the impact of the overthrow of the Romanovs and Hohenzollerns, and the Russian and German Revolutions, that full democracy triumphed in Sweden; the remaining powers of the king were annulled, complete Parliamentary rule established and universal suffrage for both men and women introduced.

Swedish life, like that of most growing democracies, has had its full share of controversy. But on one thing all Swedes have long been in general agreement. To preserve what they had built up after so much toil and turmoil, they have been determined to stay out of wars. Two centuries of national wars ending in 1814, which bled the country white and constantly bankrupted it, were enough. And nearly all Swedes are also agreed that the best way to stay out of wars is for the nation not to choose sides, as Norway and Denmark have done, but to remain neutral — in peace and war.

One cannot understand Sweden today until one confronts the national passion for neutrality and looks carefully and objectively into how it has worked under the pressure of wars raging all around and considers how much luck there has been in its success and whether it can survive in the present cold conflict between the Communist world and the West.

Neutral Sweden

When Europe went to war in 1914, Sweden had just celebrated a century of peace. The devastating four-year conflict which now ensued put Sweden's neutrality to a stern test. There were hardships due to Allied and German blockades. Food and many raw materials became scarce; the nation's economy was dislocated, though a few profited from trade with both sides. There was occasional embarrassment, as when the United States government disclosed that the Swedish Foreign Office had permitted the Germans to send messages in cipher code through the Swedish minister in Buenos Aires directing German U-boats to sink Allied ships without trace.[1] But all parties in Sweden were unanimous in supporting a policy of neutrality.

They were divided in their sympathies toward the belligerents. The Liberals and the Socialists favored the Allies; the Conservatives, whom the King had put in power, were predominantly pro-German. In fact, sentiment for the Germans was quite strong in ruling circles. There were many reasons for this. Russia was one. Sweden had been forced to cede Finland to Russia in 1809, and this still rankled most Swedes. But most important, Sweden felt that its very independence might be threatened if Russia were to win and Germany to lose.

Also there were many close ties between the Germans and the Swedes. King Gustav V, who had come to the throne in 1907, had married the daughter of the Grand Duke of Baden. Many Swedish Army officers received some of their training in Germany. Numerous Swedish scientists and professional men had studied in German universities. Business connections between the two countries were close. The Swedish upper classes — the court circles, aristocracy, big industrialists and landowners and high government functionaries — were attracted to the upper classes in Germany. German was their preferred foreign language and German books and scientific treatises were avidly read in Sweden. A few fanatical "activists," led by Dr. Sven Hedin, the explorer (Hitler named a street in Berlin after him; it sticks to this day), wanted Sweden to openly intervene on Germany's side. But the vast majority, Right or Left, felt that Sweden's interests were best served by staying out of the war.

Pro-German sentiment in Sweden was much reduced by the time Hitler started the Second World War, thanks to Nazi excesses which shocked and disgusted the vast majority of Swedes as they did decent folk everywhere. But the driving determination to stay out of the war remained undiminished. However, the test for Sweden was to be

[1] *The Northern Tangle*, by Rowland Kenney.

much severer this time and her neutrality was strained to a point where it often became decidedly un-neutral, leaving scars on her national consciousness which are still visible to a visitor who probes beneath the surface in Sweden today.

Not that she lacked good reasons for her many deviations from strict neutrality. She had many and we shall duly consider them. A nation is surely justified in going to almost any length to assure its survival as a free society. But that does not in this case hide the fact so truthfully put by Professor Scott that Sweden's policy shifed like a weathervane during World War II, and was a better indication than the stock market of how the fortunes of war were treating the warring powers.[2]

First, there was the Finnish Winter War of 1939-1940. Here the overwhelming desire of the Swedes to help the Finns resist Soviet aggression confronted their hard-rock determination to stay out of war. The result was a compromise. The Swedes quickly raised, mostly by voluntary subscription, $100,000,000 for aid to Finland. Some 9000 Swedish volunteers rushed to the front, and 20,000 more were in training to go when hostilities ceased after 100 days. Sweden dispatched to the Finns 300 pieces of artillery with 300,000 shells, 84,000 rifles with 50,000,000 rounds of ammunition; and 25 planes. Large quantities of clothing, medical supplies and food were also sent. But Sweden declined to back suggestions for League of Nations sanctions against Russia, and on February 19, the King declared, with sorrow in his heart, that Sweden could not officially involve herself in the war. Early in March Sweden and Norway refused France and Britain permission to send an Allied expeditionary force to Finland across their territories.[3] The Winter War ended on March 12 with Finland's in-

---

[2] Cf. *The United States and Scandinavia*, by Franklin D. Scott.

[3] It is likely that the governments of both Norway and Sweden suspected that a part at least of the Allied force, instead of proceeding to Finland, would halt to occupy the Norwegian ports and the great Swedish iron mines in Lapland in order to deprive Germany of Swedish iron ore, without which she could not continue to wage war.

Long after the war they found their suspicions confirmed by the publication of official Allied documents on the matter in London. These revealed that the Supreme Allied War Council, meeting in Paris on February 5, 1940, decided that in connection with sending an expeditionary force to Finland the Swedish iron fields should be occupied by an Allied force sent through the Norwegian port of Narvik, which lies but a short distance from the mines.

The Allied leaders believed that such a step would provoke German counter-

evitable capitulation, and there were qualms in many Swedish hearts that, though they had done much, they might have done even more to help their Finnish neighbors.

There was not much time for soul searching. Less than a month later, on April 9, Germany attacked Denmark and Norway and Sweden was suddenly confronted with the worst dilemma in her modern experience. Should she come to the help of her Scandinavian brethren? Or should she do what almost all nations have done at the moment of peril: try to save her own skin, by standing aside? Denmark was overrun in a day — before Sweden could possibly act. But Norway, which throughout the nineteenth century had been in union with Sweden, had, as we have seen, refused to capitulate. Should Sweden spring to the side of her neighbor and kin?

Sweden's situation, we must try to realize, was desperate. She had drained her scanty supply of arms to help Finland. She had little to fight Germany with. The lightning Nazi occupation of Denmark and the Norwegian ports had cut her off from Great Britain and the West, from whom no direct aid could therefore be expected. Russia was still allied to Germany in the Hitler-Stalin pact of August, 1939, and for that reason as well as because of Moscow's resentment at Swedish assistance to Finland in the recent Winter War, no help could be expected from the Soviet Union. Sweden was at the mercy of

---

measures in the form of an attack on Sweden from the south. Plans were therefore made for Allied troops to be dispatched to the aid of the Swedes in the South through the Norwegian ports of Trondheim and Bergen, which were connected with Sweden by rail. The Finno-Russian armistice of March 12 removed all grounds for sending an Allied expedition to Finland, and the scheme to occupy Sweden's iron fields had to be dropped, at least temporarily.

It was revived in London on March 28 at the urging of the French Premier, Reynaud, who convinced himself that by setting up a front in Scandinavia and depriving Germany of her main source of iron ore, Germany might be quickly defeated. (There was a perfectly good front on the Franco-German border, but neither side did any fighting there in this period of the "phony" war.) Hitler's lightning conquest of Denmark and Norway in April once again destroyed the Allied plans. But as late as June 8, after the Allies had begun to withdraw from Narvik, their last foothold in Norway, the Commander of the British Home Fleet received orders to prepare a carrier which would stand off Norway and send planes across the peninsula to Sweden's warm-weather iron port of Luleå at the tip of the Gulf of Bothnia and there torpedo German ore ships. The British government, however, decided the political consequences of such an attack might be too serious, and the plan was finally abandoned.

The Swedes today shudder at the very thought of how close they came to becoming involved in a war with friendly Britain.

Germany. She would fight in self-defense if attacked. But otherwise . . . ?[4]

She did not take much time to make up her mind. King Gustav sat
down and wrote a personal letter to Hitler assuring him of Sweden's
neutrality. Per Albin Hansson, the popular Labor Prime Minister,
broadcast the decision to his people on April 12.

The Norwegians were understandably indignant, for they were in
an even more desperate predicament than the Swedes. They were resentful that Sweden, which had sent arms to Finland, now banned
shipment of arms to them — and indeed forbade the export to them
even of ammunition and gasoline for their hard-pressed forces. They
did not take kindly to the efforts of the Swedish government to discourage, for a time, public exhibitions of sympathy for Norway —
there was no doubt how the Swedish people felt — nor to the government's "suggestion" to the Swedish press that it exercise restraint
in its comments on the German conquest and the way the Germans
were carrying it out. More than a decade later, I still found resentment in the Norwegian Foreign Office at Sweden's refusal, until after
the tide of war had changed, to recognize the Norwegian chargé
d'affaires in Stockholm as "Minister," which Norway's government in
exile in London had requested.

But above all, the Norwegians resented (as did the British) the
highly unneutral concessions which Sweden made to Germany as soon
as the conquest of Norway was completed. We now come to a painful matter which is still the subject of much controversy in Scandinavia — and indeed within Sweden. It shall be set down here, highly
condensed, as objectively as possible. The bare facts, so far as I could
get them (the Swedish government has not yet released the full,
documented story), are as follows:

In May, 1940, when General Dietl's position at Narvik had become
critical, Berlin asked the Swedish government to be allowed to transport arms and munitions across Sweden to Narvik. The Swedish government refused. The worse Dietl's situation became, the more Berlin threatened. The Swedes had reason to fear that Hitler intended
to attack them on June 17 in order to secure his communications to

[4] An eminent Swedish journalist and historian, on reading this section in manuscript, expressed doubts that many Swedes saw this situation as presenting a dilemma. There was never any question, he says, of Sweden coming to the help of
Norway — for the reasons I have enumerated.

northern Norway. The capitulation of the Norwegian forces and the flight of the government to London on that date, the Swedes believe, saved them from the German fury.

It spared them an attack, but it did not spare them from German pressure. As soon as the fighting in Norway was over, Berlin renewed its demands for transit facilities for both troops and war material through Sweden to Norway. And now the government in Stockholm began to yield.

In all fairness, we must again attempt to keep in mind Sweden's sorry predicament in the fateful June of 1940. It was much worse than in April. Norway and Denmark were completely occupied by the Germans. But that was not all. France, Holland and Belgium had fallen in the meantime to the Nazis too. In the brief moment of the late spring and early summer, Hitler had conquered the continent of Western Europe. Only Britain held out, and, after Dunkirk, few gave it much chance for survival. In France the venerable Pétain and the politically powerful Laval had agreed to collaborate with the Fuehrer in establishing the New Order. Italy was collaborating, and so was Russia and Franco's Spain. Moreover, with the fighting over in the North and on the Continent, Hitler had vast forces at hand to overwhelm Sweden should she prove recalcitrant.

In these circumstances, the hardheaded Swedes, who not unreasonably saw their problem in terms of sheer survival, decided not to be very recalcitrant. On June 15, Germany again prodded Stockholm for an answer to its transit demands. On June 19, Sweden, after much soul-searching on the part of the King and the members of the cabinet, gave in. On July 5, the transit agreement was signed.

It provided for the transport over Swedish railways of unarmed Nazi soldiers and war material on the condition that the number of troops moving in each direction should balance so that the German garrison in Norway would not be strengthened by the arrangement. In addition the Swedes agreed to a liberal amount of "horseshoe" traffic between the Norwegian ports of Trondheim and Narvik, whose only rail-link passes, almost entirely, through Sweden.

This so-called "leave traffic" was, of course, of immense value to Germany. By transporting fresh troops and war material by land through Sweden it avoided the risk of having them sunk at sea by the British navy and air force. In the first six months of the agreement some 140,000 German troops in Norway were exchanged and vast amounts of war goods were shipped to the German garrisons. By 1943, when the German star had commenced to fade and Sweden felt strong enough to cancel the agreement, Swedish railways had earned some $22,000,000 dollars from the German traffic, a sum which the outspokenly pro-Allied newspaper *Göteborgs Handels och Sjöfartstidningen* under its great editor, Torgny Segerstedt, bitterly suggested should be referred to as "blood money," a profit derived from Norway's sufferings. The journal suggested that the money be given to the Norwegians after the war.

For the Swedish people, and a good part of the press, had been indignant at these concessions to Germany at the expense of Norway. And both the Norwegian government in exile and the British government had protested vehemently. The unhappy feelings of the members of the Swedish government may be imagined for they were mostly Social-Democrats, who loathed Nazism and who had been very close, personally, to the Social-Democrats who composed the government of Norway. But they felt — and this was one reason for their political success — that their primary obligation was to look to Sweden's survival. As one of their notes, in reply to a Norwegian protest, explained: "All neutrality policy has its limits in the possibilities open to the neutral state."

What greatly annoyed the Allies until their successes induced Stockholm to change its policies was that the Swedish Social-Democrats in power never seemed to realize the import of what they were doing. As Professor Bruce Hopper of Harvard, who was on duty at the American Legation in Stockholm at the time, said: "It will always be difficult for a foreign observer to understand why the Swedish government did not admit that the Transit Agreement was a violation of neutrality, accepted under the threat of *force majeure*."[5]

But Per Albin Hansson, the beloved and highly respected Social-Democrat Prime Minister, would not admit it. He believed and said that Sweden's neutrality had really served Norway's best interests,[6]

[5] *Foreign Affairs*, April, 1945.
[6] There is no doubt that once the fighting in Norway was over, there were advantages to the Norwegians in having Sweden neutral and independent rather than occupied by the Germans. Norway's wartime Prime Minister, Johan Nygaardsvold, handsomely acknowledged this to Parliament a few days after Liberation, when he said: "We are sufficiently honest now to acknowledge that Sweden's neutrality was a blessing for Norway."

and he defended such favors to Hitler as transporting German troops and war material as "a burden which Sweden had been compelled to bear as the result of the war." He stoutly denied that it was a breach of neutrality. His Foreign Minister, Christian Günther, made a number of even more striking statements. "Sweden's neutrality policy," he was wont to affirm, "needs no excuses."

But the Danes, for one, smarting under the Nazi occupation, thought that perhaps it did, or that, to look at it another way, there was certainly little excuse for Mr. Günther's complacent pronunciamentos. And they expressed their feelings immediately after their liberation in a manner that both surprised and pained many Swedes. Following a cabinet shakeup at the war's end, Mr. Günther was replaced as Sweden's foreign minister by Östen Undén, who had been consistently anti-Nazi throughout the war. Mr. Günther was named Swedish Minister to Denmark. But the Danes did not want him and the uproar, especially in the Danish press, against his appointment was so strong that Mr. Günther withdrew without ever going to Copenhagen. The Swedes were taken aback at this unexpected manifestation of Danish sentiment, and in some quarters there was so much resentment that a sum of $54,000 was raised by private subscription as a testimonial to the rejected envoy; and Mr. Günther accepted it.

There was one other flagrant violation of neutrality by Sweden which aroused the ire of the Allies. Just before the German onslaught on Russia in June, 1941, the Swedish government permitted the Nazi High Command to transport an entire army division, fully armed, from Norway across Sweden to Finland to be used to attack the Soviet Union. Just a year before, the Allies recalled, the same Swedish government had bluntly turned down an Anglo-French request to send Allied troops through Sweden to Finland to fight the Russians. What Sweden would not accord the Western democracies, it now gave Nazi Germany. The Germans also demanded the right to fly over Sweden and to lay mines in certain areas of the Baltic. To what extent the Swedish government gave in to these additional demands is still not accurately known, but Professor Hopper says "It is a matter of history that Sweden accepted the most important Finnish-German demands." [7]

Obviously the vast majority of Swedes believed in helping Finland

[7] *Foreign Affairs*, April, 1945.

regain the territories which Russia had taken from her the year before, though they disliked the Finnish tie-up with Nazi Germany. Few of them seem to have given much consideration to the probability that a German victory over Russia would have made the Baltic a Nazi lake and made Sweden's chances of surviving alone as an independent, democratic nation extremely small. But the Swedes, like almost everyone else, believed that a German triumph in Russia was inevitable.

Then, toward the end of 1942, the fortunes of the titanic world conflict began to change, and with them Swedish policy. The German setbacks at El Alamein and especially at Stalingrad, plus the prodigious war effort of the United States quickly awakened the Swedish government to the realization that Germany probably was not going to win the war after all. The feeling of relief in Stockholm was immense. There had been a bad scare in February–March, 1942, when in the face of rumors that the Germans, irritated by their first reverses in Russia, might attack Sweden, the government ordered full mobilization. But by the beginning of 1943, Sweden's confidence in her ability to defend herself successfully against a German attack had greatly increased. Three years of feverish rearming had begun to show results. An army of 600,000 was continually being mobilized, and it was now fairly well trained and armed. The navy had 23 destroyers, 27 submarines and numerous torpedo boats to strengthen coastal defense. For the first time since 1940, Sweden could afford to stand up to German demands.

In August, 1943, the transit of German troops and war material through Sweden was stopped. Berlin howled and threatened, but the Swedes stood fast. The Norwegian chargé d'affaires in Stockholm was recognized as "Minister."

And now Sweden began to feel increased pressure from the Allied side — there is no easy life for a neutral. Great Britain and the United States insisted that Swedish deliveries to Germany be greatly curtailed. The Swedes argued that they had to sell to Germany in order to get coal to keep their economy — and especially their rearmament — going. But they agreed to reduce their exports to the Reich. In the spring of 1944, London and Washington pressed Sweden to halt its shipment of ball-bearings to Germany. The Swedes balked at this but finally agreed to it in October. In the meantime, beginning in the fall of 1943, the Swedish King and government had offered their services in extracting Finland from the war. Early in 1944, they were advising the Finns to accept Russian terms. Most of the initial negotiations for peace between Finland and the Soviet Union were conducted in Stockholm.

In the fall of 1944, Sweden announced that it would not give asylum to war criminals, thus spoiling any plans some of the Nazi leaders may have had to take refuge there after the war. In the spring of 1945, Count Folke Bernadotte, a nephew of the King, was able to arrange for the liberation and transport to Sweden of 19,000 Norwegians and Danes held in German concentration camps, and thus spare them the eleventh-hour horrors which were experienced by inmates of other nationalities. Finally, on May 7, the day of Germany's capitulation, Sweden broke off diplomatic relations with the expiring Third Reich.

It had successfully survived, as a neutral, the greatest war in history and one which had raged all about it. Just how neutral Sweden had really been, we have seen. Certainly she had followed a policy of naked opportunism, of cold-blooded national self-interest, of the stern will to survive under terrorizing German pressure. Exactly how great that pressure was is still not known in every detail. Men like Professor Herbert Tingsten, the brilliant, nonconformist editor of Sweden's greatest newspaper, *Dagens Nyheter*, believe the German threats were sometimes exaggerated by the Swedish government to justify their concessions to Berlin. There is no doubt, though, that on at least three occasions the government actually believed the Germans were about to attack: just prior to June 7, 1940; in the early summer of 1941, shortly before the German assault on Russia; and in February–March, 1942. Each time the Swedes hurriedly mobilized their entire defense forces. But there were numerous other periods when Stockholm feared an imminent German onslaught, and they all added up to a war of nerves that put a great strain on the nation and people. General Bengt Nordenskiöld, the extremely able chief of the air force, who slept at night on a cot in his office throughout the early years of the war, told me that on many a late evening he was alerted to what looked like a German attack and that on each occasion he would have to get his planes into the air just before dawn, though he was frightfully short of oil.

Sweden, it must be remembered, was completely dependent upon

Germany, once she had been cut off from the West, for coal and
other supplies to keep her economy from collapse. This was another
principal reason why she heeded German demands. Hitler could have
snuffed out her economic life.

Why did he spare her from that, and from invasion between 1940
and 1943? The Swedes don't know. Perhaps he calculated that, on the
whole, a neutral Sweden which supplied transit facilities and great
quantities of iron ore and badly needed ball bearings, and some other
things, was worth more to him than an occupied Sweden which, after
a costly resistance, could render its iron mines unworkable, its railways unusable and its factories unproductive.

Then there was luck. Sweden was lucky where Finland, Denmark
and Norway, which had also striven to remain neutral, were unlucky.
Recently the Swedes were reminded of that in a rather interesting
way.

In the autumn of 1952, a novel entitled *Paradise for Us* was published in Stockholm and soon became a best-seller. The author had a
quite un-Swedish name: John Burns. The scene of the story was
Stockholm in the first year of World War II. The characters were the
British and German ambassadors, and all the members of the Swedish
Cabinet, the names of whom were so thinly disguised that the reader
had no trouble at all in making out who was who. But the book was
more than just an amusing *roman à clef*. It described confidential debates and decisions of the Cabinet and the contents of highly secret
diplomatic notes and negotiations with such obvious authority and
fidelity that the reader instantly became aware that the author could
only have been a person high in government circles, with an inside
knowledge of what actually happened in the Cabinet and Foreign
Office.

But who was he? All Stockholm wondered. There was no "John
Burns" in the Cabinet or in the Foreign Office. Who stood behind the
pseudonym? The question provided the great guessing game in the
capital for months. Then, one day, in a letter to *Dagens Nyheter*,
the Swedish ambassador to the Court of St. James's let the cat out
of the bag. He was the author!

The surprise in Sweden was tremendous. Ambassador Gunnar Hägg-
löf was one of the most brilliant of Foreign Office career officials.
At thirty-five, he had been a cabinet adviser; during the war he

had held a key post in the Foreign Office and later, at forty-four had been awarded the top diplomatic post of ambassador in London. No wonder the author wrote so authoritatively!

But it was what he had to say in his novel that shocked so many Swedish readers out of their complacency about Sweden's neutrality during the war. He made it quite clear that Sweden escaped involvement in the conflict only because of a long series of lucky accidents. In fact, he denied that the Swedish government had been able to exert any influence at all on developments, and compared the venerable wartime Prime Minister, Per Albin Hansson, with the captain of ship in trouble on the high seas who refrains from appraising the passengers that he has lost control of the vessel only to avoid panic. And the author enumerated numerous happenings to prove that it was not what Sweden did or refrained from doing that saved it from the fate of Norway and Denmark but merely outward events over which the country had no control. From that the author drew some conclusions: that even for lucky Sweden there can be no paradise in a world which resembles more the lower regions. The Swedes must see that they live in great danger and that there is no guaranty that they will be lucky a third time. Henceforth they must cease trusting to luck and work out a more logical and realistic solution of the problem of survival.

Not that the book, or any other development since the war, has led Sweden to abandon her historic neutrality. She clings tenaciously, though with increasing inner doubts, to her age-old course. It is a policy which has isolated Sweden more fully — and more dangerously — than at any time in the last century and a half. Today she stands aloof and alone in the North between the belligerent East and West.

The devious wartime neutrality, which the Swedish people generally supported as a choice between life and death, but which most of them nevertheless regretted, has left deep traces in the consciousness of the nation. As a semiofficial booklet on contemporary Sweden remarks of the popular reaction to the transit agreement with the Germans: "It may be stated that the Swedish people were deeply aware of a strain on their conscience in this tragic situation." [7]

A slight feeling of guilt lingers on. I found a number of good folk who spoke frankly of their misgivings over their country's neutrality

[7] *Introduction to Sweden,* published by the Swedish Institute at the request of the Ministry for Foreign Affairs.

policy during the war. And yet they honestly were unable to see that they could have done much to help their neighbors in view of their own military weakness and Germany's overwhelming strength.

At least, as neutrals, they were able to lend more humanitarian aid to the Norwegians and Danes than would have been possible had they been occupied by the Germans. That humanitarian aid was considerable. Considering the resources of a country whose total population is less than that of London or New York, it was immense. In the case of the Norwegians and the Danes, and indeed of the Dutch and the Greeks, who also received aid, it often meant the difference between semistarvation and decent survival. During and immediately after the war, Sweden sent to these four hapless lands more than 400,000 tons of food, valued at $39,000,000, and clothing and shoes to the value of $24,000,000. Medical supplies were also provided. Refugees were welcomed and taken care of. At the end of 1944, nearly five months before the war ended, they numbered 300,-000 of whom 80,000 were children. An additional 100,000 Finnish children were accommodated in private Swedish homes. Several thousand Danish Jews who escaped the Nazi vengeance were provided for in Sweden — it was the only country they could flee to.

To sum up: during and immediately after the war government and private gifts and government credits for relief amounted to nearly half a billion dollars. During the difficult first postwar years, when Europe was still in chaos and millions hungering, the Swedes contributed an additional quarter of a billion dollars in gifts and credits for relief. Of the wartime credits to Norway and Denmark, $48,000,-000 was written off as an outright gift. The total relief, then, came to three quarters of a billion dollars, or more than 15 per cent of Sweden's annual national income — a contribution of $119 for every man, woman and child in the country. No people in Europe was more generous than the Swedes.

Sweden Goes It Alone

The Second World War left Sweden much worse off strategically than she had been at the end of the first war. In 1918, her position on the Baltic had been strengthened by a new balance of power. Both Germany and Russia were weakened, and a new independent

Poland appeared on the shores of the inland sea. Moreover the Soviet Union held but a few miles of coast on the Gulf of Finland, on both sides of Leningrad, making the Russian position on the Baltic weaker than it had been since the days of the Swedish conqueror, Charles XII, at the beginning of the eighteenth century. Germany's position was weak, too, because of the disarmament imposed on her by Versailles.

In 1945 the situation was radically — and for Sweden, dangerously — changed. Russia, the ancient enemy, had gained control of almost the entire southern coast of the Baltic — from Finland through the former Baltic states to Luebeck, in occupied Germany, at the southwest tip of the sea. And Russia, even in peacetime, was a difficult and provocative neighbor.

Sometimes it appears, to a foreigner from the West at least, that the Swedes are blind to the realities of their changed position in the postwar world. But that, even in the face of the Soviet danger, they will abandon their cherished neutrality in the foreseeable future, there is slight chance.

This stand, which leaves them outside the camp of the Western powers, does cause misgivings — at least to some. For the Swedes quite naturally consider themselves, ideologically and culturally, a part of the Western world. To a minority of them there is something wrong in their country refusing to make common cause in the defense of the West. People of this persuasion will tell you that the Swedes hope for and expect immediate aid from the West in case of a Soviet attack and they are chagrined that their country will not face up to the responsibility of arranging for that aid in advance by joining the Western alliance. I met a number of Swedes with such thoughts, but I recognize that they comprise but a small minority.

For the majority, if I understand them correctly, the risks of taking sides today outweigh those of remaining neutral. We have considered their arguments in the first chapter — their fear that NATO could not get adequate military aid to them in time if they were attacked; their belief that if they joined the Atlantic alliance, Russia would occupy more bases in Finland and thereby not only further reduce the Finns' internal freedom but, by moving up to Sweden's frontiers with Finland, make the defense of Sweden all but impossible.[8] This may be more a justification than a reason for Swedish

[8] See pp. 16-23.

policy, but the Swedes hold to it tenaciously. And they argue further that to adhere to the Atlantic Pact would make the Russians regard Sweden as a forward American base which seriously endangered the security of the Soviet Union. As Dr. Lennart Hirschfeldt, director of the Institute of International Affairs in Stockholm, has put it:

"Sweden would find herself in the extreme front line. In the event of war the country would probably be involved from the very start and become the object of concentrated campaigning. During a continued state of international tension Scandinavia as a whole would be in the foreground of the cold war and world politics would have one more center of disturbance and friction."

That is a risk the Swedes do not want to take. But is it such a risk? Some of Sweden's western friends wonder. In Oslo one is reminded by the Norwegians that when Norway joined NATO, Russia did no more than protest. Even though Norway's adherence moved NATO territory to the very border of the Soviet Union in the North, Moscow made no move into Finland.

The Swedes consider that they have modified their neutrality to some extent by joining the United Nations. Foreign Minister Östen Undén has said that Sweden will go along with UN sanctions ordered by the Security Council in accordance with the Charter — that is, when the Great Powers are unanimous. But Sweden, he has added, will reserve its decision in case the Assembly, under the Acheson Plan, should recommend sanctions.

"Sweden," says Mr. Undén, "cannot be expected to participate in sanctions in cases where a war between Great Powers has broken out or where she considers that she is in danger of being drawn into a general war."

At the deliberations of the UN, Sweden has by no means followed an exclusively Western or — much less — an American line. She approved UN action in declaring North Korea an aggressor but abstained from voting for the Assembly's condemnation of Red China — an abstention that was attacked at home by the Conservative and Liberal parties. Sweden has recognized the Peiping government and, like Norway and Denmark, has publicly supported its right to represent China in the UN.

There is no danger that Sweden will recede into the pacificism which was so strong all over Scandinavia between the wars. Sweden today is by all odds the strongest military power in the North. Her government quite realizes that while her neutrality in the last resort depends on whether the Great Powers find it to their advantage not to involve her in war, it will be greatly buttressed by a defense force strong enough to make any tempted aggressor think twice about the cost of attacking her.

That cost would be considerable today.

In time of peace, Sweden maintains only a small regular army of some 15,000 professional officers, noncommissioned officers and enlisted men, whose chief task is to train the annual contingent of from 35,-000 to 50,000 conscripts and to give one-month refresher courses to 70,000 reserve troops each year. In case of war, Sweden could mobilize three quarters of a million men, of whom about half a million would be in the field force and the rest in reserve or in special home defense units. But it takes time to mobilize a civilian army and Sweden's fate, if she is attacked, depends upon whether she has sufficient time to put a half million men in the field, suitably disposed and armed. Mobilization plans are naturally highly secret but the experience gained during the last war, when the army was called up during several emergencies, would indicate that the Swedes could put sizable forces in the field within a week or ten days. Each reservist knows exactly where he is to report, and the railroads, bus lines, trucking firms and shipping lines have exhaustive plans to transport the troops to their destination. The 100,000 members of the Home Guard keep their weapons at home and are ready for action at a moment's notice. Incidentally, service in Civilian Defense is compulsory for all citizens between sixteen and sixty-five years who have not been assigned to regular military duty.

In order to avoid what happened in Norway in 1940, when the traitor Quisling seized the radio station in Oslo and broadcast an "order" to cease fighting, there is a standing government order, issued to all troops during the war and still in force, which proclaims: "Resistance shall be made to all attacks. Any information that resistance shall cease is false and must be ignored."

For a nation of seven millions, Sweden has a surprisingly strong navy and, as is natural, it is designed chiefly for coastal defense. It comprises three cruisers, two of them of 8000 tons built after the last war, two old, but modernized, pocket battleships of 7000 tons,

24 submarines most of which are fitted with "schnorkels," 19 destroyers, 20 MTBs and numerous minelayers, minesweepers and other
small craft. In 1952, the Riksdag approved a new program of naval
construction over a six-year period which will add 50 more ships to
the navy, including 4 destroyers and 3 submarines. In addition there
is a considerable coast artillery establishment covering 700 miles of
the shoreline.

The Swedish air force is second to that of Great Britain in Western
Europe and represents an amazing achievement for such a small country. It has over 1000 first-line planes, almost all jet fighters or fighter
bombers, since the air force, like the navy, is purely defensive.

For many years the Swedes have manufactured their own jet
planes. Today most of the fighter squadrons of the Swedish Air Force
are equipped with the J-29, nicknamed the "Flying Barrel," which
it indeed resembles. This plane has an officially acknowledged speed
of 665 miles an hour. Swedish designers are making great efforts to
keep pace with the development of jet aircraft in other countries
(especially in Russia), but they have to concentrate on a few types.
A new fighter with a top speed of nearly 1000 miles an hour is being
developed and will go into production in 1957. In the meantime the
Air Force has reinforced its Flying Barrels with purchases from England of British Venom jet night fighters and with Britain's latest
and fastest jet, the Hunter IV, deliveries of which began in 1955.

While I was in Sweden I heard of highly secret tests of a new
Swedish all-weather jet attack plane, which was believed to have
exceeded the speed of sound. At the end of 1953, it was publicly
announced that the plane, known as the A–32, or the "Lance," had
gone into production at the Saab works. It is said to have a speed of
well over 700 miles an hour and a range of at least 1250 miles. Swedish
engineers believe it is probably the only relatively heavy jet in actual
production anywhere which has broken the sound barrier. It will become the backbone of Sweden's twelve specialized attack squadrons.

The air force is organized in 33 fighter squadrons, 12 fighter-
bomber squadrons and 5 reconnaissance squadrons. Its chief from 1942
to 1954 was General Bengt Nordenskiöld, a dashing and popular figure
in Sweden. Despite his years — he is over sixty — he personally takes
up a jet fighter almost daily, and during the tense moments just after
the Russians had shot down a couple of Swedish planes over the Baltic
in the summer of 1952, he jumped into a fully armed jet, checked his

ammunition belts, and somewhat to the consternation of the civilian members of the government flew over to the scene of the crime to see for himself what the Russians were up to. General Nordenskiöld, incidentally, holds the American Legion of Merit — an award, I suspect, which is not unconnected with the understanding he showed toward hundreds of American pilots who during the last war made forced landings in Sweden after their planes had been damaged over Germany. He was one of the most friendly, frank and informative persons I met in Sweden. Late in 1954, he retired and was succeeded by Major General Axel Ljungdahl, who, besides being an eminent flyer, is an amateur ornithologist.

Going it alone is not without its expense. Sweden's defense expenditures amount to $425,000,000 annually, which is one quarter of her budget and 5 per cent of the national income — approximately equal to what the NATO countries in Europe are spending.

A good deal of Sweden's surprising military strength is due to her having built up a considerable armaments industry. She is the only country in the North which has a sizable one. Today it can produce almost all of her armaments from battleships to jets to guns. Bofors anti-aircraft artillery, tested in the last war, is among the best in the world. And Bofors, like Saab, which turns out the new jet planes, has built some of its chief factories underground, where they are safe from bombing.

The story of how Sweden has built underground is a remarkable one. For reasons of military security only a part of it can be revealed. But this is enough to give a picture of how a civilized nation is preparing to exist in a bizarre subterranean world safe from the murderous consequences of the atom and hydrogen and ordinary high-explosive bombs.

Not only war-essential industrial works, including two mammoth hydroelectric power plants, but hospitals, laboratories, firefighting stations, airplane hangars, ammunition and fuel dumps, storehouses for stockpiles of crucial materials and pens for submarines and destroyers have been built into Sweden's granite hills or hollowed out of solid rock along the coast.[10] Furthermore, underground rock shelters for

[10] In 1954 it was decided to transfer gradually the Stockholm Naval Base to a number of islands in the southern part of the Stockholm archipelago, with Muskö as the center. The moving will not be completed until the middle of the 1960's.

100,000 people have been constructed since the war — and this is in addition to ordinary shelters for a million others. It would be extremely difficult, if not impossible, for an enemy today to knock out Sweden by air attack even if it were made with A- and H-bombs.

Swedish engineers calculate that you need some 165 feet of solid rock above your head to be safe from a direct hit by an atomic bomb. But only the most vital and vulnerable targets are being placed that deep. On the whole the Swedes work on the theory that the thickness of rock should be roughly 1½ times the width of a room. If it is 100 feet wide, a ceiling of from 135 to 150 feet of solid rock will do. But isn't the cost of such extensive tunneling prohibitive? Not at all. Thanks to a new process of drilling and dynamiting perfected by the Swedes, it has now become cheaper, they say, to build underground than above ground.

Still, the cost is considerable because underground construction has been so extensive. Leaving out the millions of dollars spent by private industry, the Swedish government is spending seventeen times as much per capita on civil defense as is the United States Federal government. The figure comes to $28,000,000 a year — four dollars per head — against the 23½ cents per citizen spent in the United States.

A little ingenuity has enabled the Swedes, however, to keep their costs down. For example, the mammoth air raid shelters being built for civilians in the larger towns are so planned as to earn nearly half their cost. In the granite bluffs on the south shore of Saltsjön Bay, in the heart of Stockholm, workmen were blasting a great cavern when I was there into which could be squeezed a building as large as New York's Chrysler skyscraper. It was one of five such projects in the capital, built or building, for the protection of civilians against atom and hydrogen bombs. In time of war it will be a self-contained underground city accommodating 20,000 people and complete with hospital, schools, stores, water, sewage and electric lighting and heating. In time of peace it will serve as a garage for 550 cars, with auto repair shops, filling stations, shops and even a restaurant. The income from these, it is calculated, will pay in the long run for at least 40 per cent of the cost of building, which was $3,000,000.

Aside from these large, deep, "atom-proof" caverns, which when

---

The installations at Muskö are being blasted into solid rock, with bombproof pens for destroyers, submarines and other vessels as well as subterranean workshops and repair docks.

completed will take care of 80,000 persons, there are hundreds of small shelters — one of them built under the old Johannes Church — which eventually will accommodate another 320,000 people — or 400,000 altogether, which is half of the capital's population. The other half, according to present plans, will be evacuated inland should war come.

Among the armament works that have gone underground are Bofors at Karlskoga, producing guns and ammunition; Saab at Linköping, which makes jet fighters; Bolinder-Munktell at Eskilstuna, which turns out engines; and Aga at Stockholm, which manufactures precision instruments. The Saab plant required the blasting and removal of some 5,280,000 cubic feet of granite at a cost of 40 cents a cubic foot — or more than $2,000,000.

I wondered if continued work in an underground plant didn't adversely affect one's health. There has been much debate in Sweden about this, but recently a joint study made by the Employers' and Labor Federations (a typical example of the present-day cooperation of these one-time bitter foes) found that there were no particular disadvantages to health in working in a factory underground. They made an investigation, for example, of two neighboring factories, one above ground, the other dug out of a great bed of rock, and each with a payroll of more than 500 men. The plant in the open actually had more absenteeism on account of illness. It also had more accidents and more turnover of employees. The underground plant reported more cases of brief sick leaves and slightly more visits to the company doctor for headaches, fatigue, "nerves" and similar minor ailments. But doctors and psychologists believe the somewhat higher percentage of such complaints stem not so much from a physical condition as from an initial mental state which makes a new worker a bit apprehensive of his health when he goes to work in an underground workshop. It was found that below-ground workers checked more frequently with the company doctor than did those in a normal place of work until they became accustomed to the new environment and learned that it was not harmful to their health.

Since Sweden must import nearly every drop of oil it consumes, safe storage facilities for it are absolutely necessary for national defense. These have now been built underground. Many of them have been located in abandoned mines. A former feldspar mine not far from Stockholm has been fitted up to make the largest single underground oil depot in the world — it has a capacity of 40 million gallons. There are also several thin metal vertical tanks, with a capacity of eight million gallons each, placed in holes blasted out of granite and encased in heavy concrete.

The two great underground hydroelectric power plants in Sweden are marvels of engineering ingenuity. The one in the far north at Harspränget is buried in solid rock and can continue to produce 380,000 volts in the midst of the heaviest air attack. The Kilforsen plant near the junction of the Fjällsjö and Ångerman Rivers is unique in the world. Some four million logs are floated annually down the nine waterfalls of the Fjällsjö River into the Ångerman, and the Swedish engineers had to find a way of handling them as well as generating electric power in an underground station. The solution was to build a two-mile tunnel through which the logs are floated to an artificial lake and thence dropped through a chute to the Ångerman River. In order to prevent log jams in the tunnel the roof was fitted up with rail, and a Diesel-electric suspension cable car, carrying four inspectors, cruises along just under the roof. When the inspectors spot a log jam, they press buttons which alter the speed and level of the water in a manner calculated to break the jam up. The power plant itself lies 185 feet under solid rock — a direct hit from an A-bomb would not disturb it. Water from the artificial lake drops 307 feet vertically into three turbines and surges out into an equalizing chamber and then into a discharge tunnel and thereafter into the Ångerman River. The feed tunnel, far underground, is large enough to house a five-story building: the equalizing chamber is a third larger — the biggest of its kind in the world. The Kilforsen plant represents one of the greatest rock excavation jobs in construction history. A total of 53 million cubic feet of solid rock was blasted out with 2 million pounds of explosives and a million pounds of drilling steel. Some 40 million cubic feet of earth was also removed. The whole job took seven years and cost seven million dollars. Beginning in 1954 the Kilforsen plant had a capacity of 1.2 billion kwh. annually, making it the second largest hydroelectric power station in Sweden.

Thus has Sweden built underground. The Swedes are proud of their achievement; but even so, they will tell you, they would have preferred to leave their places of work in the open air and in the sunlight and would have done so, had the world after 1945 taken a better turning. They do not feel very exultant that Twentieth Century

Man, after so much progress, is now being forced to go back to the life of the cave man of prehistoric times.[11]

Soviet Provocation

Sweden's determination to preserve a neutral position between East and West and thus to stay out of the anti-Soviet defense alliance has by no means spared her from Russian provocation and truculence. For a few tense weeks in the summer of 1952, the Swedish government wondered whether the Soviet Union was trying to provoke a serious quarrel or merely attempting to test Swedish mettle in the face of unfriendly, aggressive acts.

On June 16, the biggest espionage trial in the history of Sweden had opened in the Stockholm Magistrate's Court. The accused were Fritiof Enbom, a former Communist journalist, and six alleged accomplices, all Swedes, who were charged with having sold vitally important military secrets to the Soviet Union. All but one of the seven — he was later acquitted — confessed and implicated important officials of the Soviet Embassy whom they said had directed their work of espionage.

On that same day the spy trial opened — June 16 — two other things happened. The Swedish Prime Minister himself, Tage Erlander, protested to the Russian Ambassador against officials of his Embassy carrying out espionage and asked that the practice be stopped. And Russian jet fighters shot down an unarmed Swedish air force Catalina flying boat over the Baltic between Stockholm and a Russian airbase on the island of Dagö, north of the Gulf of Riga.

The Swedes were especially indignant because the Catalina had been searching for an air force DC-3, also unarmed, which had disappeared three days previously while on a routine navigation training flight over the international waters of the Baltic. Later its wreckage was discovered at the bottom of the sea north of the Swedish island of Gotland. Some of the parts of the DC-3, including a rubber lifeboat, were found floating on the surface by the Swedes, and their examination showed that the airplane had been fired upon before crashing, with the loss of all eight lives aboard. The Swedish government asked

[11] Swedish engineers say the two hydroelectric plants would have been built underground in any case because of greater efficiency at these particular sites.

Moscow whether Soviet fighters had done the firing. In the meantime it had protested the shooting down of the Catalina, which had managed to make an emergency landing at sea alongside a German freighter, which rescued the crew, two of whom were wounded by Russian bullets.

The Soviet response was typical. Mr. Vyshinsky, the then Russian foreign secretary, replied that the Catalina had flown over the island of Dagö, which was Soviet territory, and after refusing to land as directed had *opened fire* on pursuing Russian fighters. The Russians, he said, had merely *returned* the fire.

Now, it was shown by the Swedes beyond doubt that the Catalina was a sea-rescue plane and was completely *unarmed*. Did this fact bother the Russians? Not at all. Mr. Vyshinsky formally protested to Sweden this "gross violation of the Soviet frontier" by an *armed* Swedish military airplane!

The Swedish government also made a good case for its contention that neither of the planes shot down by the Russians had violated the 12-mile limit which Russia has claimed off its coasts since imperial times. The Stockholm government had already promptly informed the Russians that on June 13, while searching for the DC–3, another Catalina had lost its bearings in the clouds and had momentarily transgressed Soviet territory. In any event, it offered to submit to international arbitration, preferably before the International Court of Justice, the question of whether, as it maintained, two Swedish planes were fired upon by Russian fighters over indisputably international waters and that both aircraft were unarmed and that consequently neither opened fire nor were even capable of opening fire on Soviet military aircraft.

The Soviet government refused categorically to arbitrate the dispute. Instead, in its final note, it renewed its "request that severe steps be taken by the Swedish government to prevent any further violation of the Soviet frontier by Swedish aircraft."

The excitement and indignation of the Swedish public at the shooting down of the planes was bound to distract attention from the trial of the Communist spies and the revelations of the part officials of the Soviet Embassy in Stockholm had played in directing their work. The Swedes have no doubt that this was exactly what Moscow intended. Did the Soviet government intend more? The Swedish government couldn't prove it, of course, but some of its members at least were quite sure that the Kremlin believed that its brutal action might induce the Swedes to handle the spy case with circumspection, especially as regards the implication of Soviet diplomatic officials. And there were some of the government who during that tense summer believed, as they told me later, that the Russian regime may have intended to provoke another crisis in Europe to scare Scandinavia and the West. The Swedes are sure that, among other things, the Russians at least wanted to see whether Sweden would take such provocation lying down — an old tactic of Hitler's which Stalin had adopted.

In the meantime the Enbom spy trial continued throughout the last fortnight of June to the end of July. Because it involved top military secrets, most of it was held *in camera*. Indeed some of the trial documents were classified as top secret for a period of sixty years. But enough was disclosed to shock and fascinate the public.

Fritiof Enbom, a Swedish Communist newspaperman, had been a spy for the Russians since early in the last war. He served as a correspondent for a Communist newspaper *Norrskensflamman* in Boden, which happens to be a key Swedish fortress in Lapland near the Finnish frontier, and in the paper's editorial offices at Luleå, which is the chief Bothnian port for the export of Sweden's vast supply of iron ore from the far north. Just northeast of these two towns lies the so-called Kalix defense line, near the Finnish border. So Enbom was strategically located. With Russian help he set up a secret radio transmitter, but this was to be used to contact the Soviet Union only in case of war. In the meantime he had more ordinary means of communication.

The chief one was through the Soviet embassy at Stockholm. Enbom, it was brought out in the trial, made frequent trips from the North to the capital, announcing his presence to his Russian friends by sticking a hairpin, twisted in a certain manner, in the wall of a house not far from the Soviet embassy.

In 1951 he quarreled with his comrades and his Communist newspaper, and quit both the journal and the party. Moving to Stockholm he appealed to a Communist member of Parliament for help in getting a job, and was turned down. Bitter and disillusioned, he told his story to a roommate, who quickly got in touch with the Ministry of Defense. Enbom's arrest and that of six alleged members of his spy ring, including his brother and his lady friend, followed. How many military secrets Enbom and his gang were able to give to the Russians did not come out publicly, but they were reported to be numerous and important.

Enbom, who made a full confession, was convicted of selling Swedish defense secrets to the Soviet Union and also of plotting treason in the event of war with Russia. He and his chief aide received the severest sentence possible under Swedish law — life imprisonment at hard labor — and four others involved drew penalties of from seven years to eight months. Enbom was also sentenced to repay the Swedish government the money he had received through the Soviet Embassy — some $2,000 — plus interest.

An official of the Soviet Embassy who had been Enbom's liaison man with Moscow hurriedly left Sweden at the time of the spy's arrest. He had been preceded at the Embassy by several others.

Some of these Russian Intelligence agents had also worked with another Swedish Communist spy, whose trial the year before had first aroused the Swedish public to the nature of Soviet espionage. He was Hilding Andersson, a petty officer in the Swedish navy, who was found guilty of systematically transmitting data on naval installations and coast defenses to Russia.

As a matter of fact, ever since the end of the last war the Swedish government had had to contend with officials of the Soviet embassy, usually military and naval attachés, wandering about restricted military reservations, camera and notebook in hand. The government kept protesting and Moscow kept rejecting their protests arrogantly, though discreetly withdrawing the awkward culprits. But the Andersson and Enbom cases were more serious; by the time the latter confessed and went to trial, the government in Stockholm had become fed up with the misuse of the Soviet embassy as a center of espionage. It is no secret in Stockholm that the Soviet Embassy from that time on found it much more difficult than previously to carry on its spying activities.

The good-natured Swedish public was profoundly shocked by the revelations of the two spy trials and as Gunnar Hedlund, Minister of Interior, said, "had its eyes opened to the danger of Communism." Prime Minister Erlander, the leader of the Socialists, told the Riksdag that his government was taking care not to put Communists in government posts of importance to the country's security. He confessed that "we who believe in democracy find ourselves in a dilemma" — was it not the dilemma of all democratic lands? "We do not want to persecute anybody," said the Prime Minister, "because of his political opinion, but at the same time we intend to guard ourselves against treasonable elements. They are an insignificant minority, but they are there and they compel us to resort to police measures."

Disturbed though the Swedish people were, they did not become hysterical and neither did the government and Parliament. The security police redoubled its vigilance and the people seemed to accept the advice of the government that the police and the regular courts were best fitted to cope with the problem. There were no special investigations by parliamentary committees. No special loyalty oaths and tests were instituted. The Communist party, which in Sweden is a legal organization with a handful of elected representatives in Parliament (8 seats out of 380) was not driven underground.

"We prefer them in the open where we can keep tab on what they are up to," one Socialist leader in the government told me.

Is Swedish Neutrality Today an Illusion?

Granted that Sweden is doing all that is humanly possible for a nation of seven millions to make herself militarily strong, and that she is also striving mightily and sincerely to stay out of the quarrels of the rival Big Powers, the stark fact remains, as the leading military authorities admit, that the country stands little chance of remaining out of the third world war, should there be one, and even less chance of holding out alone for more than two or three months in the event of an all-out attack by Russia, which would probably cut her off from the supplies of the West.

It is scarcely a military secret in Stockholm that Sweden has only enough oil stored to last four months in case of war, and that she soon would be crippled also from the lack of coal. Both fuels she must import, having none herself. But aside from the crucial shortage of oil and coal, the Swedish High Command realizes, as one general after another admitted to me, that the Red Army could overwhelm Sweden in two months if she were left to fight alone.

General Helge Jung, Commander of Sweden's armed forces, tried to warn the Swedish public of its precarious position in a speech at Lund back in 1949. "Our possibilities of remaining outside a general conflict in the long run," he said frankly, "are, unfortunately, small." And he added: "Our strategy must be aimed at gaining time, so that we can hold vital sections of the country *until aid comes.*"

From where?

That is the core of the problem. For General Jung was hinting publicly at what both civilian and military authorities in Stockholm emphasized to me privately: that in the event of a Russian attack Sweden is counting on immediate aid from the West.

One civilian head, in answer to my question as to what kind of aid Sweden expected from a West with which it declined to work in advance, replied blandly: "If we could get from NATO quickly a supply of small atom bombs, which we could drop on the enemy with our fighter-bombers, that would be very effective."

One of the most intelligent generals in the Swedish High Command confided to me that he hoped, in case of a Russian attack, that NATO's air force would spring immediately to Sweden's side. "Our two air forces," he explained, "might then be able to hold the Russians off and eventually establish air superiority up to a line *east* of Sweden. That," he emphasized, "would be Sweden's only hope of survival."

"But wouldn't that be awfully difficult, if not impossible," I asked, "unless liaison between the two air forces were established in advance?"

"Certainly," he said, sadly.

Later I asked a NATO army officer of my acquaintance about that problem. "If the West," he replied, "is ever to be in a position to help Sweden, should she be attacked, we will have to know much more than we know now about her requirements, capabilities, organization, ordnance and plans. You can't even improvise effective help without such knowledge — and without doing something about it beforehand."

Now, the Swedish military authorities, if not all of the civilian leaders, realize this perfectly well. And I gathered from my very frank talks with them that they hope someday to convince the neutrality-obsessed Swedish public, Parliament and government that an eventual tie-up with NATO may be an absolute necessity for the country's survival. But the generals know enough about politics and public opinion to understand that such a move is politically impossible today.

Besides, up to 1954, at least, they were not convinced that NATO was strong enough to offer much military help. "Where are NATO's divisions that could come to our aid if we were attacked tomorrow morning?" one Swedish general exclaimed, brandishing his pointer at a large map in his office. "I don't believe they exist," he added.

There is an Achilles' heel to the defense of all three of the Scandinavian lands, and now the general pointed to it on his map. His pointer rested on the southern part of the Jutland peninsula, which forms the frontier between Germany and Denmark. "NATO has few if any contingents defending that frontier," he explained. "As of today, at least, the Russians would sweep in from their nearby bases in occupied northern Germany, push north through Jutland and across the islands to Copenhagen, swiftly occupying Denmark, and then cross the narrow Öresund straits and move into Sweden from the south. We will begin to believe in NATO when it has sufficient forces to block the Russians from entering Jutland. Probably NATO will need German troops to do that. But it doesn't have them today."

The Swedish general was putting his finger on one of the acknowledged weaknesses of NATO. As I would learn later in Copenhagen, it was a constant worry to the Danes, who had put their trust in NATO but who felt it offered them little protection from the south — the only land route by which an army could invade their land.

The Swedes believe the Russians could as easily occupy the northern coast of Norway from Petsamo and then move south along the western shore. One effect of Soviet forces in northern Norway and in Denmark would be to cut off Sweden from the West. This would be disastrous.

Another military reason why Sweden has declined to join in mutual defense with the West is that the government and the High Command — I heard this a dozen times from civilians as well as from generals in Stockholm — believe that, since the next war would be global, the Red Army might not think it worthwhile to bother with Sweden but would push westward across the North German plains — the historic East–West invasion routes — in an attempt to occupy the Western part of the European Continent, thus bypassing and sparing Sweden.

It is a somewhat comforting thought in Stockholm and not without basis. But there is also the possibility, which the Swedish High Command at least has not overlooked, that the Soviet Union, like Hitler's Reich, might knock off a neighbor or two, one at a time, before risking a world conflict. In that case Sweden would be a likely candidate, since its possession would give Russia great strategic advantages. If this should happen and Sweden alone be attacked, the Defense Staff is prepared for a main Soviet assault in the north across the present Swedish-Finnish border. Since it lies far to the north, most of it above the Arctic Circle, the heavy snows of the eight months' winter give the Swedes many defensive advantages. Moreover the terrain is difficult and also favors the defense. Further Russian moves might be expected in two places: an amphibious attack from the Finnish Åland islands against nearby Stockholm; a second amphibious attack halfway up the Gulf of Bothnia, whose object would be to cut Sweden in two and enable a Russian force to move westward toward the Norwegian port of Trondheim.

Sweden, one general emphasized to me, has a long frontier to defend. From the Norwegian border in the far north down along the Finnish border, the Gulf of Bothnia and around the coast line to a point just south of Oslo is longer than from Maine to Florida. It is impossible for a relatively small army to defend strongly all along such an extensive frontier. It is proving costly just to maintain a protective radar screen along part of it. Thus, the general pointed out, it would relieve Sweden immensely if NATO could really defend northern Norway and the land approach to Denmark.

And it would relieve the NATO authorities, of course, if Sweden would join up, so that mutual defense could be worked out. She may someday. There is growing sentiment for it in the military establishment, and some among influential newspapers and a small segment of the public. But the overwhelming mass of the Swedes, and especially the ruling Social-Democrat party, oppose it. There is no likelihood, barring a Russian move into Finland or some equally provocative act, of Sweden — in the immediate future at least — going with the West.[12]

[12] Recently, however, after years of public debate and secret deliberations, the Swedish government initiated negotiations with Norway for a project which would give Sweden an outlet on the Atlantic in case she were blockaded by the Russians. The project is known as the "Trondheim line." Sweden has proposed to build harbor works and oil storage installations on the northern part of Norway's Trond-

In World War I, King Gustav V had borne the chief responsibility of keeping Sweden out of the conflict. In that war he had not allowed his rather pro-German sentiments to blind him to his country's main interests. By the time of the second conflagration he had been shorn of most of his political power, but his influence was still strong. He shared the burden of keeping Sweden neutral with his Socialist Prime Minister, Per Albin Hansson, who carried the final responsibility for Sweden's policies. "Per Albin," as he is usually and affectionately referred to in Sweden, was a man of the people, a person of simple tastes and great integrity and tolerance, who enjoyed a justified popularity in the country and who was liked and respected by the aging King despite the monarch's innate political conservatism. Neither official was above criticism, but there is no doubt that they reflected the desires and hopes of the vast mass of the people.

Per Albin died in harness in 1946 at the age of sixty and was succeeded by Tage Erlander, a socialist editor and intellectual who also became head of the Social-Democrat party. But the real architect of Sweden's postwar neutrality policy is the scholarly Östen Undén, a former professor of international law, rector of the University of Uppsala and Chancellor of the Universities, which is the highest administrative academic post in Sweden. Undén is the last survivor of a remarkable little group of Swedish laborites who came to prominence with Sweden's first great Socialist leader, the late Hjalmar Branting. Undén, who had expressed his revulsion at Nazi Germany with more frankness than most Swedish parliamentarians during the war, became Foreign Minister in 1945 at the age of fifty-nine. Frankly suspicious of Big Power politics but possessed of a vast knowledge of international affairs, he has steered Sweden down a middle path in the postwar years.

Recently he summed up his views: "Such a small country as ours can rarely exert any influence on the sequence of events. Nations of our size are not usually able to help others in the event of war. We believe that Sweden makes a more useful positive contribution to peace through keeping her territory outside all military combinations rather than by entering into a defensive alliance with one or several

---

heim fjord and to lay a pipeline over the 75 miles of mountains to the Swedish frontier. Eventually, the railway line from Trondheim to the Swedish border may be double-tracked and electrified. Swedish Communists in the Riksdag have assailed the project as a mask for linking Sweden to NATO.

powerful protectors among the Great Powers. We consequently doubt that peace can best be promoted through the nations of the world lining up on two fronts. In such a world there is also a place for neutral states."

How the Swedes Live

It would be misleading to give the impression that the Swedish people are unduly concerned about these matters of neutrality, defense, and the threats of Russia and Communism. The very nature of my quest for information naturally brought me into contact with those who were most concerned, because of their responsibility for the country's future. Actually, the average citizen seemed much more interested in other things: domestic politics, the cost of living, high taxes, wages and salaries, housing, co-ops, the various arts, sports, and, above all, the progress of social welfare.

Sweden, like Norway, is a social welfare state, and most of her citizens and certainly her Labor-Farmer government are proud of it. They even point with pride to the fact that 11 per cent of the national income and one third of the government's budget is spent on social security, of which the leading and most costly features are the national pensions scheme, health insurance, and children's allowances.

Until recently sickness insurance in Sweden was handled by a large group of private benefit societies supervised and subsidized by the state. And it was purely voluntary. But soon after the war, the Riksdag passed a bill setting up compulsory health insurance and it became law in 1947. However, it remained inoperative, principally because of lack of government funds and partly because the somewhat cautious members of Parliament wanted to have another look at the whole problem.

I happened to be in Stockholm when the Riksdag — the Conservative party dissenting — voted to apply the law, as revised in 1952, beginning in 1955. On that date health insurance became compulsory for all citizens, poor or rich.

It provides three main benefits. (1) Three fourths of the doctor's standard fee, *and everyone may choose his own physician.* (2) Free hospital care, including surgery. (3) Tax-free cash payments covering from 65 to 70 per cent of the loss of earned income (up to $2,800 a year) during illness.

In addition, there are numerous other minor benefits similar to those in Norway.

The cost of compulsory health insurance is considerable and in Sweden, the people who are insured will carry directly nearly half the charges. Their insurance premiums are expected to amount to 44 per cent of an estimated total cost for the first year of $147,600,000 (738,000,000 crowns). Employers will chip in 27 per cent and the government the remaining 29 per cent. Since the state had already heavily subsidized the voluntary private health insurance societies, its burden is increased under the compulsory system by only some $32,000,000 a year.

The cost to the insured individual under the new compulsory health scheme is as follows:

There are two kinds of annual premiums which all must pay. One covers medical care, hospitalization, and surgery. This premium comes to $4.50 (23 crowns) a year.[13] Citizens earning less than $240 a year or those receiving old-age pensions are exempt from payment.

The second premium covers cash benefits while a person is ill and varies according to one's income. For the basic benefit of 60 cents a day the premium is $5.00 a year (25 crowns) thus bringing the total minimum cost of health insurance for each family or single person to $9.50 annually. But all employed persons earning more than $360 a year are obliged to take out what is called "supplementary benefit insurance," which calls for additional premiums for extra cash benefits based on present income. Housewives, students and self-employed persons may qualify for this supplementary insurance if they wish, but it is not compulsory for them.

Those in what in Sweden are termed the middle-income brackets — from $1,360 (6,800 crowns) to $1,680 (8,400 crowns) a year — will pay, for example, total health insurance premiums for medical care and cash benefits of around $20.00 a year. Those in the top income

[13] For purposes of comparison this writer finds he pays $52.32 a year for group family Blue Cross insurance which provides free semiprivate hospital accommodation for 21 days and one half the regular hospital bill for 180 days thereafter, plus full coverage of ten hospital services, including anesthesia if it is administered by a hospital employee. It does not of course cover any part of doctors' or surgeons' fees, which is by far the greatest expense.

SWEDEN

145

bracket, which the law establishes as $2,800 (14,000 crowns) or more a year, will pay total annual premiums of about $30.00. In all cases the wife and children under sixteen are covered by the basic insurance of the husband and father.

The Swedish scheme attempts to eliminate one fault of many state health insurance systems: excessive centralization. The Swedes realized that it would be unwise to let doctors and bureaucrats in Stockholm try to administer the entire scheme from the capital. The new law places the administration in the hands of so-called sickness societies, in most cases the very ones which previously handled the voluntary health plan, though they have had to submit to some reorganization to bring them into line with the new compulsory system. They are divided into two groups: local and central benefit societies. The local societies will review and pay all claims in their districts for basic medical care, and will also pay the basic sickness benefit fees for the first 90 days of illness. The central societies, one for each city or county, will reimburse the local groups for their expenditures, take over all benefit payments beyond the first 90-day period of illness and generally assist the local societies with their accounting and other administrative details.

The day before I left Stockholm a number of leading Swedish doctors gave me a cocktail party, in the course of which they went to great lengths to explain how the past and future health insurance plans worked and how these affected them in various branches of medicine. It was one of the most enlightening afternoons I had in Sweden for I had come to Scandinavia with the preconceived idea that the *doctors*, at least, were opposed to "socialized medicine." They weren't. On the contrary. They argued among themselves as to details and on how the plan could be improved, but on the system of health insurance itself they were in general and, I must say, enthusiastic agreement. Incidentally, they disliked the term "socialized medicine," which they thought was a quite misleading term. One doctor said: "You don't call free public schools 'socialized education,' do you? There is even less justification to call health insurance 'socialized medicine.'"

Maternity welfare is also an important part of the Swedish system. Until now, about 90 per cent of the mothers in Sweden have had free confinement care as well as a modest cash allowance. The new scheme makes it 100 per cent and provides a "motherhood allowance" of $54.00. Like illness itself, having babies will no longer mean an undue financial burden for the lower-income families of Sweden.

Nor will the rearing of children. Since 1948 a general children's allowance is payable at the rate of $58.00 a year for every child up to the age of sixteen, regardless of the family's income. This is not an insurance scheme, but is financed out of general revenue. Then there are special children's allowances to supplement the general allowances in cases where one or both parents are dead or the wage earner is unable to make a normal living. These come to $120 a year per child under sixteen.

Two factors must be noted here in connection with children's allowances and indeed with all these social welfare payments to individuals. The dollar figures are misleading. Roughly speaking a dollar — five crowns — will go about twice as far in Sweden as in the U.S.A. Second, each benefit in the social welfare plan must be considered in relation to the others. The children's allowances, for example, are regarded in Sweden as merely supplementing numerous other benefits enjoyed by the family such as subsidized housing for households with two or more children, free school luncheons, free confinement, free dentistry for children, health insurance, the prospect of old-age pensions and a host of other aids that come under the heading of Family Welfare Service and Child Welfare, including marriage loans, preschool care, recreation for mothers and children and social domestic aid service.

In 1952 general allowances to 1,764,000 children came to a total of $100,000,000 and additional special allowances to 30,000 children amounted to $1,700,000.

The most costly single item in Sweden's social welfare program is the National Pensions Scheme, which deals with the aged and the disabled. What the Swedish government has done since the war is simply, as one official in Stockholm explained to me, to take over the responsibility for maintaining the aged, as well as the permanently disabled, from the families themselves or the communities or charity, and charge the bill to the entire people.

Everyone in Sweden has to make a small contribution to it — 1.8 per cent of taxable income with a maximum of $36 a year — from the age of eighteen to sixty-six. But these payments come to only about

14 per cent of what is needed and the state and communities make up the rest out of general taxation. The total cost comes to $200,-000,000 a year.

Old age pension payments begin at sixty-seven years of age and they are paid according to a uniform scale regardless of other income or assets. Thus, unlike our American scheme, Swedes may continue to work after sixty-seven if they like, and still draw their full old age pension.

As the result of a 35 per cent increase unanimously voted by the Riksdag in 1953, basic old age pensions were fixed at $350 a year for single persons and $560 for a married couple. To this must be added two supplements. Payments go up with the cost-of-living index; and the municipalities provide special housing allowances. Thus an aged couple living in Stockholm may receive up to $1000 a year in pensions and housing allowances.

Considering the cost of living in Sweden, the fact that there are no doctors' or hospital bills to pay, that indeed in case of illness a pensioner will receive 60 cents a day in addition to his regular pension, and that there are numerous other benefits from the general social welfare program, such a couple is fairly well off. They are even better off if, as is the case with two thirds of them, they engage in part-time work or have saved a little for their declining days or are in receipt of public or private pensions as a result of their former occupations.

Disability pensions for those under sixty-seven who have lost two thirds of their earning capacity are the same as those for the aged. Today in Sweden there are 650,000 old age pensioners and 140,000 invalid pensioners, or more than 11 per cent of the total population.

The rest of the social welfare scheme in Sweden may be touched on briefly.

The Swedish employer has long footed the bill for industrial accident insurance. But beginning in 1955, he was relieved of that burden when the health insurance scheme took over the whole field of industrial accidents and occupational diseases.

Curiously enough, Sweden has lagged behind most other Western countries in unemployment insurance. There is no state system. The matter is handled entirely by voluntary mutual benefit societies established by the trade-unions, though legally independent of them, and subsidized by the government. Swedish employers pay nothing at all to the unemployment insurance funds. The workers themselves contribute about 75 per cent and the state the rest. Payments are made only for a comparatively brief period of unemployment, a maximum of from 120 to 156 days, and only to those who have paid a minimum of 52 weekly payments, half of them during the 12 months prior to unemployment.

A government committee was busy reviewing the whole problem when I was in Stockholm and it is expected to recommend an eventual system of obligatory unemployment insurance to which not only the workers and the state but the employers would contribute. Two reasons are given in Sweden as to why a more modern plan has not been adopted to take care of the unemployed. The first is that the government is determined to maintain full employment. The second reason is that the unions find certain obvious advantages in handling unemployment funds themselves through their own benefit societies. Almost all of the million and a third members of the industrial unions have taken out unemployment insurance in their own organizations.

Since the end of the last war, the law requires that all employees be given a paid annual vacation of three weeks.

The traditional forms of public assistance for the poor and unfortunate are disappearing in Sweden, because they are no longer needed in a welfare state. In 1941 there were still over half a million persons receiving public assistance, or 8 per cent of the population. Today that figure has been cut in half and eventually the new social security program will eliminate so-called public assistance entirely.

In the early 1930's there was grave concern in Sweden over the fall of the birth rate. Emigration to America had stopped. But for forty years births had been declining at such an alarming rate that the worried authorities bestirred themselves to do something drastic about it. Out of their concern — and their studies — came many of the reforms that were added to the new social welfare scheme and in addition a specific program that comes under the general heading of Family and Child Welfare.

Swedish policy is not concerned primarily with increasing the population but in bettering the welfare of the family so that a normal and healthy rate of procreation is maintained. Indeed in Sweden, so far as I could see, birth control is certainly not discouraged. The Welfare Agencies volunteer information about it. Contraceptives have been made even more easily available than heretofore by removing certain restrictions on their advertising and sale. All state-licensed pharmacies sell them openly. And grounds for legal abortion have been broadened.

What the Swedes desired to overcome was the tendency in modern society for families to avoid having children because of the financial burden. Their family and child welfare program has been designed to help ease that burden and also to make motherhood and family life more attractive, especially for the mass of low-income people.

To encourage more and earlier marriages among young couples, state "marriage loans" up to $600 are granted to help to furnish a home. But since the interest charge is 4 per cent and the loans repayable in eight years, this would not appear to an American to be of much advantage over a straight commercial loan. However the Swedes point out that the state does not require the kind of security usually demanded for private bank loans, and that in cases of hardship a part or all of the loan may be written off. Low-cost housing for families with children is also offered. Rent rebates or deductions on the repayments of building loans are given in proportion to the number of children.

Part-time care of pre-school children or youngsters in the lower grades is provided through state-subsidized nursery schools, infants' schools, kindergartens, day nurseries and afternoon homes. The need for these has grown in recent years because of the large number of married women who work at regular jobs and are away from home eight hours a day. There are 786 such establishments, but the number is still woefully inadequate to meet the demand. They are not absolutely free, but the fee is small.

When I was in Sweden the trains were jammed with mothers and children, most of them from working-class homes, getting off to the annual summer vacation as their neighbors in Norway do. In ways too numerous to mention here the state, the communities and various private organizations combine to help low-income families enjoy a happy holiday. Every year, for instance, the thoughtful members of the Riksdag appropriate $160,000 to be parceled out to deserving housewives in need of a vacation. In fact, the Riksdag overlooks few

150 THE CHALLENGE OF SCANDINAVIA

bets to give a helping hand to the lady of the house. In the midst of the wartime crisis of 1943, its members took time off from their worries over a German invasion to pass a Bill for a Social Domestic Aid Service. This service sends trained women to households where the mother is ill — or otherwise incapacitated — to look after the housework and the children. The state and the town councils defray this expense.

Illegitimate children are the subject of special legislation and care, though the Swedes have not gone quite as far in this field as have the Norwegians. In Sweden, a child born out of wedlock does not, as in Norway, enjoy inheritance rights, though the father is responsible for maintenance. The one exception is the so-called "betrothal child" — one born of a betrothed couple — who does obtain the full right of inheritance.

The illegitimate birth rate in Sweden is rather high, numbering from 11,000 to 12,000 a year, or 9 per cent of all births. However, in the 1920's and 1930's it was 15 per cent, and has been slowly declining ever since. Also many children born illegitimate are made legitimate by the subsequent marriage of their parents. Under the Parents' Act of 1949, paternity is established either by acknowledgment or by court action. In the majority of cases the man admits his fatherhood. Thus at the end of 1950, out of 84,393 children listed as illegitimate, paternity had been established for 76,798; and, of these, 85 per cent by acknowledgment, the rest by court decision.

The Child Welfare Committee in each community in Sweden is responsible for the appointment of a special guardian for every child born out of wedlock. The guardian, whose assignment lasts until the child is eighteen, and who must not be a relative of either father or mother, is obliged to help the mother with advice, take measures, if necessary, to establish paternity, see that the father supports the child and look after its general welfare. A father who neglects this support is severely dealt with and if he proves really recalcitrant may be sent off to forced labor in a special institution.

These Community Child Welfare Committees have been given extraordinary legal powers to deal with children. They are charged with carrying out "preventive measures" in the case of children who, in the language of an official report, "are a source of worry to parents or teachers owing to tantrums, restlessness, aggressiveness, hypereroticism, pilfering, school difficulties, etc." In the cities and pro-

vincial council areas which maintain state-subsidized child-guidance
clinics, the recalcitrant youths are first dispatched to these for psy-
chiatric observation and treatment. Trained social workers investigate the home environment of the children and consult with and
advise their parents and teachers as to how best to handle them.

If it deems it advisable the Child Welfare Committee may commit
difficult children to special classes in school or even send them off to
institutions. For youths of from eighteen to twenty-one, the law
empowers the committee "to urge the person to lead an orderly life
and to remind him of the serious consequences which may result from
his continual misbehavior." Today an average of some 5000 children
and juveniles are subject to preventive measures under the Child
Welfare Act. About 15 per cent are over eighteen.

The Act also charges the committees with what is called "protective upbringing," which is applied after "preventive measures"
have failed. About 7000 children come under protective upbringing
and they have come to the attention of the authorities because of —
to quote an official report — "viciousness or danger of viciousness, as
defined by the Act." Decisions of the committee as to what to do
with them can be taken against the will of the parents, though in
such cases they must be approved by the State Provincial Board.
However, it has been found that most of these children come from
broken homes or from parents who maltreat or neglect them. Of the
7000 children under "protective upbringing" in a typical year since
the war, 47 per cent are placed in private homes, 16 per cent in special children's homes, 25 per cent in welfare schools and 12 per cent
in hospitals. The welfare schools are run by the state, and their aim
is not to punish but to rehabilitate the character of the young
offenders. I checked on what kind of offenses were most common
among these youth. They are stealing, assault and battery, sexual
misbehavior, "work-shy misbehavior" (that is the official term), "un-
amenability to education" and "contributing to viciousness of
others."

The Difficult Problem of Temperance

The excessive imbibing of alcoholic beverages has long been a serious
and burning problem in Sweden. The winters are long and cold and

damp and dark, and to many Swedes it has often seemed that such conditions can only be coped with by resort to hard liquor, chiefly the native *brännvin* distilled from potatoes and grain and possessed of considerable potency. A century ago the annual consumption of alcoholic spirits in Sweden amounted to ten gallons for every man, woman and child in the country. The Swedes, in truth, like all the Norsemen, were enormous drinkers and as the population increased and cities grew, this was reflected in mounting crimes of violence and in an unusually high death rate from chronic alcoholism.

It was obvious that something had to be done, and all over Sweden temperance societies, strongly influenced by sister groups in America, sprang up in the latter half of the nineteenth century to demand prompt reform. In 1865 the so-called "Gothenburg system" was adopted which closed the saloons, transferred on-the-premise sale of spirits to the restaurants and restricted the manufacture of brandy to a few companies whose profits were limited by the state. In the opinion of many, the Gothenburg plan worked reasonably well; by 1910 consumption of spirits had dropped to two gallons per capita. But this was considered too much by the ardent Prohibitionists, who, fired by the success of their brethren in the United States, Norway and Finland, where dry regimes had been legislated immediately after the first war, demanded a national plebiscite. This was held in Sweden in 1922. By the close vote of 925,000 to 890,000, the Swedes voted not to try the noble experiment.

But in the meantime they had begun to try another kind of experiment designed to make the Swedish people not teetotalers, but moderate in their drinking. On January 1, 1919 — a year before the American people embarked upon complete prohibition — Sweden established by law a national system of strict control of the manufacture and sale of all alcoholic beverages. It had been devised by a remarkable figure in Sweden, Dr. Ivan Bratt, who soon gained world renown in temperance circles for his achievement. Marquis Childs in *Sweden — The Middle Way* has written eloquently of both Dr. Bratt and his system and called his chapter on them "Liquor Control That Works."

But in the uneasy period that has elapsed since Mr. Childs wrote his book in 1936, it has not worked — at least not to the satisfaction of most Swedes. There was little surprise in Sweden, therefore, when the so-called 1944 Temperance Committee appointed by the government at the request of the Riksdag, after nine years of study and deliberation, recommended in 1953 that the Bratt Liquor Control System be dropped and that the Swedish people henceforth be given the inalterable right to buy as much hard liquor, wine and strong beer as they liked or could afford.

Under the Bratt scheme they had been limited to the purchase of three liters of spirits a month at the retail stores of the government-controlled liquor monopoly and to five fluid ounces per meal in the restaurants. At the liquor stores each individual had to have his purchase entered in a passbook, to obtain which one had to furnish a great deal of information about one's private affairs, including income, family background and past drinking habits. Many Swedes objected to this prying into their private lives, and they found even more objectionable the practice of the Liquor Monopoly in employing anonymous snoopers to visit restaurants to see that no one got more than the legal thimbleful of spirits with his meal. Nor did the mass of the Swedes take kindly to the law which forbade their buying strong beer (4.5 per cent) but which allowed foreign tourists in Sweden to purchase as much of it as they pleased.

But what finally doomed the Bratt system was not its unpopularity but its failure, in the long run, to curb excessive drinking. Bootleggers flourished. The Swedes drank more and more. Three fourths of all alcoholic offenses, the Committee found, were committed by persons who did not even have a passbook. Some 200,000 persons living at the end of the last war had been guilty of alcoholic misdemeanors during the decade of 1936-1945, of whom 50,000 turned out to be habitual drunkards.

On May 22, 1954, the Riksdag, by a vote of 274 to 54, decided to abolish the liquor control system, as of October 1, 1955. Local option was retained, as was the monopoly of the manufacture and sale of spirits by government-controlled enterprises, for the Swedes were in general agreement that no one should make private profits out of the liquor business.

Prices of alcoholic drinks as well as taxes on them will remain high in Sweden, so that the government will continue to receive from their sale an annual income that averages $175,000,000 — some 12 per cent of the total revenue of the state.

I was puzzled by the strong support in Sweden, especially in Labor circles, for pricing intoxicants out of the reach of the man of modest income as one of the means of achieving temperance. Depriving a workingman of his right to a drink, while allowing a person of wealth all he wanted because he could pay for it, seemed a curious sort of democracy in a country which Labor was proudly transforming into not only a political democracy but, as they said, a social democracy. Where was the equality, the democracy — not to speak of the justice — in that? Labor leaders, especially trade-union officials, listened to my question patiently and then gave a blunt answer. Frankly, they said, they were not disturbed at pricing liquor out of the reach of the working class. They were old enough to remember, they said, when drink used to be the curse of the Swedish worker. Every Saturday night he got drunk, blew his week's earnings and was hard put to it to get back on the job Monday morning. His family went penniless. This, said the labor leaders, was no longer so. And they want to keep liquor prices high — even if it isn't exactly democratic. Indeed the Labor Party — and many union chiefs — have been in the forefront of the Swedish temperance movement. Aside from their support of many general societies they have two temperance organizations of their own: the Workers' Temperance Society with 215 locals and the Swedish Railwaymen's Temperance Society with 110 locals.

The new law reconfirmed the powers of the local Sobriety Committees to curb excessive drinking. As in Norway, these groups have an authority which never ceases to fascinate foreign visitors to Sweden.

They are empowered by special legislation to take legal action against temperance offenders, to review licenses of establishments selling liquor and to pass on all applications for drivers' licenses as well as to report infractions of the law by those driving motor cars while intoxicated.

Their primary duty, however, as laid down by the Inebriates Act, is to take measures against any person "who by reason of habitual intemperate drinking" . . .

Is dangerous to the personal safety of others or to himself;
Or neglects his lawful dependents, thereby exposing them to manifest distress, or is guilty of any other negligence of his duties;
Or becomes a burden to his family, some other person, or society;

Or is incapable of managing himself;
Or becomes a serious nuisance to his neighbors or others.

Furthermore the Sobriety Committees are duty bound to proceed against itinerants or vagrants addicted to drink as well as against persons who have been convicted of drunkenness three or more times in the preceding two years.

What measures are these watchdogs of society empowered to take? The Act outlines their general purpose as "designed to restore the abuser to a sober and orderly life." Specifically the local Sobriety Committees can place the offender under "supervision" for a period usually not exceeding one year. "Supervision" is defined by the Act as a "protracted educative and restorative process." It authorizes the committees to require an offender to spend his leisure time at some special temperance hostel after his daily work. Or he may be boarded with a suitable family. In any case, he is given a thorough education in the necessity of temperance.

If he proves recalcitrant the Sobriety Committees may resort to stronger measures. They may sentence him to forcible detention in an inebriates' institution, though he can appeal that sentence to the Supreme Administrative Court. Sojourn in these institutions may last up to two years. The local committees are given summary powers to jail drunks liable to acts of violence.

All in all, the local Sobriety Committees are kept fairly busy. They proceed against some 30,000 offenders each year, of whom roughly 13,000 are subjected to stringent measures and the rest let off with milder preventive measures. The expenses of the committees come to nearly $2,000,000 a year, of which the state defrays two thirds and the communities the rest.

In Sweden, as in Norway, the drunken driver is given short shrift. Recently a parliamentary committee recommended even more stringent legislation against driving while intoxicated. At present drivers, whether involved in an accident or not, are liable to fines or jail terms up to six months if they are found to have from between .08 and .15 per cent concentration of alcohol in their blood. If it is above that level, they can be jailed for one year. The new recommendations propose to lower the punishable alcohol ration in the blood to the Norwegian standard of 0.05 per cent — roughly the equivalent of one cocktail and one beer — and to raise the maximum jail terms for drunken driving to 2 years, and to 6 years if the driver contributes to another person's death. It also advocates suspension of drivers' licenses for as long as 8 years, or for life in exceptional cases. It asks that the police be equipped with "drunko-meters," which measure the alcohol content of the breath, in order to check up on suspected alcoholics on the highways, but it recommends that blood tests be the only legal evidence in actual prosecutions.

The present severe laws against driving after one has imbibed the equivalent of two drinks of hard liquor have kept drunken driving to a minimum, but the menace is actually growing due to the great increase in car ownership since the war — Sweden now has an automobile for every twelfth person, which is the highest rate in Scandinavia. Arrests for drunken driving increased from 3400 in 1950 to 5500 in 1952, though in some 20,000 automobile accidents annually only 3 per cent were found to be due to the driver's being intoxicated.

Such is the Swedish welfare state. Its basic philosophy — subscribed to by all parties, including the Conservatives — is that *all* citizens are entitled to a decent standard of living and that the overriding criterion is not the ability of the individual to pay for it but his need.

Though social welfare is financed partly by insurance, the Swedes emphasize that they had to face the inescapable fact that low-income groups are simply unable to provide, by their own efforts, adequate insurance protection. The ordinary principles of commercial insurance were first tried and found wanting. Nor did the Swedish Parliament, dominated though it has been in the last two decades by Labor, feel that the employer should foot a good part of the bill by large compulsory direct contributions to social insurance funds, as is done in many other countries. The bulk of the cost for social welfare, the Swedes concluded, must come out of taxation on the country's national income, to which all citizens contributed according to how much money they made and had. That it meant a redistribution of the national income was plain. Such extensive social benefits as the government envisaged were also not possible unless the country's production and wealth were increased. This was recognized, and the Swedes believe today that it is the improved standard of social welfare which, by reducing or abolishing poverty and stress and worry and poor health, has largely contributed to the nation's greater productivity.

In Sweden, as elsewhere in Scandinavia, I found a quite clear recognition that the social welfare program does not give something to the people for nothing. It merely equalizes the burden and, as they say, evens up the opportunities for a decent existence. If society, say the Swedes, can demand that you give up your life in its defense, then there are things which you can ask of society in return. Social security is one thing.

Its total cost is great. It comes in Sweden to $300 a year per family and, as we have seen, to 11 per cent of the national income and one third of the national budget. Moreover, social expenditures of the provincial councils in Sweden amount to 80 per cent of *their* budgets.

Finally, the Swedes contend that the creation of their welfare state has not stifled a healthy individualism nor a staunch spirit of self-reliance among the people. It has relieved the average person of much worry and in so doing it has released in the individual, say the Swedes, new energies to create and produce and to live a fuller life than was possible for many before. Not only the private citizen, they say, has gained thereby, but the whole Swedish nation.

A Note on Housing

It would be a whopping exaggeration, however, to say that social welfare has produced a Utopia. One is reminded of this when one looks into the housing situation, which in Sweden is considered an integral part of the social program.

Despite a record rate of construction of new dwellings since the war there is an acute housing shortage in Sweden today resulting in a severe overcrowding in the urban areas. Some 38 per cent of the inhabitants are forced to live in homes where more than two persons have to be accommodated in each room. Indeed until recently one-room apartments with a kitchen were the most sought after of all homes even by families with children. In the cities and towns one third of the dwellings still consist of only one room and kitchen, and up to the eve of the second war, a third of the housing under construction provided only that skimpy accommodation. Since the Second World War the dominant type of apartment has provided two rooms with kitchen and bath, leaving Sweden somewhat behind Norway and Denmark, where three-room flats predominate. No wonder that a family of five in Sweden still feels overcrowded in their new, bright, modern apartment.

Rents have been high and between the World Wars were often outrageously high. In 1930 a city worker and his family were forced to pay 42 per cent of their income for a two-room flat in a low-cost co-operative housing project. Today they still pay 23 per cent.

This state of affairs has long perturbed both the public and the government. Sometime after the First World War both came to the conclusion that private enterprise simply could not provide adequate low-cost housing for modest-income families and make a profit. The result was a new approach to the whole problem. The national and municipal governments, and the co-ops, stepped in to make financially feasible a decent standard of housing for families of modest means. They do the planning and much of the financing; commercial construction firms do most of the building. In Sweden the landlord, looking for profitable means of investment, has not been eliminated as he has been in Norway, but his field is becoming limited to the relatively few well-to-do.

The Swedish co-ops today account for about 15 per cent of the total new building construction and of this some 13 per cent is done by one organization called the Tenants' Savings and Building Society, known throughout Sweden as HSB from its Swedish title *Hyresgästernas Sparkasse och Byggnadsförening*. HSB is one of the lights of the remarkable Swedish co-op movement.

Founded in 1923, it now operates in the 140 leading cities and towns of the country. It works on three levels. There is a "grandmother" society, known as the National Association of HSB Societies, which functions as a national office; under it are 130 "parent societies," which organize and finance new building in their districts, and, when they are completed, turn them over to the so-called "daughter societies" — which consist of the tenants, who operate and maintain them as co-ops.

HSB has its own bank to help local societies finance new building but, like other enterprises, it borrows most of its capital from private banks and semiprivate credit institutions against first and second mortgages. A prospective tenant of an HSB co-op makes a down payment of from 5 to 10 per cent of his estimated share of the cost of a building and pays the amortization and interest on the remainder in the form of annual rent. In 20 years he becomes a fully paid-up owner of his own apartment and his rent is thereafter decreased to a sum necessary to pay his share of the upkeep of the building. In this manner a co-op resident effects considerable savings compared with an ordinary tenant and also ends up owning his own home.

The national HSB association maintains its own architects and a technical staff which is continually studying the whole field of building construction. Though it turns over the actual building to private contractors through competitive bidding it has in recent years gone in for producing some of its own building materials in order to get more prompt delivery than commercial firms could give. It owns or controls several brick factories, a piping works, joineries, a marble quarry and two plants for the construction of prefabricated houses. HSB also builds housing developments for both the state and municipalities.

HSB is not the only co-operative enterprise which has successfully brought moderate-cost housing of a high standard to the mass of the low-income groups. Two others deserve mention. One is the Stockholm Housing Society, one of the first in the field, which has built 3000 apartments in the capital and rents them to its members at a low rate. It pioneered in placing its buildings amid gardens and spacious lawns at a time in the Twenties when such surroundings were offered only to the wealthy.

The second society is known as SR (*Svenska Riksbyggen*) and is owned and run by workers in the building trade-unions. They owe their venture into the construction business to the exigencies of the second war. Its outbreak paralyzed the building trade. Private investors, who heretofore had financed the bulk of construction work, turned to other less risky fields. The building laborers were faced with mass unemployment. Meeting together to decide what, if anything, could be done, they found that the demand for housing was as great as ever. All that was needed was financing and an organization. Their own unions raised the first capital. Mortgages were secured from the state, municipalities and credit associations. Tenants paid 5 per cent down on the estimated value of their apartment. With this backing SR began operations late in 1941. In that year new building fell to 12,000 dwellings from 41,000 in 1939. In 1942 it was up to 20,500, and SR was getting a big enough share to employ many thousands of its members. To date it has built some 15,000 dwellings valued at more than $50,000,000, mostly in and around Stockholm.

This unique workers'-builder's co-op, like the bigger HSB, aims in its larger housing developments at providing a completely self-contained community. Provision is made for shops, banks, pharmacies, doctors' and dentists' offices, a post office, restaurants, café, cinemas and sports grounds — and of course for public schools. Perhaps the schools should be emphasized because American architects tell me they have sometimes been forgotten in our own large housing projects — as at Peter Stuyvesant Town in New York City, for example, where 25,000 people dwell without a single school.

The new co-op or public-financed apartment buildings in Sweden do not line the streets, but are set back in parks and are oriented to the sun. Each flat has at least one spacious private balcony — a feature in all Scandinavian apartment buildings which I am told some American architects wish was more widely copied at home. They provide a city dweller with many advantages: a pleasant place to eat in the summer, an ideal spot for sun-bathing; a bit of space for boxes in which to cultivate flowers; and above all the perfect surroundings to raise a baby in. Charles Abrams, the American housing expert, has said there are few amenities which could accomplish so much in emancipating the urban American mother from some of her parental chores as the Scandinavian balcony. He lists eight timesaving steps it would save merely in airing the baby, including the long wheeling to and from the park. A Swedish mother can get through most of her housework while the infant is sunning on the balcony nearby.

Much as the co-ops have done in creating new low-cost housing, it is the state and municipalities in Sweden which must be given even more of the credit. They provide the family with the necessary financing. It is not a give-away program. The government requires a person to take out first and second mortgages up to 70 per cent of the cost of the proposed dwelling either at private banks or state-supported mortgage banks. The state will take the third mortgage covering the rest. For those who cannot afford this method, the government will provide up to 100 per cent of the loan on easy terms. It will also offer, in needy cases, certain limited subsidies, interest and

rent rebates especially to families with children, and postponement
or elimination of amortization payments. The towns often offer
valuable aid by selling at extremely low prices land which they have
acquired. The city of Stockholm, for instance, began buying suburban land fifty years ago and in recent times has been able to sell
cheaply some twenty-five thousand acres within ten miles of the
heart of the capital for new homes.

The total amount of public aid for housing is difficult to estimate.
But some official figures indicate its extent. In 1952 the two state
co-operative mortgage banks had loans outstanding for urban building alone of half a billion dollars. In 1951, a typical postwar year, loans,
subsidies and rebates granted by the State Housing Board and the
provincial housing committees totaled $80,000,000. In contemplat-
ing these figures, it must be kept in mind that Sweden has a population of seven million. The United States, with 21½ times the number of inhabitants, would have to spend one and three quarter billion
dollars a year for state aid to housing to match the Swedish figure.

Rents in Sweden today, though relatively high by Scandinavian
standards and in relation to income, would probably appear rather
cheap to most Americans. In Stockholm, with its three-quarters of a
million inhabitants, average rents for a two-room flat with kitchen,
bath and central heating are $350 a year; for three rooms, $450 a year.
Rents in smaller communities are considerably cheaper, bringing down
the national average to $290 a year for two-room flats and $359 for
those with three rooms. These must be considered against average
family incomes among urban wage earners and white-collar workers
of $1600 a year.

*Sweden's Economy—Private Enterprise, Co-ops and
Nationalization*

Contrary to a widespread belief private enterprise is still the
foundation and the overwhelming element of the national economy
in Labor-dominated Sweden. More than two decades of political rule
by the Socialists has not changed this situation in the least. Indeed,
what little nationalization there is took place mostly under Conservative governments before the rise of the Socialist-Labor party.

Today over 90 per cent of total production is accounted for by private companies. The co-ops and the state contribute the rest.

The state, for the most part, has stepped in only where public utilities, communications and hydroelectric power were concerned — or where private investment was unattractive. Thus the government, in order to avert unemployment in the Far North, owns and operates a few pulp factories and sawmills, and a steel works at Luleå. It owns a half-interest in the great Kiruna iron mines above the Arctic Circle, but leaves the operation of them in private hands. The state and municipalities possess one fourth of the forests — property that has come down to them from the ancient kings — but the rest is owned privately, one half by individuals, mostly farmers, and one fourth by corporations.

As in all Continental countries, Sweden's railways are largely nationalized, the government owning some 93 per cent of the 10,300 miles of track, 40 per cent of which is electrified. The State railways also own and operate many of the country's bus lines. Government ownership of the trunk rail lines was voted by a conservative Riksdag back in 1854, long before a Socialist party had ever been dreamed of, so that the state's role in this field, as in the telegraph and telephone business, which is also a state enterprise, has occasioned no debate in Sweden.

Lacking both coal and oil, Sweden has been largely compensated by nature in the form of numerous lakes and swift-flowing rivers throughout the country from which one of the greatest hydroelectric power capacities in Europe is available. Today about one third of a potential 80 billion kilowatt hours per year has been harnessed, giving Sweden a per capita consumption of electric power approximately equal to that of the United States. As in America, the state has entered this field in a big way, though it has not supplanted private ownership and operation by any means. In fact the Swedes over the years have worked out what businessmen in Stockholm described to me as a "successful collaborative effort" between the private and public power business. Private companies supply about half of the electric power, the state 45 per cent and the municipalities the remaining 5 per cent. Most of the trunk transmission lines are operated by the government but its power is also distributed over private lines, and vice versa. The commercial companies and the government have divided up the country for their operations though there is usually enough competition in each district to keep prices down. At the outbreak of the last war the private and state power companies voluntarily entered an agreement for joint operation of the electric power business under the direction of an organization called the Central Operating Management. It was conceived as a wartime measure only, but proved so successful that it was made permanent after the war. By exchanging power and use of transmission lines a much more efficient and economical use of electricity was obtained. The sharing of loads reduced the need for generator capacity. Excessive power capacity in one region at certain seasons or hours could be utilized in other areas where there was a shortage. The necessity of having standby steam plants was almost eliminated, so that today they are called upon to contribute only 2 per cent of the needed electric power. The exchange of power between the various districts and companies is calculated weekly and accounts settled between them.

Cheap water power has enabled Sweden to bring electrification to nearly 95 per cent of rural households, which is about saturation point. Only about 50,000 out of one million rural homes now remain without electricity, and most of them are too remote to be reached at reasonable cost. Even threshing is done by electric power on most farms.

As recently as 1870 nearly three fourths of the population in Sweden lived from farming and forestry. Today less than one fourth do. The present century has seen a constant drain from the farms to the factories, and even since the last war the agricultural population has been dwindling by 47,000 persons a year. In a country of only seven million, this is a sizable emigration. It has transformed the social, political and economic fabric of Sweden.

Today — according to the most recent census, that of 1950 — 65 per cent of the population lives from industry, commerce and transportation. These activities contribute 67 per cent of the national income; agriculture but 16½ per cent. Of some 3,000,000 gainfully employed men and women, 56 per cent are workers — a figure which may help to explain why the Labor party, having discovered how to organize so large a group politically, is so strong in Sweden.

Yet the greatly reduced number of people on the farms produce twice as much food as in 1870, making Sweden largely self-supporting.

Aside from the farms, the natural sources of the country's economic life are forests, mines and water power, which combine to make manufacturing the chief occupation, the biggest employer and the heaviest contributor to the national wealth.

The forests, which cover 55 per cent of the land — an area larger than Great Britain — are Sweden's greatest single source of wealth. Containing an estimated 50 billion cubic feet, their products — lumber, pulp, paper, chemicals and plastics — account for one fifth of the national income and nearly one half of the exports. Before the recent war Sweden was the world's largest exporter of wood pulp, but was forced to overcut its forests during the war because of the shortage of coal and other imports, and production since 1945 has had to be reduced to 80 per cent of the estimated annual growth.

Though the war emergency depleted the forests somewhat, it also taught the Swedes much about new uses for wood. Cellulose was woven into rayon and other substitutes for silk, cotton and wool. When gasoline imports were cut off, automobiles, tractors and motorboats were kept running on gas generated from wood or charcoal. Ethyl alcohol was distilled from cellulose lyes. Sweden's extensive dairy and cattle production is dependent upon the import of fodder concentrates. When these became unobtainable, the Swedes developed a high-protein fodder from wood. They also learned how to make paints, soap, yeast, sulfa drugs and even synthetic rubber from their trees.

The Swedish wood industry has been blessed by nature in one special way. The rivers of the North, where most of the forests are, flow from the northwest to the southeast into the Gulf of Bothnia. Thus logs can be floated from the interior to the mills along the coast, from which cheap sea transport of manufactured products is available. Another advantage is that because of the direction of the rivers the lower stretches become ice-free first. If it were the other way around, the floating of logs in the spring would be hampered by ice jams. As it is now, the logs are loaded on to the ice-covered rivers during the winter, and begin to move automatically as soon as the thaws arrive.

Sweden has developed a unique system of logging waterways with a total length of 20,000 miles — twice that of the rail system — to assure a transportation so cheap that it is estimated some 180 million logs are floated down to the mills each year at a cost per log of a postage stamp for an ordinary letter.

In the seventeenth and eighteenth centuries Sweden was the greatest producer and processor of iron in the world. Today her mining of iron is second in Europe to that of France, but she has had to drop far behind in steelmaking because of her lack of coal. Today half of the blast furnaces in the country still operate with charcoal though most of the steel production is derived from coke processes and more recently from electric furnaces receiving cheap power from nearby hydroelectric plants.

Four fifths of Sweden's annual output of iron ore comes from the great mines at Gällivare and Kiruna in Lapland, far above the Arctic Circle. Kiruna, with proven reserves of over a billion tons, is probably the biggest mountain of iron in the world. Unlike most of the ore from the centuries-old mines in central Sweden, that of the north, though extremely rich in iron (60 to 70 per cent), is highly phosphorous, and therefore must be smelted with coke, which Sweden lacks. For this reason almost all of its annual output of fifteen million tons is exported, either through the nearby ice-free Norwegian port of Narvik, over which the Allies and the Germans fought so bitterly in the last war, or during the summer months through the Swedish port of Luleå on the Gulf of Bothnia. In both cases the government owns the electrified railway connecting the iron fields with the ports. The immense iron deposits were found on land belonging to the state since the time of Gustavus Vasa, but the state turned them over to a private firm to exploit. The government, in 1907, Tory though it was, demanded half the shares of the company in return for adequate hauling service on its railroads. Without transportation, the mines were useless and the company gave in. Today the state and the Grängesberg Company, one of the biggest corporations in Sweden, each own 50 per cent of the stock, each name four directors; but the chairman of the board is appointed by the company, which, in fact, manages the mines. Profits are divided and add several million dollars a year to the coffers of the state as well as to those of the Grängesberg corporation — another typical example of the mixture of private and public enterprise in Sweden.

This mining development in Lapland is by far the greatest industrial undertaking any place in the world above the Arctic Circle, and Kiruna, population 10,000, is one of the largest towns in such a northern clime. There is almost no daylight during the long Arctic winters, so that the open-pit mines have to be floodlit around the clock. It is a wild, snowbound wilderness where the Lapps still tend their reindeer, and was only made accessible to the outside world with the coming of the railroad at the turn of the century. Kiruna is a model town, with excellent schools, public libraries, concert and recreational halls, movies, shops, steam baths and modern housing, in which the homes are heated by electricity. Working conditions and pay are the best in Sweden. Kiruna also boasts, within its city limits, besides the world's richest iron mountain, Sweden's highest mountain, Kebnekajse, which rises to a height of 7000 feet.

The Swedes have concentrated on the manufacture of a high grade steel which has made the metal-working industry the most important one in Sweden. Its annual production is valued at nearly two billion dollars a year and it employs 230,000 persons or about one third of the total industrial labor force. With the exception of one steel plant, all the manufacturing companies in this group, including shipbuilding, motor cars, ball bearings, machine tools, heavy and light electrical equipment and armaments, are private corporations. I found no interest among Swedish Socialists in nationalizing any of them.

Nor does the Labor-Farmer government unduly soak the corporations by taxation. They pay somewhat less in taxes than do American firms — a straight 40 per cent on income after deduction of local income taxes which average 10 per cent — or a total of about 45 per cent.

In industry, as in farming, Sweden is a land of small enterprises. There are a few giant corporations in iron and steel, pulp and paper and engineering products, but 93 per cent of all industrial companies employ fewer than 100 workers and only 1 per cent — some 200 companies — have more than 500 persons on their payrolls. Altogether small businesses employing less than fifty workers produce a billion dollars' worth of goods a year and hire 10 per cent of the industrial working force.

Likewise on the land. Of 400,000 holdings, over 100,000 have less than 5 acres of cropland and therefore offer only partial support to the owner. Another 200,000 farms consist of less than 25 acres and do not provide a minimum standard of living to the holder. Only some 60,000 farms of between 25 and 50 acres provide a decent living, and there are only 35,000 farms of over 50 acres. Nevertheless by growing twice as much grain per acre as Americans and by taking advantage of an ingenious system of co-ops, Swedish farmers make a fair living on relatively small plots. Considering the fact that only 10 per cent of the land is arable — about nine million acres — the Swedish farmers, in feeding a population of seven million, have achieved wonders.

A Note on the Swedish Co-operatives

When I arrived in Stockholm the Swedish Co-operative Union and Wholesale Society, known throughout Sweden as KF (from its official name *Kooperativa Förbundet*), was celebrating a landmark in its half-century of history. Its annual report for 1952 had revealed that for the first time its membership had passed the million mark, and that it had done a business of nearly half a billion dollars, which it increased to three quarters of a billion the following year.

The members owned and operated and shared the profits co-operatively in one of the biggest business enterprises in Sweden. It comprised 681 consumer co-operative societies running 8200 retail stores, an immense wholesale business and half a hundred factories that produced everything from margarine to electric-light bulbs and cash registers.

Big as it was, however, it did not, as so many outside had been led to believe, dominate the economy of Sweden. Ten times as many retail stores, 80,000 in all, are owned and run by the old-fashioned little private trader and in a few cases by big private traders — mostly chains. Exact figures are hard to come by since many private owners do not publish their statistics, but the most responsible calculations I found in Stockholm indicated that independently owned stores did approximately 80 per cent of the total retail trade, the co-ops 12 per cent, and the privately owned large-scale outlets 8 per cent. In the general goods which they sell, the co-ops do 15 per cent of the retail business; and in some of the things they produce they do even better, accounting for 90 per cent of the production of edible oil, 68 per cent of the electric bulbs, 30 per cent of the automobile tires and 25 per cent of general foodstuffs.

Although the co-ops play second fiddle to private enterprise, their influence on the economic life of Sweden in the past half-century nevertheless has been immense, and their impact on the social and even cultural life considerable. Their growth in recent years has been phenomenal. Between 1936 and 1950 KF's retail trade increased by 282 per cent, and total membership was almost doubled. There is no doubt that the aggressive and shrewd competition the co-operatives have offered to private business has resulted not only in a vast improvement of products sold by both groups but in much fairer prices charged by both. In the case of outrageously high prices fixed by private monopolies the co-ops, by battling the monopolies, have brought steep price reductions which saved all families, wherever they traded, considerable sums of money.

Other writers have vividly described the epochal battles which KF launched between the world wars against both national and international trusts.[14]

It took on not only such national cartels as the margarine and flour trusts but international giants such as Unilever and General Electric, and, by starting factories of its own to manufacture their products, restored competitive prices — thus saving the Swedish consumer millions of dollars.

I found in Stockholm that KF's relentless war against cartels continues. Since the Second World War it has done much, in co-operation with other producers' co-ops, to keep down the price of bread and flour. It has tried to offset the high prices in building materials, which it believes are partly due to price fixing by semimonopolies, by producing many of the materials itself. It has entered in a big way into the production of soaps and washing materials and in this field survived the attempts of private manufacturers and retail firms to boycott its products. Recently when private suppliers of chocolates and other sweets appeared to be favoring their commercial clients over the co-ops, KF countered by setting up its own candy factory at Kalmar.

Production has become in the last few years an important part of a co-operative movement which began as a retail and wholesale business. KF now produces goods to the annual value of 150 million dol-

[14] See *Sweden — The Middle Way*, by Marquis Childs.

lars, or nearly a third of the total turnover of the affiliated retail societies. Yet because of the wartime and postwar shortages of goods,
the separate societies have had to turn to ordinary commercial quarters for many of their supplies. Some purists in the co-op movement
question the wisdom of this, but the majority, led by a very shrewd
management, has gone ahead with it, allowing its practical sense to
triumph over pure theory.

While the Swedish co-ops have taught private traders a great deal
about successful merchandising, they have not hesitated to learn all
they could from private enterprise — even from the American brand.
A recent example of this is interesting.

During the last war, when the shortage and high cost of labor
threatened the very existence of the smaller retail outlets, the Swedish
co-ops took the lead in establishing self-service shops. The experiment
was a failure. The customers didn't like the idea. Something was wrong,
but the Swedes couldn't figure out what it was. After the war, when
transatlantic travel became possible again, the Swedish co-ops rushed
a team of experts to the United States to see how the non-co-operative
American chains did it. They returned to Sweden in 1947 and advised
a complete reorganization on the American plan. It worked. The wage
bill per shop was reduced by 20 per cent and turnover of goods increased. Today there are some 1000 self-service stores in Sweden run
by the co-ops, 50 of them in Stockholm. I wandered into one of them
one day and thought for a moment it was an A & P shop. The idea is
spreading. Dry goods are now sold in this manner, and one self-service
shop in Stockholm has begun to sell furniture and bicycles.

The private traders in Sweden were slower to see the benefits of
the American example. They got off to a late start but now have
some 700 self-service shops, most of them smaller than those of the
co-ops.

There are few fields of economic activity that the co-ops have not
entered. They have gone into the oil business, for instance. But here
the National Swedish Oil Consumers' Union, known as OK from its
Swedish name, has run into difficulties. It owns considerable storage
tanks, tank cars and trucks and its own fleet of ship tankers. What it
needs, the co-op leaders realize only too well, is its own oil wells and
refineries. Without these, say the Swedes, prices and supplies will continue to be fixed by the international oil combines. The oil co-op pins

some hopes on the International Co-operative Petroleum Association, which was recently formed with the help of some independent American producers. If this international oil co-op could obtain sufficient wells and refineries, it would have a huge market among the European co-operatives. At present the Swedish oil co-op controls 7 per cent of the oil market in Sweden — enough, it thinks, to influence retail prices but not enough to determine basic prices it holds are set by the international giant companies.

Incidentally, when the Socialist government after the war proposed to nationalize the oil business it was KF which took the lead in organizing private as well as co-op oil interests to fight the measure. Albin Johansson, the veteran, shrewd, revered head of KF, personally led the antinationalization campaign.

Another interesting phase of the co-op movement since the war has been the establishment of Co-operative Burial Societies for the express purpose of reducing the price of funerals. The war brought a drastic rise in the cost of burying the dead. Complaints became so widespread that even Parliament debated what to do about it. Undertakers were accused of exploiting the bereavement of their customers by getting them to buy more expensive coffins and order more costly ceremonies than were necessary or advisable.

By 1948 the co-ops were doing well enough in this field to hold their first annual congress in Stockholm and report that twelve burial societies were in operation with several more formed and only waiting an opportunity to set up shop in suitable premises. The private morticians naturally protested this unexpected encroachment of their preserves by the co-ops, but to no avail. Today the co-ops are burying one quarter of all the dead in Stockholm and an even greater percentage in some other towns. And they have brought prices down. Formerly, the minimum price charged for the cheapest funeral by a Swedish undertaker was one hundred dollars. The co-ops offer all of theirs for between sixty and eighty dollars.

Contrary to a widespread belief, Swedish consumer co-ops do pay taxes, even though they contend that they declare no profits, in the accepted sense of that term. In 1936 Parliament established the principle that dividends on purchases paid by co-ops as well as rebates on purchases paid by private traders should not be taxed. There was one condition: that the recipient of such dividends or rebates used his purchases as a consumer and not as a distributor or producer.

But the co-ops were made subject to stiff taxation on other grounds. From 1936 to 1947 both co-operative societies and private corporations paid the same tax on net income — a straight 32 per cent. In 1947, under pressure from the farmers, the government raised the corporation tax to 40 per cent and left the co-op rate at 32 per cent, giving the latter an 8 per cent advantage over private enterprise. At the KF headquarters in Stockholm it was emphasized to me that at no time did the consumer co-operatives seek any tax advantage over private entrepreneurs; they did not ask for the 8 per cent advantage granted them in 1947. And they point out that it is not such an advantage as it first appears to be. The bulk of the retail trade, they explain, is not carried out by big corporations, which pay 8 per cent more taxes, but by small private traders who are regarded by the government as private individuals for the purpose of taxation. In the average small business, the individual proprietor thus pays a considerably smaller tax than the small co-op shop. Many of the undertakings of KF, especially on the productive side, are organized as ordinary stock companies and though they pay no dividends on profits are taxed the same as corporations on their net earnings. Probably KF could re-register these enterprises as co-ops and win an 8 per cent tax advantage over its private competitors, but it has made no move to do so.

Despite bitter conflicts with private enterprise, especially where monopolies are concerned or where the co-ops have invaded a new field of trade or production, the co-operative movement in recent years has greatly improved its relations with the private business community. There are cogent reasons for this. In many of its productive enterprises KF has to sell to private traders in order to run its factories at maximum efficiency — its own outlets are not big enough or numerous enough to absorb all its productive output. Also, in order to get at least partial control of many sources of production, so as to improve the product and reduce prices for the consumer, KF has not hesitated to invest its surplus capital in private corporations or enter partnerships with private firms. The Swedish Rayon Company, in which KF has a half interest, is an example.

This mixing in with capitalist enterprise has brought much criticism from the "purists" in the co-operative movement who vehemently insist on KF staying out of any business run for profit. They believe the co-ops should adhere to their original principles of production and distribution for use, not for profit. But the genius of the Swedes for compromise so well shown in the evolution of a conservative monarchy into a Labor-dominated welfare state is also much in evidence in the co-op movement. Its leaders share with all Swedes a practical hardheadedness. They believe that they are benefiting the consumer by working with private enterprise to some extent and by sometimes performing as profit-making capitalists themselves. The benefits, they say, go to the consumer and not to coupon clippers, of which there are none in the co-operative enterprises.

Private entrepreneurs in Sweden have mellowed too toward the co-ops. The President of the Stockholm Chamber of Commerce perhaps summed up the attitude in a long conversation one afternoon. "Private business," he told me, "now accepts the co-operative movement. The co-ops provide us with smart, shrewd competition. They are run very efficiently on business lines so far as production and merchandising are concerned. Perhaps," he added with a smile, "the co-ops have lost a little of their ideology now that they've become Big Business."

Back in 1924, Axel Gjöres, one of the pioneering leaders of the Swedish consumers' co-op movement, proposed to the Administrative Council of KF that it should launch a magazine of the highest literary and cultural content to which Sweden's best writers and journalists would contribute regardless of how they felt about the co-operative idea. The council turned him down. It was in favor of starting a highly popular journal appealing to the housewife, who made the bulk of the purchases in a co-op store. But nothing highbrow — or "literary." Gjöres and other shrewd leaders bided their time.

Today the weekly magazine which they ultimately started not only has an extremely high literary and cultural level but also the largest circulation in Sweden of any publication. Called Vi — which means "We" — it sells 650,000 copies a week (price 7 cents or $1.80 a year) and publishes the best and most promising authors, poets and journalists in the land. In fact its quality is so high that the charge has often been made that it cannot be read by the general public.

Irked by this criticism, the editors recently asked the Gallup Institute to make an investigation. Dr. Gallup's experts, after an exhaustive survey, found that the general public was not so stupid or so low-brow as many people imagined. It discovered that *Vi* was read by 45 per cent of all Swedes above the age of twenty. True they turned first, most of them, to the pictures and cartoons. But hundreds of thousands of them liked too the literary contributions and the serious articles.

One morning Editor Nils Thedin discussed his journal's success with me. "It would have been easy — and certainly tempting — to make *Vi* into a popular 'yellow' magazine of the type now prevalent," he said. "But it also would have been a disgrace — an insult to the peoples' intelligence and taste. We felt that both were higher than most editors and publishers imagined. I think we now have proved it. If you publish the best writers and journalists you have, the people will read them. And they will prefer them to trash."

Vi's editorial credo would seem to be a model for editors and publishers anywhere. Thedin ran over it for me.

To entertain and amuse without dulling the intellect.

To reflect contemporary reality, but never falsify it.

To act as a link with the cultural tradition, but never romanticize the past.

To follow the battle of ideas, but never bow with the wind.

To cultivate the ideal of community, but never relinquish the demand for the freedom of the individual.

To broaden the horizon.

Editor Thedin is one of the many co-op leaders you meet in Sweden who believe the movement has a cultural as well as economic mission. He talks enthusiastically about what KF and its associates have done to make an average home not only comfortable but esthetically satisfying. He speaks of the "wretched" furniture that used to clutter a clerk's or a worker's home and how KF furniture designers have changed all that for the better; of how first-rate artists have been brought in to design china and ceramics at KF's Gustavsberg porcelain factory.

When I saw him he was exclaiming about the results of an annual book-lottery which *Vi* and other co-op groups organize to encourage and support writers. Lottery tickets costing 30 cents apiece are sold in thousands of co-op shops and meeting places of various organizations. From the proceeds, *Vi* awards four stipends of a thousand dollars each and smaller ones to some thirty-five other writers, which he said, are second in value in Sweden to the Nobel prizes for literature.

KF itself has gone into book publishing extensively since the end of the war. In 1946 it purchased the Ehlins Company, a publisher of textbooks. In 1948 it acquired another publishing house which had specialized in children's books. And lately KF has begun to publish novels, poetry and art books. It also maintains a co-operative college, a correspondence school (with an enrollment of 90,000) and a vast system of Study Circles.

Politically, the Swedish consumers' co-operative movement remains neutral. But the growing intervention of the state in the economic and social life of Sweden has resulted in a good deal of discussion within the movement as to whether it should not reconsider its attitude toward politics and the state. Some think in terms of starting a co-op political party. Many suggest the movement affiliate itself with one of the existing parties — preferably Labor, since probably a majority of the members vote regularly for that party. But the majority argue that the movement can best serve the consumers' interest by staying out of politics while keeping an eagle eye on all legislation to see that the movement's interests are fully protected. Outright socialism, the co-op leaders realize, would wreck them. In fact they consider themselves a shining example of private enterprise.

The Agricultural Co-operatives

We have been dealing up to now with the consumers' co-ops, which emphasize, as we have seen, that they produce and distribute goods for use and not for profit.

We must now have a brief look at a quite separate co-operative movement — the agricultural co-ops. These are essentially producers' societies, and though organized collectively, are in business to sell farm products on the open market at prices which bring individual members a profit. If there is any general surplus at the end of the year, it is divided among members not according to the amount of capital stock they hold, as would be the case in a private enterprise, but on the volume of their sales through the organization. The co-operatives also handle the purchases of machinery, fertilizer, seed and other commodities needed on the farm as well as transportation of produce to and from the farm, thus effecting considerable savings in both. In fact, like the consumers' societies, the agricultural co-ops have eliminated the middleman and his profit. In the farmers' case, this has been done not only with what he sells but with what he buys.

As in Norway and Denmark, the farmers' co-operatives in Sweden are the backbone of agriculture. Membership among full-time farmers is virtually 100 per cent and today the central organization, the Federation of Swedish Farmers' Associations — known as SL — handles 90 per cent of the sales of all farm produces. Its turnover is half a billion dollars a year.

There are separate societies — twelve in all — for each branch of farming. Thus the Swedish Dairies Association accounts for the sale of 98 per cent of all milk and butter, and 94 per cent of all cheese. The Swedish Farmers' Meat Market Association sells 75 per cent of all slaughtered livestock; the egg co-ops do 65 per cent of the total egg business, and the grain co-ops a similar percentage in their field.

Like the consumers' groups, the farmers' co-operative associations have become Big Business since their phenomenal rise, after a tardy start, in the Thirties. Today they operate 600 dairies, 60 slaughterhouses, 45 meat-packing plants, 90 granaries, 500 warehouses and numerous starch factories, flour mills, sawmills, flax and hemp processing plants, and distilleries, the total capital value of which is a quarter of a billion dollars. The farmers average $579 apiece in their stockholdings in the various co-ops.

The Farmers' Federation also has a building society with 150 architects and other experts operating out of 23 regional offices, who advise and assist farmers with new buildings and alterations to old ones. Transportation of farmers' produce is efficiently organized by the co-ops, which have their own trucking combine operating over carefully planned routes. Grain and potatoes are usually transported on their own barges by cheap waterways to co-op grain elevators and storage houses built along the water routes. Transport costs have thus been drastically reduced.

Since half the farms in Sweden are too small — 25 acres or less — to support a family adequately, the government has stepped in since the war to try to solve the problem in two ways. It offers loans and subsidies for merging small, unprofitable farms into units large enough to keep a family decently. As a result the number of farm operators has been declining by 5,000 annually.

The government's second method is to encourage collective farming — not on the Russian model but on one based on a voluntary, democratic, co-operative principle. After the war Parliament appointed a special committee to study the possibilities of collective farming. Both the government and the Committee were looking for a way to get rid of the small, unprofitable farm and yet preserve the farm family and its healthy way of life. It was no easy task. After three years of investigation, the committee recommended, and Parliament, in 1948, approved, a law to encourage the establishment of co-operative collective farms. It laid down a three-point purpose: to allow the small farm, by merging into a larger unit, to reap the advantage of modern mechanized farming methods; to preserve the status of the small farmer as a landowner; and to provide the farm laborer with the opportunity of becoming a farm owner.

It remains to be seen whether collective farming in Sweden will work out. So far the experiment has not been very promising. Swedish farmers have shown an amazing spirit of co-operation in their own co-ops, but apparently they balk at the idea of the collectivization of *land*. They are not enthusiastic about some of the government rules for collectives, among which are the following:

All members are bound to contribute their labor, and are not permitted to transfer this obligation to any paid employee.

Any member neglecting to carry out his obligation to the society may be expelled.

Any members withdrawing from a collective farm forfeits his share capital unless a suitable person can be found to take over.

The farmers, I gather, do not dispute the fairness or necessity of these and many other regulations if you are going to try to make a success of a collective farm. But they are suspicious and resentful of the regimentation.

The age-old conflict between the farmer, who wants high prices for his food products, and the consumer, who wants low prices for them, has not been solved in Sweden by any means. At first the consumers' co-operative federation, KF, gave a good deal of support to the budding farm co-ops. When the private livestock dealers tried to destroy the farmer's meat co-operatives, KF arranged to buy their products and sell them in its own stores. When the fertilizer trusts insisted on keeping the prices of its products sky-high, KF bought a superphosphate factory, took the Farmers' Union into partnership with it, and in the first year lowered fertilizer prices enough to save the farmers half a million dollars.

But as the agricultural co-ops grew in size and strength they began to compete and to clash with the consumers' co-ops. Finally in 1936 the two groups signed an agreement whereby the consumers' co-ops were to turn over their dairies and slaughterhouses to the farmers and the latter their retail outlets to the Consumers' Union. But the agreement was not kept. The farmers went on opening their own retail shops and finally withdrew altogether from the agreement.

During the war the Farmer's Federation, which had replaced the Farmers' Union as the central bargaining body, approached KF and suggested a new agreement. After three years of careful negotiation a new accord was signed in 1945 re-defining the respective fields of operation between the two great co-operative movements. But it has not worked out either. The gulf between farmers and consumers has remained too wide. Not even the genius of the Swedes for co-operation and compromise has been able to bridge the gap.

The Enlightened Relations between Labor and Management

We turn now to a field where the Swedish aptitude for compromise and tolerance has been eminently successful — after a sordid era of misunderstanding and bitter conflict.

The first strike in Sweden's history was ruthlessly broken by the government, backed by King Oscar II, who did not hesitate a moment to call out the army and navy. A sawmill owner at Sundsvall, north of Stockholm, had reduced the wages of his hands from 15 to 20 per cent, and since they only came to from 25 to 80 cents for a 12-hour day in the first place, the workers went out on strike. This was in 1879. When King Oscar heard of the walkout he was outraged. There were, he exclaimed, "limits to forbearance." Troops and naval vessels were rushed to the scene. Soldiers and sailors surrounded the strikers, who were holding an open-air mass meeting in the town and were actually singing hymns when the military arrived. Thirty-six strikers were sentenced to jail, a thousand families were evicted from their company-owned homes and the rest of the working force was marched back to the mill and its members ordered to resume work.

But such suppression could not kill the idea of labor's organizing. Two decades later, individual unions felt strong enough to form a national federation and in 1898 the Swedish Federation of Labor, known as LO from its Swedish name, was established. Within ten years it had 162,000 members and had become a force in Sweden both on the labor front and in politics. In 1902 the employers countered by organizing the Swedish Employers' Association, known as SAF. Its main purpose was to handle labor relations. In the beginning this meant curbing the growing bargaining power of the unions by maintaining the "open shop" and resorting to lockouts when necessary.

A bitter struggle between labor and management now ensued. It came to a crisis in the great general strike and lockout of 1909. A depression which had started in 1907 had brought reduction of already meager wages, and several strikes had been called. Finally early in July, 1909, the Employers' Association dispatched an ultimatum to the Labor Federation warning that unless all strikers returned to work by July 25, there would be a general lockout. The workers retorted by calling a general strike for August 4. The employers beat them to the gun in many industries by enforcing an immediate lockout.

Whether by strike or by lockout, hardly a wheel was turning in Sweden by the middle of August.

At first, labor was quite confident it would win. It believed that the general strike was an invincible weapon, that management would be sure to give in to escape economic ruin and that if it didn't the consequent disaster to business would bring an end to capitalism and the beginning of socialism, which most workers desired. But events didn't work out that way. For one thing the railroad workers, though sympathetic to the strike, refused to join it. Transportation was maintained. Despite the printers' walking out, the employers managed to publish newspapers damning the unions while the labor press was silenced. The conservative government called out troops to guard government buildings, post offices, telegraph and telephone centers, and this action helped turn the public against the strikers. Not that there was any threat of violence. As the strike went into the harsh winter months and the plight of the workers and their families, short of food and fuel, became desperate, the unions maintained a strict discipline over their men and there was no resort to violence.

The employers held firm. They might be facing economic ruin, but at least they could eat, and heat their homes.

A fortnight before Christmas the unions capitulated. The hungry workers went back to work on the employers' terms. It seemed for a time that the unions had been broken once and for all. In the three years from 1909 through 1911 they had lost nearly 100,000 members, which was more than half their strength. The Social-Democratic party, which drew most of its support from the unions, suffered similarly as disillusioned, bitter workers also deserted its ranks en masse. Its membership fell from 140,000 to 62,000 and it took a whole decade to get back to the 100,000 members. Both economically and politically, labor seemed finished.

And yet its leaders, the foremost of whom was Hjalmar Branting, a formidable personality in contemporary Sweden, did not give up. Their failure taught them a hard lesson: that a direct attempt to assume power in one leap had been wrong. They saw they must proceed by more reasonable and gradual methods. The first thing to do, they decided, was to embark on a methodical long-range task of education: to teach the working class the eventual advantages of organizing collectively for bargaining with employers and to teach not only the workers but all modest-income groups, including the intellectuals, the advantages of uniting for political action. The unions spawned schools all over Sweden. The Workingmen's Educational Society, known as ABF, served as a sort of high school. Young workers began to seriously study economics and history and politics. A number of middle-class students and even instructors at the university became attracted to the labor movement and helped in the teaching.

Just eleven years after the disastrous strike, Branting, who had gone to Parliament in 1897 as the first Labor member ever to be elected to it, became Prime Minister. Politically, Labor had staged an amazing comeback. And the growth of the unions, following the end of the First World War, began to mushroom. From 1919 to 1929, LO's membership grew from 200,000 to half a million.

Yet there was no labor peace. The number of working days lost because of strikes or lockouts during the Twenties came to over five million annually. During the Thirties this costly loss was greatly reduced but it still amounted to about half a million working days annually. Then, after the war, the situation drastically changed — for the better.

In 1952, only 10,716 working days were lost by strikes and lockouts — the lowest figure of any country with free unions. Of all the wage discussions which took place that year, only one tenth of one per cent resulted in an open conflict. Some 19,540 collective agreements covering 1,251,079 workers and 96,350 employers were in force and were being kept by both sides. Something had happened to both the unions and management. What? Labor peace had finally been won. How?

I got a clue on my very first day in Stockholm. I had been invited to lunch by a group of businessmen and economists, one of whom was a director of the Employers' Association and who had just been named president of one of Sweden's largest banks. I was struck by the director's appearance. Obviously he had gone without sleep for several nights. His eyes were bleary. He looked exhausted, and yet happy. He soon explained why he was in this singular condition. He had been sitting up for sixty continuous hours negotiating with a union committee for the settlement of a strike in the food-processing industries, the most serious postwar labor dispute in Sweden since the Communist-fomented walkout in the metal trade industries in 1945. Three nights and two days of unbroken bargaining had done the trick after a five weeks' strike which had halted three fourths of the production of meat, bread, margarine, yeast, candy and fruit and vegetable canning in Sweden.

Yet as this employer told me the story he showed no bitterness or hostility toward the unions, I noticed; just the opposite. And from his account I got a picture of civilized labor-management relations which was confirmed by many subsequent talks with both sides. Three points impressed an American observer.

   1. The high degree of mutual respect and understanding between the union leaders and management. This is especially true of the relations between LO, the Labor Federation, and SAF, the Employers' Association.

   2. The ability of both groups to speak and negotiate for their respective members. At least 98 per cent of industrial labor belongs to unions affiliated with LO. And though the national unions have the last word in regard to wage negotiations, they invariably

accept the advice or the services in negotiation of the Federation. Some employers' groups remain outside of SAF, but its negotiations set the pattern for all industry.

3. The mutual wish of labor and management to keep the national government out of their disputes. They prefer to settle their differences among themselves.

The account given me of the food strike and its settlement by the sleepy but happy director of the Employers' Association is so typical in its revelation of management attitudes in Sweden that I shall set it down briefly, in his own words.

"The dispute in the food industries arose because the unions demanded wage increases despite a wage-stop agreed upon by LO and SAF. When initial talks failed, the slaughterhouse workers walked out."

Then followed a practice quite common in Sweden, though rarely if ever used, I believe, in America: a lockout by employers for a very specific purpose. Mr. B, the director, explained it as follows:

"When the butchers struck, the Employers' Association decided that the only way to settle the dispute in the entire food-processing industry was to negotiate not with several separate unions but on the highest level, that is, with the Labor Federation. So SAF, using its ample powers, locked out the workers in the other branches of the food business. This gave us a chance to negotiate a general settlement with the Federation of Labor, representing all the unions concerned, just as we represented scores of companies involved."

At this point the director digressed to discuss the general philosophy of management toward bargaining with the unions.

"You must realize," he said, "that management in Sweden is all for good strong unions. We have learned how to deal with their responsible leaders. Organized labor gives us something stable to work with and enables intelligent negotiations to take place. The LO, for example, has a number of brilliant economists on its staff as well as elected officials who know the facts and problems of business; we couldn't get by with any nonsense with them, even if we tried. In our bargaining to settle the food strike, we were talking with responsible men. They knew as much as we did about the relations between wages, prices and inflation. They knew the ins-and-outs of the food business. They were shrewd, tough bargainers and so, I suppose, were we. Finally we hammered out an agreement."

I could not help being impressed by the tolerance and good will toward organized labor of this spokesman for the employers, and later I was to receive the same impression from union leaders when they spoke of their differences with management. No doubt this mutual spirit is one of the secrets of labor peace and understanding in Sweden. But it is buttressed by something more specific.

In 1936, it became evident to both employers and labor that Parliament was likely to pass legislation compelling labor peace through the intervention of the state. It would seem at first thought that since the Labor party dominated the Riksdag and the government, the trade-unions would have welcomed such action. But this was not the case. In order to forestall the government, the central federations of the unions and employers began negotiations to set up their own machinery for settling their differences on a nationwide scale. The talks, initiated in 1936, took place at a seaside resort near Stockholm called Saltsjöbaden. There in a big resort hotel the representatives of labor and management argued all day, but relaxed for dinner and cards together in the evening. They became unusually well acquainted with each other and in the course of two years of bargaining hammered out what turned out to be a new foundation of labor-employer relations which is known throughout Sweden as the Saltsjöbaden Basic Agreement. It was signed by LO and SAF on December 20, 1938, and has since been hailed by labor and many enlightened industrial leaders throughout the West as a model of its kind. Gerard Swope, former president of General Electric, who headed a Commission appointed by President Roosevelt to study industrial relations in Sweden, called it a "new high in voluntarily negotiated agreements between employers and workers."

It is a remarkable document. It establishes a uniform system of negotiations to handle labor disputes; a general practice to be followed in dismissals and layoffs; limitations on secondary boycotts. It attempts to minimize resort to strikes and lockouts and to give some guarantee against the interruption of essential public services during labor disputes. Supplementary agreements have been added from time to time, such as those covering factory safety committees in 1942; occupational training in 1944; labor-management "enterprise councils" in 1946; and time and motion studies in 1948. The Basic

Agreement was also amended in 1947 to bring it up to date. It has become a practical, living document which reflects the changing conditions and problems of the times.

The setting up of "enterprise councils" and of time and motion studies represents a joint attempt by labor and management to increase their co-operation beyond the mere field of bargaining on wages and conditions of work. There are today councils in some 3000 firms employing three quarters of a million workers in which management meets regularly with employees' representatives to discuss means of improving production. No doubt these regular meetings have given the workers a better insight into the problems of management. Even more important they have given the workers a sense of participation in the running of an enterprise which previously was denied them. Also employers say they often learn a great deal from the employee's suggestions.

However, both sides admit that progress has been slow. The unions say that in too many cases employers hold back essential information about the business. Management feels that too few workers are equipped or willing to do much thinking about some of its complicated problems. But both sides agree that a useful channel of communication between them has been opened up.

Joint time and motion studies are more important in Sweden than in the United States because 75 per cent of Swedish workers are on piecework. Here again both workers and employers prefer it that way; they agree that piecework provides a necessary incentive and increases both individual wages and production. As recently as 1953, the Labor Federation approved what it called "the present trend toward more and more piecework in industry, as piecework is an incentive of the greatest importance, particularly in a country with small wage differentials."

In general, piece rates are worked out by negotiations between management and unions on the basis of joint or separate time and motion studies. In some firms the scale is so detailed and complicated that it takes a booklet of from 50 to 100 pages of fine print to reduce it to words and figures. The Joint Agreement of 1948 between the labor and employers' federations lays down "principles and motives" for determining piece rates and sets up a joint Board to handle disputes which cannot be settled locally in the plant. In this field too, co-operation between labor and management seems to be paying off.

No objective foreign observer can linger in Sweden very long without being impressed by the sense of responsibility of the trade-union movement, especially as it is reflected in LO, the national federation. One finds very few of the abuses common in some other lands. The unions are democratically run and the elected officials strike one as men of responsibility, maturity, intelligence and utter honesty.

They showed these qualities strikingly in 1949 when in the face of threatened inflation they courageously volunteered to recommend a wage-stop for their members. They didn't have to. In fact, overfull employment in Sweden put them in a unique bargaining position where they could have demanded — and got — further wage increases from employers, most of whom were quite ready to grant them. But the union leaders realized that another round of wage increases would result in another round of price increases. So LO and TCO (the latter representing the white-collar workers) made a voluntary agreement with SAF and other employers' associations not to ask for wage rises that year. This wage-stop was voluntarily extended through 1950. One result was that the official cost-of-living index, which had stood at 166 in December, 1948, jumped only one point, to 167, up to June, 1950. Employers generally credited LO with the main contribution to this brake on inflation. Said one of them: "If there had been no strong central labor federation to tell workers what sound economic policy should be, it would have been impossible for employers to convince workers of this." [15]

It must not be imagined that the labor leaders were, as the Communists charged, selling out to the employers. They were merely showing a grasp of economics and a sense of responsibility. When the effects of the devaluation of the Swedish crown in 1949 and the inflationary pressures of the Korean war a year later began to be felt, LO demanded further wage increases at the end of 1950. By January of 1951, it had obtained general raises ranging from 8 to 17 per cent. The following year it asked and received further wage hikes of 10 per cent to keep up with the inflation caused mainly by the Korean war.

In recent years the leaders of the Labor Federation have learned a great deal about wages and their relation to the national economy, and they have been blunt in sharing their information with their

[15] *Industrial Relations in Sweden,* by Charles A. Meyers.

members. An exhaustive report presented to the 1951 Trade-Union Congress by LO contained such statements as this:

"The total wage increase in a country cannot, in the long run, differ appreciably from the increase of production in industry as a whole. . . . If wages of all workers rise more rapidly than productivity increases, then prices are bound to rise. An inflationary price trend caused by too rapid wage increases should, if possible, be avoided, as it disrupts the economy."

Finally, since the war, the Swedish Federation of Labor has faced up to the problems created by the achievement of full employment, which both it and the Labor government made their main goal after 1945 when it was generally feared that peace might bring, as it had after 1918, economic stagnation and mass unemployment.

Full employment, the Swedish unions feel strongly, has been one of the great blessings in an otherwise bleak and uneasy postwar world. But even full employment has its problems and — strangely enough — according to the unions, its drawbacks.

In a remarkable, exhaustive study called "Trade-Unions and Full Employment" presented to the 1951 Congress, and brought up to date in 1953, the Swedish Federation of Labor once more showed its sense of responsibility by boldly considering those problems and drawbacks.

"Experience in Sweden and elsewhere," it said, "has shown that full employment, let alone 'overfull' employment, creates a set of disturbing phenomena in the labor market: excessive labor turnover, increased absenteeism, a higher rate of accidents, and less occupational training. Thus an increased rate of employment may be assumed to result in a progressively declining rate of increase in productivity until a point is reached where any additional demand for labor must be feared to lead to an actual decline in the national income."

These were the sober words not of some primitive, unreconstructed, selfish, reactionary, old-school capitalist but of one of the most progressive and powerful trade-union movements in the West! And they were backed up by a blunt look at some facts.

Labor Federation statisticians found, for example, that the total labor turnover in Swedish industry had averaged 50 per cent annually since the war. That meant that every other Swedish worker changed jobs each year. This in turn brought an increase in the frequency of accidents, since most accidents occur when men are new at a job. LO also found absenteeism greatly on the increase and concluded that it had hurt production more than labor turnover. It discovered that full employment tended to draw workers from basic industries, especially from jobs that were heavy, dirty or otherwise unattractive, and reminded its members that this could bring about an imbalance in the country's economic structure which could diminish production and halt industrial progress.

Also, LO recognized that in a social welfare state dominated by a Labor party and a Labor government many of the original tasks and objectives of the trade-unions have been taken over by the state. What functions were left to the trade-unions? For one thing, LO answered, a responsibility to help maintain political, social and economic democracy; to use their power to maintain not only a fair share of the national income for the wage earner but a stable economy. The trade-unions, said LO, naturally desired the closest co-operation with a Labor government, but they intended to retain their complete independence from the state and in fact were against the intervention of the state, even if it was run by Labor, in the affairs of the unions.

Finally, said the federation in summing up its attitude, "a trade-union movement independent of the state has an essential task to fulfill in the community even if it is increasingly developing towards socialism, lest the entire community should be overrun by centralized bureaucracy. Uncontrolled bureaucracy can easily develop into a ruling class which regards power as a means of promoting its own interests." Against that, said LO, the unions would fight.

On January 28, 1954, there was an unusual attendance at the Labor Court in Stockholm, which was hearing the complaints of a couple of stockyard employees. Into the courtroom strode King Gustav VI Adolf, the Prime Minister, half the members of the Cabinet, the chiefs of the Federation of Labor, the Confederation of Salaried Workers and the Employers' Association and a hundred other prominent citizens.

The occasion was the twenty-fifth anniversary of the founding of the Labor Court. The presence of so eminent and varied a gathering was proof of the success of this Scandinavian institution in handling one field of labor-management relations. As in the other northern lands, legislation recognizes two kinds of labor disputes: those over wages and working conditions, which are settled by collective bargaining; and those over the interpretation and application of collective agreements, which the law considers binding on both parties. The latter are settled — irrevocably — by the Labor Court.

In Sweden this tribunal consists of eight members appointed by the government: five representing workers, salaried employees and management, and three considered as impartial. Of the latter three, two members must have had judicial experience in the ordinary courts and one must be an expert in labor relations. In a quarter of a century the Swedish Labor Court has settled 3000 cases, 75 per cent of them by unanimous verdict. It has the sole power to impose suitable damages in case of breach of a labor contract.

In the beginning, as Axel Strand, the president of the Federation of Labor, said in his address to the anniversary celebration, the trade-unions bitterly opposed the very idea of the court. In fact they protested its advent by staging a one-day general strike. "But the fears that were then felt in labor circles," Strand said, "have not come true. We have long emphasized the positive importance of the Labor Court."

Everyone else present agreed.

Business and Prophets

Sweden's chief economic problem can be summed up easily: how to achieve a balance of trade at a level high enough to maintain prosperity. A small, highly industrialized country like Sweden, without coal or oil, must export heavily in order to import the raw materials it must have to live. In this it faces two specific difficulties: because of inflated domestic prices and a consequent relatively high wage standard Sweden is finding it increasingly hard to compete in the world market with her exports. German competition especially is taking away business from her. Secondly, Sweden is at the mercy of world markets over which she has no control. In 1953, for example, prices for goods imported by Sweden rose 5 per cent; prices for goods Sweden sold abroad declined by 1 per cent. Since Sweden imported $172,000,000 dollars more of goods than she exported, this disparity in prices was keenly felt. Actually, receipts from shipping more than balanced her trade.

Every businessman and banker I talked with in Sweden emphasized the country's dependence on the United States — not on her trade with us, which is relatively small (6 per cent of her exports, 10 per cent of her imports) but on the continuance of American prosperity. Professor Erik Lundberg, the dynamic, fiercely independent director of the Institute of Economic Research, summed up this attitude for me in one sentence: "An American recession could mean a Swedish depression."

It was the Socialist government's undue fear of the American economy taking a nose-dive after the late war which resulted in some monumental miscalculations in Stockholm with consequences which almost proved disastrous.

The chief miscalculator, ironically enough, was one of the most brilliant men in Sweden and its foremost authority on the United States. Professor Gunnar Myrdal, Socialist Minister of Commerce in the postwar governments of 1945-1947, knew America well. He had been a lecturer at Harvard, a wartime economic adviser to the Swedish Embassy in Washington and, as director of a comprehensive study of the Negro question in America financed by the Carnegie Corporation, had written in the early war years a classic book, *The American Dilemma*, the most exhaustive inquiry into this American problem ever penned. In Stockholm, where Myrdal is a controversial though much admired figure, his critics say that, while in America, he came under the influence of "pessimistic" American economists who were sure that the United States would have a fearful depression after the second war, as it had had after the first.

Despite the fact that neutral Sweden emerged from the war in 1945 unscathed, strong and relatively prosperous in a Europe which was ravished, devastated and bankrupt, Myrdal and his socialist colleagues convinced themselves that Sweden's position was in danger and that it must take steps to protect itself against a terrible world slump which an American depression was sure to bring about. He and his friends in government took two steps. One, they embarked on a policy of cheap money, expansion of credit and other inflationary moves at home. Also to make Sweden less vulnerable to inflation abroad, especially in the United States, they raised the value of the crown in July, 1946, by 16 per cent. Second, and this was the brain child of Myrdal, the Swedish government, convinced that little business could be done with a slumping or inflationary America, and knowing

that Germany, formerly Sweden's biggest trading partner, was pros-
trate and that Great Britain, Sweden's second best customer, was flat
on her back for the moment, looked about for new trade possibilities.
Myrdal cast his eyes on the Soviet Union. She was not subject to
these infernal capitalist depressions. She needed many of Sweden's
products. And she and her satellites had the oil and coal Sweden had
to have to run her own economy.

Myrdal therefore negotiated a billion-crown ($280,000,000) deal
with Russia. The Soviets were to receive credits for that amount over
a five-year period and could purchase their machinery direct from
Swedish manufacturers, who were guaranteed payment by the Stockholm government. There was quite a furore in Conservative and
even in Liberal circles in Sweden, and the United States made an
official protest. The American argument was that Western Europe,
which the United States was doing so much to keep alive, ought to
have first call on Sweden's products, which it needed badly.

Actually the Russians used up only half the credit by the time the
agreement ran out in 1952. Professor Myrdal, somewhat chastened
by the turn of events, departed the government in 1947 and took a
post as secretary general of the Economic Commission for Europe in
Geneva. In the meantime Sweden's deliberately continued domestic
inflation made it increasingly difficult for her to sell her goods
abroad, especially in the dollar market. Torrential rains in 1946 and
a drought the next year ruined the harvests. Government policies and
controls which were designed for abundance deteriorated into plans
for mere economic survival. By 1947 Sweden's foreign exchange reserves built up during the war were exhausted; in that year the deficit
in the trade balance amounted to $400,000,000. Signs appeared on
the walls of Stockholm: SAVE FOR WORSE TIMES AHEAD.

By 1948, Sweden was ready for Marshall Plan aid. She received no
direct grants, but was accorded loans and conditional aid in the form
of dollars for goods she shipped to European members of ERP. This
amounted to $106,000,000 from 1948 through 1951. In the latter year,
thanks to her own efforts, and the general world recovery that followed the Korean war, Sweden promptly informed the United States
that she needed no further aid. In 1954 Sweden continued to enjoy
full employment, and a reasonably balanced trade, and businessmen,
bankers and trade-unionists, though uneasy about the signs of an
American recession, were mildly confident of the future.

By Scandinavian and European scales, the standard of living in Sweden is relatively high. Sweden has more cinemas in relation to population than any country in the world, and more radios than any other country except the United States. It tops all European countries in the number of telephones, and Stockholm, with one phone for every inhabitant, is ahead, in this respect, of New York.

A motor car is, as in all European countries, still something of a luxury, though Sweden ranks seventh among the nations in the number of automobiles in proportion to population. It produces 35,000 motor cars annually, including American models assembled in the country, though the United States has lost to Germany and Britain its prewar position as the leading exporter of automobiles to Sweden.

The Swedes, like the other Scandinavians, get about mostly on bicycles, and not even a cabinet minister is entitled to a car of his own for official use, much less allowed one by the government for private use. Per Albin Hansson, the late and revered Prime Minister, always journeyed on a streetcar from his suburban home to his office. The summer I was in Stockholm the students of the university presented the Socialist Prime Minister, Tage Erlander, with an Essex, vintage of 1930, but he returned it with thanks. He has a car of his own, a small but modern Swedish Volvo; as a rule, however, he leaves it to Mrs. Erlander, who is a schoolteacher, and he, like his predecessor in office, takes a streetcar from his suburban apartment to the seat of government in the center of the city.

On the whole, the Swedes eat well, the average daily consumption of 3190 calories being slightly above even that of the United States and considerably higher than that of France or Italy. But the diet is high in carbohydrates and low in proteins, minerals and vitamins, this being largely due to climatic reasons: it is impossible to grow fruits and vegetables in Sweden except during the short summer season, though the canning and freezing of these foods has made much progress since the last war.

Incomes, in terms of dollars, may at first seem rather low, though not when it is remembered that a dollar (five crowns) buys twice as much in Sweden as in the United States. Few Swedes earn very much, but nearly everyone seems to have a fairly adequate income. The average income is $1400 (7000 crowns), one of the highest in Europe. Nearly half of the inhabitants make between $800 and $2000 a year and only one in ten makes more than $2000. Just four persons in a thousand earn more than $10,000 a year. All this reflects a remarkable leveling in income and wealth, and this condition is what most Swedes seem to prefer. They look with disfavor and even suspicion on those who get rich quick. On the other hand, they are revolted at poverty — for anyone. That is one reason why they support so strongly the social welfare state.

Taxes and Taxes

Swedes, both rich and poor, pay higher taxes than Americans and, like all other peoples, they groan under the load. Being a highly organized race, the Swedes have a "Taxpayers' Association," which tries to protect not only its 50,000 members but everyone else who pays taxes, although, as the august president admitted to me one afternoon when I called at his office, it has been a losing battle.

What disturbed him most — and what indeed is a sore point with businessmen or anyone else who has a nest egg — is the capital levy.

Most Swedes, like most Americans, pay three kinds of direct taxes: a local income tax, a local real property tax and a national income tax. But in addition to these a Swede also pays a stiff national tax on his capital.

There seems to be a widespread prejudice in Sweden, which is reflected in Parliament whenever it writes its tax laws, against income on capital. It is taxed much more heavily than income from earnings. In fact, it is assessed at such a high rate that a man earning a good salary often finds that the tax on his supplementary income from interest on his capital is higher than that income.

The president of the "Taxpayers' Association" gave me an example. He cited the case of a married man with an earned income of $20,000 a year who also receives $4000 from a 3 per cent yield on his capital. His tax on his capital income (income and capital taxes) will come to $4039— or $39 more than the income itself. If he had made $6000 from his investments (3 per cent on a capital of $200,000), his loss would be $411. It would seem that the state was taxing the more wealthy coupon clippers out of existence.

A general tax reduction in 1952 raised the tax-exempt level on capital from $6000 to $10,000. On any capital holdings above that figure a Swede pays a capital levy varying from 6 to 18 per thousand, regardless of yield. Taxable capital includes almost every imaginable kind of asset such as land, houses, stocks and bonds, bank claims and even such personal property as jewelry, automobiles and sailboats.

The municipal income tax amounts to a straight 8 to 10 per cent assessment, depending on the locality. The national income tax is graduated, but single persons earning up to $1200 a year or married persons making up to $2400 pay an overall tax of 12 per cent. Those who make less than $600 a year, if single, or $800, if married, pay no national income tax. Under the 1952 tax reforms, the national government cannot take more than 65 per cent of a man's income, nor the national government and municipalities together more than 80 per cent.

Taxes have increased greatly since the war. According to a survey made by the Institute of Economic Research, all taxes — direct and indirect — amounted to 15 per cent of a family's expenditures in 1938-1939. In the period between 1951 and 1953 they amounted to one quarter.

A good many citizens in Sweden reminded me that while their taxes were considerably higher than those in America, they bought a great many services which in the United States had to be financed privately, if at all. Not only are churches, hospitals and schools in Sweden financed exclusively out of taxation but so are about 85 per cent of the social services, which include, as we have seen, free medical care and old age pensions. If the average American, it was suggested, would add to his taxes his voluntary contributions to his church, to hospitals, and to various charitable and civic organizations he helps support through the Community Chest, and then tack on his family's medical expenses and his private insurance premiums, including annuities he hopes will provide for him in his old age, then the total bill would probably come to about the same amount a Swede pays in total taxes.

Parties, Politics and Government

On the morning of October 29, 1950, King Gustav V passed away peacefully at Drottningholm Palace at the age of ninety-two, in the forty-third year of his reign, the longest in Sweden's history. He had managed to preserve the monarchy over an expanse of nearly half a century which saw Sweden transformed by a peaceful political and social revolution that took from him all of his powers to rule and gave them, during the last two decades of his life, to the democratically elected representatives of the people — mostly the working class — leaving the King a mere figurehead though a respected one and, to most Swedes, a beloved one.

The roots of Swedish democracy go far back in time. Local self-government under law developed in the Viking era, and as early as the eleventh century a German commentator remarked that "the Swedes have kings of ancient lineage, but their power depends on the verdict of the people." Provincial assemblies sometimes elected kings in the Middle Ages, and what may be regarded as the origin of the national Parliament dates back to the fifteenth century.

In 1809, following a twenty-year period of "Gustavian Absolutism," the last ever exercised by a Swedish king, a new Constitution was hammered out which is still in force, making it the oldest written Constitution in Europe. But it was not until 1865, when the Four Estates — nobles, clergy, burghers and peasants — on which the Swedish Parliament had been based, were abolished and the present system of a bicameral Riksdag, without class distinctions, established, that the road was open for the gradual establishment of parliamentary democracy.

Even as late as 1907, however, the year Gustav V came to the throne, only 10 per cent of the population had the vote, which was based on a property qualification; and it was not until the end of the First World War, after the Russian and German revolutions had overthrown the Romanovs and the Hohenzollerns (two events which duly impressed the Swedish ruling classes) that the Conservatives gave in to the incessant pressure of the Liberal and Labor parties and universal suffrage for men and women was established. This was the moment too when Gustav V relinquished his remaining powers to the Prime Minister, who thereafter became the chief executive of the realm.

Today in Sweden one is impressed by the tranquil and balanced quality of parliamentary, democratic life. The Swedes are the only northern people who have retained a parliament of two houses. The Upper and the Lower House of the Swedish Riksdag each has equal power; they differ only in the way they are organized. The 150 members of the Upper Chamber are elected indirectly by provincial and city councils for terms of eight years, one eighth of the membership being renewed annually. The Lower House, which has tended in recent years to become the political center of gravity in Sweden, has 230 members who are elected every four years by direct, universal suffrage.

The two houses do provide a certain check and balance in parliamentary affairs. Every measure introduced in the Riksdag must be approved by both chambers, though urgent matters on which the Houses disagree are decided by joint divisions. The standing committees, which do most of the hammering out of legislation, are always joint committees consisting of an equal number from each chamber. Incidentally, the Swedish Parliament has more journalists and teachers than lawyers in it; and while members say proudly that the Riksdag truly represents a cross-section of the population, I noticed that only one tenth of the 380 members of the two houses were women. Admittedly, that is a high percentage compared to most Parliaments in the West, including our own.

Since 1917, the Social Democrats have comprised the largest party in Sweden, and since 1932 they have been, with the exception of four months in 1936, in power—either alone or in coalition with the Agrarians. (During the Second World War, they also took in the Conservatives and Liberals to form a national government.) Possessing an absolute majority in Parliament after the 1940 elections for the first time in history, the Socialists formed their own government at the war's end in 1945. The general elections of 1948, however, reduced their strength in the Lower House to just short of a majority — 112 out of 230 seats — and in 1951 they took in the Agrarians (in a deal which the Conservatives and Liberals charged was somewhat cynical) to form a new government under the Socialist leader Tage Erlander. In the elections of 1952, the Laborites lost a further two seats and the Agrarians four seats (from 30 to 26), but they continued their coalition government. Thus the Swedish government today is run by farmers and workers, with the latter, because of their far greater political strength, dominating.

Why is Labor so dominant in Sweden? Before we attempt to answer that question, we must glance at the opposition parties.

The Conservative party, representing the well-to-do classes — leading businessmen, bankers, civil service career officials and officers of the army — polled more than half a million votes in 1952, thereby increasing its representation in the Lower House from 23 to 31 seats. It stands, as is natural, for the protection of private industry and free enterprise and opposes state controls and further socialization. It is in favor of social welfare on the condition that the resulting tax burden does not stifle business. Though it is lively, as the last election showed, it has been unable to find the kind of mass following which could return it to office.

More successful in this respect since the war has been the Liberal party, which once — from 1900 until 1914 — was the biggest party in Sweden. It became hopelessly split over the question of Prohibition in the 1920's, and broke in two. In 1932 the party was almost destroyed when it was revealed that its leader, Carl Gustav Ekman, who was Prime Minister, had accepted secret funds from the Swedish match king, Kreuger, whose financial empire was then crashing amidst a scandal that rocked the international financial world.

After the last war, however, Liberal fortunes revived. This was partly due to a weariness with the Socialists felt by many and partly because of the dynamic leadership furnished by the new party chief, Bertil Ohlin, a professor of economics. In 1944 the Liberals, known as the People's party, polled 400,000 votes and won 26 seats in the Riksdag; four years later they more than doubled their vote (882,000) and secured 57 seats, becoming the second largest party. In 1952 the Liberals polled nearly a million votes, almost as many as the Conservatives and Agrarians combined. On the whole, they represent the urban middle class, the tradesmen, and the professional and intellectual groups. They form the only Liberal party in Europe, I believe, which has made progress since the war.

The Communists have not flourished in Sweden, though towards the end of World War II they had a brief spurt due largely to the enhanced prestige of the Soviet Union as a result of its successful stand against Nazi Germany and its alliance with the West. In the 1944 elections the Communists polled 318,000 votes — 10 per cent of the total — and sent 15 members to the Lower House of the Riksdag. Four years later their vote decreased to 6 per cent and in 1952 they received but 164,000 votes, or about 4 per cent of all ballots cast, reducing their delegation in the Lower Chamber to 5 members. They have 3 representatives in the Upper House. Their fall was due partly to Swedish reaction to Russia's behavior after the war, including the shooting down of Swedish planes by Soviet flyers and the revelations that the Russian embassy in Stockholm was the center of espionage activity against Swedish security. Part of the Communist decline is also due to the militant anticommunism of the trade-unions and the Labor party.

I questioned Conservative, Liberal and Labor politicians about their attitude toward the question of outlawing the Communist party and banning Communists from government employment. Their common answer may be summarized as follows: they have never considered banning the party, because they believe it would be undemocratic and impractical. They believe it is easier to handle an open Communist movement than one driven underground. Government employees found to be Communists are not fired — there is no agitation in Sweden for this — but they are quietly weeded out from sensitive posts and put into positions where they can do no damage — either by espionage or by sabotage.

The success of the Labor party in Sweden is due to a number of factors. The party appeals to the low and modest income groups, which comprise the majority of the population. It has the support of the highly organized trade-union movement with its more than one million members. The relationship between the labor unions and the party is a close one. The unions can join the Social Democratic party *collectively* so that every member of the union becomes automatically a member of the party unless he specifically declines. Still, only one third of the party's membership of over half a million comes from such collective affiliation and only one sixth of the total membership of the unions pays dues to the party.

The two labor organizations, the unions and the party, are quite separate; but among the leaders there is what might be called a great deal of interlocking. Thus Axel Strand, President of the Federation of Labor, is First Vice-President of the Upper House of the Riksdag, and leader of the Social-Democratic party group in that Chamber. He is member of the National Committee of the Labor party; in short, he ranks among the first half dozen leaders of the party and can have a post in the Cabinet any time he wishes.

The Socialist party has also been lucky in its leaders. Hjalmar Branting, the first Labor prime minister, and Per Albin Hansson, who in 1925, when Branting died, succeeded him as party leader, were men of great stature and widespread popularity who easily dominated Swedish politics between the wars. Incidentally both of them, as well as the present Labor prime minister, Tage Erlander, started life as journalists.

Erlander is not so spectacular or brilliant as his two predecessors. Born in 1901, the son of a schoolteacher and organist, he received a B.A. degree in social studies at Lund University in 1928. He was elected as a socialist to the Riksdag in 1932, and from 1931 to 1937 supported himself as an editor of a Swedish encyclopedia *Svensk Uppslagsbok*.

On the death of Per Albin Hansson in 1946, Erlander was chosen to succeed him both as head of the Labor Party and Prime Minister. A shy and modest man, he told newspaper reporters as he acceded to the leadership of the government: "I'm just an average person. There is nothing exciting to write about me."

Three final reasons may be given for Labor's success at the polls. It is by far the best-organized party. Besides an energetic Youth League and a Women's League, it maintains active organizations at the local level and recently — to combat the Communists — has set up militant groups in factories, unions and even city blocks. Also it has an energetic press, including a number of daily newspapers.

Secondly, its championship of neutrality in foreign affairs and social welfare at home has responded to what most Swedes want from their government. Finally, it benefits from the old law that nothing succeeds like success. It has convinced large numbers of people that it can govern the nation responsibly, successfully and well.

An antisocialist editor of one of the great liberal daily newspapers perhaps summed this up best when he told me:

"The majority of Swedes feel that, on the whole, the Labor governments have done pretty well. When the bulk of our people compare their present prosperous status — all the social welfare gains, better housing, paid vacations, higher wages, good schools, a more equal distribution of wealth, and all that — with what it was under previous governments of the so-called 'bourgeois' parties, they are inclined to give Labor most of the credit and therefore most of their votes.

"Their feelings in this regard," the editor added, "are strengthened when they visit countries like Italy and France (and our working class people have become great travelers) and see how much worse off the common people are under so-called 'middle-class' governments there. They come home and say, Well, our Labor government has given us a pretty good deal after all."

Administration in Sweden is not, as in most countries, the exclusive business of the prime minister and the various government ministries. It is shared with some fifty so-called administrative agencies, staffed by civil servants and surprisingly independent of the government. These bodies are not responsible to any individual cabinet minister or ministries, but rather to existing laws which were laid down in the seventeenth century. The permanent officials who preside over them, with the exception of the top man, cannot be removed by the government and in practice even the head of the board is rarely dismissed. In Sweden, civil servants enjoy a security of tenure which must be envied by their brethren in certain other democratic lands. The Constitution stipulates that they cannot be fired except after formal trial and conviction in a court of law. When the great King Gustavus Adolphus came to the throne in 1611, he made a solemn pledge to that effect, and the tradition has held ever since.

The Institute of Economic Research, under the leadership of Professor Erik Lundberg, is a good example of the independent administrative agency in Sweden. Unlike our own Council of Economic Advisers, which works closely with the President and tends to reflect the thinking and policies of the Administration, the Institute of Economic Research is completely independent of the government in power. Indeed it often puts out statements on the economic and financial aspect of problems which are highly annoying to the government. Yet Lundberg, whose integrity and outspokenness are universally admired in Sweden, never has to fear that some irate politician can get him fired from his job.

Local government, which goes back to ancient times, is of great importance to the Swedes. For centuries the townships were based on the early medieval parishes, which were built around the village church and whose communal councils looked after local affairs. After the last war, the Riksdag, in the face of much opposition from many local parishes which clung stubbornly to their ancient ways, voted to merge the smaller communes into larger units of from two to three thousand souls, thereby reducing their total number from 2,381 to 821. Also to further local government, Sweden is divided into twenty-four provincial districts (*län*) and six city districts — Stockholm, Göteborg, Malmö, Norrköping, Hälsingborg and Gävle. Each provincial district has a governor, appointed by the national government, and there are provincial and — for the six cities — city councils whose members are elected in the communal elections every four years midway between the national elections. It is these councils which elect the members of the Upper House of the Riksdag. Thus local politics exercises a constant influence on Parliament.

A Popular, Scholarly, Hard-working King

Gustav VI Adolf, King of Sweden, came late to the throne. He was sixty-eight when his father, Gustav V, died in 1950. At an age, then, when most kings are coming to the end of their reign, the present Swedish monarch began his. His life up to that moment, however, had not been idle. For half a century he had diligently set about learning all he could about the job which one day would be his. He had traveled widely abroad and twice visited America. He came to know every nook and corner of Sweden. Often he acted as regent for his aging father.

But he did more than prepare for the throne. He became a distinguished scientist — an archaeologist — in his own right. Had he not been in line for the succession, he might easily have earned his living as a professor of archaeology at the university or as a curator of a museum. He participated in, and later led, a number of scientific expeditions to Greece, Egypt and China. At home, until he was sixty-eight, he led the simple, modest life of a scholarly country squire. He and the crown princess had an apartment in the Royal Palace in Stockholm, a small château at Ulriksdal outside the capital and a summer home, a rambling, English-style country house, in the southernmost province of Skåne.

Both the King's first wife, who died in 1920, and the present Queen were English. The former, the late Princess Margaret, daughter of the Duke and Duchess of Connaught, was a granddaughter of Queen Victoria, and the present Queen, who is a sister of Earl Mountbatten, is a great-granddaughter of Victoria. When as crown prince the present monarch married Princess Margaret in 1905, he was the first member of a Swedish royal family to wed British royalty in five hundred years. Most of them, at least in recent times, had taken their spouses from the numerous courts that, until 1918, dotted Germany.

The Swedish royal family is, of course, Swedish only by adoption. Its origin is French—and *petit bourgeois* French, at that—going back to Jean Baptiste Bernadotte from the Béarn district in the Pyrenees mountains, who began his distinguished career as an army sergeant and rose to be one of Napoleon's foremost marshals and the Prince of Ponte Corvo. Invited by the Riksdag to succeed a childless Swedish king, Karl XIII, Marshal Bernadotte became Crown Prince Karl Johan in 1810, and, quickly taking over the royal power in all but name, turned *against* Napoleon, thereby not only saving himself from sharing the French Emperor's fate but achieving an initial success for Sweden which assured the future of the Bernadotte dynasty. In return for Swedish aid against Napoleon, the Allies took Norway from Denmark and joined it with Sweden. This compensated for Russia's having grabbed Finland from Sweden in 1809, with Bonaparte's encouragement. Bernadotte was crowned King Karl XIV Johan in 1818.

King Gustav VI Adolf is the sixth Bernadotte to rule Sweden. His eldest son and heir apparent, Prince Gustav Adolf, was killed in an airplane crash at the Copenhagen airport January 26, 1947—it was in this accident that Grace Moore, the American opera singer, also lost her life. The Prince had four daughters and one son. The latter, Carl Gustav, born in 1946, is the youthful Crown Prince today.

Two other sons of the King, as well as the only son of his brother, Prince Wilhelm, have married commoners and thereby renounced their rights to the throne.[16] Their marriages to women outside of royalty attracted a good deal of attention in Scandinavia.

---

[16] Actually, according to changes made in the Law of Succession in 1937, a Swedish prince can marry a *foreign* commoner without forfeiting his right of succession, that is, if the King and government give their consent to the marriage. Why is a prince penalized if he marries a Swedish woman? One eminent Swede explained to me that this is because close family relations between members of the ruling royal family and private families in Sweden "would cause difficult problems," as he put it, in such a case. Strangely enough, there is nothing in the law to prevent the King himself from marrying a commoner, even a Swedish one, though my eminent friend assured me that such a thing was not likely to happen. In the case of Prince Sigvard, it was explained to me that though he is presently married to a Dane, he lost his succession rights before the law was changed in 1937 when he married a German girl.

Sigvard, the second son of the King, who was born in 1907, inherited the Bernadotte artistic strain and, after taking an academic degree at Uppsala University in 1929, enrolled at the Royal Academy of Art, where his great-uncle, Prince Eugen, a brother of the then King Gustav V and a professional painter, was a leading figure.[17]

Soon Prince Sigvard began to make a name for himself in the field of industrial art, specializing in designs for silverware, textiles, furniture, ceramics and theatre settings. In 1943, he married Sonja Robbert, the daughter of a Danish shipowner. Given the title of Count Bernadotte of Wisborg, he now lives with his wife and children in Copenhagen, where he pursues his artistic work.

The King's fourth son, Carl Johan, born in 1916, figured prominently in the American press shortly after the end of World War II. In 1946 he renounced his rights to the throne and married Kerstin Wijkmark, a journalist. The couple lived for some years thereafter in New York, where Count Bernadotte was engaged in the import and export business. They now make their home in Stockholm and have two adopted children.

Prince Lennart, the only son of Prince Wilhelm, brother of the present King, also sought marriage outside of royal circles. In 1932 he married Karin Nissvandt, with whom he has had four children. He has been active in various fields such as choral societies and glee clubs. For a time he was head of the Swedish Boy Scout movement and has long been chairman of the Swedish Children's Day Societies. A frequent contributor to the daily newspapers and weekly magazines, and editor from 1939 to 1951 of the magazine *Foto*, he is also a film director and since 1947 has managed his own cinema firm, *Artfilm*.

Though Sweden has had such renowned ruling queens as Christina, the law adopted for the Bernadottes in 1810 provides for male succession only. Second in line of succession, after the present child Crown Prince, is Prince Bertil, the only living son of the King who has not married a commoner. Born in 1912, he is unmarried. The last in the existing line of succession is the King's only brother, Prince Wilhelm.

Crown Prince Carl Gustav will not come of age until 1967, when the King will be eighty-five. Should King Gustav VI Adolf die before

---

[17] In 1954 an exhibition in New York of fifty water colors by the late Prince Eugen was highly praised by the critics.

1967, the Riksdag would appoint a regency to rule Sweden until the Crown Prince reaches his majority. Aside from the Communists, who naturally oppose the monarchy, there are a few in Sweden — mostly liberal intellectuals — who believe that after the present King passes away, Sweden ought to consider the possibility of becoming a republic. These persons are small in number and not very vociferous, though apparently they add a certain spice to contemporary life in Sweden today. They tend to follow the lead of Professor Herbert Tingsten, the editor in chief of *Dagens Nyheter*, the country's most widely read and most influential daily newspaper — it is generally regarded as the *Times* of Sweden.

Tingsten, the country's leading journalist, is a controversial figure in the land. Rather jovially he denied during a long talk with me that he was, as many charged, "antimonarchist." He explained that he just couldn't get as "steamed up" about the monarchy as did so many other Swedes, who, he thought, were growing more "lyrical" than ever on the subject since the war. He said he felt the late King was inclined to throw his weight around too much despite his lack of constitutional power to do so. He regretted that King Gustav V wrote Adolf Hitler a letter expressing the hope that Nazi Germany would not attack Sweden after it had invaded Denmark and Norway. He was not pleased, he said, at the attempts of the government to hush up the "Haijby Affair." [18]

[18] Professor Tingsten's newspaper was one of the few in Sweden to give prominence to this affair, though every editor I talked with, both in Stockholm and the provinces, discussed it at length. It involved an ex-convict and blackmailer named Kurt Haijby and his alleged personal relations with King Gustav V, and came to light only after the aged monarch's death in 1950. In brief, the story is this.

Haijby, who had been in and out of jail after various convictions for robbery and forgery, is said to have met the then seventy-four-year-old King in 1932 when he called upon him in connection with an application for a liquor license for a restaurant. Some years later he embarked upon a long career of trying to blackmail the Court, threatening to divulge his alleged relations with the King. Officials of the Court and a high-ranking police officer in Stockholm tried to hush the man up by paying him blackmail. The total sum paid over the years was reported in the press as varying from $20,000 to $35,000. So far as is known, the King knew nothing of these payments.

According to the accounts in the Swedish press, court circles succeeded in sending Haijby off to Germany shortly before the war after he had threatened, during court questioning on a suspected homosexual charge, to publish some articles. In Germany he was reported to have got into trouble over some bellboys in a hotel and been sentenced to nine months in jail. Returning to Sweden in 1940, he made fresh demands for money from the Court. Apparently they were met, at least in

The king, it is clear, is not immune to debate or criticism in democratic Sweden. But so far as I could ascertain, Gustav VI Adolf is immensely popular among the vast majority of Swedes, including Labor. He is highly respected for his fairness, his considerable abilities, his capacity for hard work and his devotion to duty. (When he assumed the throne in 1950, abstaining from the pomp of a formal coronation, he took as his royal motto DUTY ABOVE ALL.)

King Gustav VI Adolf celebrated his seventieth birthday on November 11, 1952. Among many evidences of affection was a birthday gift of nearly a million and a half dollars raised largely by popular subscription. It was typical of the King that he announced the money would be put into a project known as "King Gustav VI Adolf's Seventieth Anniversary Fund for Promoting Swedish Culture."

---

part. The payments, it was later revealed, were lumped together in the royal accounts under the heading of "Contributions to Charity."

When the old King died in 1950, Haijby sent a threatening letter to the new King, who promptly turned it over to the government. Haijby was then sent to an asylum for observation.

In the meantime the story had leaked out and was published, first, in a small anticommunist syndicalist journal in Stockholm, *Arbetaren.* The government asked the Lord Chancellor's office to investigate, and, in the spring of 1952, the Lord Chancellor, assisted by a Supreme Court Justice, made a report to the government. Their findings, but not the material on which they had based them, were made public. Their conclusions were that Haijby's charges against certain officials had been carefully examined and the Lord Chancellor had not found further action called for. The government agreed, and justified its refusal to publish the report on the grounds that it consisted of uncorroborated allegations which had not led to legal proceedings. (In part, because of the statute of limitations.)

In December, 1952, Haijby was tried for blackmail before the Stockholm Magistrates' Court. The trial, as is traditional in blackmail cases in Sweden, was held in secret and the records of the proceedings impounded and ordered not to be made public for seventy years, until 2022. Haijby was found guilty of blackmail under aggravating circumstances and sentenced to eight years at hard labor, the severest sentence allowable under the law. In March, 1953, the Court of Appeals reduced the sentence to six years.

The Swedish reaction, according to what several editors told me, was interesting. In the first place, the public was not nearly as interested as the editors had expected. And its concern was not with the alleged charges but with the fact that officials of the Court should try to take the law into their own hands by paying blackmail and by sending Haijby off to Germany and then getting him confined in an asylum. The public, which in Sweden has a fierce feeling for justice under law, felt that the principle of equality before the law had been abused by the Court officials.

Dagens Nyheter ran several editorials on the affair, arguing that in democratic Sweden the details of the whole episode should be given the public, and criticizing the government for trying, as it charged, to hush the matter up.

The Prevalence of Culture in Sweden

The King's interest in promoting culture is shared by an amazingly high proportion of his seven million subjects. The arts, literature and learning are matters of serious and lively interest in the kingdom and are the concern not of a few highbrows but — so it seemed to me — of broad masses of the population. The writer, the artist, the professor are highly regarded in Sweden. The term "egghead" is unknown, and is not likely to come into the Swedish language, even in that used by politicians in the Parliament, for there is no feeling at all of derision for the intellectuals — just the opposite.

The Swedes still read books; much more than do Americans; and they see more of the legitimate theater than we do; and though comparative statistics are lacking, they think that perhaps they buy more original contemporary paintings than Americans buy — enough, at any rate, to support a healthily large number of living artists.

An American visitor to the Riksdag is likely to be surprised at finding that the politicians in Parliament are interested not only in taxes, foreign trade, containing the Russians, beating the Communists and, of course, winning elections, but also in doing something about furthering the broad aspects of culture. For this purpose they vote sizable sums that derive from an ingenious series of state-run lotteries. Thus in 1952, to take a typical year, Parliament voted to pay out of the Lottery Fund $2,000,000 for opera and the theater, $250,000 for symphony orchestras, and a further quarter of a million dollars to promote such activities as art exhibitions, choral groups, historical societies and the appearance of an Icelandic theatrical troupe.

During the years that immediately followed the last war lively debates took place in both houses of Parliament over the publishing and reading of books. Many members felt that Swedish publishers were not giving the public all it wanted in good literature; that they were pricing books out of the reach of too many persons; and that, in effect, publishing was in such a poor state that perhaps a state-owned publishing house might have to be set up to remedy the situation.

Finally, the government set up a special committee of publishers, authors, booksellers, educators and state officials to look into the matter. It came up in the end with what the Swedes believe to be the most exhaustive study of the subject ever made in any country. It concluded that the state had better, at least for the time being, stay out of the publishing business.

But most interesting were the facts learned about the buying and reading of books. A special Gallup Poll made for the committee showed that 63 per cent of all adult Swedes were regular readers of books — a proportion second only to Iceland and far higher than in the United States.[19]

Unlike most other Western peoples, including Americans, the Swedes were found to spend more money in the purchase of books than for any other reading media. Newspapers were second to books, and magazines third. Also 60 per cent of book readers said they preferred fiction to nonfiction — a trend that is just the reverse of that in America.

Relative to population, Sweden publishes annually far more titles than the United States. With only one twenty-third of our inhabitants, Swedish publishers brought out in 1953 some 4000 new titles — nearly one third as many as were published in America.

Although Sweden has relatively more movie houses than any other country in the world, the films have by no means driven out the legitimate theater. Sweden today boasts 623 theater houses or a ratio to movies of 1 to 4 against 1 to 70 in the United States. There is in fact a boom in live entertainment. This is due not only to a surprising interest of the masses in stage offerings but to three uniquely Scandinavian — if not uniquely Swedish — institutions in addition to the traditional state and civic theater. These three institutions are known as the People's Parks (*Folkets Park*), the People's House (*Folkets Hus*) and the National Theater (*Riksteatern*). In the organization of the first two, the Swedish Labor movement has played a leading role.

The People's Parks offer entertainment at low cost during the three-and-a-half-month summer season. Each of the 250 parks in the enterprise has a roof-covered theater without walls — it usually doubles as a dance floor. In a typical season these park theaters offer 1500 performances and draw twelve million cash customers. Musicals, comedies and variety shows usually pay their own way, but the state chips in $100,000 a year to encourage entertainment that otherwise

[19] Almost four times higher, in fact. Dr. Gallup found that in 1953 only 17 per cent of our people in America were regular book readers.

might be too expensive. The backers of the summer park theaters say they do not try to push culture down the throats of reluctant customers as if it were medicine. They offer plenty of vaudeville acts and such American attractions as the Delta Rhythm Boys. But they have also found a growing demand not only for such American musicals as *Call Me Madam* and *Kiss Me Kate* but for the famous Vienna Ballet, which recently played a whole season at the Swedish parks, and for the plays of Strindberg, Sweden's greatest playwright. Actually, more people see Strindberg's plays in the park theaters than in all the permanent theaters of the country. The casts are purely professional and each summer at least 2000 actors and artists find regular employment in the park theaters.

The People's House, largely an enterprise of the Labor movement, is the wintertime version of the summer park theaters. A national organization, it operates 600 People's Houses, each of which, besides a theater, usually contains offices for the trade-unions. Fourteen theater groups play the chain, offering opera, light opera and stage plays. Some of the bigger houses, such as the one in Gothenburg, which was recently opened by the Prime Minister, have permanent companies.

The third institution providing bargain-priced theater entertainment is the National Theater, which is quite separate from the state and civic theaters. It was born in 1934 during the depression, with the objective of not only giving employment to professionals in the theater but of reviving what at that time looked like a dying art by bringing it to the farthest reaches of the hinterland. The National Theater is primarily a state-subsidized booking office. It maintains twenty-two permanent road companies, which give an average of 1300 performances in 375 separate communities during a season. The smaller towns each has its own committee which books, at fixed rates, as many offerings as wished from the central program agency in Stockholm.

The directors of the National Theater are frank about their long-range objective, which in the words of one of them is nothing less than changing the cultural pattern of the nation toward more serious entertainment. This, they say, is not so difficult as it might seem. While the public still turns out in biggest numbers to musical comedies, Shaw's *Pygmalion* was a solid hit as was Tennessee Williams's *Streetcar Named Desire*. Also popular with National Theater audiences have been plays by Chekhov and Pär Lagerkvist, the latter a Nobel

Prize winner and generally considered to be Sweden's most eminent living playwright and novelist.

Finally, there are the two state theaters in Stockholm, the Royal Opera and the Royal Dramatic Theater, on a par with the best of their kind in the world, and five civic theaters, subsidized by municipalities, in other large cities. The civic theater in Malmö is the largest in Europe and attracts over half a million paid admissions a year — twice the number of the population. In cities like Malmö and Gothenburg attendance in the civic theaters has increased fivefold in the last ten years. Besides its state-subsidized theaters, Stockholm, with a population of three quarters of a million, supports fourteen privately owned playhouses all of which are continually open during the long winter season. (New York, with ten times the population, had twenty-four theaters open in 1954.)

Salaries in the Swedish theater are low by American standards. An experienced professional earns around $250 a month, a star perhaps twice that much, though the repertory system does not generally promote stars. Still, employment is regular and actors and directors get much more experience in a variety of plays than do their counterparts on Broadway. Swedish stars, incidentally, especially in the films, tend to emigrate to America. Among the graduates of Stockholm's Royal Dramatic Theater, or of its famed school of acting, are Greta Garbo, Ingrid Bergman, Viveca Lindfors, Signe Hasso, Marta Toren and Mai Zetterling. In recent years the Metropolitan Opera of New York has engaged at least six singers, including Kerstin Thorborg and Jussi Björling, from Stockholm's Royal Opera.

Artists in a civilized society, it is generally recognized, should be able to live from their creative efforts, and in few countries that I know is this more truly appreciated than in Sweden — especially among businessmen, labor leaders and the politicians in Parliament. The government, supported by all parties in the legislature, believes in subsidizing art. It raises the necessary funds not by taxation but, as the Swedes say, painlessly — through national lotteries.

The main one, operated by the state, is a monthly lottery which sells annually 15 million tickets yielding a total of $39,000,000, of which $19,000,000 is distributed as prizes. Some two and a half million dollars of the remainder goes, as we have seen, to support the opera, the theater, music and other cultural enterprises. When I was in Stockholm, arrangements were being made to launch a special lottery to raise one million dollars for the benefit of the Royal Dramatic Theater, which will be thoroughly modernized in time to celebrate its fiftieth anniversary in 1959. The original construction of the theater in 1908 was also financed by a lottery, which realized six million dollars.

A further scheme, borrowed from Denmark, was recently proposed by the government to add to the income of writers, whose sales of books in the original are necessarily modest because of Sweden's small population. As we shall see in the next chapter, the Danes originated the idea of compensating authors for their books used by the public libraries. The Swedish plan calls for government contributions of three fifths of a cent for each book loaned by a public library. Two thirds of this goes to the author himself and one third to a special fund for the support of needy and deserving writers administered by the Swedish Authors' Fund. Since the public libraries in Sweden loan on an average seventeen million books a year, the authors will benefit by some $100,000 a year from this plan. Whether the bookkeeping will absorb most of the fund remains to be seen. The Danes thought a similar scheme of their own would, and dropped it for a more simple and ingenious plan.

I found in Sweden a brisk business in the selling both of original paintings by modern artists, who thereby are enabled to earn a decent living, and of good reproductions of both contemporary and classic art. Business and professional men with a little extra money on hand at the end of the year tend to buy paintings not only to adorn the walls of their homes but as gifts to associates, relatives and friends. Moreover, employers and trade-unions co-operate in organizing company art clubs. The employees pay ten or fifteen cents a month, the employers chip in an equal amount, and joint purchases are made through experts. There are ninety-four such company art clubs in Stockholm alone, with 18,000 individual members, their collective purchases of art works totaling over $55,000 annually. In many cases the paintings are distributed to members by lot. One of the clubs at a Stockholm bank recently exhibited its purchases over a period of five years. Besides paintings by a dozen leading Swedish artists, there were works from Picasso, Chagall, Leger, Maillol and Laurens.

Perhaps the biggest boost to artists has been the formation of a

Society for the Promotion of Art. Dues-paying members include 15,-000 organizations and clubs (largely from the trade-unions and the co-ops) in addition to several thousand individuals. The society arranges art exhibitions and sells good reproductions and lithographs at reasonable prices. There is also the Swedish National Federation for Instructive Art, which arranges traveling art exhibitions which circulate throughout the country. The art shows of these two organizations are responsible for many sales of paintings and sculpture.

If the creation and appreciation of art is one of the glories of Western civilization, then the Swedes would seem rather to shine in it. True they have not produced any great geniuses either in painting or in music. But as a people they have accepted art as a living force not just for the few but for the many. It has greatly enriched them.

The influence of Strindberg, the one hundredth anniversary of whose birth was celebrated throughout Sweden in 1949, dominates Swedish writing. In one of his plays, *After the Fire*, a character named Ericson remarks: "It's horrible, don't you find life horrible?" And the Stranger replies: "Yes, horrible beyond all description."

Nowadays Swedish critics find their contemporary creative writers echoing that gloomy view of life. There is a paradox there. Gunnar Ahlström recently pointed it out in a brilliant essay on contemporary Swedish writing:

> In this green and pleasant land, the writers seem to have no share in the standard of living that others find so stimulating and inspiring. Instead of plunging into the collective ecstasies of a leisured society, they roam the thistles and brambles of the periphery, wearing the hair-shirt of individualistic tribulation. They seem to go out of their way to collect grievances and fears, intimations of aloneness and causes for unrest, crises and writings on the wall. The attitude toward society is correspondingly negative and critical. Swedish literature today can by no means be geared into any public health system or social welfare scheme.[20]

No wonder that Kafka, after Strindberg, appears to have the greatest hold on the new generation of Swedish writers. They strike foreign critics who know their work as not only highly introspective but often morbid. That might explain why Faulkner is by far the most popular American author among Swedish writers and why perhaps

[20] From *Life and Letters* (London, 1949).

in 1949 he, rather than Hemingway (who had to wait until 1954) was selected among Americans to be awarded the Nobel Prize.

The Swedes are avid newspaper readers. They buy daily a total of three and a half million copies, or one for every two inhabitants. Swedish dailies average fewer pages than their American counterparts but publish about the same amount of news and devote considerably more space to general cultural subjects. The largest newspaper in the country, *Dagens Nyheter*, with a daily circulation of 300,000, is generally considered to be one of the best journals in Europe. Though it is owned by Bonnier, the largest publishing combine in Sweden, its editor in chief, Professor Tingsten, is the real boss of the paper. Recently he expressed his concern to me about newspaper chains in other countries forcing their editors to write according to orders from the management. Such a practice, he maintained, would be unthinkable in Sweden where, he said, it is taken for granted that the editor is the real head of the paper.

The Swedish press, except for the organs of the Labor party and the Communists, is mostly privately owned. As elsewhere in the North, nearly all papers back a political party but their political influence is by no means in proportion to their circulation. The Liberal press, for instance, has 48 per cent of the newspaper circulation but receives only 21 per cent of the vote. The Labor press has only 17 per cent of the circulation but polls 48 per cent of the vote. In other words, most people who vote for the Socialists don't bother to read the Socialist press. Apparently they prefer to read the "bourgeois" papers, which give them more news and features but which obviously do not influence them politically.

The freedom of the press in Sweden is guaranteed by the Constitution and by statutes in law, but this freedom was somewhat curtailed during the Second World War due to pressure from Berlin. Reviving an old statute which had been regarded as defunct, the government, presided over by a Labor prime minister, confiscated a good many editions which contained allegedly derogatory comments on Nazi German leaders from Hitler on down. Whether this bow to Hitler really appeased the Fuehrer is to be doubted, judging by my own observations in Berlin at the time. In all fairness, it must be added that newspapers containing violently pro-Nazi pieces were also confiscated.

Such is Sweden, a homogeneous nation of rather industrious, self-reliant, reasonable men and women, practical and yet not without idealism, and who have reason to be proud of the society they have built and the good life it has provided not for the few but for the many.

They are not without human faults. A century ago Bayard Taylor described the Swedish people as friendly, decent, but stiff and conventional, with a weakness for everything foreign, and envious among themselves. He noted the complicated system of titles by which they addressed each other, their fondness for schnapps, convivial singing and banqueting and gymnastics.

A Swedish author has recently observed that this description is not too much out of date,[21] though my own impression is that while Taylor would not feel exactly lost if he were to return to Sweden today, he would be amazed at the changes. Political and social democracy has revolutionized Swedish society, though not even two decades of Labor rule nor fifty years of the growing co-operative movement have completely melted the stiffness and the conventional in the Swedish temperament, nor abolished by any means class distinctions and the fondness for identifying everyone by their professional titles.[22]

One finds a certain morose streak in these admirable people.[23] Gustavus Vasa is said to have described his Swedes as "a slow people, full of passions." Oscar Levertin, a Swedish author, has written of the loneliness and eternal longing of the Swedes.

One foreign diplomat in Stockholm explained to me what he thought was a historical reason for certain Swedish characteristics, and in doing so attempted the difficult — if not impossible — task of summing up the differing qualities of the three Scandinavian peoples.

"For centuries," said he, "the Norwegians faced West and liked what they saw. Their contacts were mainly with the English, and later the Americans — that is, with Anglo-Saxon civilization. The Norwegians became an individualistic and spontaneous people. The

[21] *Introduction to Sweden.* (See Appendix.)

[22] The formality of the Swedes is perhaps best illustrated by their use of the third person plural in direct address to anyone they don't know or to anyone who has a slightly higher official rating. Thus, if a Swede in a train wanted to ask the time he would not say "Could you tell me the time, please?" but "Will my fellow-passenger have the goodness to tell me the time?" using the third person plural verb form.

[23] The annual suicide rate in Sweden is 16 per 100,000 inhabitants — somewhat higher than that of the United States, which is 10.

Swedes faced East and did not much like what they saw — the Russians. They fought with them over the centuries, and perhaps the battle is not yet over. This experience tended to make them reserved and gloomy. The Danes are closer to the heart of the continent of Europe and are thus somewhat more cosmopolitan and European than the Swedes and Norwegians."

Be that as it may, the Swedes have achieved a way of life that places them high indeed among the civilized peoples of the West. They seem to have taken to heart the advice of Ovid: "You will go most safely in the middle."

Postscript

In Stockholm you find the headquarters of what is undoubtedly the most successful example of Scandinavian co-operation on a practical, commercial level — the Scandinavian Airlines System.

No country of seven millions such as Sweden, not to mention lands of three or four millions such as Norway and Denmark, has the resources to operate a world airline. But even before the last war was over, a remarkable group of far-sighted, imaginative Swedes, Norwegians and Danes became convinced that their three little countries could do it together. So confident were they that, even before any company had been formed and while Denmark and Norway still lay under the Nazi occupation, they placed the first contract for post-war DC-4's on Thanksgiving Day, 1943, in the Douglas offices in Santa Monica, California. To help bind the deal, the occupied Danes smuggled out a guarantee of $750,000 from the National Bank of Denmark. Before the war had come to an end the Scandinavians had also negotiated landing rights in New York with the American government.

Today, after overcoming incredible difficulties — political, national, ideological and financial — SAS, as the Scandinavian Airlines System is known, is the fifth largest of the world's 230 commercial airlines, plying routes to the five continents, serving 69 cities in 40 countries and linking the Scandinavian capitals to the United States, South America, South Africa, the Near and the Far East, as well as to the rest of the European continent and England. In a typical year (1953) SAS carries 670,000 passengers and flies 59,000,000 paid miles and does a total business of $45,000,000 showing a gross profit of $5,000,000.

SAS represents a typical Scandinavian compromise. It is an amalgamation of the Danish, Norwegian and Swedish national airlines into a consortium of which Sweden controls three sevenths and Norway and Denmark each two sevenths. Each nation's participation is made up of 50 per cent private capital and 50 per cent government capital. Actually a group of free-enterprisers who pioneered the formation of the company hold the key management positions, but half the board members are appointed by the respective governments, so that Socialist planners sit next to such financial tycoons as Sweden's Marcus Wallenberg and not only get along but share a common pride at the phenomenal growth each year of this strangest of all Scandinavian enterprises. The official language of SAS, incidentally, is English.

Having linked Scandinavia by conventional air routes with the leading cities of the five continents, SAS is now busy pioneering short cuts to Los Angeles and Tokyo over the North Pole.

Ever since the old Vikings pushed across the northern seas to Greenland and America, long before Columbus, the Scandinavians have been exploring the arctic paths. In 1906 Roald Amundsen, the great Norwegian explorer, forced his little ship *Gjöa* through the Northwest Passage at the tip of North America. He had hoped to open a new shipping route between Europe and America's West Coast and Asia, but his three-year voyage convinced him that this was not practical. There was too much ice. The going was too slow.

Exactly two decades later, in 1926, he flew the airship *Norge* from Spitsbergen to Alaska *over* the Northwest Passage, discovering that if seagoing vessels could not profitably traverse the polar route, airships and planes could. Others soon began to prove it. Sir Hubert Wilkins in 1928 flew a plane from Point Barrow, Alaska, to Spitsbergen. In 1938 the Russians twice flew planes from Moscow to the West Coast of America, demonstrating to the public that the shortest and quickest route from the Soviet capital to San Francisco and Los Angeles was over the North Pole — a fact that became rather ominous a few years later with the knowledge that the Soviet Union was producing atomic and hydrogen bombs.

Recently SAS has shown that the northern route is practicable for commercial flying. Until 1952 it was not feasible because the great distances between airfields prevented airliners from carrying a pay load. But with the opening up in 1952 of the United States Air Force base at Thule in Greenland, the dreams that the engineers and management of SAS had been entertaining suddenly came true. Two chartered flights in 1952 and a third in 1953 — all with DC–6B's — showed that pay loads could be successfully flown from Los Angeles to Oslo, Copenhagen and Stockholm in 18 hours of flying time, a saving of at least 10 hours over the conventional route from our West Coast via New York.

In 1953 SAS flew a DC–6B, chartered by the Norwegian Defense Department to carry relief personnel to the Norwegian Field Hospital in Korea, from Oslo to Tokyo over the Northwest Passage in 34 hours and 55 minutes of flying time. SAS engineers say this can be cut to about 30 hours, thus saving 15 hours over the present route in the opposite direction via Rome and Bangkok.

The Scandinavians point out that more is saved here than merely a day's time for busy passengers between Scandinavia and Los Angeles or Tokyo. Lower fares are made possible by the shorter distance. And airlines can achieve further economies by being able to utilize their planes and personnel better over the shorter routes.

Commercial flights over the polar wastes require, of course, new navigational instruments and techniques, since the magnetic compass does not function in the proximity of the magnetic North Pole. The Pfund's Sky Compass, one of the most important inventions in this field, enables the navigator to take course instructions on the sun when it is below the horizon by means of the polarized light in the sky. The Greenwich Grid System and the method of gyro steering are, of course, the basic foundation of polar navigation.

For SAS's first commercial flight from Los Angeles to Copenhagen by way of Edmonton, Canada, and Thule in November, 1952, Eclipse-Pioneer constructed a special gyro-system called the "Polar Path" control system. It consisted of an extremely precise directional gyro which could be linked electrically to the PB–10 automatic pilot and so steer independently of magnetic influences.

In spite of all technical advances, however, the stars, SAS pilots emphasize, are still the best aids to navigation in the Arctic.

SAS found that winter is the best time to fly the Arctic route, for two reasons: the weather is more stable than during the summer and navigation is easier because the stars may be used day and night. The entire flight from Edmonton to Copenhagen was made in darkness.

The United States government raised one stumbling block for a time to the plans of the Scandinavians to provide regular commercial air service over the Arctic between Los Angeles and Oslo, Copenhagen and Stockholm. SAS had hoped to inaugurate the scheduled service in May of 1954, but the authorities in Washington refused to give it terminal rights in Los Angeles. They suggested Seattle in its stead. This was because the domestic airlines wished to carry the Scandinavian-bound passengers themselves between the southern California metropolis and Seattle. But SAS, backed by the three northern governments, protested that the saving in time over the arctic route would be largely lost if passengers had to change planes in Seattle. Newspapers in Oslo, Stockholm and Copenhagen carried some strong editorials on the subject and the ambassadors in Washington of the three kingdoms called at the State Department and made a vigorous joint protest.

During the summer the American government offered to reconsider its stand and on August 6, after lengthy negotiations, an agreement was signed permitting SAS to use Los Angeles as its terminal for an experimental period of three years. Reciprocal rights for an American line to use the Arctic route were also given. Scandinavian Airlines immediately announced that it would begin in the fall a scheduled service over the arctic route, operating two weekly flights in each direction between Los Angeles and Copenhagen, with intermediary stops at Winnipeg and Greenland.

CHAPTER IV

Denmark

IT HAPPENED so quickly in the early morning hours of April 9, 1940, that there was no time for the easygoing Danes to take stock or to do anything about it. This ancient kingdom of four million pleasant, peaceful, rather sophisticated, and happy and harmonious people was overwhelmed by Hitler's barbarians in the course of a few hours. By 6 A.M., it was all over, and the bewildered King Christian X, in accordance with the decision of a dazed government, gave orders for what little armed resistance there was to cease.

Denmark, in truth, had no defense. The country was too small and flat, and the largest part, Jutland, lay open by land to Hitler's powerful Panzers. The idea of being able to hold out against a strong, aggressive neighbor such as Germany had long been given up by the Danes. The quick defeat in 1864 by Bismarck's Prussia, which had resulted in the loss of Schleswig and Holstein, had convinced the Danes of their helplessness in the face of a rising, militarist Germany. Neither the Swedes nor the Norwegians, despite all their romantic Scandinavianism, had come to Denmark's aid, as expected. Neither had France or Britain, despite their growing uneasiness over the Germans.

So the Danes abandoned the hope of finding survival in futile wars. They disarmed. In the 1920's even the fortifications of Copenhagen, the capital, were dismantled. Pacificism, neutrality and support of the League of Nations became the watchword. No wonder that Denmark fell, like overripe fruit from a tree, so easily to the Nazi hordes.

The lightninglike capitulation without a fight to the Third Reich and the five long years of Nazi occupation, during which it seemed to many Danes that the existence of the land as a sovereign nation had come to an end for good, marked the lowest ebb in the kingdom's centuries-old history which had seen Denmark, at times, the leading country of the North and one of the great powers of Europe. (In 1013 Denmark had conquered England and a Danish king had ruled over the forced union of the two countries.)

But there had been low points before this Nazi occupation, as every Dane recalled. There had been the long period of monarchial absolutism from 1660 to 1849. Long after most other monarchs in Western Europe had had their powers curbed by parliaments, the Danish king ruled under the Regal Law (*Kongeloven*), which has been called the most unequivocal formal delineation of absolutism found in the annals of mankind.[1] To even suggest a change in the Regal Law was considered treason, and the law itself forbade any amendments.

The opening years of the nineteeenth century saw Denmark sink into the depths of defeat, impoverishment and despair. In 1807 the British, ostensibly to forestall Napoleon, bombarded Copenhagen, reducing large parts of the capital to ruin. Denmark was forced to surrender its great fleet. King Frederick VI then made a catastrophic decision. He joined the war on Bonaparte's side. In 1813 the Danish State went bankrupt. The next year it was forced by the Allied coalition against Napoleon to cede Norway to Sweden after a union which, as we have seen, had lasted four hundred and fifty years.

The period which ensued, from 1814 to 1830, is described by Danish historians as the poorest in Denmark's modern history. The nation was bankrupt, the fleet surrendered, the beaten army disorganized, the national territory more than halved by the loss of Norway. Agriculture, deprived of the English and Norwegian markets, was paralyzed. Business was at a standstill.

Gradually over the next half-century the Danes strove to rebuild their shattered state. In 1814 a revolutionary Educational Act brought compulsory schooling for all children between six and fourteen. This act, by educating for the first time the children of the peasantry, which formed the overwhelming majority of the population, was to have great social, economic and political consequences. The July Revolution of 1830 in France induced King Frederick VI in 1834 to grant consultative provincial assemblies — the first breach in the royal absolutism which had long held Denmark back. The revolu-

[1] *The Democratic Monarchies of Scandinavia*, by Ben A. Arneson.

tionary fervor which swept Europe in 1848 forced Frederick VII to grant a free Constitution in 1849 which gave Denmark a parliamentary form of government based on equal suffrage, thus bringing an end, without a shot being fired, to a royal absolutism which had lasted for nearly two centuries.

With political freedom came prosperity on the farms and in business and shipping. But the country's comeback did not last for long. All through the century Denmark was plagued by the question of Schleswig and Holstein, of which Lord Palmerston once remarked that only three men had ever understood it. One was dead, another mad and the third, he himself, had forgotten what it was all about. The two duchies belonged to the Danish kingdom, though Holstein was also a member of the German Confederation, and except for North Schleswig, the population was predominantly German.

Now two wars were fought to decide their destiny. In 1848 the two duchies revolted and were assisted by Prussia until the great powers obliged the German state to withdraw. The Danes triumphed in a hard-fought war which lasted two years. But the triumph was short-lived. In 1864, Bismarck, the new leader of Prussia, persuaded Austria to join him in settling the question of Schleswig and Holstein once and for all. Austrian and Prussian troops, in overwhelming strength, crossed the Ejder and though the Danes fought stubbornly and valiantly (as they did not do, or were prevented from doing, in 1940) they were overwhelmed.

Denmark was forced to cede both duchies. This meant the loss of two-fifths of her territory and a million inhabitants, of whom 200,000 were Danes mostly concentrated in North Schleswig. Prussia promised that a plebiscite should later decide the fate of North Schleswig, but the promise was not kept. Half a century later the victorious Allies in the war against Germany remembered the promise and the Versailles Treaty called for the plebiscite. Some 75 per cent of the inhabitants voted for Denmark, which again took possession of North Schleswig in 1920.

The defeat of 1864 and the loss of Schleswig and Holstein appeared to doom Denmark once more to oblivion. An intense feeling of national humiliation and utter despair gripped the nation. Many felt that it must soon succumb completely to the power and appetite of the Prussians. Georg Brandes, the great literary critic, and the liberal intellectuals grouped around him, came to the conclusion that there was nothing left in Denmark upon which to build.

But this was an error in judgment. From some inner strength in the Danish people there now began an almost miraculous resurgence. Its source of inspiration was Bishop Nikolai Frederik Severin Grundtvig, a creative genius who became the spiritual founder of modern Denmark and one of the most remarkable men Europe threw up in the nineteenth century.

Grundtvig was a person of broad and heroic dimensions. He was a poet, preacher, historian, philosopher, educator, hymnist and statesman. Under the stress of violent mental conflicts, at least three times on the verge of insanity, he fought his way, as one Danish historian has put it, from one point of view to the other through poetry and philosophy, through mythology and history, to a living Christianity and a fiery belief that the Danish people, especially the peasants and workers, had it in themselves to live a decent, fruitful, Christian life. His stirring sermons, his inspiring hymns, his eloquent writings stirred the Danes from their torpor and despair.

And he was practical enough throughout his long and stormy life to see that, above all, the people must be educated if they were to understand their heritage and to participate intelligently in the mass cultural awakening and in the successful working of the new democratic way of life — not only in politics, but in economics, agriculture and social affairs.

It was Grundtvig who inspired the founding of the Danish Folk High Schools, that unique system of adult education which has helped transform not only Denmark but all the northern countries into one of the most literate and enlightened groups of societies on earth. They grew out of Grundtvig's conviction that children's schools were not enough, and neither were a few universities which, in his time, were principally concerned in turning out officials well versed in Latin and Greek. What was most needed, he thought, were schools for young adults, where farmers and workers could become educated to the duties, opportunities and responsibilities of citizenship and of their position in life.

"Only barbarians and tyrants," he said, "can imagine that this root and kernel of the people — tenants and freeholders, large farmers and small ones, workers of all kinds, sailors and tradesmen — does not need any more enlightenment than can be obtained behind the plow, in the workshop, on the boat and behind the counter."

Born in 1783, Grundtvig, a man of immense vitality, lived to be eighty-nine years old. He had a son by his second wife when he was seventy, and a daughter by his third wife when he was seventy-seven. Though he battled the academics, he was a noted scholar himself, learning German, English, Hebrew, Greek, Latin and Old Norse in order to be able to go directly to the original sources for his historical works. He performed, says one Danish historian, the work of three generations. He left a mark on Denmark — and indeed on all the North — that still shows indelibly today.

"From 1864, when the Prussians licked us, until recently, we have had no foreign policy except a burning desire to be left alone." Thus a Danish historian summed up Denmark's position to me, during a conversation in Copenhagen.

For a considerable time the little kingdom's wishes were respected. Prussia turned on bigger game: on Austria in 1866 and on France in 1870. Denmark was left alone to try once more to recoup her fortunes in peace.

Her progress was immediate and rapid, despite bitter internal political struggles. For a time the Conservatives, led by the large landowners, managed to set the clock back. In 1866 they succeeded in getting rid of the free Constitution and substituting a new and less liberal one, which enhanced their powers, especially in the Upper House of Parliament. Though reduced by 1884 to a small minority in the Lower House, whose members were elected by direct suffrage, the Conservatives, backed by the King, refused to resign from office. It was not until 1901, when they were outnumbered 90 to 8 in the Lower House, that the Conservatives and the King gave way and true parliamentary government was restored. The intense struggle for political power between the two Houses of the Danish Rigsdag, incidentally, came to an end during my stay in Denmark when the citizens, in a nationwide plebiscite, voted to *abolish* the Upper House and transform Parliament into a unicameral legislature whose members were elected directly by popular vote.

In the midst of violent political strife, however, trade, industry and, above all, agriculture began to flourish. Farming was the backbone of the nation, which possessed no coal, oil or iron of its own.

Export of grain, principally to England, was the basis of Danish prosperity. Then in the 1870's, Denmark's agriculture was threatened with catastrophe. The opening up of grain exports from North America and Russia brought prices down by half in the world markets. Danish farmers, with their relatively small plots, simply could not meet such competition. Their answer to it was to revolutionize their centuries-old agriculture. Overnight they turned to raising pigs, poultry and cows for the production of bacon and eggs and butter. Today these are the products which are the basis of Denmark's economy, whose export enables her to pay for an expanding industry and trade, and which have brought her as high a standard of living as you find anywhere in Europe.

The revolution in Danish agriculture which preserved the nation could not have been carried out had it not been for three fundamental developments. First, the freeing of the peasants from their feudal obligations and their establishment as independent farmers owning and working their own land. Second, the high degree of education of the farmers as the result of the Folk High Schools and the Agricultural Colleges. Third, the setting up by their own voluntary collective action of the most remarkable agricultural co-operatives in the world.

By the turn of the century Denmark was well on the way to becoming what it is today: a farmer's co-operative commonwealth. It was not an idyllic paradise. But it was a good and healthy society. Its only requirement was that it be left in peace.

The First World War threatened that position. But Denmark, like Norway and Sweden, managed to survive as a neutral. In fact, the Danes, as did the other Scandinavians, managed to get along fairly well during the war by trading with both sides.

The period between the beginning of the first war and the advent of the second was marked by enlightened reforms — political and social — in Denmark. The Liberals (or Radicals as they were called in Denmark) and later the Social-Democrats dominated politics. In 1915 a more liberal Constitution was enacted providing universal suffrage for both men and women over twenty-five in the elections to the Lower House. The right of the king to nominate members for the Upper House was abolished, and this citadel of the Conservatives became more representative and democratic through a system of indirect election by citizens over thirty-five.

Also during the war the judiciary system was modernized, local government completely democratized, entail and feoffment abolished, a third of the holdings of the big estates broken up and given to farmers who would themselves work the soil, state regulation of business and finance instituted and industrial-labor legislation, including the eight-hour day, introduced.

But the first war's end brought trouble. There was an economic crisis, a general lockout and a general strike. There was ferment in the urban masses as the result of the German and Russian Revolutions. The Social-Democrats demanded the abolition of the Upper House, disarmament, nationalization of communications and monopolies, progressive taxation and more social security legislation. In 1920, when the King abruptly dismissed the Radical government of C. T. Zahle, the Socialists called for a Republic and the trade-unions decreed a general strike in support of it. Denmark seemed on the verge of a revolution. But cooler heads on all sides prevailed, an interim compromise government of civil servants was set up, and by 1924, when the Socialists emerged for the first time as the largest political party, the country was quiet enough to accept its first Labor government under Thorvald Stauning without anything untoward happening.

Prime Minister from 1924 to 1926 and from 1929 until his death in 1942 during the German occupation, Stauning, who began life as a cigar sorter and union organizer, overshadowed all other political figures in Denmark for a generation. A bluff, bearded Viking, vigorous, forceful and shrewd, he was essentially, like most Scandinavian Labor party leaders, a man of the middle and in foreign politics he was especially cautious. His tragedy, like that of most Scandinavian and European statesmen of the time, was that he thought Hitler's Germany might be appeased. He refused stubbornly to rearm or to consider the possibilities, slim as they were, of a united Scandinavian defense against Germany, remarking in a speech at Lund University in Sweden in 1937: "Denmark is not the watchdog of Scandinavia." He gambled to the end on Hitler's good will. The German invasion and occupation broke him in spirit, though he continued doggedly in office until his death.

But it was under his guiding spirit that the great social reforms of the 1930's which transformed Denmark into a welfare state were achieved. On the whole, Denmark was a nation of contented, well-fed, civilized people, with no concern except to go about their business and improve their lot, content to leave world politics to the great powers, when tragedy struck suddenly on the night between April 8 and 9 of 1940.

The Nazi Conquest of Denmark

Warnings to the government in Copenhagen from the Danish legation in Berlin became more and more ominous that spring. Yet Denmark (like Norway) did nothing about them. True, there was not much a pacifist, unarmed, unfortified country of four millions could do against the might of the Third Reich. But it is strange that Denmark did even less to protect herself than she had done in 1914 when the Kaiser's Germany threatened her.

In that year Denmark had mobilized 55,000 troops. At the beginning of the Second World War in 1939 it had called up 32,000 men. Curiously, as the danger from Hitler increased the size of Denmark's army decreased. When the Germans struck with one armored division and 80,000 men, the Danish army numbered just 14,000 men, half of them raw recruits.

Possibly Prime Minister Stauning and Foreign Minister Munch, both of whom had staunchly opposed the slightest rearmament, believed in the nonaggression treaty which they had signed with Germany on May 31, 1939. Hitler, egged on by Roosevelt, had offered such pacts to all the four northern countries that year, but only Denmark had accepted.

On April 4, 1940, the Danish Minister in Berlin, whose reports of imminent danger seemed to leave his superiors in Copenhagen strangely unmoved, sent his naval attaché, Captain Kjölsen, home to warn the government that all signs pointed to the Nazis' attacking Denmark within a few days. Even this dire warning fell on deaf ears. The Danes just couldn't believe it. Four days later, on April 8, they saw with their own eyes a German naval force of one hundred ships steaming northward through the Great Belt between the islands of Fyn and Zealand. On the same day came reports of large concentrations of German troops and armor along the Danish border in Jutland.

General W. W. Prior, the Danish Commander in Chief, who in the next twenty-four hours was to be one of the few in authority to insist on fighting, however hopeless the odds, demanded immediate mobilization. But the complacent Stauning would hear none of it. The most he was willing to do was to order certain security measures and to place the under-strength army in a state of readiness for action. Even these inadequate precautionary measures were not carried out because that afternoon the German envoy called on the Danish Foreign Minister and protested that such military measures would be an inexcusable affront to the friendly German nation! He assured Mr. Munch that all reports of threatening German troop movements were false. Germany, he said, would never attack Denmark. Didn't they have a nonaggression treaty?

A few hours later, at 4 A.M. on April 9, the same German Minister called on the same Mr. Munch and while German bombers roared overhead informed him that in order to forestall a British invasion of Denmark, German troops were at this moment crossing the Danish border in Jutland and landing on the principal islands. Germany, he assured the Danish Foreign Minister, was doing this merely to protect Denmark. If there were no resistance Germany would guarantee Denmark's territorial integrity, political independence and neutrality and would neither interfere in domestic affairs nor erect fortifications or bases on Danish soil.

While the Nazi diplomat was at the Foreign Office pronouncing Denmark's doom, German troops were landing from an innocent-looking freighter a few blocks away in Copenhagen's harbor. The vessel, disguised as a coal ship, had passed the coastal forts manned by the navy without being challenged, much less fired upon. In fact, Admiral Rechnitzer, commander of the Danish navy, in contrast to General Prior, apparently had no intention of molesting the Germans. Neither his ships nor his naval installations on shore fired a shot throughout the length and breadth of the island kingdom.

The German troopship moored without interference at the Langelinie quay and small detachments immediately set out for two nearby objectives: the citadel, whose fortifications had long been dismantled but which served as army headquarters, and the Royal Palace of Amalienborg. At the citadel the Germans planned to capture the army commander in chief; at the palace, of course, the King.

But General Prior, who had been convoked before daybreak to the

War Ministry, which was already choked with bad news, left the citadel a step ahead of the Germans and thus avoided capture. At the War Ministry he soon realized, among other things, that the Germans were about to seize the King. He thereupon called out the Royal Life Guards, ordered the issue of live ammunition to them and instructed them to resist the Germans. Then he hurried to the Palace.

Amalienborg Palace lies but a short distance up the harbor from the citadel. Of pleasing rococo design, it consists actually of four palaces, built around a spacious square and overlooking the port. Shortly after 4 A.M. on April 9, King Christian X was awakened and told that the Prime Minister had arrived with some important information. As he hurriedly dressed he saw through the window that the Life Guards were being issued live ammunition and thus knew, as one aide later put it, that something serious was afoot.

He was greatly surprised. According to Lieutenant Colonel Th. Thaulow, a Guards officer and a confidant of the King,[2] the royal table on the previous day had certainly been full of talk about the war, but it was mostly about a German troop transport which had been torpedoed off the south coast of Norway (just north of Denmark) and about the Nazi naval ships which that day had steamed through the Belt seemingly bound for Norway. When someone at the table expressed the fear that Germany might invade Denmark instead of Norway, the King had dismissed the idea with a smile.

"He really didn't believe that," Colonel Thaulow later reported. In fact, according to this Guards officer, the King had gone that evening, "confident and happy," to the Royal Theater.

Now a few hours later he was being informed by a startled prime minister that it really had happened. Shots that began to be heard at the approaches of the palace emphasized that the unbelievable news was true. The handful of Life Guards was going into action. They easily repulsed the first attempt of a German detachment to take the palace.

Upstairs the King was conferring with his Prime Minister, Foreign Minister and his military leaders. Only General Prior urged that the Danes fight. Colonel Thaulow says that the King asked "whether our soldiers had fought long enough," and that General Prior answered that in his opinion they had not. In fact, the General urged that the

[2] *Denmark During the Occupation.* Copenhagen.

royal family and government should leave for the nearest military camp at Høvelte to escape capture. Though General Prior did not know it, this was approximately, as we have seen, what the Norwegians were doing in Oslo at precisely the same hour.

The case of the Danes was, of course, much more hopeless. The King and government had no mountains to flee to, nor could they expect help from England as could the Norwegians. In January that year Winston Churchill had made that plain when he told a group of Scandinavian journalists: "Sweden and Norway have a ditch across which they can feed the tiger, but Denmark is so terribly close to Germany that it would be impossible [for us] to bring aid."

At any rate, the King and the government believed that the situation was completely hopeless and that further sacrifices of Danish blood would be a futile and inexcusable gesture. At 6 A.M. the King, in accord with the government but against the advice of the army commander in chief, ordered all resistance to the Germans to cease.

The fighting around the palace stopped, as did a few minutes later the skirmishes in Jutland where the main German blow had fallen and where detachments of one Danish division had put up sporadic resistance.

Before most Danes had finished their hearty breakfasts the occupation was complete. And it had been one of the most lightning conquests of a sovereign power in history. It was over before the good-natured civilians of this kingdom knew what had happened. Later, when they learned of Norway's gallant resistance, a feeling of shame and guilt came over many of them. Yet the majority felt that the King and government had taken the most civilized course. This feeling was strengthened two months later when they saw not only Norway but Holland and Belgium and even France go down. What good, they asked, had it done these other peoples to fight? The spilling of blood, the snuffing out of many lives, had not saved them from subjugation to the Nazi Germans.

The "Model Protectorate"

At first the Germans made quite a fuss about occupied Denmark being a "model protectorate," and they behaved with relative — and unexpected — decency. Because the Danes had not really resisted, as had the scrappy, unreasonable Norwegians, and because the Stauning government promptly promised "loyal co-operation," Hitler appeared in the beginning anxious to show the world that there were rewards for nations wise enough not to try to defy Teutonic might.

The King, the government and Parliament were ostensibly allowed to function. The administration of justice and even the censorship of press and radio were ostensibly left in Danish hands. Not even Denmark's 7000 Jews were molested — at first. Despite the Fuehrer's loathing of it, democracy, apparently, was to be allowed to exist in Denmark. It was not long before a majority of Danes began to believe that they were still sovereign and that the occupation, though unpleasant, was not so bad after all.

Prime Minister Stauning, who had brought the opposition Conservatives into a coalition government, was quite accommodating. To some Danes he often seemed more than that: he seemed unnecessarily obsequious. This lifelong Socialist never tired of appealing to his countrymen for loyal co-operation with the Germans. By the end of the year, he was describing Denmark as the happiest country in Europe. On New Year's, 1941, he expressed agreement with the German lie that the Nazis had only occupied Denmark to forestall the British. In the spring of 1941 he was quite prepared to recognize Hitler's preposterous "New Order" in which Denmark, he said, would co-operate "quietly and willingly." In November, 1941, he signed, under pressure from Berlin, to be sure, the Anti-Comintern Pact, which aligned "neutral" Denmark with the Berlin-Rome-Tokyo Axis.

He was enthusiastically supported in these policies by another strong man, Erik Scavenius, whom he had brought into the coalition government to replace Foreign Minister Munch after the surrender. Scavenius had been the pro-German Foreign Minister during the First World War. Even his enemies, of whom I found many in Denmark, doubt, however, that he was ever pro-anything. A man of arrogant mind, who believed that almost all Danes were living in a sort of Hans Christian Andersen fairyland oblivious to the realities of the world which he himself saw so clearly, Scavenius was certain that Germany would win the war and rule Europe and that it was his duty to procure for Denmark as good a place as possible in the "New Order." To his credit it must be said that unlike almost all other "collaborationists" he never attempted later to deny what he had done. From the first, his attitude was that if by any chance he proved wrong, he would take the responsibility.

John Danstrup, a young Danish historian, offers an interesting explanation of why even those leaders of the democratic parties who detested the Germans approved the official policy of accommodation and co-operation with the conquerors.[3] They hoped that by doing so they could prevent the *Danish* Nazis from taking over and destroying the fabric of national democratic life from within. In the 1939 election the Nazis had won 2 per cent of the votes and captured three seats in the Parliament. Their leader, Frits Clausen, was a joke. But behind the ragged group of Danish Nazis, Danstrup says, "waited the activist agrarian wing and people with capital and influence who at the opportune moment would jump over the fence. They were preparing a Nazi coup with the support of the German Embassy."

It never came off, despite extensive German aid, thanks to the alertness of the democratic parties, which joined together in a Committee of Nine to thwart the Nazi designs. In a free national election held in the spring of 1943 in which 90 per cent of all registered voters cast their ballots, the Danish Nazi party again received only 2 per cent of the votes. The Danes affirmed their adherence to a democratic system. Before many more months passed, the period of collaboration between the royal government and the Nazi regime would come to an abrupt end.

From the very first there had been a few Danes in high office who had declined to believe in the officially sponsored fiction that the royal government of Denmark exercised true sovereignty under the Nazi occupation. The foremost of these was Henrik Kauffmann, Danish Minister in Washington. With a personal courage and foresight shared at the time by no other Dane in such an official position, he dared to defy his King and his government, not to mention Adolf Hitler, for the ultimate good of his country and the Allied cause. Because his strange story has never before been fully told, it shall be set down, briefly, here.

[3] In his *History of Denmark* (Copenhagen), and in conversation with the author.

The Case of Henrik Kauffmann

Kauffmann had been in his post as Danish Minister to the United States scarcely a year when his native land was overrun by the Germans. His reaction to it was immediate, clear-cut and, considering his position, courageous. It got him into difficulties with his King and government from the very first.

A few hours after the Danish capitulation in Copenhagen he went on the air in Washington and broadcast that as representative of his King and country, he would work for one thing alone: the re-establishment of a free and independent Denmark. Strange as it may seem, that pledge did not go down well in government circles at home. They were already deluding themselves that Hitler had left Denmark free and independent; there was nothing for the Minister to re-establish.

The Danish envoy's press conference the same day displeased the Copenhagen government even more. He was peppered with some very blunt questions by fifty newsmen. Would he obey instructions from Copenhagen which originated from the Danish Foreign Office but which to him were clearly due to German pressure?

"Certainly not!" he answered.

And he added — most undiplomatically, the staid Danish Foreign Office must have thought — that he found himself in the same position as a man whose father had been kidnapped by *gangsters*. Such a man had to use his own best judgment as to how to proceed; and that was exactly what he intended to do.

Kauffmann freely admits that he disobeyed his government's orders from the very first day of the Nazi occupation. He was told on that day to instruct Danish ships to attempt to reach neutral ports, preferably those in lands friendly to Germany such as Spain and Italy. Instead, he advised them to go to Allied harbors or to remain in American ports. It was plain to him, if not to his superiors in Copenhagen, that Denmark was no longer free, that its decisions were made under duress and were therefore not valid — at least insofar as he was concerned. He so informed both his own government, which refused to believe him, and the American government, which though still neutral, did believe him.

He was quite sure he would be fired forthwith. Actually his dismissal did not come for a year, not until he had taken the unprecedented step on April 9, 1941 — the first anniversary of the occupation — of signing an agreement with Secretary of State Cordell Hull providing for the United States to take over the defense of Greenland until Denmark became free. In this historic treaty the United States freely recognized the sovereignty of Denmark over Greenland. And Minister Kauffmann, in a cablegram to Copenhagen, carefully explained that he signed the agreement "acting on behalf of the King of Denmark in his capacity as Sovereign of Greenland."

Kauffmann admits that "various legal doubts could be raised about the constitutional validity of the Greenland Agreement." "But Hitler," he reminds you, "had created a situation without any precedent, and one would have been badly handicapped if one felt strictly bound by precedent."

The reaction of King Christian and his government in Copenhagen to the Greenland agreement was highly explosive. The Greenland Treaty was denounced as void, and Kauffmann was immediately recalled and ordered to return to Copenhagen at once, his place to be taken temporarily by a Mr. E. Blechingberg, Counsellor of Legation, as Chargé d'Affaires.

Henrik Kauffmann refused to be fired. He declined to step down even when his Foreign Minister, the inimitable Scavenius, so ordered. He even defied his King, to whom he had given the oath of allegiance, when he tried to get rid of him — and Christian X certainly tried. For a Danish diplomat of conservative bent and aristocratic background such as Kauffmann to disobey his King was unheard of; and to have to do so sorely tried the Minister. Soon he had to bear the humiliation of being openly disowned by the monarch. His own government officially denounced him as "being guilty of abuse of the King's name" and with having set up what it called "the Kauffmann Usurper Government" in opposition to "the lawful government appointed by the King."

There now followed one of the most extraordinary diplomatic exchanges of the war. This took place, it can now be revealed, not only between the foreign secretaries of the two countries, Cordell Hull and Erik Scavenius, but between the heads of state, King Christian X and President Roosevelt.

On April 19, 1941, the President, addressing the King as "Great and Good Friend," acknowledges a letter from the monarch apprising him of Kauffmann's dismissal, but replies rather bluntly that "Mr. de Kauffmann remains in the view of the Government of the United States the representative of the Royal Danish Government in this country." Furthermore the President assures the King that Greenland will be held in trust until such time as the Danish government "ceases to be subjected to duress on the part of an occupying nation."

On April 26 the King replies, addressing President Roosevelt as "Dear and Great Friend." "I am anxious to let you know," says Christian X — the letter is countersigned by Scavenius — "that the news about these unjustified measures (regarding Greenland) have caused Me deep disappointment and grief." And he goes on to say:

> I have instructed My Minister for Foreign Affairs to further develop to Your Secretary of State the points which Your message occasions Me to emphasize, viz: *That* My former Envoy Extraordinary and Minister Plenipotentiary Mr. Henrik Kauffmann by arbitrarily signing the agreement . . . on the defense of Greenland has exceeded his authority as Accredited Minister and has acted against the Danish Constitution, for which reason he has no more My confidence, *that* the said agreement is invalid in point of Danish constitutional as well as international law . . . , *that* Mr. Kauffmann after his dismissal from the public service is a private person without any authority whatsoever to represent Denmark, and *that* it would not chime in with Our mutual wishes for maintaining all ties that may promote Dano-American interests, if the Government of the United States continues to recognize him as Denmark's official representative, as this would be tantamount to rendering diplomatic contact between Denmark and the United States at Washington impossible and thus a very important tie would be broken.

Ten days later, on May 5, President Roosevelt answers his "Great and Good Friend." His tone is firmer.

> I am greatly distressed that Your Majesty has found it necessary to characterize as unjustified the measures which the Government of the United States deems it essential to take no less in the interests of Your Majesty's sovereignty over Greenland than for the protection of the Western Hemisphere. I trust that I am not mis-

informed as to the true feelings of deep friendship and of common ideals which the people of Denmark have for the United
States of America or that they have any doubt that the Government of the United States will not live up to its undertakings with
respect to Your Majesty's sovereignty over Greenland.

The President notes "with regret" His Majesty's statement that
it is inexpedient to deal "through Mr. de Kauffmann even though
this Government recognizes him as Minister of Denmark at Washington." That recognition, Mr. Roosevelt makes clear, will continue, but
if the King prefers he may deal henceforth through the American
Chargé d'Affaires in Copenhagen. That was the only concession the
President would make.

In the meantime Counsellor Blechingberg has broken with his chief
in the Danish Legation in Washington. On May 13, on orders from
the Danish Foreign Office, he tries to fire the Danish consul-generals
in New York, Chicago and San Francisco because they have sided with
Kauffmann. Like their Minister, the consul-generals decline to be
fired. And on June 3, Secretary Hull backs them up, as he has Kauffmann, by notifying Scavenius that the United States "would find it
out of the question to recognize any other person, or any other diplomatic officer . . . except Mr. de Kauffmann." A few days later the
discouraged Mr. Blechingberg packs his bags and, accompanied by two
vice-consuls of similar mind, returns to Copenhagen.

Finally on December 12, 1941, the Danish Government addresses a
Note Verbale to the United States full of bitterness and sarcasm. It
expresses the "greatest anxiety" that the United States would appear to be recognizing two Danish governments, "one being the lawful Government appointed by the King, recognized by the people,
and domiciled in Denmark, at which foreign powers (including the
U.S.A.) maintain legations, the other being the 'Kauffmann usurper
Government' which on the basis of certain ideas of duress . . . has
obtained the authority which the lawful Government in Copenhagen would normally be able to exercise through its (law-abiding)
Minister in Washington."

The note reiterates what Scavenius and the King had stoutly
maintained in their communications to Washington, that the "lawful
Danish Government . . . composed of all the great political parties
. . . is directing all affairs in the country. In all essential respects the
powers of State — legislative, judiciary and executive — [continue] to

function independently and without interference from the occupying power."

This of course was not true, as Kauffmann and Hull and Roosevelt were sure. No king and government under the Nazi heel could possibly be free, sovereign and independent. But it was not until after the war that specific proof of the lie, in so far as it concerned Kauffmann, was forthcoming. A damaging German document was uncovered.

It revealed that on April 12, 1941, as soon as Berlin heard of Kauffmann's signing of the Greenland Treaty with the United States, the German government sent a six-point ultimatum to the Danish Government. Germany demanded:

"1. A formal declaration whether the King or any member of the Danish government had any previous knowledge whatsoever of Kauffmann's signing the Greenland Treaty.

"2. The immediate recall of Kauffmann by the King.

"3. The immediate dispatch of a note to the American Chargé d'Affaires in Copenhagen in which Minister Kauffmann must be completely disavowed, his recall confirmed, the Greenland agreement declared void and the sharpest protest made against the American action.

"4. A public statement to the Press by the Danish Government stating that Minister Kauffmann acted against the will of the King and government and without authority, that his recall is a consequence, and that the Treaty is void and that the sharpest protest against the American action has been made."

All these demands the Danish King and Government promptly obeyed, while maintaining to the United States that they were acting on their own on behalf of a "free, independent and sovereign Denmark"!

Two German demands were not carried out. One ordered a law taking away Danish citizenship and confiscating all property of any Dane abroad who acted against "the interests of Denmark or the decrees of the Danish government." The second commanded the Danish government to take legal proceeding against Kauffmann for treason and to deprive him of his citizenship.

Neither Christian X nor Scavenius would go so far, but there is no doubt that Minister Kauffmann was in disgrace with the King and government, which he had sworn to serve and which, from the highest motives of patriotism, he found himself forced to disobey.[4] He was aware that many persons at home, especially among the complacent politicians and government officials, took a high critical attitude toward his conduct. Some agreed with the Germans that he was a traitor.

His vindication, of course, came in the end with Allied victory and the liberation of Denmark. It was complete and to him it must have been sweet.

He was named a member of the "Liberation Government," which consisted of nine representatives of the political parties and an equal number from the Resistance. He was one of the representatives of the Resistance abroad.

Returning home a few days after the liberation, he was immediately received by the King who had tried so unsuccessfully to sack him, and thanked by the monarch for what he had done for the country. The King officially reinstated him in his position as Danish Minister in Washington. On May 16, 1945, the Danish Parliament *unanimously* ratified the Greenland Treaty, which he had signed four years before on his own hook. And, finally, he was officially confirmed as Chairman of the Danish delegation to the United Nations Conference in San Francisco, where he won Denmark's recognition as an Allied power.

He remains today Denmark's ambassador in Washington, a modest, charming and popular figure in the capital.

The Not So Model Protectorate — 1943-1945

The year 1943 marked the end of the loyal co-operation of occupied Denmark with Nazi Germany and the beginning of a serious Danish Resistance movement. Later than the other conquered peoples, the Danes finally came to the realization that further compromise with the Teutonic tyrants was imposssible, if they were to retain any shred of self-respect and honor.

True, the changing fortunes of the war that year undoubtedly helped to bring the Danes to their senses. With the exception of the

[4] His only property in Denmark, consisting of securities deposited in a bank, was confiscated, and the Minister of Justice, as Kauffmann learned after the war, gave orders for his arrest as soon as he set foot on Danish soil.

incurable Scavenius, Danish politicians began to see that Germany might not win the war after all and that little Denmark was not inexorably condemned to be a vassal state in Hitler's unspeakable New Order. But it was the growing brutality of the Germans in their dealings with the Danish government and people which brought the "model protectorate" to an end and, with the King and government finally declining to function further, culminated in a reign of terror by the Wehrmacht and Gestapo during the last two years of the occupation.

Already in December, 1941, the first Danish parachutists had been dropped from British planes to organize the Resistance. Within a year they had succeeded in setting up not only an espionage network with radio communication to London but in establishing sabotage groups to blow up railway lines and factories serving German military interests. By 1943, the organized sabotage was effective enough to provoke the Germans into demanding that the Danish government declare a state of emergency and hand over all saboteurs to German military courts. The government, which had now been taken over under German urging by Scavenius, as Prime Minister, thundered against the saboteurs. But the King, the Parliament and the government flatly rejected the German demands.

Now the workers began to revolt. Angered by the excesses of the "Schalburg Corps," a Danish S.S. outfit composed largely of ex-convicts — who had been recruited with the approval of Scavenius to fight for the Fuehrer on the Russian front, but who had been brought back to guard factories against sabotage — the workers called general strikes in Copenhagen and various other towns. The most serious one was at the shipyards at Odense, birthplace of Hans Christian Andersen. There a German officer lost his head, fired into the crowd, and was trampled to death by an infuriated mob. Sabotage spread all over Denmark and was especially effective in Jutland where rail lines were dynamited nightly.

On August 27, 1943, Dr. Werner Best, the Fuehrer's plenipotentiary in Denmark and a former S.S. officer, returned to Copenhagen from Hitler's headquarters and on the next day presented an ultimatum to the Danish government. He demanded that it proclaim a state of emergency, prohibit strikes and public assemblies, institute a curfew at 8:30 P.M., set up drumhead courts for violators of law, and impose the death penalty for sabotage, attacks on German troops and the possession of arms. "The Reich government," said Dr. Best, "expects the acceptance of these demands by the Danish government by 4 P.M. today."

It received, instead, an outright rejection of them. Even Scavenius was no longer able to carry the day for the Germans. The King congratulated his government on its decision.

At 4 A.M. on the following day, August 29, General Hannekin, the German military commander in Denmark, proclaiming that "the latest events have shown that the Danish government is no longer capable of maintaining law and order," formally took over power. He decreed a state of emergency, a curfew at nightfall, prohibition of public assembly and the death penalty for striking. He ordered the arrest of hundreds of prominent citizens as hostages. And finally he gave orders to overpower the Danish army and navy and intern its members.

Here the navy, under a new commander, Vice Admiral Vedel, regained some of the prestige it had lost by its inaction when Denmark was occupied. The Admiral ordered the scuttling of all naval vessels, and thanks to his secret and careful preparations the order was successfully carried out under the noses of the Germans. An attack was also made on the summer castle of the King at Sorgenfri, a few miles north of Copenhagen. Two German bullets penetrated a window in the King's study, but he was unharmed.

In Copenhagen, Dr. Best summoned the newspaper editors: "In this ridiculous little country," he scolded them, "the press has inoculated the people with the idea that Germany is weak. You thought you could give us everything from bombs to poison. You have received requital during the night. Each editor will be responsible with his head for seeing that the people are no longer poisoned."

After three curious years, the conquerors and the conquered had at last found each other out.

The Germans made one more attempt to obtain a Danish government that would do their bidding. On August 30, Dr. Best asked the ever-persevering Scavenius to form one. He was willing, but he could find no one else to join him. The King declared he would refuse to appoint any Cabinet not approved by the Rigsdag. From August 29, 1943, therefore, Denmark was governed by the German military, with a few Danish departmental heads merely maintaining a skeleton administration.

A new Danish government, however, was being formed underground.
That autumn the leaders of the four main Resistance organizations
joined together to form the Freedom Council. These groups were:
The Ring, a youth organization which had been established in 1941 by
a young philologist, Frode Jakobsen, and Christmas Møller, a Conservative party leader, who escaped to England in 1942; Free Denmark, an
all-party group which set up the underground press; *Dansk Samling*
(Danish Union) a nonparty, Christian organization which operated
both openly and underground; and the Communist party. Two special sabotage groups, the noncommunist *Holger Danske* and the Communist *Bopa*, also joined the Freedom Council, as did the Danish
leader of Special Forces, whose headquarters were in London. The
Council's M-Committee amalgamated the various military units and
established close contact with SHAEF, with Special Forces in London and with the Allied governments, including Russia.

One of the most effective leaders of the Freedom Council was a
quiet, contemplative, Communist professor of neurology at the university, Mogens Fog. Captured by the Gestapo in 1944, he failed to
break under torture and miraculously escaped in March, 1945, when a
pin-point R.A.F. bombing destroyed Gestapo headquarters in Copenhagen, where he was imprisoned. He immediately resumed his post
with the council.

The Danish Resistance movement, especially in the beginning, appears to have been predominantly a coalition of Communists and
Conservatives. The part the Communists played explains their popularity at the war's end, when in the first elections after the liberation
they gained 18 seats in Parliament, mostly at the expense of the Socialists, who — with notable exceptions — had refrained until near the
end from taking an active part in the Resistance. The Communist
strength would soon be dissipated, thanks to the truculence of the
Soviet Union and the subservience of Danish Communists to Moscow.
But the Communist record in the Resistance greatly impressed the
Danes and this helps to explain, I think, an attitude of tolerance towards them that one still finds among so many noncommunists in
Copenhagen today.

In December, 1943, the Freedom Council publicly laid down the
gauntlet. In "An Open Letter to the Commander in Chief of the German Forces in Denmark," which was widely publicized in the illegal

press, the council declared: "We who are fighting for the liberation of our country cannot by any form or threat of violence be coerced into passivity toward the enemy. . . . Our reply to the [German] fight without quarter is: Fight without quarter!"

It did just that. By the war's end it had organized a military force of 56,000 men, and it had 16,000 Danes in training in Sweden. Its sabotage groups carried out 2160 major operations against rail lines, 785 against factories working for the Germans, 431 against German military installations and depots and 167 against ports, shipyards and ships. The Council's Press Committee saw to the publication of 235 illegal papers with a total circulation during the occupation of 26 million copies. In addition it established a news service which was able to send out to London, via Sweden, news of what was happening in Denmark. Events taking place in Copenhagen in the afternoon or evening were published in the press of London, New York and other Allied capitals the next morning.

As was inevitable, the Nazi masters, pondering the failure of the "model protectorate," came to the conclusion that the Jews must be to blame. There were only 7000 in Denmark, but nevertheless the Germans decided to liquidate them. Fortunately their plans leaked out and when on the night of October 1, 1943 — the Jewish New Year — the Gestapo swooped down to arrest them all, they found only 1000. The other 6000 were taken in and hidden by Danish families until they could escape over the Sound to Sweden. Most of those who were caught ultimately perished in German concentration camps.

Now the German terror came into full swing. Scores of alleged saboteurs were executed. When they could not be apprehended, leading citizens held as hostages were shot. The Germans gave the young toughs of the Schalburg Corps free rein to pillage, plunder and blow up the homes, shops and factories of patriotic Danes. Kaj Munk, Denmark's great pastor, poet and playwright, was cold-bloodedly murdered by German police. The Danes answered by stepping up their sabotage. They began to liquidate informers.

On June 26, 1944, three weeks after the Allied landings in Normandy, which stirred the Resistance to new efforts, the climax came in Copenhagen. The Germans imposed a curfew from 8 P.M. The workers at the great Burmeister and Wain's shipyards walked out, informing the Germans that they were not on strike but since the curfew made it impossible for them to work in their gardens during the evening, they would have to do so during the day.

At this time of year in the capital, daylight lasts until nearly midnight. The populace refused to get off the streets at 8 P.M. as the curfew demanded. The Germans started shooting them down. Barricades sprang up in the narrow streets. On June 29, Dr. Best tried to quiet the people by raising the curfew hour to 11 P.M. But this announcement was offset by the news that the Germans had executed eight hostages in Jutland. The next morning there was a general strike in Copenhagen. Communications, transport and shops shut down. Dr. Best retaliated by bringing in military reinforcements to surround the city. He shut off gas, water and electricity. This time, he boasted, he would starve the unruly Danes into submission.

The Freedom Council now took charge of the uprising. Street fighting continued under its direction. The general strike went on. At the end of five days of chaos the Wehrmacht weakened and offered to negotiate a settlement. The Freedom Council was now strong enough to dictate its own terms. It demanded the removal of the Schalburg Corps and of the state of emergency, calling off of the curfew and no reprisals.

The Wehrmacht accepted.

From this day on, the power of the Freedom Council was established not only in the minds of the Germans but, what was more important, in the minds of the Danes. The Resistance was succeeding.

There were setbacks, of course. And a price to pay. The Copenhagen uprising cost the lives of 88 Danes — many more than had been killed in the armed forces the day the Germans invaded Denmark — and there were 700 wounded.

On September 19, the Germans seized all police stations throughout the land, arrested 2000 police on duty and carted them off to concentration camps in Germany. Some 5000 escaped the German net, and went underground. The day also marked the third German assault on the residence of the King, who had returned to Amalienborg Palace in Copenhagen. There was sharp fighting between the guard of 52 police and the Germans before the King, for the third time, was forced to order cease-fire.

From that day to the end of the occupation, eight months later, the country had no police; but the self-restraint of the Danes kept lawlessness down to a minimum. The Germans were amazed. The behavior of the Danes recalled an incident on April 9, 1940, the first day of the Nazi occupation, when General Kaupisch, the German Commander in Chief, had called on one of Copenhagen's mayors, Dr. Ernst Kaper, at the City Hall. As the two stood at a window looking out over the square where they could see the populace calmly proceeding to work, the German general exclaimed: "What excellent discipline!" "Not discipline," replied the Dane, "but culture!"

On the evening of May 4, 1945, came word of the surrender of the German army in Holland, Northwest Germany and Denmark to Field Marshal Montgomery's 21st Army Group. British troops set foot on Danish soil the next day and, on May 6, the first Allied contingents reached Copenhagen. They found the Danish Resistance forces in control, busy arresting traitors and some of the worst of the Germans such as Dr. Best. The liberated populace was in delirium.

That summer, after the celebrating was over and the Germans were gone, the Danes settled down to the job of reconstruction. Fortunately the economy of the country, based on agriculture, was intact, though the soil had been depleted by lack of fertilizers. Damage to property had been relatively light. There was plenty of staple food. Transportation and industrial production were soon restored.[5]

There was much pondering to do too. Had the Danes learned the necessary lessons from their brutal experience? Resistance leaders such as Editor Arne Sørensen wondered. Denmark's prewar policy, he wrote a few months after the Liberation, "had been built on the theory that in case of war one should go into hiding in order to survive. The

---

[5] The cost of the German occupation was estimated at $2,300,000,000 (11,500,000,-000 crowns at the then rate of exchange). At the Conference in Paris in the autumn of 1945, the Danish government reported claims for reparations to that amount. When eight years later I asked the Danish Minister of Finance how much in reparations Denmark had actually received from the Germans, he smiled and said: "Not much." He promised to send me a breakdown of the actual figure, which he later did. From the disposal of German assets, from receipt of a few German ships and a small amount of machinery through the Inter-Allied Reparation Agency, and from the disposal of German assets in Sweden, Denmark received a total sum in cash and goods (mostly goods) of just $43,000,000 — or about 2 per cent of what the German occupation cost. In addition the German government at Bonn agreed in 1953 to pay Denmark in annual installments over 20 years some $23,000,000 for the expenses of the hundreds of thousands of German refugees who were quartered in Denmark — at Danish expense — during the last years of the war. This sum covers about one third of the actual expense to the Danes.

struggle for liberty grew out of the opposite view. If liberty has to be regained, somebody must be ready to die for it."

The chances of this view prevailing did not seem to him "so good" and he remarked bitterly that "the only members of the Resistance who will remain, with certainty, popular with everybody are those killed by the Germans, while the rest of us frequently meet strong headwinds from those who would not fight."

His pessimism, fortunately, was not borne out. The old policy of neutrality, after all, had proved to be a terrible delusion. Most Danes saw that. And they saw too that Denmark, by itself, simply was not strong enough to resist an aggressor. It could survive only as a member of a larger body that did have the resources and the power to deter aggression. At first the Danes hoped the United Nations organization might prove to be that body. As *that* hope dwindled, they looked to a Scandinavian Union for protection, only to see the Swedes make that promise impossible. In the end, as we have seen, they reluctantly allied themselves with the West in NATO.

But the fates had decreed that a new potential aggressor was to quickly replace Germany at Denmark's very doorstep — Soviet Russia — and, as I was to find when I came to Copenhagen, a sense of uneasiness, almost of helplessness, despite the guarantees of the NATO Alliance, began to spread over this once happy-go-lucky land.

The Land and the People

Denmark is the smallest and most southerly of the Scandinavian countries. Its area — 17,000 square miles — is one-tenth that of Sweden and about half as large as Indiana with a population, slightly greater than the Midwest state, of 4,300,000, a quarter of whom dwell in Copenhagen. Southerly though it is in relation to the rest of Scandinavia, the twilit summer nights remind one that this is a northern clime, and a glance at the map shows that Copenhagen has the same latitude as central Labrador.

Denmark is not, like the other northern lands, a continuous land mass. Jutland, which comprises somewhat over half its territory, is a peninsular extension of the European mainland and this land connection accounts for the Danes' being closer to the intellectual currents

of Germany and the rest of Western Europe than their Scandinavian
neighbors. To the east of Jutland lie the islands which make up the
rest of Denmark. There are 500 of them, of which 100 are inhabited,
but the only sizable ones are Fyn, connected by a bridge over the Little Belt with Jutland, and Zealand, the largest of the islands which is
reached from Fyn by ferry across the Great Belt, and on the east
coast of which lies Copenhagen.

The two Belts and the sound between Zealand and Sweden are the
outlets from the Baltic to the North Sea, and for more than a millennium have constituted important and strategic international waterways over which the Scandinavian and European powers have
fought. This position makes Denmark the "gatekeeper of the Baltic,"
as she has often been called, and explains why Britain and especially
Russia, for the past two centuries at least, have been interested in
seeing that first Prussia and then Germany did not overrun the little
kingdom and seize permanent control of the straits.

There is something idyllic in the gentle-rolling, low-lying landscape
with its neat and luscious fields of grain, the trim white farmhouses
and attached barns with their thatched roofs and red window frames,
and the little villages along the winding lanes dominated by the
square towers of the country churches. The land seems as sunny and
joyful as the people. And one might add, as modest. For here there
are no soaring mountain ranges as in Norway. As the poet Bishop
Grundtvig said in his first national song:

> No towering peaks thundered over our birth:
> It suits us best to remain on earth.

The highest point in Denmark, in fact, is only 564 feet and most of
the land is but a few feet above sea-level.

It lacks, as we have seen, the minerals, the timber and the water
power which add so much to the wealth of Norway and Sweden;
and there is no coal or oil either. All ores and fuel and most lumber
must be imported.

There remains only the soil to support this nation. It is not particularly fertile in itself, though the Danish farmers have made it so. As
one of them remarked to me: "It doesn't give us something for nothing. But if you work it good, it gives you quite a lot."

It yields enough, in fact, not only to feed the Danish population but to provide the country's leading source for export. Before the last war agricultural products furnished 72 per cent of all Danish exports. Today the figure has fallen to 62 per cent, but it still amounts to twice the value of sales of industrial goods abroad and twenty times that of fish — the other two main exports.

To achieve such a prodigious production from a relatively small acreage, Danish farmers obtain harvest yields which are phenomenal. Compared to those in the United States they are, per acre, more than three times greater in wheat, two and a half times in barley and rye, and twice as great in potatoes. Most of the grains and root crops — all that is not needed to feed the people — goes to feed cows, pigs and chickens, the raising of which is the chief source of income of the Danish farmer and, together with the processing into butter, bacon and eggs and their marketing, the principal industry of this farmer's commonwealth.

Its amazing success is due, of course, partly to the ingenuity, skill, perseverance and education of the Danish farmers. But there is another immensely important factor: the genius of the Danish farmers for co-operation. Farming in Denmark today is a vast co-operative enterprise which, in its extent, has no parallel in any other country. The Danish farmer believes it is the chief secret of his success.

The first co-operative dairy was set up in 1882, the first co-op bacon factory in 1887, and from then on the movement spread rapidly throughout the land. Today, 1300 of the country's 1500 dairies are co-ops, receiving 90 per cent of Denmark's total milk supply from 90 per cent of the nation's farmers, and doing an annual business of $280,000,000. The co-op bacon factories handle 90 per cent of the slaughtered pigs and have a yearly turnover of $290,000,000. Both types of co-ops are concerned not only with the processing of their respective products but with the mass marketing of them at home and abroad. Thus ten co-operative export societies handle the sales of more than half of all exported butter, and the bacon co-ops have their own firm, the Danish Bacon Company, with headquarters in London, where 90 per cent of Danish bacon exports are sold.

The co-operative bacon factories had a hard time of it at first. Whereas dairying in the late nineteenth century was a comparatively new enterprise, privately owned slaughterhouses were already well established and they tried to stifle the new competition of the co-ops with every trick in the bag. They declared a price war. They offered farmers premiums to sell to them. They tried to buy the co-ops out. They even induced the banks to refuse credit to the co-operatives. In one town the local public health authorities ruled that a co-operative bacon factory in the town constituted a danger to public health and forbade it to operate!

But the farmers were not to be put off. They, like the dairymen — in Denmark the average farmer raises both cows and pigs — had become convinced of the advantages of the co-op. They saw four principal ones:

1. By selling and buying (seed, feed, fertilizer, machinery, etc.) co-operatively they eliminated the middlemen and thus canalized profits back to themselves.

2. Their mass sales gave them an influence on the market they did not previously have.

3. The co-op gave them an incentive to improve and standardize their product, since the benefits would be returned to them.

4. The handling by the co-op dairy and bacon factory of the processing which they had previously been doing — inefficiently — on their farms released them from a great deal of labor which they could henceforth employ directly in growing livestock and feed.

I spent some time visiting farms and co-op dairies and bacon factories on the island of Zealand. One was immediately impressed to see that not only the homes and the dairies but the slaughterhouses and the barns were as spotlessly clean as a modern hospital. I could not even detect any odor in the cowbarns or the pigpens. The neat, white farmhouses were flanked by brightly colored flowerbeds. Beyond, the grain lay ripening in the fields, as thick as I have ever seen.

The Danes are about the most hospitable and friendly folk in the world. Farmers and managers of co-op dairies and bacon factories, after showing me through their places, dropped their work to have a chat about their problems over drinks and cigars, which they inevitably offered. They spoke in a general way first: of how small and middle-sized holdings dominate Danish agriculture, and they were proud that 95 per cent of the farmers own and run their own farms. These are small by our American standards. One half of them are under 25 acres; and yet, on a plot of that tiny size, many a Danish family, by intensive cultivation, ingenuity and some financial help from the government, keeps enough cows, pigs and chickens to make a decent living. Most of the other farms vary from 25 to 150 acres, and provide an extremely good living. Less than 5000 farms out of a total of 208,000 have more than 150 acres.

A manager of a dairy co-op, after showing me around, exchanged his wooden shoes for slippers, took me across the road to his home and, over drinks, pastry and cigars, discussed his business. Most of his butter went to England. Indeed the United Kingdom, he said, took 75 per cent of all Danish exports of butter as well as 85 per cent of eggs and 90 per cent of bacon. He appreciated this trade but thought the British government, which negotiates with Denmark for the entire amount at fixed prices, might well raise those prices a little. But his chief complaint was against the United States. Congress, he said, had severely restricted the import of Danish cheese. It was a severe blow to the Danish dairies and the farmers who supply and operate them.

"How does the United States expect us to pay for what we buy from her if she won't let us sell her anything?" he asked.

For the Danish farmers since the war were buying a great deal from America: oil fodders and fertilizer and tractors and machinery with which to rehabilitate their land and stock, which had deteriorated because of being shut off from the rest of the world during the war. But most of their income came from Britain in sterling, and pounds were not freely convertible into dollars. This was the dilemma when the Marshall Plan came to the timely aid of Denmark as it had to Norway.

Nearly half of the Marshall Plan funds for Denmark went to buy American commodities for the Danish farmer — above all feed, fertilizer, tractors and agricultural machinery. This help restored Danish agricultural business to above the prewar level and these farmers I was talking with said they greatly appreciated it.

However, contrary to a view I had gained at home, this American aid was not a gift to the farmers themselves. They had to pay normal prices for what they got in Danish currency. But they were thankful, they said, to be able to make the purchases. Now, however, with the end of the Marshall Plan aid, they confront their old problem: a dollar shortage. To keep up their livestock, which is the basis of the nation's economy, the Danes need to import 7 per cent of their feed. At the present this is only available against purchases in dollars. The Danes have sterling, from their sales to England, but this cannot buy what they need. This was their unsolved problem when I took leave of them.

Among other things, the standardization of livestock and poultry impressed me. By careful and selective breeding the Danish farmers have succeeded in producing cows, pigs, chickens and eggs that are so uniform in size and body that when you see them arriving at a meat factory they have the appearance of having come off an assembly line as precise as one turning out motor cars in a Detroit plant.

This is a great help in marketing, but here too there are problems, as one manager of a co-op bacon factory reminded me. The English, he said, must have their bacon lean, and so the Danes bred a long, thin-backed, lean pig to please their chief customers. But the Germans, he said, who are coming back into the market, insist on having their bacon fat. And that necessitates another kind of porker.

The Danes must surely be the most highly organized farmers on the face of the globe. There is space here only to list the remaining agricultural co-operatives: the Co-operative Egg Export Association with 60,000 members and an annual turnover of $17,000,000 (it has succeeded in destroying Denmark's former reputation abroad for bad eggs and with it, the old joke that Hamlet's line "there is something rotten in the State of Denmark" applied to its eggs); the Co-operative Poultry-Dressing Stations, with a membership of 85,000 and an annual turnover of $1,000,000; the Danish Farmers' Society for the Sale of Cattle, with 86,000 members and an annual turnover of $15,000,000; the National Federation of Danish Co-operative Cattle Export Associations, with 40,000 members and an annual turnover of $13,000,000. There are smaller co-ops for the production and marketing of seed, fruit and vegetables.

There are numerous co-op purchasing societies to handle the buying of almost everything the farmer needs. Thus the Co-ops for the Purchase of Feed have 100,000 members and buy annually $47,000,000 worth of produce. There are 1600 local co-ops organized as the Co-operative Fertilizer Association, which purchases yearly $21,000,000 worth of fertilizers. There is a co-op to buy coal to furnish the power for the co-operative dairies and bacon factories. Finally, in contrast to Norway and Sweden, almost all farmers belong to consumers' co-ops, and through them make not only most of their general purchases but buy their insurance and do their banking.

Aside from the agricultural co-ops, there are a multitude of other farm organizations all united in the Agricultural Council. The owners of small, medium and large farms each have their separate national organizations. So do the cattle breeders, with 25,000 members; the cattle breeders employing artificial insemination, with 97,000 members; the horse breeders with 25,000 members; and the members of the milk-recording societies, who number 67,000.

The Danish Folk High Schools

At first I did not understand. One farmer after another kept remarking that there was a very close connection between their success in organizing agriculture on a co-operative basis and the Danish Folk High School. They told of how Sir Horace Plunkett, the Irish land reformer, visiting Denmark to study agricultural methods, found to his surprise that the efficiency and prosperity of the Danish farmers and their co-ops really went back to a cultural institution: the Folk High School. Instead of investigating agronomy, he found he first had to study rural adult education.

"It is something to look into," the farmers advised me, "if you want to understand Denmark."

For more than a century the Folk High School — the first one was opened in 1844 — has been the mainspring of the cultural emancipation of the rural people. It has taught them not only how to think for themselves but has given them an understanding of life, of society, and of how to cope with their myriad problems. There have been few farmers, I was told, who have not during some part of their life come into contact with the Folk High Schools.

What this institution has meant to the country folk has been best summed up perhaps by Anders Nielsen, a farmer and one of the leaders of the agricultural co-op movement: "It has filled in and leveled the cleavages in society and thereby paved the way for common endeavor. It has sent students out into life with an increased love for the country and its achievements, riper and more thoughtful, more receptive to life's teaching, and therefore better equipped to understand and to make their way. . . . It can be stated as a fact that not only the co-operative movements but the cultural position of the Danish farmers as a whole rests on this foundation. . . . It has taught the people to think and to use their powers so that not only the individual but the whole community is benefited." [6]

The Danish Folk High Schools lie quite outside the country's regular public school system. They are privately run. They hold no examinations and confer no degrees. Courses are held for young men, who have completed their formal obligatory schooling, during the five winter months — November through March — when they are not needed on the farm. The young women attend in the three summer months, May through July, though some of the winter terms have recently been made co-educational.

The teaching, especially in the opening weeks, is in the nature of a refresher course of subjects acquired in elementary school: arithmetic, writing and the Danish language. Then come courses in history, geography, literature, English, economics, physics, chemistry, botany, agronomy and sociology. Usually there are practical studies such as farm bookkeeping, hygiene, plant and soil chemistry, mechanics, and drawing. Lectures, as Grundtvig advised, play an important part, the aim being not so much to impart exact knowledge as to open up new cultural horizons in literature, history, politics, social subjects and religion. Most of the great Folk High School teachers, many of whom also have become prominent in Parliament, government and the co-op movement, have achieved national reputations by their eloquence on the platforms. They seek in their lectures, they say, not to find pat answers to the questions of the universe but to stimulate the raising and the pondering of questions by the students.

Since most of these board and room at the High School during the term, there are many discussion groups outside of school hours and a great deal of community singing as well as gymnastics and sports. Farmers appear to have toward the Folk High Schools they attended an attitude similar to that of many Americans toward their college: their stay there was one of the best, most fruitful times of their lives.

If it was the versatile Grundtvig who conceived the idea of the Folk High School, it was Kristen Kold who pioneered in the practical development of the institution in the middle of the last century. The son of a cobbler, he has been called "a rustic blend of Socrates and Pestalozzi," and Grundtvig thought he was Denmark's and perhaps the world's greatest educator of his time.

[6] *Living Democracy in Denmark*, by Peter Manniche.

Kold opened his first school in 1850 at Ryslinge on the island of Fyn in a building 45 by 25 feet which served as both schoolroom and living accommodations for his fifteen students, himself and family. Living conditions were Spartan and he himself lived mostly on bread and milk. The Ministry of Education declared his school "unfitted for a healthy and practical development of young people from the peasant class." But he persisted, and soon students began flocking to him from all over the kingdom. He was a man of immense vision and inspiring eloquence, and yet of a practical enough nature to work out a pattern for the Folk High Schools which still stands.

He, like Grundtvig, was principally interested in educating young farmers — for they believed that this most numerous and most important, economically, of the classes was destined to lead and dominate a new Denmark as soon as it became democratic and the people truly free. Hence the Folk High Schools at first were exclusively rural. These early leaders did not foresee the growth of the proletariat in the cities and the rise of the Labor movement as industrialization set in.

It was left, therefore, to others to introduce the Folk High School idea into the cities and larger towns. The Labor High Schools differ from the Folk High Schools in that they are primarily day schools where the students do not live in, and their curricula put more emphasis on industrial economics and labor problems and tend to stress more book learning. They have not become, however, as some feared, mere instruments of superficial political agitation for Socialism, though most of their students and teachers are Socialists.

"On the contrary," one of its principals recently said, "one of our tasks has been to combat cheap phrases and viewpoints and to help our young people obtain views that are genuine and lasting. Our principal study is man himself."

But the main source of adult education for workers in Denmark is the Workers' Educational Movement, founded in 1924 with the financial help of the trade-unions and the Social-Democratic party. It has a Folk High School of its own at Roskilde, is part owner of another at Esbjerg and conducts, among other things, one thousand study circles, as well as numerous book circles. Its evening schools have an attendance today of 200,000.

Finally there is an International Folk High School at Elsinore, scene of *Hamlet*, which under the leadership from 1921 to 1953 of Peter

Manniche, has been eminently successful in applying the Folk High School ideal to international education. It draws students from forty-four nations, including the United States.

Though the Folk High Schools are completely independent of the state, the Danish government generously contributes enough to keep them fairly free from financial worries. The state support of fifty-five recognized institutions covers half the salaries of the teachers, 35 per cent of the cost of new books and a good part of the tuition of needy students.

"The greatest gifts of life — spiritual and cultural values — are for everyone," Alfred Poulsen, for twenty-five years the chairman of the Union of Folk High Schools, once said; "and the task of the Folk High Schools is to guide the young to make these gifts their own."

No one who has journeyed through the lovely Danish countryside and talked with the people on the land can doubt that this task has been achieved with considerable success.[7]

Consumer Co-ops and Others

Unlike in Norway and Sweden, it is the producers' societies which dominate the co-operative movement in Denmark, because of the extent to which the farmers have combined to process and sell their products. Nevertheless the consumer societies are of great importance. Both groups adhere to an over-all organization, the Central Co-operative Committee. And the 1984 local consumers' co-ops, with a total membership of 446,000 and yearly sales of $120,000,000, all belong to the Danish Co-operative Wholesale Society, from which they purchase nearly all their goods.

Actually total membership in all co-operatives is more than two million, but since many farmers belong to two or more societies — producer, purchasing and consumer — the number of separate individuals in the co-op movement is about 450,000 — which, when their families are taken into consideration, represents about half the population of the country.

While such agricultural co-operatives as those dealing in the pro-

[7] The Folk High Schools are not the only means of adult education in Denmark. The Public School system maintains residential youth colleges, evening Folk High Schools, small-holders' schools, gymnastic schools and an adult educational league.

duction and sale of milk, butter and bacon do the bulk of the nation's business in these products, the consumers' societies handle only about 10 per cent of Denmark's retail trade, thus leaving this field pretty much to private enterprise. However, they form together one of the big businesses of the land and the Co-operative Wholesale Society, which supplies them, is the largest of all Danish enterprises in the wholesale distribution of goods. Its annual turnover amounts to $85,-000,000.

I spent a morning tramping through the immense Copenhagen headquarters of the Wholesale Society — an experience much the same as visiting Montgomery Ward in Chicago. It is a vast and teeming enterprise run on strictly business principles. A good many of its goods are manufactured by the society itself, which has numerous factories of its own turning out clothing, textiles, footwear, furniture, flour, canned foods, margarine (the Danes export most of their butter and many content themselves with margarine), soap, toilet articles, candy, cigarettes and cigars, for a total value of $25,000,000 a year.

From the Copenhagen headquarters and the scattered factories goods flow out to sixteen wholesale branches situated all over the country, and from them to the 2000 odd retail outlets. The transportation division is a beehive of activity. One visits various other departments: the architects' and engineering office which helps local stores plan new building or adopt their premises to expanding trade; the advertising office which supplies copy, layouts, store signs and other material to the network of retail shops; a central laboratory which tests all goods, whether purchased or manufactured, before they are put on the retail market.

The organization of the consumers' co-ops in Denmark is similar to what we have seen in Norway and Sweden. One of the chief differences is the growth in Denmark of the Labor co-operatives. For years the Labor movement, despite the success of the consumers' co-ops among the rural folk, opposed them as a matter of Socialist principle. Under the influence of the German Socialist, Lassalle, the workers at first decided that the co-operatives offered no solution to their problems, and they would have none of them. However, toward the end of the last century, exasperated over the high price of bread, they began to organize bakeries as joint stock companies. In 1899 when a nationwide lockout caused widespread unemployment in the building trades, the workers combined to set up construction companies of their own. Though these were co-operative ventures, they were formed as joint stock enterprises.

It was only after the turn of the century that the Labor movement discarded its theories and turned to organizing retail co-ops in the cities and larger towns. Their success was rapid. Today they have more than fifty outlets, organized in the Union of Urban Co-operative Societies, with a membership of 100,000 and an annual business of $12,000,000. All these belong to the Co-operative Wholesale Society, thus linking them with the main Danish co-op movement. Supported by the Labor party and the unions, the workers' co-operative movement has now branched out into many fields. It maintains 37 co-op canteens doing an annual business of over $2,000,000; coal and coke societies, insurance societies, a dairy, a brewery, a bank, hairdressing salons and a loan society — altogether 442 enterprises conducting an annual business of nearly $50,000,000.

Banking and insurance have been successfully taken up by the Danish co-operators, though the struggle in these fields at first was a hard one, due to the hostility of private financial circles. The first bank established by the Central Co-operative Committee was forced to close in 1925, when it became unable to weather the business slump after the First World War. But a second one, established later in the same year, the Danish Co-operative and People's Bank, fared better; and today, with a $2,000,000,000-a-year business, is the fourth largest trading bank in Denmark. The co-op movement has also established a chain of so-called "village banks." Some 54 of the odd 100 of them are federated in a national union and have a turnover of $100,000,000 a year, making them one of the country's large financial institutions.

Standing somewhat separate from the general co-op structure are the co-operative first and second mortgage credit associations, which dominate the mortgage market in Denmark.

Finally, the Danish co-ops, like all the others in Scandinavia, pay taxes, though for a long time those which sold only to members were generally held exempt from income tax. The law did not catch up with them until 1941 when a direct income tax was levied on all retail societies and, in some cases, on productive and marketing organizations.

In 1949, however, the tax system was changed and all co-ops, with-

out exception, were made subject to a tax on their capital and property. Actually in terms of income this works out to a state and local
income tax on retail co-ops of 27 per cent, on producer and purchasing co-ops of 11 per cent. This tax "reform" came mainly as the
result of vigorous agitation by private enterprise, which objected to
being discriminated against in taxes.

Private Enterprise in Denmark's Economy

Despite more than two decades of Labor political rule, interspersed
by periods of Agrarian-Conservative governments such as the one in
power from 1950 to 1953, and despite the strength of the co-operatives, private enterprise dominates the industrial and commercial life
of Denmark. Neither the powerful trade-unions nor the ruling Social-
Democratic party have ever been much steamed-up about nationalization of industry — or about Socialism, for that matter.

Their stress has been on reform: higher wages, better working
conditions, paid vacations, social welfare, progressive income and inheritance taxes and enough regulation of the economy to assure full
employment. In practice at least, if not in theory, they have been
quite willing to let capitalism thrive.

It has.

For a country whose only natural resource is agriculture, the extent of manufacturing is surprisingly large. Almost every scrap of
raw material to be processed, every ton of coal or barrel of oil to
provide the power to turn the machinery of production, must be
imported from abroad. Yet industry, public utilities and handicrafts
contribute one quarter of the gross national income — even more
than agriculture, which accounts for one fifth. Commerce and banking provide for somewhat less than agriculture, and shipping and
transport about one tenth. Thus one third of the people live off
industry and handicrafts, one fourth off farming and one fifth off
commerce and transport.

Denmark's main problem of existing on the present prosperous and
enlightened level may be stated quite simply. It must sell enough
farm products abroad to be able to import the raw materials it needs
to manufacture the multitude of things necessary for modern life. It
could of course easily keep its four million odd people alive — well fed,
even — on its own resources. But unless it can export from one fourth

to one third of its national production — chiefly agricultural goods — it is doomed to be reduced to a primitive pastoral state, which it once was.

That is why foreign trade is so absolutely necessary to its survival, and why Denmark today has the biggest foreign trade per capita of any nation in the world — five times that of the United States. To live, it must trade.

And because world trade for the last forty years has been a precarious business, hamstrung and restricted by quotas, tariffs, currency inconvertibility, war and cold war, Denmark's position has been more precarious than most of its easygoing, life-loving people have realized. An increase in world prices of raw materials which she must purchase overseas, unaccompanied by a compensatory rise in the prices of the food products she sells, as is often the case, hurts her; if the difference is too great, it can destroy her.

There is a further complication, which we have already considered in connection with the farmers. Great Britain, since the end of hostilities, has taken the bulk of Denmark's exports, as she did before 1940. But prior to that date the Danes could take their pounds sterling and convert them freely into dollars to buy what they needed any place in the world. Since the war, that has been impossible: sterling has not been convertible into dollars. Thus Denmark is in the position of having to sell in a sterling area and buy many essentials in a dollar area. She has the funds in sterling from her exports to import what she needs, but she cannot use those funds because they cannot be transferred into dollars.

This has been her dilemma since 1945. Although production, exports and imports increased rapidly in the next three years, often surpassing pre-war figures, the truth was that by 1948 Denmark had virtually exhausted her modest foreign exchange reserves as well as her credit possibilities. She was, as the government admitted, in a very serious economic situation as 1948 came to an end.

It was then that the Marshall Plan came to her rescue — in the nick of time. It did not by itself save her, by any means. But it greatly helped. In the two crucial years of 1949-1950, it made available to Denmark $196,000,000. This was 10 per cent of her total imports. But American help was more important than that figure implies. It enabled Denmark to buy what she sorely needed in the only place it was available — the dollar area. It reduced her imbalance of payments.

It helped her to renew her agricultural and industrial plant. Through the European Payments Union and the Organization for European Economic Co-operation (OEEC) it enabled her to increase her natural trade with the countries of Western Europe. It helped keep employment at a high level.

Marshall Plan aid, which totaled $275,000,000, virtually ceased in 1952. And Denmark is once again confronted with the old nightmare: the dollar gap.

She is profoundly grateful for the generous help America provided, as was made almost embarrassingly clear to me not only by cabinet members but by everyone else I talked to: farmers, workers, businessmen, eminent scientists and others.

But as one cabinet member said to me: "It would be fine if the idea behind the Marshall Plan could now become practical enough for Denmark to be given an opportunity of earning on the American market the dollars she needs to keep her economy going. This," he added, "would be the best proof that the Plan had been successful."

I did not detect any great hope in his declaration. Danish butter and bacon and ham and cheese are delicious. Americans, if given a chance and the right price — and the price is good — would certainly buy them. But our storage houses are full of American butter and cheese, and the meat supply here is more than adequate. The Danes say they were encouraged to believe after the war that they could sell 20,000 tons of butter a year to the United States, which would have yielded $15,000,000 annually, and also that they could sell here a considerable amount of cheese. But the amount of cheese was restricted by Presidential order, and import licenses were refused altogether for the butter.

Since the war we have sold to Denmark much more than we bought from her — in 1951 nearly five times as much, in 1952 twice as much. More recently the balance has been a bit more even due largely to sizable purchases of Danish dairy products by the United States armed forces in Germany, to special efforts of Denmark to sell in the dollar market, and by drastic reductions in Danish imports from America. But the balance has been achieved at the cost of a heavy curtailment of trade between the two countries.

Business establishments are small in Denmark. One half of the 100,000 registered enterprises are operated by the proprietor and his family. There are only 19,000 firms employing more than five men. There is also a leveling of incomes, which we have seen in the other Scandinavian lands. The words of Grundtvig are especially true of Denmark: "Few have too much and still fewer too little."

The average income is $1000 a year. This may seem low by American standards, but when you consider that prices, in dollars, are about half ours, and that a Dane receives many social security benefits not available to an American and that a large part of the people live in rural places where the cost of living is relatively cheap and where they can grow a good deal of their food on their own garden plots, it will be seen that the Danes have a pretty good living standard. Nearly half the people earn between $450 and $1000 a year, one fifth between $1000 and $3000, and only one per cent over $3000.

Income taxes are fairly steep by American standards. For married persons with two children they come to 7 per cent on incomes of $700 a year; 15 per cent on $1400; 23 per cent on $3600; and 28 per cent on $7000. There is the same fiscal practice in Denmark as in other Scandinavian lands of boosting the tax on incomes derived from capital and real estate. Thus a taxpayer's income may get an increased assessment of from 25 to 50 per cent if it comes from capital and property. Still, the government extracts more in what may be called consumption taxes than in income tax. They amount to 56 per cent of total state revenue against 42 per cent from income tax.

Social Welfare in Denmark

Although in many respects Denmark handles its social welfare differently from Norway and Sweden, the philosophy behind it is the same: that society should give *all* its members, regardless of fortune, a reasonable amount of security and well-being.

Because of the innate aversion to compulsion among the Danes, they tend to make their social security system more voluntary than is the case in the other Scandinavian countries. And employers are let off relatively easy. They do not, for instance, have to contribute to health insurance or old age pensions and pay only $2.00 a year per worker to unemployment insurance, which is handled directly by the trade-unions with the financial backing of the state.

Modern social welfare in Denmark dates from 1933, when the entire system was overhauled by Parliament in a series of four Acts known as the Social Reform. The legislation, largely the work of K. K. Steincke, Minister for Social Affairs, and one of Europe's leading social reformers, is the charter of social welfare in Denmark today. There is space here to sketch only the salient points wherein the program differs from that which we have seen in Norway and Sweden.

The Danes say they are proud that their Health Insurance system, though comprehensive, is voluntary. Actually, it is only partly so. For under a law passed in 1950, all persons between twenty-one and sixty are required to become members of an approved health insurance fund or a state-controlled health insurance society. But citizens who are not in the top income groups may choose whether they shall become an *active* or a *passive* member. This distinction, as it is made in Denmark, takes a bit of explaining.

Active members belong to state-approved but self-owning, self-governing, health insurance societies, and receive, in return for an average premium of seven dollars a year, the following benefits:

1. Medical care.
2. Hospital treatment, including surgery.
3. Daily cash payments during illness.
4. Maternity aid.
5. Assistance on funeral expenses.

But you cannot be an active member if your yearly income, after income tax, exceeds the pay of a skilled worker — a figure fixed annually by the government in conformity to the current wage scale. At present it is $1585 in Copenhagen, $1470 in provincial towns and $1330 in rural areas. That is the first condition. There is a second one. You cannot receive this kind of health insurance if your capital exceeds $4000 for single persons or $5500 for married persons.

Nevertheless 80 per cent of the total population — some 2,460,000 persons — are active members and receive, for the nominal premiums of seven dollars a year, the full benefits enumerated above.

Some 10 per cent of the population, ineligible for active membership because their income or capital exceeds the limit, are passive members. They pay a fee of $1.50 a year for this privilege — there is a slightly higher annual fine if one neglects to join. They do not receive any medical benefits, but are eligible to become active participants should their income at any time fall below the limit. Also they must be passive members in order to qualify for old age pensions later. They may — and almost all do — join a health insurance society, which though supervised by the state receives no financial help from it. Such organizations operate on strictly insurance principles and charge an average of twenty dollars a year. Even for the relatively well-to-do, medical care is infinitely more cheap in Denmark than in the United States. The reason for this, aside from the insurance benefits, lies in the hospital system. As elsewhere in Scandinavia almost all hospitals are public institutions supported by the state or the municipality. Their charges are only nominal, so that even if you pay your own expenses the cost is extremely low. The maximum charge for ward patients is a dollar a day; at many of the best hospitals in Copenhagen it is half that. And this nominal charge includes surgery, anesthetics, therapeutic treatment and other services.

How this works out for persons earning more than a skilled worker was explained to me by the ranking permanent official of one of the ministries in Copenhagen. He had recently had a hernia operation. The total cost of that and the hospital treatment came to just $5.70. His annual insurance in a private society cost him $20.00 so that he figured the total cost of the operation amounted to roughly $25.00. However, since both his wife and children had been ill during the year and had required the attention of a doctor, their medical treatment, covered by his insurance, was included in that low figure.

Thus in Denmark, as elsewhere in Scandinavia, medical and hospital expenses, whether for workers, farmers or what we call in America families of modest middle-class incomes, are so low that they relieve all citizens of financial worries and undue burden in regard to them. And the less well-to-do are helped relatively more than those who are more fortunate. This is one of the underlying ideas of Danish social welfare.

A Dane can have a *doctor of his own choosing* though in some societies his choice is limited to a panel of doctors living within a six-mile radius. Usually a doctor receives a fixed annual fee from the society for each person choosing him — whether the physician finds it necessary to treat him or not. In some cases, the society pays the doctor according to services rendered. No physician can have more than 2500 persons on his panel.

Fundamentally, the 1600 health insurance societies which handle the nearly two and a half million active members are co-operative ventures subsidized by the state. The state does not own or operate them; the members do.

And they pay the bulk of the annual cost of $22,500,000 — about 70 per cent, with the state chipping in 25 per cent and the municipalities 5 per cent. Cash benefits paid during illness are low compared to Sweden, coming to between fifteen cents and a dollar a day.

Unlike the health system, old age pensions in Denmark are not a matter of insurance. The costs are covered entirely by the state and the municipalities, out of taxation, and the public makes no direct contribution to them. They are payable to women over sixty and men over sixty-five, come to roughly five hundred dollars a year and are adjusted annually to the cost of living. Pensions and allowances are reduced when the pensioner has other income exceeding half the basic pension. Over half the total population above the required age receive old age pensions which total $65,000,000 annually. The state and municipalities also pay $35,000,000 a year to support some five hundred exceedingly pleasant homes for the aged or to defray part of their rent in private apartments.

Incidentally, the state is much concerned that everyone in Denmark get a decent funeral. In cases where insurance does not cover funeral costs or there is no other private means, the law obliges the local authorities to pay them at public expense and expressly stipulates that no such funeral may be plainer than is customary among people of small means and that in no case may persons buried at the public expense be placed in a separate part of the cemetery.

In Denmark unemployment insurance is voluntary in principle, as the Danes say, but scarcely in practice. This is because the trade-unions themselves handle this phase of social security and they require all their members to maintain unemployment insurance. They themselves operate the unemployment funds, of which there are 67 separate ones with some 600,000 active members — practically 100 per cent of the organized workers. But these funds, by law, must be kept quite separate from ordinary union funds. Workers pay into them an average of 50 cents a week and receive unemployment compensation of $1.35 a day for from 90 to 160 days. The state and workers share the cost of the system on what amounts to a 50-50 basis.

In case of prolonged unemployment there is what is called a continuation fund which operates when the general insurance funds

cease. To this the employer must contribute two dollars per employed worker a year, but three quarters of the cost is borne by the
state and municipalities. Accident insurance, or workmen's compensation, is the responsibility exclusively of the employer, who is required by law to take out appropriate insurance in an ordinary or a
mutual company, approved by the government.

Disability insurance is a peculiar Danish institution. It is compulsory for all persons who are obliged to be a passive member of a health
insurance society. Premiums are practically nominal — $1.50 a year —
and benefits are similar to old-age pensions. The state bears the bulk
of the expenditure and local authorities and employers also chip in.
Actually, the most important part of the scheme is not the modest
remuneration but the measures which the state takes under it to
rehabilitate the disabled so that they can earn a living. Thus the
government pays the full cost of curative treatment, artificial limbs,
glasses, invalid chairs, new tools as well as retraining in a suitable
trade. In some cases, even, the state will help an invalid to set himself
up in business. The idea is to make the disabled self-supporting.

Maternity aid and child welfare in Denmark is similar to that we
have seen in Norway and Sweden. Here too there are Child Welfare
Committees in each community with authority to deal with negli-
gent parents and juvenile delinquents. These committees, which are
elected, may remove any youth under eighteen from his home, regardless of the parents' or child's wishes, for the following reasons: bad
behavior; exposure to neglect or abuse by the parents; if the child
needs special treatment which cannot or will not be given in the
home. The decision to remove a child from its home must be taken
by a two-thirds majority of the committee and may be appealed by
the parents to the National Board of Child Welfare, though the
appeal may not delay the action taken by the committee. The board
is not a court. It consists of a chairman, who must have the qualifications of a judge, two members appointed by Parliament, one by the
Ministry of Social Affairs, and the Chief Inspector of Child Welfare.
The board's decisions are final, and cannot be appealed to a court of
law. The Danes feel strongly that juveniles should be kept out of the
law courts as much as possible.

In Denmark, as in the other Scandinavian lands, the illegitimate
birth rate is rather high, and the law lays down a number of interesting regulations governing the responsibility of the father. In the

first place, an unmarried woman who has become pregnant may, after the sixth month, take proceedings against the man whom she considers to be the father of the expected child. In this she is assisted by the Maternity Aid institutions. Not later than a month after the child is born, the woman must inform the Chief Constable of her district of the name of the father. If the man admits it, or is held by the Court after due process to be the father, he must assume support of the child until it is eighteen. Such a child receives the same legal rights as legitimate children, including the right of inheritance.

In one particular, the Danish law goes further than that of the other northern lands. Even if it is not proved conclusively in court that a man is the father of an illegitimate child, he will be considered responsible for partial support if the court finds that he has had sexual relations with the mother — unless the man can prove that such relations could not possibly have produced an offspring. Such a case usually involves a woman who has had relations not with one man but with several subsequent to pregnancy. Danish law provides for just this contingency. If a number of men have had that experience, *each* of them is held liable for three fifths of the cost of supporting the child in reasonably good circumstances. The mother must herself provide the other two fifths. The extra contributions, in case of several men paying them, are turned over to the Child Welfare fund. These men, however, do not have to give their name to the child nor accord it the right of inheritance.

I found no sentiment whatsoever in Denmark for Prohibition or even for complicated laws regulating the sale and imbibing of alcoholic beverages such as were in force so long in Sweden. The Danes have solved the temperance question in a very simple — and they think reasonable — way. They have taxed strong drinks out of the reach of most people. In addition there are normal regulations concerning the number of public houses serving alcoholic beverages, the responsibility of the proprietors insofar — to quote the Licensing Act of 1939 — "as lawfulness, morality and sobriety" are concerned, and the prohibition of the sale of hard liquor to minors. Finally there is a fairly strong temperance movement.

These reasonable measures have been quite successful. Not so long ago — toward the end of the nineteenth century — Denmark was the hardest-drinking country in the world. Consumption of pure al-

cohol per person was nine quarts a year — a world's record. The
number of licensed houses serving spirits averaged one for every 200
souls in the kingdom. In 1882 an official report on *Drunkenness in
Denmark* declared: "It may be regarded as proved to the hilt that
drunkenness is spreading deep into our social life and that it is the
cause of many accidents and crimes as well as of deserved and unde-
served suffering."

But the good work of the temperance societies, the stricter licensing of bars and the progressive increase in taxes on spirits soon
brought a steady decline in the consumption of alcohol. By 1915 it
was down to six quarts a year per capita and by 1925 down to three
quarts. It is slightly under that today.

The Danes are chiefly beer drinkers, their brew being of a fine quality. Beer is also rather heavily taxed, though not out of reach of the
modest income groups.

The cost of social welfare to the state — and hence to the taxpayers
— is considerable. It amounts to nearly half of the national government's budget and about 10 per cent of the net national income. And
though Denmark, like every other NATO country, has had to increase
sharply its expenditures on defense — they are ten times what they were
before the war and three times more than in 1945-1947 — the Danes
take pride in the fact that their government still spends twice as
much on social welfare as on the military.

A Note on Housing

Denmark, like the other Scandinavian countries, has a vigorous
housing program backed and partly financed by the state. Yet the
Danes say they have been careful not to fall for the temptation of so-
cializing the housing industry. Almost one half (47 per cent) of the
new housing is still constructed by private builders, though 36 per
cent of it with state support. Of the rest 47 per cent is built by co-
operatives, largely operated by the trade-unions, while the state and
municipalities account for 6 per cent of new building.

There is, however, no question of direct state aid to housing, except
in the relatively few cases of homes for the aged and for farm workers. What the state does is to loan money on third mortgages only

after a prospective builder has borrowed the maximum amount on first and second mortgages from the credit associations, which, as we have seen, are co-operative ventures. The state charges 4½ per cent annually on its housing loans, of which one per cent is for amortization, the rest for interest. In addition the government suspends building taxes for the first twenty-two years on all nonprofit projects.

Today in Denmark there are three kinds of what are called "Social Housing Associations" sanctioned by the Ministry of Housing:

1. Profit-sharing housing societies organized on a co-operative basis for the purpose of building and administering dwelling accommodations for the use of members.

2. Non-profit building associations which, in close co-operation with local authorities, build and administer blocks of flats available to the general public.

3. Housing societies which are stock companies with limited profits organized to construct and administer dwellings that are available to all.

Since 1933 the law provides that all profits and savings made by these three groups cannot be passed on to the tenants but must be spent on new construction, the aim of the government being to achieve eventually the self-financing of new housing and to prevent the increment from capital invested by the State accruing to individuals instead of society as a whole. Moreover, in all three categories the Housing Ministry retains the right to control rents and inspect balance sheets.

The largest of the co-operative housing societies have been formed by the trade-unions. There is a special reason for this development in Denmark. It goes back to just before the First World War, when wild speculation in real-estate development and consequent crashes led the banks to become wary of financing new building. The result was to curtail new construction and cause widespread unemployment in the building trade. It was here that the trade-unions stepped in. In 1912 they organized the Workers' Co-operative Housing Society, the largest such co-op venture in Denmark. Later they formed the Workers' Co-operative Building Society which, though a nonprofit organization, does not require occupants of its flats to be members of the society or put up capital,[8] as is the case with other co-op building organizations.

Private builders in Denmark have suffered from the sharp increase of building costs since World War II and the squeeze in which they have been caught between these rising costs and rent controls. In 1939, for instance, 88 per cent of all construction was done by private firms and only 13 per cent of their housing received state aid. By 1951 their share had fallen below half and more than a third of it had state support.

There is less overcrowding in Denmark than in Sweden. Two thirds of the dwellings have two or three rooms, not including kitchen. Still, five years after the end of the past war there were 13,000 flats in Copenhagen with more than two inhabitants per room.

Average rents are modest compared to American standards. In Copenhagen they come to $130 a year for a three-room apartment. But in new housing they average considerably higher — $200 for two rooms. In relation to income, however, rents are a little cheaper than they were before the war. Today they account for 16 per cent of a skilled worker's income against 20 per cent in 1940; for an unskilled worker rents take 20 per cent of income against 25 per cent in 1940.

I found the new housing developments in Copenhagen impressive. I visited one project containing 150 apartments of from one to four rooms set in a beautifully landscaped park. The architecture of the four-story buildings was modern and simple. The rooms, flooded with sunlight, were tastefully decorated, the colors harmonious, the ceilings finished in wood. The whole development was designed for modern living in which the wife, as well as the husband, often has a job outside the home. On the ground floor was a reception office which kept track of telephone calls and took care of deliveries. Next to it was a delicatessen shop. Here the wife, returning from work, could buy all manner of cooked foods and thus be spared the drudgery of cooking. For those too tired even to set a table, there was a pleasant restaurant with tables outside on a terrace overlooking the gardens. Soft drinks, beer, wine and liquor were sold by the delicatessen and served in the restaurant. There was a day nursery for the young

---

[8] Usually a "member" of a co-operative housing development pays a membership fee of $5.00 and buys shares equal to from 3 to 5 per cent of the estimated value of the dwelling he plans to occupy.

children. There was a domestic service bureau to provide someone to do the housework, if desired.

And there were innovations which gave the occupants facilities for entertaining and putting up visiting relatives which they could not ordinarily enjoy in their small apartments. On the top floor of each block were excellently appointed "social rooms" of various sizes where one could entertain a large or small group of friends in complete privacy. There was no charge for their use and meals and drinks could be sent up from the restaurant below. On the roof garden there were several separate sections where, in the summer, one could also entertain.

Finally each building in the series which made up the development had two guest rooms.

"These are mostly for mother-in-laws," my guide, a housing expert, smiled. "They can now visit their families without crowding up and getting into everyone's hair. They like having a room of their own, and our experience is that their families like it even more."

Although vast apartment buildings such as I have just described dominate housing in Copenhagen and the larger towns, I saw a number of pleasant one-family housing projects. One row of these, well within the city limits, was flanked by family gardens on one side and a park on the other. Venturing into one of the homes I found it to have four rooms, kitchen and bath. It was obviously occupied by a middle-class family. The lady of the house explained that their rent came to $250 a year, which was about 10 per cent of their income. The great bulk of Danes, wage earners and salaried employees, however, make between $1400 and $1500 a year.

The Achievement of Labor-Management Peace

In Copenhagen, as in the other northern capitals, I consulted with leaders of the Confederation of Labor and the Employers' Federation and learned how in Denmark they had worked out, after much costly strife, a detailed system of collective bargaining which might well serve as an example, if not a model, for the rest of the world. It has not completely eliminated strikes and lockouts. But it has brought an era of relative labor peace which few other countries have experienced.

As far back as 1899, shortly after they were founded, the two federations representing workers and employers were brought together as the result of a disastrous work-stoppage caused by a nationwide lockout. They not only settled that dispute but negotiated that year what has since become known as the "September Agreement." It is still, more than a half century later, the charter of collective bargaining in Denmark and though it has been amended over the years, stands today as the foundation of fair and amicable relations between industry and its workers.

These two far-sighted organizations also have been responsible for all the labor legislation enacted in Denmark in modern times. Parliament, in effect, has told them to first reach agreement on the whole complex system regulating their relations. Then when they have hammered out a compromise between themselves, the Rigsdag has enacted it, when necessary, into law. Unlike conditions in Norway and Sweden, where the unions at first bitterly opposed the establishment of a Labor Court to interpret collective contracts, the Danish Labor Federation approved it, working out the structure of the tribunal first with the employers' organization before it was established by law.

Such remarkable co-operation between labor and management could never have been attained had not the respective federations achieved power to speak for their respective members. Actually the Danish Employers' Federation is a more closely knit organization than the Labor Federation and has more authority not only to negotiate but to discipline its members. It can force an employer who belongs to it to lock out his workers whether he is involved in a labor dispute or not, and regardless of his wishes. It can fine him up to $15,000 for disregarding such an order. It can compel a member to break off all business relations with a nonmember who tries to benefit from a lockout or a strike. And no member firm may resign from the Federation during a labor dispute.

The Employers' Association is well financed, for the purpose not only of carrying out successful bargaining with the unions through a permanent staff of professional labor experts and economists but of providing a partial compensation to firms affected by strikes and lockouts. The initiation fee in the federation is 1 per cent of the total wages paid out by a company in the previous year. Annual dues are one fourth of 1 per cent. A further one fourth of 1 per cent has to be paid into the federation's strike and lockout fund. In case of a work stoppage a firm is granted from the fund a sum equal to 25 per cent of the wages it would have had to pay had there not been a cessation of work.

The Danish Federation of Labor, though possessing considerable power by American standards, is the least centralized of the three Scandinavian labor organizations. This is largely because 40 per cent of the total federation membership is concentrated in one organization, the Laborers' Union, which consists of both skilled and unskilled workers in several fields, being similar in this respect to the British Transport and General Workers' Union which is so dominant in Great Britain. This powerful organization has been able to prevent the federation from assuming the authority to bargain for all. The result is that the various national unions negotiate their own collective contracts and call their own strikes; and though the central federation must at least be advised of the progress of negotiations and strike plans and can exert considerable influence on their outcome (partly because of its control of a central strike fund), it lacks the centralized bargaining power of its Swedish and Norwegian counterparts. However, in the basic agreements with employers it has been able to negotiate for all of its members.

Through the Labor party it also wields great political power. Legally, the two organizations are quite separate. The Danish trade-unions do not even permit so-called collective affiliation with the political Labor party, as is done in Norway and Sweden. The Danish Labor party is actually a federation of some 1360 local clubs with over 300,000 members, of whom the majority are trade-unionists. However, these local clubs are affiliated in their respective localities with the central trades and labor councils and they work closely together.

On the national level, the Labor Federation elects one member to the executive committee of the Labor party and one to the party council, which is the real ruling body of political labor. The party, on its part, elects two members to the executive Committee of the Labor Federation. So there is an interlocking.

There is also direct financial support of the party by the trade-unions and the federation. The latter contributes to the party's national campaign funds, and gives liberally to the Copenhagen Socialist daily, *Social Demokraten.*

Trade-union funds, incidentally, are often swelled by the success of the Labor co-operative enterprises. A brewery in Copenhagen, for example, co-operatively owned and operated by the capital's unions, does an annual business of four to five million dollars a year.

After the Second World War the Communists made a bid to capture the Danish trade-union movement but after some initial success their attempt failed. They benefited for a short time by their splendid record in the Resistance but the numerous strikes which they engineered and their subservience to Moscow quickly lost them most of their support among the workers, who in Denmark are decidedly not revolutionary nor interested in Marxism. Also increasing prosperity, bringing with it higher wages and nearly full employment, and the vigorous reaction of the dominant Socialists in the unions, helped to terminate Communist ambitions in the trade-union field. By 1950 they dominated but a dozen or two locals, and none of the national unions.

Until recently Danish law accorded only a two-week paid vacation to all employees compared to three weeks in Norway and Sweden. But in 1952 the Labor Federation made its own agreement with the employers to increase paid vacations to three weeks; and a year later Parliament followed suit by amending the Holiday Act to that effect though it did not go into force until the summer of 1954.

Economic and political power, a visitor from America senses, fills the organized Danish workers with a certain pride. They feel, not without reason, that collectively they are one of the main pillars of the nation. They are highly conscious of the opportunities such a position gives them and also, it must be added, of the responsibilities.

The September Agreement of 1899 between the Employers' and Labor Federations carefully separated the two kinds of disputes between unions and management: those over "interests" and those over "law." The first concerns the substance of contracts, especially wages, hours and working conditions. The second deals exclusively with interpretation of contracts.

Conflicts over interests are settled by direct collective bargaining, according to a comprehensive set of rules for negotiation agreed upon between the two federations in 1936, after eleven years of talks over the conference table. The most noteworthy feature of this agreement is that if direct negotiations between unions and management break down a state mediator is called in to try to effect an accord.

This is a key moment in collective bargaining in Denmark. If the mediator cannot get an agreement he is empowered to draft what he thinks is a fair compromise proposal. That draft, and that draft alone, must then be submitted to both sides for a secret referendum of their members. This practice prevents either labor or management from misrepresenting the issues by preparing its own version of what is to be voted on. If both sides ballot to accept the mediator's proposal, it is written into a collective agreement. If one group or both reject the proposal, they may then, but only then, resort to a strike or lockout. In practice they seldom do.

Settlement of *interpretations* of collective agreements differs somewhat in Denmark from the practice we have seen in Norway and Sweden, where a Labor Court has exclusive jurisdiction in such matters. The Danes handle this problem in two ways. They have a Labor Court, or "the Permanent Court of Arbitration." Each federation chooses three members and jointly they select a neutral presiding judge. Thus, unlike in the other Scandinavian countries, where the state appoints the members of the Labor Court, the tribunal in Denmark is really a creation of organized labor and management.

However, it is a statutory body and has exclusive jurisdiction over *breaches* of collective contracts. Its decisions have complete legality, are final, and cannot be appealed to the ordinary courts. It assesses fines for damages or as a penalty not only upon employers and unions but on individual workers — a practice which has increased respect for it by all parties. An individual worker or employer, however, has no standing in the court. His case must be presented through his respective national federation.

Whereas the Labor Court handles only *breaches* of agreements, the *interpretation* of them is left to a network of industrial arbitration boards which consist usually of two representatives of each side and an impartial chairman jointly selected by them from a panel of judges from the ordinary courts. Thus interpretation of contracts is really a matter of private arbitration between labor and employers. Its decisions do not therefore have legal force, as do those of the Labor Court, though they are almost always accepted by the losing party. If they are not and the losing party declines to abide by the decision, then the case is taken to the Labor Court, not as an appeal, but as a breach of contract.

In no case can a dispute before either the Labor Court or an arbitration board be used to bring about a strike or a lockout. In Denmark I found that both unions and employers, though they were often bitter if decisions went against them, agreed that this method of settling interpretation and breaches of contracts was not only equitable and fair but had contributed much to labor peace.

A Note on the Cultural Life

The Danes, one soon senses, are a people who have learned how to enjoy life. The "melancholy Dane" must be largely the creation of fiction writers; or at least he has disappeared from real life in recent years.[9] Workers, farmers, businessmen, editors, writers, artists, professors — even the few aristocrats in their ancient castles behind the moats, whom I also visited — have a light and sunny disposition, being much given to joking and good-natured banter. I heard much hearty laughter in this country.

Life is simpler than ours. The Danes lack many of our gadgets, especially the motor car. The bicycle is still the chief mode of locomotion — for men, women and children. Country roads and the new city streets all have special lanes for cyclists, but in Copenhagen they swarm through the narrow, winding ancient thoroughfares, which a pedestrian crosses in their wake at considerable though not mortal peril. Everyone in Denmark, including the King and Queen, august cabinet members and bishops, rides a bicycle; and a visiting American, used to driving a car even to reach a drugstore around the corner, is likely to be fascinated to find, at the conclusion of an elegant luncheon or dinner, the ladies and gentlemen setting off for home or office on their bikes, the chic full skirts of the ladies billowing in the breeze which invariably blows in from the nearby sea.

Lovers, I noticed, have perfected a technique of riding arm in arm — or holding hands — as they weave through the heavy traffic of the capital on their respective bicycles. Whole families may be seen cycling off for a week end or a vacation in the country or at the seaside, the mother and father, say, carting a baby and a three-year-

[9] Against this personal appraisal must be noted a suicide rate that is four times as high as in the United States. Every year in Denmark an average of 1000 persons commit suicide.

old in a basket in front of the handle bars and perhaps a slightly older child on a carrier behind while the other (riding) members manage a load of suitcases, blankets, provisions and — often, if they are going camping — parts of a tent. Because Denmark is one of the levelest lands in Europe, cycling demands no heavy exertion and it gets people around the realm with what the Danes think is reasonable speed.

The pace of life in Denmark is slower than ours, the pressures of living less — and the Danes say they prefer it that way. One finds few "worriers," and I never heard a businessman or politician complain of ulcers.

In Copenhagen, where one fourth of all Danes live, people of every class relax in the summer time at Tivoli, an amusement park in the very heart of the city. There is nothing comparable to it — in my experience — anywhere else in the world. It is much more than an "amusement" park. To be sure it has its roller-coasters, merry-go-rounds and Ferris wheels. But it also has half a dozen of the capital's finest restaurants, with great terraces overlooking pleasant gardens. It has band concerts, but it also has a fine symphony orchestra with conductors and guest artists of world renown. It also has — I stumbled across it one balmy summer evening while roaming through the vast park — an open-air pantomime theater which is the last home of *Commedia dell'Arte* in Europe.

The country's greatest drama house is the Royal Theater in the Kongens Nytorv Square, where three permanent companies perform plays, operas and ballet. Indeed, the Royal Ballet is one of the two or three best in Europe. The Royal Theater has an annex, known as "The New Stage," with an excellent repertoire. The government subsidizes the Royal Theater to the extent of some half-million dollars a year, and one condition for such support is that it give at least fifty performances annually in the provinces. There are also a dozen private theaters in the capital.

With its fine theaters, excellent restaurants and cafés, frequent concerts, remarkable art galleries and smart shops (along the narrow, winding Stroget street which runs from Kongens Nytorv to Town Hall Square) Copenhagen, with reason, has come to be known as the "Paris of the North." Perhaps, since the end of the past war, at least, it has become even gayer than the French Metropolis of Light. During the pleasant summer months it is packed with visitors and the excellent hotels are quite incapable of adequately taking care of the influx.

In their pursuit of happiness, the Danes (like the French) put much store in good eating. They are hearty eaters, and they eat well — both at home and in restaurants, of which there are a large number of good ones both in the capital and the provinces. Perhaps this is a good place to sample what the Danes eat — in a general way it goes for all the Scandinavian peoples.

Breakfast is not very hearty by American standards. It is "Continental" — that is, it consists usually merely of coffee and rolls, though both are likely to be better than is obtainable anywhere else in Europe. If you ask for some of the wonderful Danish bacon and eggs you are liable to be informed that they are obtainable only in England, which buys most of them.

Lunch brings the national dish — *smørrebrød*. There are about two hundred varieties of this — all sorts of smoked, cooked and pickled fish, shrimps and meat as well as assorted cheeses atop buttered rye or white bread. This is a meal in itself and is invariably accompanied by beer and usually by *schnapps*. Sometimes the supply of *smørrebrød* is deliberately cut down so that a warm dish of meat or fish may be served.

Then follows cheese and some delicious (but fattening) Danish pastry.

The evening meal is customarily served between 6 and 7 P.M. and the Danes, for some reason, call it *Middag*, or midday meal. The main dish is meat — beefsteak, pork chop or veal cutlet — with plenty of vegetables and, in summer, a green salad. Sometimes a fish dish is substituted for meat, the supply of fish being abundant and the cooking of it superb. Among Danish specialties are *stegt Aal* (fried eel), *kogt Torsk* (boiled cod), *Flaeskesteg med Rødkaal* (roast pork and red cabbage), *Engelsk Bøf* (English beefsteak, cooked in a manner the English never knew) *gule Aerter* (a pea soup served with pork, sausages or even pickled goose). Danish soups take some getting acquainted with. One, popular in warm weather, is made of fruit juices and is too sweet; another, *Øllebrød*, is, as the Danish name makes clear, made of beer and rye bread.

A meal in a private Danish home, I found, is inevitably a lavish feast. An uninitiated guest does well to indulge sparingly in first servings, for there will be several more, and unless they are liberally partaken of, he will be regarded by his host as either ailing or displeased with the food.

In Denmark, as elsewhere in the North, I found a remarkable respect and even enthusiasm for the cultural life. The cultivation of arts and letters might almost be called a national passion; and in Copenhagen I got the impression that writers, artists and intellectuals are rated higher in general acclaim than businessmen and bankers, poorer in worldly goods and bank accounts though they may be and inevitably are.

The Danes read and buy books on a scale that long ago disappeared in America. Except for Iceland, Denmark publishes more books in relation to the number of inhabitants than any other nation in the world. With a population only half as large as New York City, Danish publishers bring out 3500 titles annually — roughly, a third as many as publishers in the United States. The average Danish book sells 5000 copies — as many, that is, as the average American book — though our population is forty times greater. Danish publishers have made strenuous efforts not to price books out of the market (as some believe American publishers may have felt forced to do). The average book sells for a dollar and standard editions, of course, like almost all books sold on the European continent, are paper-covered, which is one of the reasons, though not the only one, why they can be sold at a price within the reach of those who read.

The support of arts, letters and science by both the state and private sources is little short of amazing. Out of the $2,000,000 a year the state earns from its betting pools on soccer-football games, a quarter is budgeted for "general cultural purposes." In addition to a half-million dollars a year for the Royal Theater, the national government pays out $200,000 to encourage art and artists. Each year the Ministry of Education presents a number of aspiring, needy writers, painters, sculptors and composers with stipends ranging from $200 to $1400. Many established authors, artists and composers receive a life pension from the state of $750 a year — and there are no strings attached either in theory or in practice.

Private enterprise does even more to encourage art and science. In the first place, individuals are in the habit of buying not only books but contemporary works of art. In the second place, some of the great private fortunes made in business have in recent years been turned over to the advancement of art and science.

The outstanding example of this is the great Carlsberg Foundation. It is unique — in many ways.

Carlsberg, as every connoisseur of beer knows, is one of the great breweries of the world, its brews being popular not only in Denmark and Europe but on the other four continents. It was founded by a very remarkable Dane, J. C. Jacobsen, Ph.D., in 1847, and carried on through the turn of the century by his equally distinguished son, Carl, also a Ph.D., who for some years ran his own plant, the New Carlsberg Brewery, in competition with his father. Each of them bequeathed their brewery business to foundations for the advancement of science and art.

Not the least unique result of these bequests is that the Carlsberg Foundation, presided over by five learned professors chosen by and from the members of the Royal Danish Academy of Science, today owns and operates the Carlsberg breweries, one of the most flourishing businesses in Denmark, all of whose profits go to art and science. Probably no other brewery in the world has such an academic management or so disposes of its profits, and when I inquired of one of the plant managers how on earth a bunch of professors could run such a huge commercial enterprise, he replied that they did very well, as a glance at the profit sheets would show.

Actually, in order to prevent fluctuation of income, about a third of the profits are set aside for augmenting the Foundation's capital outside the brewery, chiefly by purchase of government and credit-society bonds. Nevertheless that portion of the brewery's annual profits spent on art and science comes to some three quarters of a million dollars. And since 1872 the total amount expended by the Foundation has amounted to nearly $15,000,000.

Not that the professorial Board of Directors has let the brewery run down in its enthusiasm for supporting science and art. Between the wars, one manager told me, the professors allotted $13,000,000 for new construction and equipment. And since the war, the manager added, his academic bosses have been most liberal in their spending on plant renovation. Indeed on a visit to the Carlsberg breweries I saw a new bottling unit which had just arrived from America and which, I was told, was one of the biggest, most ingenious and hygienic things of its kind in existence on the globe. The professors had insisted on their managers having it in order to keep up with new business.

J. C. Jacobsen, the founder of the Carlsberg breweries, had been mainly interested in science; his son, Carl, developed a passion for art. Thus the original Foundation set up by the father was devoted to promoting science and today comprises three sections: the Carlsberg Laboratory of Chemistry and Physiology; the Research Center for the Natural Sciences, Mathematics, Philology, History and Philosophy — which includes the Institute for Biology; and the Museum of National History at Frederiksborg Castle.

The so-called New Carlsberg Foundation, established by the son, is devoted to the encouragement of art. Its chief glory is the New Carlsberg Glyptotek in Copenhagen, which houses one of the world's largest and richest art collections. This foundation also devotes considerable sums to the purchase of art works for other Danish museums, to the commissioning of decorations for public buildings and to the study of art. It also makes liberal grants to living artists.

The two Carlsberg breweries were amalgamated in 1906 under the ownership of the parent Carlsberg Foundation. Actually the New Carlsberg Foundation remains separate, with its own board of directors. But profits from beer are divided about equally between the two organizations — and thus between science and art.

Finally, the elder Jacobsen willed that his town mansion and gardens should be occupied by Denmark's most distinguished private citizen, to be selected by the Academy of Science. The first occupant was the noted philosopher Harald Høffding. The present one is Niels Bohr, the atomic physicist who played an important part in the development of America's first atom bomb following his flight from the Nazis. I had, incidentally, one of the most enlightening afternoons of my life with Professor Bohr, one of the truly great men of our atomic age.

Philosophers, scientists, artists and writers are indeed honored in this kingdom.

The Danes have an interesting literature of their own, but it is little known outside of Scandinavia because so little of it has been translated into the principal languages. A few nineteenth-century writers — above all, Hans Christian Andersen, the spinner of fairy tales —

achieved world renown. Kierkegaard, the fiery philosopher and antitheologian, has recently become widely read abroad, hailed by some as the father of postwar Existentialism. And there was the great critic, Georg Brandes, who toward the end of the last century transformed Danish culture by stormily and successfully battling romanticism, and whose six-volume work, *Main Currents in Nineteenth-Century Literature*, is regarded as a classic in the Western world.

Danish critics speak passionately of three contemporary authors who, they feel, are less known abroad than they should be. Two are Nobel Prize winners: Henrik Pontoppidan, who died at the age of eighty-six in 1943 during the Nazi occupation, and Johannes V. Jensen, who was seventy-seven at his death in 1950. Pontoppidan is generally regarded as Denmark's finest modern author, whose novels, only one of which has been translated into English, constitute a moving description and a severe judgment of his native land in recent times.

Jensen was a sort of Danish Kipling who, unlike most of his contemporaries, glorified, as one Copenhagen critic has written, "the machine, imperialism, the City and Wall Street, High Finance and Darwinism." He was also a passionate enthusiast for the United States of America. Indeed, his first visit to our shores was a milestone in his literary career and four books on the subject, two of which were novels, helped launch him on the road to success as an author.

The third writer is Martin Andersen Nexø, the first and greatest of the country's proletarian writers. Born in 1869 in a slum tenement in Copenhagen, the son of a drunkard father, he worked as a farm hand, shoemaker and finally as a bricklayer before he turned to writing. In Scandinavia, he is hailed as the Danish Gorki.

Danish writers face a difficult problem. Their audience is limited to some four million Danes and three million Norwegians, who can read them in their own language. The nationalism of the Norwegians, however, make them prefer Norwegian editions. Of the seven million Swedes, many read Danish with ease, but most prefer translations. Only occasionally, it seems, is a Danish book translated into English, French and German, where it can enjoy a wider circulation.

This condition necessarily limits a writer's income. But the problem of the author's existence in modern society is very much in the minds of the Danes, and they have done a great deal to try to solve it.

As we have seen, the state itself gives extensive grants to writers, and the state, and to a lesser extent the booksellers, have recently hit upon an ingenious scheme to increase the income of authors. Members of rental libraries maintained by the bookstores pay an annual fee of fifteen cents which goes to a benevolent fund maintained by the Danish Society of Authors for needy members.

Much more important is a plan put through by the Danish Parliament after the last war by which 5 per cent of the funds given by the state for public libraries is credited to a special fund for authors. It was realized that to try to pay a writer a small fee for every loan of his book from a public library would necessitate so much bookkeeping as to absorb most of the fund for this purpose. So a far simpler scheme was worked out. At the end of the year, each public library in the country is obligated by law to render a statement showing the number of books of each living author on its lending shelves. It is not necessary to enumerate specific works: just the total number of volumes by each author. Nor does it make any difference whether the books have circulated or not.

The Authors' Society, which administers the fund's accounts, then works out a table showing the total number of books of each author on all the library shelves. Then 5 per cent of the state grant to libraries is pro-rated to the authors, according to the number of books each one is represented as having in the libraries. At the present time, a fee to authors of about four cents per copy is paid annually on a little over one million library books. This, of course, is in addition to the regular royalty at the time of sale.

The feeling of the Danes for culture and its relation to life was typically expressed on the occasion of the visit of Winston Churchill to Copenhagen in 1950. The Danes, grateful to the great English Prime Minister for all he had done to help liberate them from the Nazi tyranny, presented him with a statue of Victory. It was not a representation of Allied victory over the Nazi Germans, but of the triumph of culture over brutal force.

A word about church, press and movies.

Not until the middle of the nineteenth century was religious liberty granted in Denmark. Until 1849 all Danish subjects had to belong to the Lutheran State Church. Today the Church, to which the King must adhere, retains 97 per cent of the inhabitants, though far from that percentage may be called regular churchgoers. Parliament has legislative authority over the Church. Citizens entitled to vote for Parliament elect representatives to the parish congregational councils, which administer local church finances and often select the pastors.

The press of Denmark is lively and independent, though almost all newspapers serve as organs of one of the political parties — Conservative, Liberal or Labor. Copenhagen has more daily newspapers than New York, twelve in all, of which the leading ones, in circulation, influence and amount of news, are *Berlingske Tidende,* Conservative, and *Politiken,* Social Liberal.

The Danes are great moviegoers (there is only a limited television broadcast in Copenhagen and extremely few receivers) and Hollywood films dominate the market. In 1950, an average year, 205 out of the 284 new films shown were American; only 13 were Danish. Out of some 54,000,000 movie admissions sold annually, it is estimated that 38,000,000 are for American movies. This accounts sometimes — I often heard it said in Copenhagen — for some very curious ideas prevalent in Denmark about the state of civilization in the United States.

The Trials of a Small Kingdom in the Atomic Age

Throughout the summer I was in Denmark the good citizens kept trekking to the polls. There was a national election on April 21, 1953, for the Lower House (Folketing) of the Rigsdag. This was necessary because of the requirement that a newly elected Lower House first approve the new Constitution before it could be voted on by the people in a plesbiscite. On April 28, the indirect election for the Upper House (Landsting), which the new Constitution was to abolish, took place. Neither election brought any important change in the political lineup, the Socialists maintaining themselves as the largest party in each house but still in a minority — with 61 seats out of 151 in the Lower House, and 33 out of 76 in the Upper House.

Since all political parties except the Communists favored the new Constitution, its approval by the people was a foregone conclusion. Actually it just squeaked through in a national plebiscite held May 28. The law provided that it had to be approved by more than 45 per cent of all eligible voters. The vote in favor of it was 45.76 per cent.[10]

On June 5, 1953, the 104th anniversary of the ratification of Denmark's first liberal Constitution, which had wiped out royal absolutism, King Frederick signed the new Constitution.

It is the newest of all democratic constitutions, and it is an interesting document.

For one thing, it boldly makes provision for the delegation of national sovereignty "to international organizations set up by mutual agreement with other states for the promotion of international rules of law and co-operation." This was a historic step for such a nationally conscious nation as Denmark, and it was not taken without much debate and reflection by the lawmakers. The issue was somewhat similar to that which was raised for Americans in the debates on the Bricker amendment.

The Danish parliamentarians had been much impressed by a recommendation of the Inter-Parliamentary Union in the summer of 1952 that member countries amend their Constitutions so as to enable them to delegate authority to international organizations. The Danes, in writing their new Constitution, did so. But the surrender of national sovereignty, as the then Prime Minister Erik Eriksen emphasized to Parliament, is a serious matter. And the makers of the new Constitution were careful to spell out very strict safeguards to prevent woolly-minded world-government fanatics, as one Danish politician put it, from giving away too much too carelessly.

Danish sovereignty can only be delegated to world bodies set up by mutual agreement. Such a step must be embodied in a bill which has to be passed by a five-sixths majority of all the members of the Folketing. If a majority less than that is obtained, the bill may be submitted to a national referendum of the electorate. In that case, a simple majority of the voters, if they represent more than 30 per cent of the electorate, decides the issue.

The new Constitution, among other things, provides: that Greenland has become an integral part of the kingdom, and is therefore no longer a colony; that all privileges attached by legislation to nobility,

[10] In 1939 both Houses of Parliament had overwhelmingly voted for a new Constitution which provided, among other things, for a unicameral legislature somewhat similar to that of Norway. But it failed to receive the approval of the necessary 45 per cent plus of the electorate.

280 THE CHALLENGE OF SCANDINAVIA

title and rank shall be abolished; that in the future no fiefs, entailed land or estates shall be created; that "the members of the Folketing shall be bound solely by their own consciences and not by any directions given by their electors"; and "that censorship shall never again be introduced."

The two most fundamental changes in Denmark's new Constitution abolished the Upper House of Parliament, leaving the country with a unicameral legislature, and provided that a woman may inherit the throne.

The Danes say there were solid reasons for both innovations. For half a century up to the end of the First World War the Socialists and Liberals had clamored for the abolition of the Upper House. Their objection was that it was a citadel of privilege and reaction and had no part in a democratic kingdom. But as the farmers and workers assumed more and more political power, they were able to dominate in recent years the Upper as well as the Lower House, and their agitation ceased. By the end of the Second World War, however, all the political parties were agreed that the Upper House had become unnecessary.

That decision left them, though, with one problem: the necessity of finding some kind of check on the decisions of a single House of Parliament, a safeguard that had been automatically provided by a two-chamber system. The Danes were much concerned to protect the rights of the minority. They first considered adopting the Norwegian or Finnish types of unicameral legislatures, but finally hit upon a scheme of their own. If a minority of at least one third of the members of Parliament objects to a bill that has been passed, they can demand that it be submitted to a national referendum. If a majority of the voters, who must number at least 30 per cent of the electorate, agrees with the parliamentary minority, the bill is killed. Certain Acts are exempted from this proviso, such as those dealing with appropriations, taxes, treaties and the powers of the king.

A Ruling Queen for Denmark

The most popular feature of the new Constitution was that annulling the requirement of male succession to the throne and providing that a daughter of a monarch would become the rightful heir if there were no sons.

The Danish lawmakers make no bones of the fact that this change, while generally desired, was also made to meet a specific and current situation. At one stroke it eliminated the then legal heir to the throne, Prince Knud, the fifty-three-year-old brother of King Frederick. In his stead it put the thirteen-year-old, oldest daughter of the King, Princess Margaret (Margrethe in Danish) next in line for the succession. If she survives her father, she will become the first ruling Queen Denmark has had in five centuries. And as Queen Margaret II, she will bear the name of the most illustrious Danish monarch in history. It was Queen Margaret I, as we have seen, who at the turn of the fifteenth century united Denmark, Norway and Sweden under one crown for the first and last time. That Queen Margaret died in 1412.

The decision of the Constitution makers to provide for female succession to the throne was taken — so I was informed in Copenhagen — after it was learned that Queen Ingrid, mother of three daughters, would not be having any more children. The Prime Minister at the time, Erik Eriksen, publicly stated that the change was in line with the achievement by women of equal status with men in all aspects of Danish life. It was natural, he stated, to carry this development a step further and enable a woman to ascend the throne.

There was also the influence of events in England. The very summer the people voted on the new Constitution, Elizabeth was being crowned Queen of England and the Danes followed the coronation ceremonies in London with avid interest. If so mature a people as the English took pride in having a ruling Queen, why shouldn't the Danes have the opportunity in similar dynastic circumstances? It was a question I often heard put in Copenhagen that summer. The more the people in Denmark thought of it, the more an affirmative answer appealed to them. Besides, said the Danes, Margaret, like Elizabeth in England, bore the name of a great queen.

I heard a good deal of talk in Denmark that the beautiful and strong-willed Queen Ingrid, daughter of King Gustav VI Adolf of Sweden, had been influential in having the law of succession changed. It would have been natural, certainly, for her to wish to see her own daughter inherit the throne.

The influence of recent dynastic history in England is further seen in the provisions of the new Danish Constitution governing royal marriages. According to Article 5 of the Succession to the Throne Act, neither the monarch nor his heir can marry anyone they please. The king, it is stipulated, "shall not enter into marriage without the consent of the Parliament." Moreover, if "a person entitled to succeed to the throne" (so reads the Act) "enters into marriage without the consent of the King given in Council of State" (that is, in agreement with the Cabinet) "the person in question shall forfeit his right of succession to the Throne for himself and the children born of the marriage and for their issue."

The Danish lawmakers, it was obvious, wanted no "Simpson affair" to complicate the dynastic affairs of the kingdom.

Princess Margaret had just turned thirteen when she learned that, if the new Constitution went through, she would replace her uncle as heir to the throne. One heard many stories in gossiping Copenhagen that summer about her reaction to the news. One account had her expressing keen disappointment. "I wish I were an ordinary girl," she was reported to have exclaimed, "who could grow up like everyone else and marry a man named Olsen!"

She first heard of what was afoot when she picked up a morning newspaper and read on the first page an account of a lively debate in Parliament over the question of succession. She was horrified, it was later reported, to learn that she might one day become Queen of Denmark. She rushed to her father with a torrent of questions, including, it was said, one about what was to happen to Uncle Knud. Her usually easygoing father was disturbed. He tucked the newspaper away and told her to forget it. For several months he contrived to keep the daily newspapers out of her reach. Then he sent her, with her two younger sisters, off to England with Queen Ingrid. It was there that her mother confided to her that the new Constitution, if and when it was adopted, would make her one day eligible to become Queen Margaret (Margrethe) II.

Princess Margaret is described by those who frequent royal circles as a typical blue-eyed, blond Danish girl, with a mind of her own and — as her father once said in a broadcast — "with certain bad habits, like all other children." She was born on April 16, 1940, seven days after the Nazi Germans occupied Denmark, and she is said to have, as would be natural, indelible memories of that unhappy time when her father, as Crown Prince, and her grandfather, the King, were virtual prisoners of the Teutonic conquerors. The Germans were still in occupation when, on her fifth birthday, she entered kindergarten. At seven, she was enrolled in a fashionable girls' day-school in down-town Copenhagen from which she will be graduated in 1958. She has above average grades but she is no wonder child and, on the insistence of her father and mother, is treated just as are the other 1200 girls in the school. Her favorite subjects are history and botany; and like all royal children in Scandinavia she is a good linguist. Her Swedish mother has taught her Swedish and — as befits a great-granddaughter of Queen Victoria — has also taught her English. She is presently mastering German and French in school. Like all Danish schoolgirls she must study sewing and cooking, which are compulsory subjects. She is said to be bored by the first and fascinated by the second. The Danes say Princess Margaret looks like her mother, who is strikingly beautiful, and takes after her father, a genial, salty, modest and democratic man who enjoys considerable popularity in the kingdom.

King Frederick IX (Christian Frederik Franz Michael Carl Valdemar Georg — to give him all his Danish names) was born March 11, 1899, and succeeded to the throne on the death of his father, Christian X, April 20, 1947. He married Princess Ingrid in Stockholm May 24, 1935. Besides Princess Margaret, the royal couple have two other daughters: Princess Benedikte, born in 1944, and Princess Anne-Marie, born in 1946.

The King was trained in the navy and still has a chestful of tattoos, which once were photographed — to the shock of some and the amused delight of others. A big, strapping man of six feet six inches, he leads a strenuous physical life, going in for underwater swimming, rowing, tennis and hunting. He is also an enthusiast for hefty daily setting-up exercises, which he first learned by mail from a London practitioner by the name of Henry Walsh.

But his chief delight outside of working hours is music. He is an accomplished pianist and since the war has been diligently learning the difficult art of conducting symphony orchestras. He now conducts two public concerts a year of Denmark's leading orchestra, the State Radio Symphony Orchestra, and also, at times, handles the baton for the Royal Chapel Orchestra. On the seventieth birthday of his father-in-law, the King of Sweden, he added to the celebration by conducting the Swedish Court Orchestra. Photographs of Frederick, rehearsing an orchestra in his shirt-sleeves, have now become common in the Danish press.

The King and Queen, who occupy a modest apartment in Amalienborg Castle in the heart of Copenhagen, lead an informal life for the most part. When the children were younger, Frederick could often be seen, at the side of the Queen, pushing a pram through the streets of the capital. Now he cycles with them.

The Danes say theirs is the oldest kingdom in Europe. The monarchy is an ingrown part of their life. Now that it has adjusted itself to modern democracy, including the prevalence of Labor governments, there is no sentiment, even among the Socialists, for a republic.

The Importance of Denmark to the Defense of the West

Tiny land though it is, with only a relatively handful of inhabitants, Denmark is of immense importance to the security of the West — for two reasons:

1. Her strategic position both on the northern flank of NATO's continental defense line, and at the entrance to the Baltic Sea, whose southern and eastern shore is now mostly occupied by Russia.

2. Her possession of Greenland, which guards the principal air-approaches to Canada and the United States from the Soviet Union.

Denmark, as the world learned in 1940, has not the faintest chance of successfully defending herself by her own efforts for one day against a big power. The Nazi occupation taught the Danes that there was no security in neutrality. Since 1949 Denmark has, therefore, as we have seen, sought security in NATO. The decision was made by a Labor government, but it was supported by the Conservatives and the Agrarians. Among the Danish people themselves, there were many doubts. Gallup Polls showed that in 1949 just 47 per cent of the people approved. In 1952, some 50 per cent liked the idea, but a year later the figure had dropped to 47 per cent again.

Denmark's membership in the North Atlantic Alliance has not

brought easy sailing for her. She has been beset with problems aris-
ing from it, and has been something of a problem herself to the
NATO High Command.

To begin with, Russia has never ceased blustering, protesting and
threatening because little Denmark has had the temerity to remain
an active partner in the Western coalition. The Danes have not been
cowed by Moscow's belligerence, but that is not to say they are unaware of the frightening fact that Soviet air bases in Germany are
but ten minutes' flying time from Denmark's chief cities and towns;
that Russia's much vaunted "Baltic Gibraltar" on the German island
of Rügen contains, among other things, launching sites for improved V-2 rockets which can easily reach Copenhagen eighty miles
away; and that with her bombers and rockets the Russians have the
power today to pulverize Denmark within a few hours, no matter
how savagely NATO forces retaliate, atomically or otherwise, later
on.

"Sure, you will eventually liberate us, as you did the last time,"
one Danish editor told me, summing up an attitude I heard often
expressed. "Only — this time there will be nothing left to liberate."

Moscow's war of nerves on the Danes goes on unceasingly. Danish
fishing smacks in the Baltic are halted in the open sea and hauled
into Russian-occupied or Polish ports. In the spring of 1953, when
two Polish flyers succeeded in landing their MIG-15's on the Danish
Island of Bornholm, the Polish government demanded the immediate
return of both planes and the pilots. When the Danish government
gave the pilots asylum and moreover allowed Allied experts, including Americans, to examine the first modern Russian jet to fall into
their hands intact before crating it and shipping it back to Poland,
the Warsaw Communist government — egged on by Moscow, the
Danes have no doubt — raged and fumed against Denmark.

In October 1952, just as NATO defenses in Western Europe began to shape up to something, the Soviet government sent a sharp
note to Denmark accusing her of following an aggressive policy by
allowing armed forces of other NATO countries to be stationed on
her territory. The Danish government replied promptly and courte-
ously to the effect that Denmark had no aggressive designs on Russia
or on any other land and that moreover, in the words of the note,
she "would never permit Danish territory to be used for starting an
attack."

Molotov considered the calm Danish reply unsatisfactory and in January of the next year, dispatched another note, which was even sharper than the first. Once more mighty Russia accused tiny Denmark of being "aggressive." Once more the Soviet Union vehemently protested "the stationing of foreign troops from the NATO bloc, which pursues aggressive purposes."

Actually, Denmark has never allowed NATO troops from other countries to be stationed on her soil. This indeed is the main bone of contention between the Danish government and the SHAPE Command in Europe, and, it might be added, between Copenhagen and base-hungry Washington.

Ever since NATO's meeting in Lisbon in February, 1952, SHAPE's generals have badly wanted to bolster their northern Continental flank by stationing two American Saber-jet fighter wings in Denmark. After all, they argue, the presence of 200 of America's best jet fighter planes in Denmark would be a deterrent to the very threat which the Danes say they fear the most: that of being wiped out by Russian bombers before Allied forces could intervene. If the logic of this seems unanswerable to SHAPE commanders and American diplomats, it is not so considered in Denmark. The Danish government, whether Conservative-Agrarian, as it was between 1950 and 1953, or Labor, as it was after 1953, has steadfastly refused to let the Americans in. Work on the two airfields in Jutland, at Vandel and Tirstrup, which were suggested by SHAPE as suitable for the American flyers and which NATO offered to modernize at its own expense so that they could be used by Saber-jets, was delayed.

It cannot be said in Washington, which was more than annoyed by the Danish attitude, that Denmark did not make its position clear from the first. Back in 1949, when the Danish Parliament was debating whether to join NATO, Gustav Rassmusen, the then Foreign Minister, gave a solemn assurance: "The question has been raised," he said, "whether Denmark, in fulfillment of her obligation under Article 3 (of the NATO treaty) . . . can be expected to face demands to grant foreign powers military bases in peacetime. *To this I can reply with certainty that there will be no question of establishing foreign bases in Denmark.*"

This declaration was hailed by people of all parties. Rassmusen spoke for a Labor government, but the Conservative-Agrarian government which held office for a three-year period that began shortly thereafter likewise wouldn't agree to letting the Americans have the two air bases. As one of the Conservatives, a leading member of the Cabinet, explained to me, it would have cost them too heavily at the crucial elections which were coming up in 1953.

Actually they lost those elections to Labor, which then took office. During the election campaign the Labor party leader, Hans Hedtoft, kept emphasizing that "as conditions are, we cannot accept this proposition." His first speech to that effect, on June 23, 1953, came as something of a bombshell, for a few days before General Matthew B. Ridgway, on a farewell tour of the NATO countries, had in Copenhagen bluntly told the Danes that it was necessary to station British or American forces in Denmark because "the northern flank [meaning Denmark] cannot itself provide sufficient strength to meet Soviet aggression."

The Danes know this perfectly well, as several of them, from generals to politicians to editors, frankly admitted to me, though not for quotation. They also know that it is politically impossible to do what they recognize is obvious and necessary.

Hedtoft, after he again became Prime Minister toward the end of 1953, summed up the Danish position in a public address: "We stand solidly with the NATO community," he said, "prepared to carry out our part of the burdens, but of course we reserve the right to make known our points of view within the community. It is on the basis of such an independent appraisement that the present government, in the circumstances, has not wished a long-term stationing of Allied air forces on Danish soil. I know very well that from military-technical points of view a series of arguments may be advanced in favor of it, but there are also military considerations that may lead to an opposite view. The question cannot, however, be resolved on the basis of military views alone. *First and foremost there are political considerations.* The determining reason for our position is that it should not be undertaken in an international situation such as the present one, nor could it be consumated against the present international background without causing a split within the people . . ."

In other words — first, the Danes, like most peoples, don't like foreign troops, even friendly ones, permanently attached to their soil; second, and most important, the Danes fear Russian reaction to having American-manned airfields so close to Russian bases — and, in fact, so close to the Soviet Union itself.

The Danes, for their part, have some doubts about NATO. They are painfully aware that the 42-mile waist of the Jutland peninsula, the only land approach to Denmark, has been left virtually undefended. Despite all the talk at SHAPE about strengthening the northern Continental flank, they remind you in Copenhagen, NATO has not stationed enough ground troops there to halt the Russians for ten minutes. The Danes are realistic enough to realize that, given the present shortage of man power among the Allied nations, it is necessary to have German troops fill in the gap on the northern flank. One general in Copenhagen put it to me this way: "Distrustful as a century of experience has made us of the Germans, we should now like to see them brought into the Western military coalition. Until they are, and can furnish at least three divisions, with armor, to help defend the Jutland approach, we will remain quite defenseless on land. In that respect, NATO has left the biggest part of Denmark (Jutland) undefended."

To be sure, it allotted a handful of troops in the beginning to Jutland in an area in Germany just south of the Danish border. The force consisted of a Norwegian brigade of 3500 troops, a Danish unit of 1500 men and a British armored-car battalion. Then, at the beginning of 1953, the SHAPE command decided that the Norwegian brigade was needed at home, where Norway has a common frontier with Russia to defend. The Danes were asked to fill the gap with an additional 2500 men. The Copenhagen government agreed and then, under Socialist pressure, hesitated. There followed a bizarre chain of events which culminated in a most embarrassing incident: a mutiny in the Danish army!

Early that year the government decided to extend the period of the draft from twelve to eighteen months. It also decided not to send the extra contingent to Germany to replace the Norwegians. Actually, because of the shortage of barracks, it meant to extend service for only about half the draftees that year. But with an additional 2500 troops, who were to have been quartered in Germany, on its hands, it prepared an announcement that only 40 per cent of the current draftees would be retained for an additional six months of training. The rest would be released in May, in time for work on the farms.

Unfortunately the announcement, containing a reasoned explanation for the move, which was sent to the troops through army channels, was delayed in transmission. The soldiers first heard of it through a broadcast. The reaction of the 40 per cent who were to be held for an additional half-year was violent. In fact, some eight hundred of them in a dozen scattered camps, mostly in Jutland and on Bornholm, mutinied.

Several hundred mutinous troops, completely out of hand, set out from their Jutland garrison vowing they would "march on Copenhagen." In vain did their junior officers attempt to stop them. General Allerup, commander of the Second Division and chief of the forces in Jutland, sped down from his headquarters in an automobile to personally head off the insurgents. Meeting them at a crossroads, he got out of his car, stood calmly in the middle of the highway blocking their further progress and proceeded to address them. Within a few minutes he had restored the mutineers to their senses and talked them into returning to their barracks. There is no court-martial in the Danish army, not even for mutiny, but the ordinary courts meted out a large number of prison sentences ranging from a few weeks to eighteen months. Most of these, however, were reduced by the government. But the proposal for eighteen months of military service was dropped for the time being.

For a small nation, whose rather pacifist people remain skeptical of the possibility of any real defense of their country, Denmark has done a good deal since the last war to arm itself. One fourth of the annual national budget — some $143,000,000 — is earmarked for defense in comparison with 9 per cent before the war. A three-year program involving Danish expenditures of nearly $400,000,000, which was almost matched by U.S. Mutual Defense assistance, was calculated to bring the Danish defense forces up to the following strength by the summer of 1954: a field army of 100,000 men, local defense units of 25,000 men and a voluntary Home Guard of 50,000 men; an air force of eight fighter and fighter-bomber squadrons flying old American jets, and a total personnel of 15,000 officers and men, with most of the pilots trained in the United States; a navy of small vessels, including submarines, suitable for coastal defense and manned, at full strength, by 20,000 men.

One drawback about the army, one SHAPE officer lamented to me, is that in May, when one conscript class finishes its training, and the next class has not yet reported, Denmark has no army-in-being at all.

Greenland and the Security of the United States

Denmark's principal contribution to the defense of the United States has been its co-operation in regard to Greenland. This vast ice-covered island, the largest in the world apart from the continent of Australia, has, with the advent of the long-range bomber, become one of the chief keys to the direct defense of North America against aerial attack from the Soviet Union. It lies athwart the shortest air route between European Russia and all of Canada and the United States. An adequate number of radar stations scattered over Greenland's snowy wastes can give suitable warning of any attempted air attack against the United States from the North. An adequate number of interceptor planes stationed on the bases we have now built in Greenland far above the Arctic Circle can, with any luck in the weather, stand a fair chance of warding off — or at least crippling — a Soviet bomber offensive against North American cities and industrial areas. Finally, from our own bases in Greenland, our long-range planes are today capable of carrying out retaliatory attacks on the principal cities and industries of European Russia.

As a matter of fact, the strategic value of Greenland to the United States, especially in relation to Russia, was grasped by a few statesmen in Washington long before the days of the airplane. Secretary of State William H. Seward, under President Andrew Johnson, wanted to purchase Greenland as a strategic base against Russia shortly after the Civil War, but his plan was howled down by Congress and the press as a foolish whim. It was bad enough, they said, for him to have squandered the American taxpayers' money by purchasing Alaska from Russia in 1867 for $7,200,000 — a transaction that was angrily denounced at the time as "Seward's Folly."

So Greenland, which had first been settled in the year 985 by Eric the Red, remained under the sovereignty of Denmark, which from the beginning of the eighteenth century until the advent of the Second World War closed it to all foreigners and established a government monopoly for its trade.

The Nazi occupation of Denmark in 1940 cut off the mother country from its great colony. There was immediate concern in Washington lest the Germans establish weather stations in Greenland or, what would be infinitely more dangerous, submarine bases and perhaps even an air base.

This American concern led, as we have seen, to President Roosevelt and Secretary of State Hull negotiating an agreement with Henrik Kauffmann under which the United States took over the defense of Greenland for the duration of the war. Actually we built two air bases on the island, Bluie West 1 at Narsarssuak on the southern tip of the island, and Bluie West 8, at Sondrestrom 400 miles further north, which served as staging points for ferrying American planes to Europe and as bases for planes on antisubmarine patrol in the North Atlantic.

Scarcely less important were the weather stations we set up in Greenland. Meteorologists have long known that much of the weather of the North Atlantic and of Europe is, as they say, "made in Greenland." Weather forecasts from the Greenland stations were of great value to the Allies, especially to the convoys plying the submarine-infested North Atlantic and even more so to the British and American bomber commands in England, whose devastating attacks on Germany were timed on the basis of the prognostications of the weathermen. I remember from my own experience in Berlin how handicapped the Germans were by the lack of regular facilities in the North Atlantic for calculating the weather. One of the first accomplishments of the Americans when they took over the defense of Greenland in 1941 was to destroy a secret German weather station there.

There was one condition in the Kauffmann Greenland agreement which was to embarrass the United States after the war. It was stipulated that the arrangement would be discontinued when both parties agreed that the "present danger" to the American continent had ceased. The "present danger," of course, referred to Nazi Germany.

And though the Danish Parliament, as we have seen, unanimously ratified the Kauffmann treaty immediately after liberation, it was not long before the Danish government was reminding the United States that Germany no longer constituted a threat to the Western Hemisphere. In fact, the Danish Foreign Minister frankly told the American Secretary of State that Denmark wanted the United States to get out of Greenland entirely.

This, the United States was reluctant to do. A new "danger" had risen, in the form of an aggressive Soviet Russia which was known to be developing the atom bomb — and later, the hydrogen bomb. The most advantageous place, the State Department reminded the Danes, to intercept a Russian attack with such bombs on the United States was midway on the shortest air route between the two countries, which was Greenland. Also in case of an East-West war, Denmark could not possibly defend Greenland. Only the United States could do that. Finally, in 1947 the Pact of Rio de Janeiro placed Greenland inside the security region of the Western Hemisphere. That added a further burden on the United States to defend it.

But all the efforts of the American government to negotiate a new treaty with Denmark for the continuance of American bases in Greenland were rebuffed in Copenhagen. Then, in 1949, the impasse between the two friendly democracies was fortunately solved by the exigencies of the NATO pact. The Danish government saw a way out of being caught between the bitter rivalries of Moscow and Washington. It announced during the parliamentary debate on joining the North Atlantic Alliance that while it would not grant Greenland bases to the United States, it might well grant them to NATO. This was ultimately done. On April 27, 1951, an agreement for the joint defense of Greenland within the framework of NATO was signed. Denmark was relieved, its conscience cleared. NATO took the responsibility for the Allied bases. In practice, of course, it was the United States which built up and manned them. The way was clear for the construction of the great arctic base at Thule, on the coast of northwestern Greenland, which was completed in the summer of 1954. The old bases at Bluie West 1 and 8 were improved. Radar warning stations were established, as well as several new weather stations, including one on a 36-square-mile chunk of ice that, when this was written, was drifting within 200 miles of the North Pole.

The geologists, as well as the soldiers, are busy in Greenland these days. They suspect it may contain valuable deposits of important and strategic metals. For some years Greenland has been the world's only source of natural cryolite, which is of great importance in the making of aluminum. It is mined at Ivigtût, and about half of its production shipped directly to the United States, the rest to Denmark. Since the war important deposits of lead, zinc and wolfram have been discovered on Greenland's ice-bound and almost inaccessible east coast. In 1948, the finding of uranium was reported.

The prospect of finding uranium in Greenland may have had something to do with Danish complaints that American geologists had been discovered at work far from the confines of American bases in the recent postwar years. This caused some irritation in Copenhagen until the chief of the United States Northeast Air Command visited the capital in November, 1953, and assured the Danish government that henceforth American geologists would adhere strictly to the regulations that no scientific expeditions could work in Greenland without the permission of the government in Copenhagen.

Politics and People — A Final Note

The trek to the polls in Denmark that summer of 1953 came to an end in the autumn, resulting not only in a new Constitution but in a new government.

In the elections of September 22, for the new unicameral parliament, the Social-Democrats won 74 seats out of 179 against 72 seats for the Agrarian Liberal-Conservative coalition which had ruled since 1950. The Socialists, therefore, took over the government under the leadership of Hans Hedtoft, who became Prime Minister.

Unlike the state of affairs in Norway — and occasionally in Sweden — the Labor party in Denmark has never been able to win a majority in Parliament. This is in part due to the relative over-representation of the rural districts and in part to the failure of the Socialists to capture as large a slice of the middle-class and farmer vote as they have in the other two Scandinavian nations.

In fact, in postwar Denmark no single party or likely coalition of parties has been able to obtain a Parliamentary majority, so that the Socialists and the Agrarian Liberal-Conservative coalition, which have alternated in power since 1945, have had to function as minority governments each with the tolerance of the other.

The failure of the Communists in Denmark is worth noting. Because of factors already mentioned — their splendid record in the Resistance and the popularity of Russia for its part in defeating Nazi Germany — the Danish Communists polled 255,000 votes and won 18 parliamentary seats in the first postwar elections in 1945, mostly at the expense of the Labor party. In 1947 their vote dropped to 140,-000, with 9 seats, and in the 1950 elections they lost a further two seats. In the 1953 voting, they were reduced to a hard core of just under 100,000, an inconsequential minority with little more than a nuisance value so far as open politics are concerned. I found the Danes alert to the danger of the conspiratorial nature of the Communists and of their subservience to Moscow, but not unduly excited about their role in politics, and in the labor unions, from which their influence has been all but eliminated. There is no agitation in Denmark to outlaw the Communist party, nor is there any law which could send its leaders to jail by holding them guilty of conspiring to overthrow the government by force. The government, however, keeps a close watch on the Communists for possible espionage and sabotage.

All three leaders of the three principal political parties in Denmark are of humble origin. Erik Eriksen, born in 1912, the son of a farmer in south Fyn and educated in a Folk High School, has been an enlightened member of the Agrarian Liberal Party all his life and served with distinction as Prime Minister in the coalition with the Conservatives from 1950 to 1953. Ole Björn Kraft, the conservative leader who became Foreign Minister in the coalition government, is the son of a provincial prison official and was born in 1893. Outside of his political activities, he is a journalist of note. He is an ardent though enlightened nationalist and as a youthful student organized a campaign against the sale of the Virgin Islands to the United States in 1916. For years he swam against the current by advocating a strong military defense, and his influence on the Conservative party has been decidedly liberal and progressive. During the occupation the Germans were so displeased with him that they ordered his assassination. The attempt failed, though not before a German had pumped his body with five bullets. His life was saved by blood transfusions given by his wife.

Hans Hedtoft, the dynamic and eloquent leader of the Labor party and twice Prime Minister since the war, was born in 1903, the son of a tailor. He was in Labor politics since the age of sixteen, when, as a lithographer's apprentice, he became chairman of his union in Aarhus. At nineteen, he was secretary of the Danish Social-Democratic Youth movement, and at twenty-four became its chairman. A protégé of the redoubtable Stauning, he was elected head of the Socialist party on the latter's recommendation in 1939 when he was only thirty-five. His violent opposition to Fascism as well as to

Communism earned him the enmity of the Germans, who forced him out of his party leadership in 1941. He immediately went underground and with Ole Björn Kraft, the Conservative, edited a Resistance paper, *Danske Tidende*. He was also active in the underground army, once disguising himself as a ship's pilot to slip across the Sound to Sweden to arrange with Swedish authorities for a supply of arms for the Resistance forces. The fact that he was one of the few Socialist leaders to take an active part in the Resistance has enhanced his popularity in the country since the war.

His joining forces with an antisocialist Conservative such as Kraft to edit an underground paper was typical of Hedtoft. He is no narrow, doctrinaire Socialist. The Danes still remember a famous speech of his (he is Denmark's greatest orator, with the sonorous voice of an organ reminiscent of the late Briand) in 1939 when he exclaimed: "Rather democracy without Socialism than Socialism without democracy!"

As Prime Minister he never hesitated to put national above party interests and almost single-handedly, when the negotiations in 1949 for a Scandinavian defense alliance broke down, he pulled his reluctant party behind him to support Denmark's joining NATO.

Possessed of a good understanding of foreign politics, Hedtoft liked to remind his people that Denmark is confronted not only with a Russian problem but a German problem. As to the Soviet Union, he publicly expressed the hope that eventually the Big Three powers may negotiate a settlement with Moscow. In the meantime he refused to budge an inch before the truculence of the Kremlin.

"Our right to accept aid from the Allies," he said recently, "is indisputable. Neither the Soviet government nor its local agents have a shadow of moral or legal right to tell Denmark what we must do or must not do."

The Danes remember not only Hitler but Bismarck, and I found no confidence in Copenhagen that the Germans had really changed, following their catastrophic defeat in 1945. Hedtoft recently reminded his fellow citizens in a public speech that "the solution of the German problem, so decisive for us, has been deferred." [11] It is a problem

[11] Hedtoft died of heart attack on January 29, 1955, while attending a meeting of the Nordic Council in Stockholm. He was succeeded as Prime Minister and leader of the Social Democratic party by H. C. Hansen, who had been foreign minister. Hansen, 49, is a former typographer and was for many years general secretary of the Socialist Party.

the Danes have lived with for centuries and they believe they will have to go on living with it for a long time to come.

Now to it has been added the Russian problem, and the bitter conflict between East and West which catches Denmark in the middle and on the front line should armed hostilities break out. A less well-balanced people might be expected to be weighed down by such problems, and by others which have been discussed in this chapter. But the Danes, conscious of their long and troubled history and of their ability to survive so many vicissitudes, face the future with admirable fortitude and even with cheerfulness. At heart, they seem a happy people, sophisticated and determined enough to get the best out of life, such as it is.

And so we take leave of this democratic, co-operative farmers' commonwealth and turn to the last of the four northern countries, which, though completely different in language and race from the three strictly Scandinavian nations we have been considering, nevertheless has been closely tied to them by geography, history, culture, religion and a similar way of life.

CHAPTER V

Finland

W<small>HEN</small> I arrived at Helsinki, Finland was in the midst of another political crisis, brought on chiefly by a recurrent economic crisis; and yet on my first evening in the capital, before I scarcely had time to open a suitcase, I was whisked off by some good friends in the government, which was about to tumble, not to a political meeting but to a gala concert of the Helsinki City Symphony Orchestra led by Leopold Stokowski and playing a program of Sibelius, whom most Finns honor — though he is an artist, a composer — as the first citizen of the land. No one would talk that evening of Finland's dire troubles — political, economic, Russian or Communist. The music was too overwhelming, the pale midsummer night in this city by the Baltic waters too enchanting.

The Finns, as sturdy a people as there are on the planet, have lived from one crisis to another almost continually since they won their independence from a collapsing Russia in 1917.

There was a bloody and savage civil war between the Whites and the Reds in the very first shaky days of national freedom. There was a serious fascist movement between the wars which almost overthrew the Republic, as a similar one had in Germany. And between 1939 and 1944 there were two disastrous wars with Finland's giant neighbor, the Soviet Union. Finally, in a bizarre turn of events, the Finns were forced to fight a bitter field campaign against the Germans, in which the retreating Nazi forces, until then allies of the Finns against the Russians, destroyed $300,000,000 worth of Finnish property in the north, scorching the earth into an utter wasteland.

As a result of war, every seventeenth married woman in Finland between fifteen and forty-five years of age was a war widow, every twenty-fourth child under eighteen was a war orphan, every sixteenth man between twenty and fifty was disabled and every ninth citizen had lost his home permanently to foreign conquest.

But that was not quite all.

The Soviet Union took from Finland one tenth of her territory, including her only ice-free port at Petsamo on the Arctic Ocean. Nearly half a million Finnish refugees from the lost territory — all departed voluntarily rather than live under the Soviets — had to be resettled in a smaller Finland. And finally, Russia saddled Finland with a reparations bill that was crushing for so small and impoverished a nation — nearly $600,000,000 worth of goods in postwar prices, which the Finns paid off on schedule and without a whimper.

Moreover, in 1948 the Soviet Union forced on this disarmed republic of slightly over four million population a treaty of "nonaggression," a customary preliminary employed in the past by Nazi Germany and Soviet Russia before taking over an independent country. Fortunately, Finland was not taken over, possibly because the Kremlin was taken back by the world reaction to the Communist coup in Czechoslovakia a few months before. But Finland's sovereign freedom in foreign affairs was further contracted.

That the Finns have survived such vicissitudes as a free people, and that their splendid little nation has maintained its independence and democracy — the only country in Europe bordering the Soviet Union except Norway to do so — is one of the miracles of our uneasy age.

The Finns

Though the Finns are an ancient people, they won their national independence very late in history. Who the Finns are or from whence they came about the time of Christ to this beautiful but not very fertile northern land of forests, swamps and 60,000 lakes, with its severe climate — for one third lies above the Arctic Circle — we do not know for sure. The most widely held theory among ethnologists and historians is that as a tribal, nomadic people they migrated westward from somewhere between the Urals and the Volga. Part of this group eventually settled in the rich Hungarian plain and became known as Magyars or Hungarians. Others pressed farther north, settling first on the southern shore of what is now the Gulf of Finland, which became known as Estonia. Those who remained there became Estonians. The rest pushed still farther north across the Gulf or around the neck of land between the gulf and Lake Ladoga to a region they called *Suomi*, which has remained to this day the native word for Finland. And these tribesmen became known as Finns.

Thus they were a race apart from the Slavs, Teutons, and Norse, with a language which had no resemblance to that spoken by the other three peoples, who were to struggle for more than a millennium for supremacy in the Baltic regions. It was this apartness which helped preserve them, small in numbers though they were, as a separate people. Eight centuries of rule and occupation by first the Swedes and then the Russians failed to assimilate them into the one race or the other. With a stubbornness and obstinacy which provoked and frustrated their foreign rulers, and which can only be called monumental, they clung to their individuality as a people.

And they clung to their language, though at one time, around the turn of the eighteenth century, it appeared to be dying out as more and more Finns came to speak Swedish, which was the official language of the land, employed exclusively not only in government and business but in the schools. Indeed Finland's great national poet, Johan Ludvig Runeberg, did not know enough Finnish to write in it. His poems of the Finnish nationalist revival, which appeared in the third and fourth decades of the nineteenth century, were written in Swedish, as were his verses which later were to become Finland's national anthem.

The great Finnish national folk epic, the *Kalevala*, was only published in 1835. Though its colorful runes were sung and spoken by village bards for a thousand years, it was not until two or three years before 1835 that a remarkable figure, Elias Lönnrot, son of a drunken rural tailor, who had worked his way through the university to become a physician and who practiced his profession in isolated Karelia, began to put them down in written Finnish. A literary genius, he conceived the idea of wielding the folk tales together on Homeric lines after the manner of the *Iliad* or the *Odyssey* — embellishing them, rearranging them and inventing his own names for heroes as he went along.

The impact of the publication of the *Kalevala* on the Finns was overwhelming. Overnight they became conscious that they possessed, after all, a heritage of poetry and song and that their native language, so scorned by the Swedes and Russians and even by their own educated classes, had in it the possibilities of a rich and colorful and poetic written expression.

The appearance of the *Kalevala* had an impact on the world outside too. Translations soon appeared in Swedish and German; and it was from the latter that Longfellow, intrigued by the *Kalevala's* trochaic tetrameter, took its meter and some of its themes for his much paler *Hiawatha*. The English translation of the folk epic did not appear until the end of the nineteenth century. Today the work is available in twenty foreign languages and is required reading in the schools of Japan. It is generally recognized as one of the great epic poems of the world.

Lönnrot, himself, though a classical scholar, was not academically inclined. However, he was prevailed upon to give up his wanderings and medical practice in the wild, outlying regions and take the chair of Professor of Finnish at Helsinki University in 1853. For the last eighteen years of his life he devoted himself to propagandizing his native language, to establishing its grammar, syntax and vocabulary and to compiling a monumental Finnish-Swedish dictionary.

The language which Lönnrot restored to life so vividly is a difficult one for foreigners. It is completely different from the Aryan tongues from which the European languages derive. It has no articles, no gender, no letters *b,c,f,q,* or *w.* It has no prepositions, their absence being compensated for by fifteen declensions of nouns which are: the nominative, genetive, partitive, ablative, elative, illative, allative, accusative, translative, comitative, essive, inessive, adessive, abessive and instructive. Yet those outsiders who have managed to learn Finnish say it is easy to pronounce, for the good reason that every written letter is articulated.

A Capsule of Finnish History

So far as the written record goes, Finland's history begins with its conquest by Sweden in 1152 and the rule of the Swedish kings, which lasted for six and a half centuries until 1809, when the country was taken over as one consequence of the Napoleonic wars by Czarist Russia as a grand duchy.

The warlike Swedes came across the Sea of Bothnia to Finland in their trim Viking boats to Christianize and colonize and they were successful in both undertakings. The Swedes did not swamp Finland with any mass emigration; they were too few in numbers for that. They settled mostly in the coastal districts and only a few aristocrats took big estates farther inland. By 1362 Finland had become one of many Swedish provinces, with the right to send a delegation to the capital to elect the king.

That Swedish colonization and rule brought great benefits to the Finns, there is no doubt. For one thing, it spared them from being conquered by the German Knights of the Sword, who enslaved the peoples of Estonia and Livonia across the Baltic. It spared them from being taken over by the Tartars who conquered Novgorod and founded modern Russia. It preserved them from the serfdom which feudalism imposed on most of Europe, for Sweden was a nation of free peasants and treated the Finns on the land as such.

And it gave the Finns great positive gains, bringing them into the fold of Western civilization, making of them first Roman Catholic and then Lutheran Christians, educating them in schools and in a fine university at Turku, laying the foundations of a national economy by the exploitation of forests and mines, the development of agriculture and metal-working, the building of towns and roads and the establishment of a postal service.

Also, the Swedish conquest gave birth to a unique race which played a dominant part in the development of Finland to our own day, though its importance is now beginning to dwindle. This race came from the intermarriage of the warm-blooded, adaptable, extra-verted Swedes with the phlegmatic, obstinate, introverted Finns. The result of this intermixture was a people who came to be known as Swedo-Finns and who settled most thickly in the islands and along the coast and river valleys of Western Finland across the Bothnian Sea from Sweden. Separated by geography from the mother country they grew different in outlook from the native Swedes; separated by the barrier of language from the Finns they never became completely assimilated in Finland, as Finns.

Yet they became the leaders not only of the cultural, commercial and political life of Finland but of the inexorable drive for Finnish national independence. It was quite logical that one of them, Rune-berg, should become the great national poet and that another, Baron

Gustav Mannerheim, should be hailed as the George Washington of his country. It was Mannerheim, scion of an old Swedo-Finnish family which spoke Swedish in its home, who, more than any other, was responsible for the founding of the independent, noncommunist Finnish nation in 1918 and for its preservation as such after the two disastrous wars with the Soviet Union between 1939 and 1944. And it was Mannerheim, it might be added, who helped keep Finland from becoming in 1918 that German satrapy under a Hessian king which most Swedo-Finns, in their folly, passionately desired and worked for.

If the Swedes brought many benefits to the Finns, they also brought them unmitigated misery by forcing them into the unending wars which Sweden fought with Russia between the end of the fifteenth century and the beginning of the nineteenth. In most of these wars Finland was not only the battleground but a great source of cannon fodder for the imperial Swedish armies.

From 1570 until 1809, when Finland was annexed by Russia, there were five wars between the Swedes and the Russians which lasted for a total of sixty years. During the Thirty Years' War, Finns made up one third of the armies of the victorious Gustavus Adolphus. Even while Charles XII was leading his Swedish forces into the heart of Russia, Peter the Great was devastating Finland from Lake Ladoga to the Gulf of Bothnia. Scandinavian historians call that struggle the Great Northern War, but to Finnish writers it is known as the Great Wrath. For four centuries Finland had no more than a generation of peace. No wonder that war with Russia became ingrained in the Finnish people so that it was part of their blood. This bitter fact of their existence must be taken into account when we consider their feelings during the Winter War which the Soviet Union cold-bloodedly provoked against Finland in 1939 and their motives in joining Nazi Germany in war on Russia two years later.

Finland under Czarist Russia

Strangely enough, Czarist rule in Finland was at first surprisingly liberal and quite unlike that in the other Russian territories such as Poland, the Ukraine and the Baltic provinces.

What was to prove the last of the seemingly interminable wars between Sweden and Russia had ended in a Russian conquest of Finland and, by the terms of the Treaty of Fredrickshamm, Finland, after six and a half centuries of Swedish rule, was ceded to Russia in 1809.

To the surprise of the Finns, Emperor Alexander I, the "autocrat of all the Russias," immediately declared his intention of ruling Finland as a constitutional grand duke; this guardian of the Orthodox Church proclaimed himself the protector of the Lutheran faith in Finland; this absolute monarch whose word was the law in Russia promised to be bound by Finnish law.

Thanks to him, the Finns found that they had much more self-government under the Russians than under the Swedes. They had their own legislature, their own executive council called the Senate; they had their own laws, courts, church, schools and university. They controlled their own customs, ports, postal services and currency. They were excused from military service and yet given the military protection of a great state. Their people on the land, who comprised the vast majority, were free peasants as opposed to the serfs in the rest of Russia. In 1812 the Czar generously returned to Finland its ancient province of Viipuri (Viborg), whose borders reached almost to the Russian capital. No wonder the Finns were pleased with the change.

Or were they? The Swedo-Finns certainly were, for Alexander in effect had turned the country over to them. In fact, it is probable that the Czar was under the belief that he had annexed a Swedish province. After all, when he visited Finland he found that the language, the culture, the church, were Swedish.

But the mass of the people were purely Finnish, and to them there was little change. They were still at the mercy of the landowning Swedo-Finns, who completely dominated the country and whose very language they could not understand. They were still a subject race. And the gulf between the two peoples caused increasing hostility, which, as the nineteenth century developed, was given vent in two bitterly opposed parties, the *Svekoman* or Swedish party, and the *Fennoman* or Finnish party.

Yet, bad as their relations with one another were, neither liked the Russians. They were keenly conscious of the gulf between a people who belonged fundamentally to the East and themselves, who were a part of the West. This feeling of malaise was summed up by a young instructor at the University of Turku, Adolf Ivar Arwids, son: "Swedes we are no longer; Russians we can never be; there- fore we must become Finns."

Thanks first to the blind Russification policies of the last of the Czars and then to the revolution which overthrew him, Arwidsson's exhortation was soon to become a reality.

When Nicholas II was crowned in Moscow in 1895, one of the two officers of the Chevalier Guards who walked in front of him in the traditional march from Uspenskij Cathedral to the Kremlin Palace was a handsome young Finn, Baron Gustav Mannerheim. He shared the hopes of most Finns that the new emperor would disavow the policy of Russification, which shortly before had begun in Finland.

The hope was shattered. In 1898 Nicholas named General Nikolai Ivanovitch Bobrikov, a brutal and reactionary tyrant, as Governor General of Finland, and assigned him the task of bringing the Finns into line with the other harassed subjects of Mother Russia. Bobri- kov suspended the Constitution, virtually closed down the Diet, abol- ished freedom of speech, the press and assembly, disbanded the Finnish army and ordered the conscription of Finns in Russian units, dismissed Finnish judges and officials and replaced them with Rus- sians and attempted to substitute Russian as the official language. His reign of terror ended only in his assassination in 1905 by a young Finnish patriot.

The Russian defeat by Japan and the revolutionary uprising in St. Petersburg in 1905, which shook the Romanov throne, brought some relief to the Finns. The Czarist government promised to re-establish a constitutional Finnish regime on even a more representative basis than heretofore. The Finns themselves drew up a new Constitution, abolishing the outdated Four Estates and establishing a new single- chamber Parliament to be elected by popular vote of all citizens above twenty-four years of age — not only male but female. Thus the Finns were the first to grant full suffrage to women, and in fact the new Parliament, on paper at least, was easily the most demo- cratic in Europe. In the first elections to the new assembly in 1907, the Social Democrats won 80 out of 200 seats, making them not only the largest party in Finland but the strongest parliamentary Social- ist party in the world.

In St. Petersburg, the government became highly alarmed at what the new democracy was up to in Finland. Steps were quickly taken to suppress it. A new policy of Russification set in. It lasted from 1909 until 1917, when the Russian Revolutions gave the Finns the opportunity they had been seeking for so long: to break away from Russia and found their own sovereign state.

The Birth of Independent Finland

As it has been with almost all nations, the birth of free Finland was not accomplished without much pain and bloodletting. Actually, because of the disintegration of the Russian Empire, national independence itself was won with unexpected ease. On July 18, 1917, four months after the Czar had been deposed, the Finnish Diet proclaimed that it had taken over the executive power of the monarchy except for foreign affairs and military matters. The provisional Kerenski government, so weak and confused and dilatory in most things, reacted to the Diet's action with surprising rapidity and firmness. It dissolved the Diet and called for new elections. This was a fatal move for the Russians because the old Finnish Parliament had a Social-Democrat majority, and the Socialists, though desiring Finland's full autonomy, wished to maintain some ties with a Russia which they envisaged becoming a Socialist Republic and one which would help them to maintain their own dominant position in Finland.

In the new elections the Social-Democrats were reduced in the Diet from 103 out of 200 seats to 92; they had lost their majority. And when the new assembly met in November, 1917, a few weeks after the October Revolution had carried the Bolsheviks to power in Russia, it promptly, on the fifteenth, declared that the supreme power in Finland belonged to the Finnish Parliament. On December 6, the Diet, now captured by the middle-class parties under the forceful leadership of the nationalist Per Svinhufvud, who had just returned from exile in Siberia, formally proclaimed Finland an independent, sovereign state.

At this fateful moment, the Finns took to quarreling among themselves. They had, at last, their complete independence. It was quickly recognized by several powers, first of all by the new Soviet Union. Indeed Leon Trotsky personally conveyed formal recognition on behalf of the Russian government on January 4, 1918. No doubt he would have preferred to give it to a more revolutionary Finnish regime. But by this time he was filled with contempt for Finland's Social-Democrats. "Never will it be forgotten," he bitterly reproached the Finnish Socialist leader, Kullervo Manner, "that you did not seize power in November." In fact the not very well known — at that time — Bolshevik Commissar for National Minorities, J. V. Stalin, had gone to Finland and urged the Finnish Socialists to seize power, by force, if necessary, and had promised Russian support.

But the Finnish Socialists, lacking the ruthlessness of the Russian Bolsheviks, had hesitated. They realized that their social, political and economic gains might be jeopardized by the rule of the Finnish middle-class and peasant nationalists. But having preached for eighteen years, in the old Social-Democratic tradition inherited from Germany, that they intended to come to power by peaceful, constitutional, democratic means, their leaders could not bring themselves to seize it by armed force.

Then a chaotic turn of events forced them to try, when it was too late. The country was overrun by Russian soldiers, sailors and workers who had been stationed in Finland during the war and who now revolted. Roving the countryside, shooting their officers and looting, they helped provoke a terrible chaos. One reaction to this was the formation of the White Guard, which attempted to restore order. The Red Guard, which the Socialists had formed during the 1907 general strike, was also revived. But soon the Social-Democratic party lost control of it. It was taken over by the extremists, by Russian revolutionaries and by hooligans, who grabbed control of the party at the same time.

On January 28, 1918, they struck. In what can only be described as a *coup d'état*, they seized government buildings in Helsinki and on the next day proclaimed a Socialist Workers' Republic under the leadership of Manner, the Social-Democrat leader and president of the Diet.

Immediately they found themselves faced with a Civil War. Several anti-Marxist members of the government, led by Svinhufvud, had managed to escape from the capital and make their way to Vasa on the Ostrobothnian coast, where they set up a Committee which proclaimed itself the only legal government of Finland. They appealed to Sweden and to Germany for help and in the meantime worked feverishly to increase the strength of the White Guard. By a stroke of fortune, the magnitude of which was only to be fully grasped over the next quarter of a century, they placed in command of the White Guard General Gustav Mannerheim. He was little known in Finland, for he had passed his entire career in the service of the Imperial Russian army. Now, at fifty-one, he was to begin a new career which would give him a unique position in Finland for a generation, causing him to be hailed by a majority of his fellow-citizens first as the liberator of his country from the Reds and then as its savior from the Russians. He proved to be not only a great military leader but, as time went on, an astute statesman.

For a good many years, I think it is true to say, Mannerheim was looked upon with a great deal of skepticism and suspicion by the liberals of the Western world, who believed him to be a narrow reactionary — if not a fascist — of the worst kind. Recently there has been a reassessment of his personality and his career. The publication of new material about his role in the Civil War, in the formation of the Republic and in the two Russian wars has revealed a great deal about him which was not previously known. And he has added to our knowledge by his memoirs, which were written shortly before his death in 1951, and published in an English translation in 1954.

I have read a good deal of this material, and it makes reasonably clear, I think, to any fair-minded observer, that Mannerheim, while certainly a staunch Conservative, as would be natural for a Swedo-Finnish aristocrat and especially for one who served for thirty years as an élite officer in the Czarist army, was far from being a primitive reactionary. Actually he emerges as a statesman of the first rank, who not only understood the designs of Communism and the Soviet Union but also the blind, hopeless inadequacies of the Extreme Right, both in his own country and in Imperial and Nazi Germany. Indeed it may be said that he saved Finland from both extremes. The fact that the Soviet Russians — and, it is said, Stalin above all — had a high respect for this uncompromisingly anti-Communist Finn is perhaps one of the highest tributes that has been paid him.

Mannerheim's career from the very first bordered on the fabulous. Expelled from the Finnish Corps of Cadets for having taken French leave, he astounded his family and friends by enrolling in the Niko-laevski Cavalry School in St. Petersburg and on graduation obtaining a commission in the Chevalier Guards, the most exclusive regiment in the Russian Imperial Guards, whose colonel in chief was the

Czarina — with whom, and with the Czar, he soon became on as friendly terms as any young officer was ever permitted. His rise in the Russian army was rapid — an extraordinary happening for a Finn. Transferring from the Guards to the Cavalry, in order to broaden his military experience, he served in the Russo-Japanese war of 1904-1905 as a Lieutenant-Colonel of the Nezhinski Hussars.

This campaign in Manchuria aroused his interest in Asia, and also his intellectual curiosity, which seems to have developed steadily in a manner not shared by many of his fellow Russian officers. In 1906, the General Staff in Petersburg offered him the unusual mission of riding on horseback through the whole of Central Asia from Russian Turkestan to Peking. Throwing himself, by way of preparation, into the task of learning Chinese, map-making, weather observing, photography, not to mention the fundamentals of philology and anthropology, he made the 1800-mile trek in two years, halting often to sketch maps, photograph, take weather data, measure the cephalic indexes of the Kalmucks, the Kirghiz, the Sarts and other Asiatic tribes, and generally to inform himself about the state of affairs in the then little known and vast area of Central Asia.

Certainly, as this Asian interlude suggests, Mannerheim was no ordinary, sluggish or empty-minded Czarist army officer. But as yet he had no great interest in Finnish nationalism. For the next six years, until the outbreak of the First World War, he led the life of a dashing Russian cavalry officer, dining and wining and flirting in Russian and Polish aristocratic circles, fond of pretty women and pure-bred horses, thoroughly at home and happy in the frivolous and sophisticated upper-class world that was so soon to crash, and brilliant enough in his profession to rise rapidly in the army.

At the outbreak of the First World War, he was a major-general and served actively at the front until the 1917 Revolution, when, as a Lieutenant-General and Commander of the 6th Cavalry Corps, he saw his troops melt away in defeat, mutiny and revolt. Miraculously escaping the fate of many another Czarist general, he made his way back from the front to St. Petersburg and, leaving Russia, in whose service he had spent his entire adult life, for the last time returned to Helsinki and his native land.

He was just turning fifty-one. The only world he knew had collapsed. He was now pressed into the service of a new one that was determined to save itself from the Communist revolution — the world of the grim, dour peasants and bourgeoisie of Finland who were gathering at Vasa as the Whites, to battle the Reds.

It was, like all civil wars, a bitter and savage struggle with atrocities, according to neutral accounts, about evenly divided. In a brilliant four months' winter campaign that ended May 16, 1918, Mannerheim, with the timely aid of arms from Sweden and Germany and the help of Swedish volunteers and one division plus one regiment of regular German army troops under General von der Goltz, won it.

The victorious Whites were in no mood for conciliation. They regarded the Reds as traitors who deserved extermination. How many Red Guards were shot out of hand has never been accurately ascertained; most non-Finnish historians merely put it at "several thousand." Some 80,000 Reds, including many women, were incarcerated in concentration camps, and of these 8000, according to the official *Finnish Encyclopedia*, died. Apparently, they were left to die by starvation. Almost all who survived — 70,000 prisoners — were tried on political charges in the courts, all but 700 of them receiving prison sentences; and 125 were condemned to death. Battle casualties among the Finns on both sides were 24,000 killed.

The Civil War — or the War of Liberation, as it is officially called in Finland — left deep scars in Finnish society for a generation, and they are still visible in the ideological gulf between the middle classes and the workers, which is much wider than in the other Northern countries which we have observed.

Fantastic Interlude: 1918

Mention must now be made of a fantastic interlude in Finnish history which took place at this time. The victorious Whites, under the curious belief — in 1918! — that Germany was winning the World War, decided that Finland should have a German prince as its king!

Mannerheim himself had opposed the sending of German troops to help the Whites in the Civil War, though he had acquiesced in their use when he learned that the Nationalist government, fanatically pro-German as it was, had negotiated for it in Berlin, without his knowledge and contrary to his advice. Now, almost single-handed in the late spring of 1918, he opposed the idea of a German king for Finland

and warned the government in Helsinki against its pro-German policy — which threatened, in his opinion, to make the country a dependency of Germany. Then, as later, he appears to have had no more illusions about the Germans than he had about the Russians. He saw the necessity of saving Finland from both.

Per Svinhufvud, a stolid nineteenth-century figure whose persecution and exile in Siberia by the Russians had turned him into a blind pro-German, had no doubt at all that Germany was winning the war and that Finland must align herself with her. In vain did Mannerheim caution him. The stubborn Svinhufvud went ahead and Mannerheim, disgusted by the turn of events, resigned as Commander in Chief at the end of May and promptly left Finland.

In May the Diet had been convoked, with the Social-Democrats excluded, and had elected Svinhufvud as Regent. One of his first acts was to request Kaiser Wilhelm II to graciously allow one of his sons to become King of Finland. The German Emperor apparently did not think the job was big enough for one of his sons. He suggested, instead, his brother-in-law, Prince Friedrich Karl of Hesse, who, liking the prospect, immediately set to work on the not easy task of trying to learn Finnish. On October 9, 1918, the Diet by a vote of 75 to 25 elected the Hessian Prince King of Finland.

Prince Karl, unlike Svinhufvud and his royalist Finnish colleagues, knew how badly the war was going for Germany and how shaky the House of Hohenzollern and the houses of all the German princes had become. He delayed coming to Helsinki to ascend the throne. The downfall of Germany and the flight of the Kaiser to Holland a month later made the journey superfluous.

Thus Finland was saved from its folly — from becoming a vassal state of Germany — by Allied victory. Svinhufvud resigned, and General Mannerheim was recalled from abroad and named Regent to succeed him.

"This was certainly one of the greatest ironies of my life," Mannerheim muses in his Memoirs — "to be made Regent on the proposal of the very government whose disloyal attitude had sent me into exile after a work of liberation completed under my leadership." [1]

So ended a somewhat ludicrous chapter in their history, which most Finns today would prefer to forget.

[1] *The Memoirs of Marshal Mannerheim.* Quoted throughout by permission of E. P. Dutton & Co., Inc., New York. (1954.)

Finland between the Wars

With World War and Civil War over, and the aberrations of the monarchists defeated by events, Finland settled down to the immense task of constructing a democratic nation. The first job was to establish a Republic.

Elections for a Constituent Assembly were held in April, 1919. The Social-Democrats, restored to legality, again became the largest party, with 80 seats. A new Constitution, based on the liberal Parliamentary Act of 1906, was drafted under the direction of the Progressive leader, K. J. Ståhlberg, Professor of Law at Helsinki University, and was ratified by the Assembly on July 17.

It has withstood the pressure of events, internal and external, fairly well and is the basis of the Finnish Republic today. It contains a Bill of Rights similar to our own, except that it guarantees legal protection of the health as well as the wealth of Finnish citizens, and of their labor as well as of their personal liberty. It declares that governing power is vested in the people as represented in the unicameral Parliament (called *Eduskunta* in Finnish, *Riksdag* in Swedish — both languages are decreed official) and in the presidency, which exercises the executive authority.

The President of Finland is given far greater powers than it is customary to accord a chief executive in Europe, though not much greater than those held by the American President. If he vetoes a Parliamentary bill by withholding his signature, it can only be passed unchanged by a new Diet after a new election. The President can dissolve Parliament at his will, and order new elections. He possesses extensive rights of issuing administrative decrees, subject only to their not contravening the law. He appoints the Cabinet members, who do not have to be members of parliament. He is commander in chief of the army and he directs foreign policy. He is chosen for office for six years by an electoral college of 300 members (there are only 200 members in the Diet) elected by popular vote.

There are, however, considerable checks on the President's powers. He has no authority over the Budget, which is the concern of Parliament exclusively. All his decisions must be countersigned by a cabinet minister. All his acts are subject to review by the Chancellor of Justice, who, if he decides that the President has exceeded his Constitutional rights, may indict him before Parliament, which can — by a three-fourths vote — hale him before the Supreme Court on a charge of high treason.

Having chosen a unicameral legislature, the Finnish lawmakers found it necessary to create some kind of check and balance which a dual chamber would have provided. They created a scheme of *delaying* action. A bill, to pass, must first have a majority of the whole house after three readings. Then it must be approved by a Grand Committee of 45 members, which often acts as a check on ill-considered, hasty legislation. Finally, if a minority of one third of all members opposes a bill, it can hold it up until it is passed by a new House after a new election.

There are other checks on both the Diet and on the Cabinet. The latter is obliged to balance its budget. It cannot raise a public loan without the consent of Parliament. The Diet can only amend the Constitution by holding a new election and then getting a two thirds majority in the House for it. However, if the matter is declared urgent, a five-sixths majority of the Diet may pass an amendment without resort to a popular election.

Both the Chancellor and the Assistant Chancellor of Justice, who are appointed by the President, sit in the Cabinet. And the Chancellor and the Solicitor General, the latter elected by the Diet, have joint powers similar to those of the United States Supreme Court in deciding the constitutionality of all acts of the Parliament, the Cabinet and the President.

Though his ultra-conservative friends — the ones who had wanted a German prince for king — urged him not to, Mannerheim, in his role as Regent, signed the new Constitution making Finland a Republic on July 17, 1919. Eight days later, on July 25, the Diet, which on this occasion only was to elect the President, convened. By a vote of 143 to 50, it chose Professor Ståhlberg over General Mannerheim. The author of the Constitution thus became the first President of the Republic of Finland.

Declining the proferred post of head of the defense forces because the new President and government would not give him the free hand he demanded, Mannerheim once again went into retirement. He was no Boulanger; he had no burning ambition for political power. But he seems to have had a sense of personal destiny.

"I asked myself," he reports in his Memoirs, "what Fate would have in store for me next."

He was to wait ten years for an answer.

On the whole it was a decade of remarkable progress. In December the first amnesty law was passed, declaring 40,000 Red prisoners guiltless and releasing them, as well as 3000 others, from the crowded prisons and concentration camps. The Social Democrats thereupon gave a solemn pledge henceforth to confine themselves to constitutional methods and, as evidence of good faith, expelled the left-wing Communist minority from the party.

On October 14, 1920, formal peace was made with the Soviet Union by the Treaty of Dorpat. Russia ceded Finland the ice-free port and nickel mines at Petsamo on the Arctic Ocean and confirmed Finnish possession of Finland's ancient province of Viipuri (Viborg) stretching down the Karelian Isthmus to within a few miles of Leningrad.

The democratic Republic of Finland was dominated by the middle class of the cities and towns and by the farmers in the years between the World Wars, much as in the United States. The greatest difference, perhaps, was that Labor organized itself, as in the other northern lands, in the largest single political party. But the middle-class majority saw to it that the labor unions were severely restricted. Union membership was relatively small. By the eve of the second war it numbered only 70,000 — about a fifth of the labor force — and many industries, including the largest, that of wood processing, were unorganized.

The majority of Finns were frugal and prudent and, by Scandinavian standards, their pace in building up their state was somewhat slow. True, as the Americans learned, the Finns paid their war debts on schedule and to the full, being unique among the Europeans in this respect. But as to social welfare, in which the other northern peoples were making such notable advances, the Finns were inclined to leave the field to voluntary efforts, especially to those of the employers, who not ungenerously saddled themselves with many social welfare obligations for their employees. The co-operative movement, on the other hand, flourished, and in Finland it soon had more members per capita and a bigger share in business than in any other country in the world.

The Finns, at least in theory, were as strong advocates of private enterprise in business as Americans. But they were not so sure as Americans about the advantages of free competition. Capital was scarce and profits modest, and business firms tended to work together in their respective branches to avoid price-cutting and undue competition for markets.

Despite their devotion to private enterprise, the Finns were not averse to seeing the state take an increasingly important part in business. It was not long before the government became an important stockholder in many private companies. By the end of the interwar period, the state owned the railroads (as was customary in most European countries), the armament factories, the largest electric power system in the country (producing one third of the nation's electricity), and the liquor monopoly. It owned 40 per cent of the forest area[2] and controlled the major share of the wood processing industries. Here again it was the shortage of private capital which forced the state to assume such large ownership. The Conservatives, as well as the Liberals and Socialists, accepted it more or less as inevitable.

Finland was — and is — a rural land. In 1936 four out of five Finns lived in country districts and three out of five were employed on the land — either on farms or in the forests, or both. And it was in its *land policy* that the Finnish nation achieved its greatest success in the days of its infancy.

The rocky soil of Finland is not very fertile. Much of the land is covered by 60,000 lakes or by countless swamps, and even the cultivated areas, as one soon learns on visiting farms, must be drained and kept drained — usually by wide ditches every ten or fifteen yards, which take up a great deal of space on a Finnish farmer's small holdings and make efficient cultivation difficult.

But the Finnish governments in the first days of independence had an even greater agricultural problem on their hands than that of mediocre soil and a harsh climate. The human condition of the people on the land was intolerable.

Of the nearly half a million families who lived from the soil, only a fourth owned what they tilled. A third were tenant farmers. The rest, nearly a half, were agricultural workers. The tenants and laborers were each divided into two groups. Some 70,000 of the 160,000 tenant

---

[2] State ownership of the forests derived from the sixteenth century when all uninhabited wilderness was declared the property of the Crown.

families were *torpparit*. That meant that their leases could be revoked at the discretion of the owners. The farm laborers numbered 207,000, but only 70,000 of them had, also at the will of the owners, cottages and vegetable plots, which gave them a roof of their own and an opportunity to secure their own food. The rest were completely landless and, for the most part, slept in the barns.

Obviously in such an agrarian country, where the peasantry was the backbone of the nation, something had to be done, now that Finland was freed from the feudal control of Russia.

In October, 1918, nearly a year before the proclamation of the Republic, a Land Purchase Act provided for state loans on easy terms to peasants who wished to own their own land. Prices of acreage were set at 1914 values, which meant they were cheap. The big landowners complained, and most of them declined to sell at such prices. So in 1927 the government, then led by Kyösti Kallio, the aggressive leader of the Agrarian party, which represented small farmers, took a further step. It passed what is known as the *Lex Kallio*, which simply forced the large landowners to sell or face expropriation of up to half of their uncultivated land. The threat brought action and actual expropriation was never carried out. But the big estates were broken up into small holdings for farmers, who acquired ownership and who worked the land themselves.

The number of independent farm families quickly increased as the following rough table shows:

In 1910,	125,172.
In 1920,	182,373.
In 1929,	255,395.
In 1938,	300,000.

Unlike the situation in America, or in other countries with vast areas of agricultural land, small family holdings have proved more efficient than large ones in Finland. Output per acre on typical farms of 25 cultivated acres (the average farmer usually owns, in addition, 50 to 100 acres of forest to provide him firewood and lumber) has been as much as three times that of farms of 100 to 200 acres.

Between the wars Finland shared the political and economic uncertainties of most continental European democracies. There were periods of prosperity and depression. Politically, there were constant shifts, so that successive governments rarely averaged more than a year in power. No single party came close to having a majority, as the Socialists had had for a brief period during the First World War. The Finns had to learn the political art of compromise. Governments were usually built around a center coalition of Agrarians and Progressives which alternated in depending for Parliamentary majorities on either the votes of the Conservative Right or the Socialist Left. Problems and disputes, both internal and external, continued to arise, and were heatedly debated in the press and Parliament.

As was perhaps inevitable, there was fierce controversy between the pure Finns and the Swedo-Finns, the latter fearing that they would be swamped and their dominant position in the country destroyed, since they were outnumbered 9 to 1. The Constitution had guaranteed the linguistic, economic and intellectual rights of both groups, "in accordance with *identical principles.*" As soon as national independence was won, they fell out on how to interpret the term "identical principles," the Swedo-Finns contending that it meant "on a basis of equality," the Finns arguing that it meant "in proportion to their numbers."

Finally a compromise was hammered out in a law passed in 1922. Unilingual and bilingual districts were established, a unilingual district being defined as one in which there was a language minority of less than 10 per cent. Thus were created 454 Finnish-speaking communes, 36 Swedish-speaking (exclusive of the Åland Islands, where Swedish was the language), and 64 bilingual. There was a bitter argument over education, the extremists among the Finns demanding that Swedish-language secondary schools receive only 10 per cent of state funds, in exact proportion to the linguistic population. In the end, they received a generous 20 per cent.

It is difficult for a foreigner to understand the linguistic conflict in Finland. Religion does not enter in; both groups are Lutheran. It is not even a racial question, since a great many Swedo-Finns have as much Finnish blood in them as the Finnish-speaking Finns, being descended from natives who merely learned Swedish and took Swedish names at a time when it was necessary for personal advancement in a country ruled by Sweden.[3] Aside from the Åland Islands and a few

[3] Often brothers in a Swedo-Finnish family carve out separate careers, one in Finland and one in Sweden. Thus Mannerheim's brother became a Swedish businessman in Sweden. One evening in Stockholm, after several hours of talk with

coastal districts, there is no single area in Finland where the Swedo-Finns are consolidated. Swedish-speaking communities are scattered all over the country. Helsinki, the capital, is overwhelmingly Finnish-speaking (though the street signs are in both languages), but the surrounding country is Swedish-speaking.

Probably, as J. Hampden Jackson, an English writer on Finland concluded,[4] the issue is primarily a class struggle. The language conflict serves, he thinks, as a disguise for the economic conflict between the old ruling Swedish-speaking class and the numerically superior Finnish-speaking Finns.

The Finns, like the Americans, tried the Prohibition experiment after the First World War, and, like us, finally gave it up about the same time as a hopeless failure.

It makes a curious story in Finnish history. The Finns, according to the records at least, were not the hard drinkers that their brethren in the adjoining northern lands were. In fact, they drank per capita only one sixth as much as the English, and seem to have been, despite their harsh climate, just about the most sober people in all of Europe. Yet the Prohibition movement in Finland got an early and vigorous start. Back in 1907, the Diet passed the first Prohibition Bill in history. It was annulled by the Senate (the then Finnish executive) on the ground that it "infringed existing treaties." Two years later the Diet passed a second bill outlawing the sale of alcoholic drinks. It failed to go into effect because the Czar, mindful of the Russian vodka business, neglected to sign it. Kerenski found the Act among his accumulation of papers when he came to power in St. Petersburg. He signed it in May, 1917, on condition that it not go into force for two years.

On June 1, 1919, six months before America, Finland began its "noble" experiment. Drinking began immediately to increase. Convictions for drunkenness rose from 12,200 in 1910 to 87,191 in 1927, and 101,500 in 1929. The legal imbibing of alcoholic drinks (for "medical purposes," that is) increased from 1.7 million quarts in 1920 to nearly five times that in 1927. Rum runners, operating from across the

---

Carl Adam Nykopp, editor of one of Sweden's biggest daily newspapers, I was surprised to hear him say that he was the brother of Johan A. Nykopp, the Finnish Minister in Washington, who had impressed me as being the most Finnish of Finns.
4 *Finland,* by J. Hampden Jackson.

Baltic to the network of islands which stud the Finnish coast, made a killing. The more the government did to curb them — and it did everything conceivable — the more the smugglers prospered and the more the Finnish people drank. Finally the government put the issue up to the people. In December, 1931, 70 percent of the electorate voted in a national referendum to abolish Prohibition. In February, 1932, a law was enacted to that effect and the liquor business was handed over to a state monopoly, as in Sweden. Drinking in Finland became normal again.

In foreign affairs the new Finland had a comparatively easy time. It maintained as little contact as possible with the Soviet Union; only one railway connection between the two countries was kept open, and it carried little traffic either in goods or passengers. Finland's only wish with regard to Russia was to be left alone. It therefore accepted the Soviet Union's offer, made first in 1926, for a nonaggression pact guaranteeing the Dorpat frontiers. The treaty was signed in 1932 for three years, and renewed at the end of 1934 for a period lasting until 1945.

Finland's only dispute with a foreign power was with Sweden, over the possession of the Åland Islands, which Napoleon had once said were the key to Stockholm. Lying midway in the Bothnian Sea between Stockholm and the southwest coast of Finland, but connected with the latter by the Turku archipelago, whereas a 30-mile-wide deep water channel separated them from Sweden, the islands were inhabited by Swedish-speaking Finns, who, after the war, desired to be associated with Sweden though the Islands had always formed a part of Finland. The controversy, which strained relations between Sweden and Finland to the point where Stockholm withdrew its minister from Helsinki and talk of war flamed up in both countries, was given to the League of Nations, which Finland had joined in 1920. The League in 1921 decided in favor of Finland, but as a favor to the Swedes, the Islands were demilitarized and the Islanders given a measure of Home Rule.

So Finland remained at peace with the world, and the Finns, whose divisions of Civil War days were being gradually healed, remained at peace with one another. The year 1926 saw the first Socialist government in power under the co-operative leader, Vaino Tanner. The

Social-Democrats now consistently polled more votes than any other party.

Then, as the third decade of the century began, the country, like all others of the West, was hit by an economic depression and, like some others, by what was far worse: a strenuous fascist movement that suddenly rose up to threaten the very existence of the democratic Republic.

The Fascist Bid for Power in Finland

In Finland it became known as "the Lapua Movement," and as in Germany and elsewhere it sprang up ostensibly to fight Communism. But whereas in Germany this motive had been merely a pretext to destroy democracy, in Finland it was considerably more genuine — at least in the beginning. The Finnish Communists were not only fairly strong and well organized, with a vigorous press, a growing foothold in the trade-unions and from 18 to 27 out of the 200 seats in Parliament during the first decade after the war, but, as a disciplined Fifth Column of the Soviet government, they represented an especially dangerous threat to most Finns, who believed that Finland's mighty neighbor was using them to undermine the Republic in order to take it over as an integral part of the Russian Communist Empire.

At least 90 per cent of the Finns — all but the Communists, that is — did not want to be taken over again by Russia, especially by a Soviet Russia. And they did not intend to sit idly by while their own Bolsheviks tried to destroy their Christian faith and their democracy.

In November, 1929, a small spark — or so it seemed — set off a mighty explosion. This happened in Lapua, a small town in Ostrobothnia, from which Finnish fascism took its name. Lapua had been the scene of Swedo-Finnish victories over the Russians in the imperial wars; it had been a stronghold of the Whites in the Civil War; and last, but not least, it was the center of the Pietists, an ascetic and fanatical religious sect which saw in Communism the enemy incarnate of the Christian religion and which was determined to exterminate it.

Into this town tripped, one day in November, 1929, about 400 members of the League of Communist Youth, some of them armed, all of them attired in red shirts hanging blouselike over their trousers in Russian fashion, and all of them determined to hold a Communist propaganda meeting in this savagely anticommunist stronghold. Their train was met at the station by a crowd of angry farmers who had been stirred up to a high pitch by their Pietist pastors. They attacked the youths, seized their arms, tore off their shirts and gave them a severe beating.

It was not the first roughing-up the Communists had experienced but it was spectacular enough to make news that spread like a conflagration throughout Finland. On December 1, the angry country people held a mass meeting in Lapua under the leadership of Vihtori Kosola, who from that moment on took over the reins of what was to become the fascist or Lapua Movement. A farmer, Kosola had been imprisoned in St. Petersburg during Czarist times for his Finnish nationalist activities. He had no love for the Russians and only fanatical hatred for the Communists. At this meeting, Kosola demanded that the government enforce the law banning Communists.

Similar meetings were held all over Finland and in March, 1930, they reached a climax at a Congress in Lapua where a formal organization to fight Communism was founded under the name of *Suomen Lukko*, or "Finland's Lock." The Lapua Movement was now launched under the leadership of a fighting organization. Deputations were sent to Helsinki to urge action against the Communists and were sympathetically received by the President and Prime Minister.

Then, taking a clue from Italy and Germany, the Lapuans turned to direct action. They smashed Communist printing presses, kidnaped Communist leaders, beat them and deposited some of them on the far side of the Soviet frontier, where — ironically — they were invariably arrested by the Russians as spies and sentenced to hard labor.

On July 7, Kosola, who was beginning to consider himself a Finnish Mussolini, staged a "March on Helsinki," as the *Duce* had done nearly a decade before when he "marched" on Rome — though actually making the trip in a Pullman car. Twelve thousand Lapuan peasants arrived in the capital and were warmly received by President Relander, General Mannerheim and Prime Minister Svinhufvud. Mannerheim was still in retirement, but the sixty-nine-year-old Svinhufvud, who had been out of office for eight years, had been called back on July 2 by the President to form a National Government of all the anti-Marxist parties.

He, as well as the other two, was much impressed by the zealousness of the Lapuans, whose most eloquent spokesmen on this occasion was the Pietist Pastor Kares, a fiery, demagogic clergyman who had long thundered against the evils of Bolshevism from his famed pulpit in Lapua. "We demand," Pastor Kares told the Government, "vigorously, unconditionally and with no room for compromise, the expulsion of Communism from this country . . . We demand the cessation of petty party calculations in Parliament and the creation of combinations and laws which will ensure the existence of strong and lasting governments in this country . . . We demand that a patriotic workman be allowed to maintain himself and his family in peace by his labors . . . We are ready to fade again into obscurity, but only on the day we see our demands on the road to real fulfillment . . ."

The Lapuans thus insisted not only on the suppression of the Communists but for the first time threatened, though in veiled language, the democratic processes of the Parliament and the power — such as it was — of the labor unions. The fascist tendencies of the Lapua movement were developing.

So far as its demands for abolishing Communism were concerned, Prime Minister Svinhufvud moved rapidly to meet them. The very next day, on July 8, he arrested the 23 Communist members of the Diet and asked the House to approve immediately three bills which he thought would effectively outlaw a party "working for the overthrow of the state." Lacking a five-sixths majority necessary to pass the bills, which were, in effect, amendments to the Constitution, Svinhufvud, on July 15, called for new elections, which under Finnish law would permit approval of his anti-Communist legislation by a two-thirds majority of the new Parliament.

The election campaign that summer was conducted amidst a reign of terror by the Lapuans. Now they turned not only on the Communists but on the Socialists, who though bitterly anti-Communist had declined to back the bills unless some changes were made. The head of the Social-Democrat party was kidnaped by them, and threatened with death. Fascist hooligans broke up Social-Democratic party meetings, smashed printing presses, seized issues of newspapers and campaign literature. The government did nothing to restore order, and Svinhufvud would later argue that, had he tried to do so, the Lapuans would have plunged the country into another Civil War.

The October elections gave Svinhufvud his required majority — by one vote — and on November 11, 1930, the bills were passed which at

last effectively destroyed the Communist movement. A two-thirds majority of the Finnish people had shown in their votes that this was
what they wanted. Up to this time, they had generally backed the anti-
Communist aim of the Lapuans. Now that this had been achieved,
they saw no further need for the Lapuan movement and they expected it to "fade again into obscurity," as Pastor Kares had promised.

But it did not fade away. It now shed its pretenses and, backed by
powerful financial interests and by a number of army officers, set out
confidently to set up a fascist dictatorship. It set loose a new reign of
terror. One Lapuan group of extremists, led by General Kurt Wallenius, until recently Chief of the Army General Staff and now secretary
general of the Suomen Lukko organization, kidnaped former President Ståhlberg and his wife. Since Ståhlberg was one of the most
eminent and generally respected men in Finland, this outrage shocked
the country. There were many more such actions, and they began to
build up popular resentment, especially after Wallenius was acquitted in the courts of complicity in the Ståhlberg kidnaping, although
he had made a full confession of his guilt.

In the spring of 1932, General Wallenius and his Lapuan fascists
made their supreme bid for power. They had planned an armed *coup
d'état* for the middle of March, but their plans were spoiled by a pre-
mature rising in February, at which, after breaking up a lecture by a
Socialist speaker at Mäntsälä, the Lapuans sent an ultimatum to the
President demanding the resignation of the Cabinet. They also began
to concentrate armed forces for a march on the capital.

Svinhufvud, who had become President in the election of January,
1931, was a Conservative, the hero — next to Mannerheim — of the
White victory in the Civil War; but he was no fascist. And now he rallied the country against the Lapuans. Tanks and artillery and regular
army reinforcements were brought in to defend Helsinki. And in an
impassioned broadcast the aging President warned the rebels that they
had been betrayed by a few extremist leaders and appealed to them to
lay down their arms and support the democratic Republic. His moving
broadcast was highly effective. Some 6000 armed Lapuans laid down
their arms and dispersed to their homes. Only a hard core of 400 held
out at Mäntsälä under General Wallenius. They were surrounded by
government troops and finally surrendered without firing a shot.

Thus was fascism finally put down in Finland. It had come perilously close to triumphing. In the summer of 1932, six months before Hitler came to power in Germany, the Finnish Parliament passed several laws for the protection of the Republic. Meetings of the Lapuan movement and two similar organizations were forbidden, and all parties were prohibited from organizing para-military formations.

Finnish fascism, like that in other lands, had fed of course not only on popular opposition to Communism but on the economic depression which set in at the beginning of the Thirties. Finland's prosperity depended largely on her export of wood products. When the world market in these commodities collapsed, Finland joined in the world slump. Worst hit of all the classes were the small farmers, who suffered not only from falling prices but from the lack of employment during the winter in the forests or woodworking factories. Without that employment they could scarcely exist. It was this group, which was naturally anti-Communist and anti-Russian anyway, which furnished the mass support of the Lapuan movement.

Surprisingly enough much of the fascist leadership was furnished by the Lutheran pastors, especially the Pietists. In a country where 98 per cent of the people are Lutheran, they had much influence and they genuinely felt that the Communists were out to destroy the Christian religion and the Lutheran Church. It was through many of these pastors that the Lapua movement, in its infancy, became in part a religious movement, stern and uncompromising. And this religious tinge contributed greatly to its mass support.

Economic recovery, which began in Finland in 1932, helped to dampen enthusiasm for the fascists. Exports increased that year for the first time since 1928. The Lapuans, though virtually outlawed, changed their name and tried to come back by Parliamentary means in the remaining years of peace. They formed the "Popular Patriotic League," more familiarly known as IKL, from its Finnish name, and managed to win 14 seats in Parliament in 1933 on a vague platform of abolishing the party system. In the last elections before World War II, in 1939, IKL lost half of its fourteen seats, and retained only a small nuisance value.

Finland had returned to a democratic balance. It was fairly prosperous. In twenty eventful years it had firmly established itself as a free and sovereign nation. Only the menacing proximity of Soviet Russia — something the Finns had to live with from day to day and were never allowed to forget — disturbed the minds of the people as the third decade of the twentieth century drew to a close.

The Winter War

On April 14, 1938, shortly after the *Anschluss* whereby Germany took over Austria, a Second Secretary of the Soviet Legation in Helsinki by the name of V. Jartsev urgently requested to see the Finnish Foreign Minister, Rudolf Holsti. Jartsev was known in the capital to be a special emissary and, as was soon learned, he acted without the knowledge of the regular Russian Minister. Holsti promptly saw him the same day.

His news was highly interesting and even somewhat startling to the Finns. He had been empowered, he said, to discuss in the utmost secrecy the possibilities of a closer understanding between the two countries. The Soviet Government wished to respect the independence and territorial integrity of Finland. But it was plain to Moscow that Germany was contemplating an attack on the Soviet Union, which involved operations through Finland. What would Finland's attitude be in case of such an attack?

Having asked a question, Jartsev issued a warning. If Germany were allowed to use Finland as a base for attack against Russia, the Soviets would not hesitate to advance into Finnish territory. However, if the Finns put up armed resistance to the Germans, they could count on Russian military and economic aid. And in this case, Jartsev added, the Soviet Union would withdraw its troops after the war and leave Finland completely free.

The Russian envoy mentioned another matter. Moscow, he said, believed that in the event of war Finland's fascists would try to seize control of the government in order to aid Germany. Russia wanted certain guarantees against this happening. When Holsti asked what guarantees were envisaged, Jartsev gave no clear answer. There the conversation ended, except that the Second Secretary requested that it be kept completely secret, even from his own Minister. Unfortunately, the Finns kept it so secret that even the inner circles of Parliament knew nothing of it, leaving them, as well as the Press and public, unprepared for events which would shortly follow.

The highly confidential talks with Jartsev continued all that spring and summer. On August 11, the Finnish government presented him a draft for a treaty with Russia in which Finland formally declared it would not permit any foreign power to obtain a foothold on its territory for an attack on the Soviet Union and Moscow reiterated its assurance that Russia would respect Finland's territorial integrity. Russia was also asked to give its approval to the joint remilitarization by Sweden and Finland of the Åland Islands, which would augment Finland's ability to defend itself (especially against Germany) and thus help to preserve its neutrality.

This was not enough to satisfy the Russians. A week later, on August 18, they replied by demanding a written undertaking that Finland would repel a German attack and agree to accept Russian armed assistance. They agreed to Finland's fortifying the Åland Islands only if Russia could control the use of the fortifications. Finally, they asked for facilities on the Finnish island of Hogland (Sursaari) in the Gulf of Finland on which to build an air and naval base. In return, the Russians offered to guarantee Finland's independence and territory and to conclude a favorable trade treaty. The Finnish government rejected the proposals on the ground that they would be a breach of Finland's sovereignty and neutrality.[5]

When in March, 1939, Litvinov initiated fresh proposals asking that the Finns lease three islands and two skerries in the Gulf of Finland to Russia so that it could better defend the Leningrad Passage, Mannerheim, who was now Chairman of the Council of Defense, advised the government not to reject them out of hand. But it did, on March 8. Undaunted, Litvinov sent a special emissary, Stein, to Helsinki to discuss — again in great secrecy — the matter further. He offered Finland 183 square kilometers of land on the Eastern frontier in exchange for the islands. Again Mannerheim advised meeting Stein halfway.

I was of the definite opinion [he wrote later in his Memoirs] that we were bound to meet the Russians in some way if this was likely to lead to improved relations with our mighty neighbor. I discussed Stein's proposal with Foreign Minister Erkko, but

[5] This account is taken largely from *The Memoirs of Marshal Mannerheim*, pp. 292 ff. There is also an account of it in a work by an anonymous Finnish author: *Finland and World War II, 1939-1944*. Edited by John H. Wuorinen. Copyright 1948. The Ronald Press Company. Mannerheim's version seems more complete and objective.

could not bring him to share my views. I also visited the President of the Republic and Prime Minister Cajander, to lay my views before them. I said that the islands were of no use to the country and that we had no means of defending them, as they were neutralized. Nor would Finland's prestige suffer should we agree to the exchange. On the other hand, the islands were of real importance to the Russians, as they commanded the entrance to their naval base at the Bay of Luga, and by leasing them we should draw advantage from one of the few trumps we held. But I met with no understanding.[6]

It was pointed out to him, Mannerheim says, that any government which accepted the Russian proposals would immediately fall. To this Mannerheim, always supremely confident in himself, replied that he was willing to risk his popularity in so vital a matter by placing himself "at the disposal of the government."

But I went still further and expressed the opinion that it would be to Finland's advantage to offer to move the frontier nearest to Leningrad westward by five or six miles against a reasonable compensation. Even in 1811, when the country of Viipuri (Viborg) was reunited with Finland, there were many who considered that the frontier ran too close to the metropolis on the Neva. (St. Petersburg)[7]

Since a few months later the Russians would try to justify their attack as a legitimate effort to free Leningrad from the threat of Finnish guns, some have speculated that, had Mannerheim's advice about withdrawing the frontiers from close proximity to Russia's second largest city been accepted by his own government, the future might have turned out differently. At this stage, the spring of 1939, the Russians had not even put forth such a proposal. Had Finland volunteered it — so the speculation goes — Russia might have been appeased.

"I insistently warned against Ambassador Stein being allowed to depart with empty hands," Mannerheim declares. But his views were not shared by the unyielding Finnish government, and on April 6, Stein departed, his mission a failure. This may well have led, as Mannerheim implies, to a hardening of sentiment in Moscow which soon was to prove disastrous to the Finns.

[6] *Memoirs,* p. 300.
[7] *Memoirs,* p. 301.

But it was Germany's unprovoked attack on Poland, on September 1, 1939, unleashing the Second World War, which radically changed Finland's situation for the worse.

On August 23, Hitler had made his pact with Stalin after one of the most fantastic turn-abouts in the experience even of these two opportunistic dictators; and war had inevitably followed. On September 17, Russia began its occupation of the Eastern half of an already defeated Poland, and immediately set out to achieve a long-dreamed of aim: to make the Eastern Baltic a Russian lake. To accomplish this, the independence of Estonia, Latvia and Lithuania on the southern shore, and of Finland on the northern shore — which the Soviet government had solemnly recognized in 1920 and reaffirmed in later nonaggression treaties — had to be snuffed out. In pursuit of this design, the Russians acted swiftly and ruthlessly.

They hastily summoned the unhappy foreign ministers of the three so-called Baltic states to Moscow, and on September 29 and October 5 and 9, respectively, forced Estonia, Latvia and Lithuania to sign treaties of mutual assistance which gave the Soviet Union naval, air and army bases in the three countries and made it only a matter of time, which proved brief, before Russia would swallow them up completely.

After the Baltic states, it was Finland's turn. On October 5, the day of the signing in Moscow of the "treaty" with Latvia, the Finnish government was requested by the Soviet government to send its foreign minister to the Russian capital within three days to discuss "concrete political questions which have become urgent through the outbreak of war."

The Finns, understandably enough, hesitated to put their heads into the jaw of the Russian bear with undue haste, and on October 8, when the three-day time limit had run out and not even a reply had been sent to Moscow, Molotov warned the Finnish government to get a move on. It finally did, but not until Mannerheim, who had followed Russian moves in the Baltic states closely, called up several classes of reserves in what he later would admit to be "a camouflaged mobilization." This quick and firm action, as well as subsequent ones of preparation, were soon to save Finland from the complete disaster which shortly overtook the Baltic states, when they were simply occupied and annexed by Russia without the firing of a shot.

On October 9, Juho Kusti Paasikivi, an able banker, jurist and diplomat, who would become a beloved President of Finland in the difficult postwar years, left for Moscow at the head of the Finnish delegation. He knew the Russian language and he knew the Russians, but these excellent qualifications were not to prove of much use. Stalin and Molotov made the following demands: the lease to Russia for 30 years of the Hanko Peninsula (which commands the mouth of the Gulf of Finland from the Finnish side); cession of part of the Karelian Isthmus above Leningrad; demolition of fortifications on both sides of the frontier on the Karelian Isthmus (which would have robbed Finland of her main defenses against a Soviet attack); cession of several islands in the Gulf and of the Finnish half of the Fisher Peninsula, on the Arctic near Petsamo; compensation for lost territory to be made by giving Finland a small slice of Russian Karelia.

The Finnish government, stunned by the extent of the Soviet demands, felt that to accept them would be to leave Russia free to take over Finland any time it desired. It therefore rejected them, but in the ensuing talks which continued, at intervals, until the middle of November offered considerable concessions to Russia in a desperate effort to reach an agreement.

Mannerheim, who had no illusions about the Russians or about the ability of a small nation such as Finland to hold out indefinitely against such a colossus of a neighbor, continued to advise giving the Russians as much as possible without destroying the country's power to put up a good fight in self-defense. He proposed that the government cede the islands in the Gulf of Finland to Russia and even give up territory on the Karelian Isthmus near Leningrad. But he firmly opposed giving Russia a foothold in the hinterland of Finland by leasing them Hanko. And it was principally on this point that the negotiations broke down in Moscow midway through November, after the Finns had agreed to give up the islands in the gulf and move their frontier as much as twenty-five miles backward from Leningrad.

The Finns were heartened by the publication of a message which President Roosevelt sent M. I. Kalinin, President of the Supreme Soviet, on October 16, expressing "the earnest hope that the Soviet Union will make no demands on Finland which are inconsistent with the maintenance and development of amicable and peaceful relations between the two countries and the independence of each." But they were not surprised at the Soviet reaction which Molotov expressed in a belligerent speech on October 31, in which he advised the President of the United States to concern himself with the independence of the Philippines rather than with that of Finland.

The Finns, of course, did not expect any more effective help from faraway, isolationist America than that of timely words. Nor could they, as the result of a conference of the Nordic states at Stockholm which took place during the Moscow negotiations, count on very much aid from their Scandinavian neighbors. President Kallio had joined the Kings of Norway, Denmark and Sweden at Stockholm full of hope that the four northern countries might present a common front against Moscow. But all he got was a pious resolution, and that of a negative nature. Finland, though few persons in Helsinki seem to have realized it, was now isolated and completely on its own. The men in the Kremlin understood this very well.

For them there remained but the little task of provoking an incident, and this they did, though with great and apparent clumsiness. On the evening of November 26, Molotov protested to the Finnish envoy in Moscow that on that same afternoon Finnish artillery had fired on Russian troops in the village of Mainila on the Karelian Isthmus, killing four Russian soldiers. He proposed that Finnish forces therefore be withdrawn from twelve to sixteen miles behind the frontier.

"This," Mannerheim would later write, "was the provocation I had been waiting for since the middle of October." To try to avoid it, he had ordered, several weeks before, the withdrawal of all artillery out of range of the Soviet frontier, and had personally seen that this was done. Actually three Finnish observation posts had pin-pointed the shots at Mainila, ascertained that they had been fired from the Russian side, and had noted it down in their records. The Finnish government therefore rejected the Soviet protest but offered not only to have impartial investigators make a check on the spot — or, if Russia preferred, to examine the incident jointly in accordance with the existing boundaries convention — but also to discuss a reciprocal withdrawal to an agreed distance from the frontier.

The Soviet government made no answer. The next day, on November 27, it unilaterally renounced its Nonaggression Pact with Finland. On the twenty-ninth it broke off diplomatic relations, declaring that "as is known," Finnish troops were "continuing" their attacks against Soviet defense forces. This was exactly the kind of Big Lie which Hitler had used so cynically to justify his attack on Poland on

September 1. On November 30, Helsinki was bombed and, in Mannerheim's words, "the Russians commenced regular operations with overwhelming force on land, sea and in the air."

It was naked, unprovoked, inexcusable aggression. Thus began the Winter War.

It lasted for one hundred and five days during the coldest winter but two recorded in those parts since 1828. For two months one of the world's greatest military powers was stopped cold — outfought and outgeneraled — by one of the world's smallest nations. It seemed like a miracle. And yet Finland's stubborn defense was due to the heroism and discipline of its people, fighting for their survival — alone.

There was help from the outside world, it is true, but it was strictly limited, and most of it came — or was promised — too late. The United States loaned $30,000,000 — for civilian supplies, since sending arms would have violated American neutrality laws (though as the Finns noted, arms were sent a few months later to Britain, despite those laws). The United States also placed an embargo on the export of strategic materials to Russia. And among the foreign volunteers was a Finnish-American Legion, three hundred strong, which reached the front on the last day of the fighting.

The Swedes, who had most to lose if Russia overran Finland and placed the Red army on the Swedish frontier, furnished the most help in arms and volunteers, though the firm refusal of Sweden to allow the transit of Franco-British troops across the territory, or to consider sending regular forces, caused considerable resentment in Helsinki. The Swedes made much of German "warnings" against their intervening in Finland, but there is no evidence even in the Swedish White Book of any such warnings; and Prime Minister Hansson acknowledged in the Riksdag on January 17, 1940, that "we have been subjected neither to warning nor threats by Germany."

Altogether 11,500 foreign volunteers, according to Mannerheim, reached Finnish soil. Of these Sweden furnished 8000, many of whom, with 725 Norwegians, saw active service in the north, where they were badly needed. (Denmark's battalion of 800 got to Finland, but never to the front.) The Swedish government also furnished, as we have seen, considerable arms: 80,000 rifles, 50 million cartridges, 112 field guns and howitzers, 300,000 artillery shells, 104 A.A. guns, 85 antitank guns with ammunition, 25 planes and large stores of oil.[8]

On February 5, 1940, after the tide of the war had begun to change, the French and British governments offered to send a small expeditionary force if the Finns formally asked for it and if Norway and Sweden would grant transit facilities. But it was not until March 7, one week before the end, that General Ironside, Chief of the British General Staff, was able to inform Finland that a force of 57,000 men was ready, and that the first division, of 15,000 troops, could reach Finland by the end of March if Norway and Sweden would allow them transit. Actually, five days previously on March 2, both countries had refused consent to transit on the grounds that it would violate their neutrality. Both London and Paris seemed annoyed that the Finns delayed in formally *asking* for their troops, and on March 8, Prime Minister Daladier, of France, addressed the Finnish government as follows: "We have waited for several days for Finland to make her appeal, so that we can come to your aid with all the means at our disposal. It is difficult to understand why this request is still postponed."

But there were good reasons, as the Finns well knew. One was the refusal of the Swedes and Norwegians to allow Allied troops to cross their territories. But the principal reason was that time had run out for the Finns. On February 1, the Russians, having reorganized and reinforced their defeated forces, threw a vast army into the struggle on the Karelian Isthmus under the direct command of Moscow's most illustrious general, Marshal Timoshenko. The Finns were simply overwhelmed by the weight of Soviet infantry, tanks, artillery and bombers which outnumbered their own many times. On February 11, there was a Russian break-through in the center of the first Finnish line of defenses at Lähde on the Isthmus. Temperatures that registered as much as 70 degrees below zero froze the waters of the Gulf of Finland and Lake Ladoga so solidly that the Russians were able to send tanks across them and threaten the Finns from the rear.

On February 22, Mannerheim advised the government "to try to arrive at a compromise with the Kremlin." His armies were still intact, but were being slowly driven back and decimated by incessant Soviet attacks. He realized that no appreciable help from the West

[8] These figures from Mannerheim agree essentially with those furnished by the Swedish government, as given on page 115.

was forthcoming and that Finland's only hope was to attempt to negotiate a peace while it still had considerable fighting forces in being.
And he knew that Moscow, worried by its unexpectedly heavy losses
in men, arms and prestige at a moment when it was growing increasingly distrustful of Nazi Germany, was not averse to discussing peace,
though undoubtedly on the harshest terms.

From the first day of battle the Finns had tried to re-establish contact with the Kremlin in order to bring a halt to the war. At first,
Moscow ignored these overtures. On the second day of its aggression,
the Soviet Union had set up the absurd fiction of "the Democratic
People's Government of the Finnish Republic" with its "temporary
capital" at Terijoki, a frontier hamlet evacuated by the Finnish forces.
Its "leader" was O.W. Kuusinen, an exiled Finnish Communist who
had been prominent in the Civil War. Russia promptly "recognized" this nonexistent government and went through the shenanigans
of concluding with it a "nonaggression treaty." For nearly two months
Molotov insisted that Russia could only deal diplomatically with this
"Finnish government."

But on January 29, 1940, he sent word through Sweden's Foreign
Minister that the Soviet Union, after all, was prepared to talk about
a settlement with the "Ryti-Tanner government." (Tanner, the Social-
Democrat leader, had become Foreign Minister in the Ryti Cabinet
on the outbreak of war.) But Molotov made it clear that its peace
terms would go far beyond its previous demands. What would the
Finns, he asked, be prepared to cede after so much bloodletting?

Steady contact was now resumed at Stockholm, through both the
Swedish Foreign Office and the Soviet Ambassador, the redoubtable
and Bohemian Madame Alexandra Kollontai. On February 23, the
Russians informed the Finns that their minimum conditions were the
leasing of Hanko and a return to the frontiers of Peter the Great, as
laid down at Nystad in 1721. This meant giving up all of the Karelian Isthmus, including Viipuri (Viborg), Finland's third largest city
and one of its chief industrial centers and ports. Moscow added that
if its terms were not immediately accepted, subsequent ones would
be even more severe.

In desperation, the Finns once more appealed to Sweden. On February 27, Tanner saw the Swedish Prime Minister in Stockholm and
asked again that Sweden permit the transit of Franco-British troops
and, if possible, send more direct aid, especially troops, herself. Hans-

son's reply was in the negative. Moreover, he urged Tanner to make peace at once, regardless of the harshness of Russia's terms, to avoid Finland's complete destruction.

The next day, on the twenty-eighth, matters reached a climax. The Russians demanded a reply to their terms within forty-eight hours. On the same day the Finnish Prime Minister, accompanied by four members of the government, hurried to Headquarters to ask Mannerheim his advice.

The General frankly told them that it was necessary to conclude peace without delay.

> I told them that I did not think we should allow bitterness over the hard conditions to blind our judgment. The Army was not defeated, and this gave us a chance of discussing peace. Were a military catastrophe to occur, our chance would be lost.[9]

On March 8, a Finnish peace delegation arrived in Moscow. As it had feared, it soon found the Kremlin raising its demands. The Russians now demanded further slices of Finnish territory in northern Finland as well as the ceding of the Finnish part of the Fisher peninsula, near Petsamo. In Helsinki, the government hesitated to accept the Soviet conditions. Again it turned to Mannerheim. On the next day, March 9, "he felt compelled" as he puts it, "to give the government categorical advice to conclude peace."

On the eleventh, the government gave its delegation in Moscow full powers to conclude peace — on whatever terms it could get. That evening, though, the government also made a frantic, eleventh-hour appeal to Sweden begging the Swedes, for the last time, to give transit to Allied troops. It also asked whether Sweden in case peace was made, would join Finland in a defensive alliance after the war. The Swedish reply to the first supplication was a flat No; as for the second, it said it was prepared to examine the possibilities.

On that eventful day, too, the Western Allies made a last-minute effort to stave off the inevitable. Both the French and British governments publicly renewed their intention of coming to the aid of Finland with an expeditionary force — though how it was to get there, they did not say.[10] But it was now much too late.

---

[9] *Memoirs.*

[10] One can only speculate how World War II might have turned out had the Allied expeditionary force got there and France and Britain thus become bellig-

Late in the evening of March 12, 1940, the Finnish delegates in Moscow put their signatures to a Treaty of Peace. Fighting stopped the next day at 11 o'clock and at midnight Mannerheim issued his last Order of the Day, ending: "We are proud in the consciousness of a historic mission which we will continue to fulfill, which is the defense of that Western civilization which has for centuries been our heritage. But we have also paid to the western countries the debt of this heritage to the uttermost farthing."

The Winter War cost Finland dearly. A country with half the population of New York City lost 24,923 killed, missing and died from wounds, and 43,557 wounded. (Russian losses were estimated by Mannerheim at 200,000 killed, though the Soviet government never revealed the actual figure.) One tenth of the cultivable land of Finland was lost, and room had to be found for half a million Finns from the ceded territories, few of them being willing to remain under Soviet rule.

Moreover, though it had preserved its sovereignty by the heroic fighting of its soldiers, Finland was now at the mercy of Russia. The Finns took some comfort in the eloquent praise which had been bestowed upon them for what they had done. There were, for instance, the ringing words of Churchill:

> Finland alone—in danger of death, superb, sublime Finland!—shows what free men can do. The service that Finland has rendered to humanity is magnificent . . . We cannot say what Finland's fate will be, but nothing could be sadder to the rest of the civilized world than that this splendid northern race should at the end be destroyed and in the face of incredible odds, should fall into a slavery worse than death.

By one of those ironies with which the history of mankind is so full, Churchill's government would — within little more than a year — declare war on the government of "this splendid northern race."

For the war between Russia and Finland was really not over. It was shortly to be resumed — with consequences even more disastrous for this little people whom Churchill, Roosevelt and almost everyone else in the Western world had so stanchly admired and praised.

---

erents against the Soviet Union. Very shortly Great Britain (France having been defeated and forced out of the war) would be fighting side by side with Russia.

The Second Finno-Russian War — Finland Joins with Nazi Germany

It would have been less than human for the Finns not to have wished to regain their lost territories and to rid themselves of the pistol which Russia held loaded and aimed at the heart of Finland by its possession of the Hanko base — should a favorable opportunity arise. Moreover, by the winter of 1940-1941, the Finns had good reason to believe that the Soviet Union intended shortly to swallow Finland up, as it had the three Baltic States during the summer of 1940, when Germany had been busy conquering the western part of Continental Europe and Scandinavia.

Nevertheless, the course of events — as distinguished from the motives — which led Finland to join Nazi Germany in the attack on Russia in June, 1941, is still shrouded in a certain haze. Even the authoritative Finnish apologia which Professor Wuorinen has edited frankly admits that at many important points the explanation of the events themselves remains hypothetical.[11] Tanner, the Social-Democrat leader, who like many other distinguished Finns served a prison sentence after 1945 as a "war criminal" for his alleged part in the second war, told me in Helsinki that to this day he has never learned the whole story of how Finland got into the conflict side by side with Hitler.

That there was resentment in England and America at the democratic Finns joining up with our principal enemy in the great global struggle was only natural, despite the understanding in both Allied countries for Finland's legitimate urge to win back what Russia had stolen after a barbarian aggression. Finland had much to answer for by the choice she made — and for which in the end she would have to pay so dearly.

But there is a Finnish case. And it is only fair to set it down, briefly, at this point.

In June, 1940, the Finns had watched with growing apprehension how Russia brazenly annexed Estonia, Latvia and Lithuania and brought them under a cruel dictatorship, deporting tens of thousands of their citizens to destinations unknown — but which could be im-

[11] *Finland and World War II*, p. 102.

agined. Was not Finland, it was anxiously asked in Helsinki, to be the next on the list?

Soviet pressure on Finland began immediately to increase. A number of new demands were made, including one that the Petsamo nickel mines, one of the largest in the world, should be handed over to Russia. On June 14, two Soviet fighters shot down in cold blood a Finnish passenger plane over the Baltic, with the loss of all aboard.

But it was at the meeting in Berlin of Molotov with Hitler and Ribbentrop early in November, 1940, that the Soviet Union made clear its designs on Finland. Molotov bluntly told the Germans that Russia regarded it as its "duty once and for all to decide and clear up the Finnish question.[12] In plain language, that meant liquidating the Finnish nation, and Hitler, of course, realized it. His secret plans for "Barbarossa," the attack on Russia, were already being developed by his General Staff. He did not want the Soviets to gain a new foothold on the northern flank; he wanted it eventually for himself. He therefore asked Molotov to wait "for six months or a year" before moving against Finland.

The full details of these conversations did not reach Helsinki until May, 1941, when the Germans revealed them in order to induce Finland to join her in the attack on Russia. But enough became known to the Finns in the next few months to make them more uneasy than ever about Russia's designs and to look desperately about for possible aid from outside. Then by a series of remarkable diplomatic blunders, the Kremlin succeeded in throwing Finland into Germany's waiting arms.

Finland had looked first to Sweden for aid and the Swedes, in October, had surprisingly offered to discuss not only a defensive alliance but a union between Sweden and Finland on the understanding that Finland was not planning a war of revenge against Russia. The Finns agreed to this condition and negotiations began, but twice in December, Moscow expressed its opposition to them so categorically and so threateningly that they had to be dropped.

Then at the turn of the year, Russia cancelled its trade treaty with Finland and stopped all deliveries of supplies. It was this which, more than anything else, threw Finland into Germany's arms. For, cut off

---

[12] We know this from the German memoranda on the conversations which form a part of the secret documents of the Reich captured toward the close of the war. See *Nazi-Soviet Relations, 1939-1941. (Washington, 1948.)*

from the West by the Allied and German blockades, and now cut off from Russia, Finland's only remaining source for food, oil, coal and metals was Germany. The Germans were very happy to step in and help. Thus Finland became dependent upon Germany for its very physical survival. And economic dependence brought with it, as it invariably does, political pressure from the benefactor.

The first step in the chain of events which brought Finland into the war on Germany's side began in August, 1940 — and seemed harmless enough to the Finns. They were asked by Goering to do what Sweden had just obligingly agreed to do — to permit the transit of German troops and war material through their territory to the German forces in northern Norway. In return, the Germans promised Finland not only more general goods but, for the first time, war material. Russia, still allied with Germany, made no objection whatsoever.

It was this transit agreement which was to enable Germany to have two strong divisions in Finland on the eve of the attack on Russia, one ostensibly being withdrawn from northern Norway and the other en route to replace it. Both divisions, supported by a third, transported from Norway to Finland across neutral Sweden, promptly headed East toward the Finno-Russian frontier.

Now, it is the official Finnish contention that there were absolutely no agreements of any kind, either military or political, between Nazi Germany and Finland for the latter country's entry into the war in June, 1941. In view of this categorical assertion, it is interesting at this point to look into the nature of the contacts between the Finns and the Germans, as revealed by exclusively Finnish sources, Mannerheim above all.

Aside from the talks about transit, these contacts began in January, 1941, when the Chief of the Finnish General Staff, General Erik Heinrichs, went to Berlin at the invitation of the German General Staff to give a lecture about the Winter War. During the visit General Halder, the German Chief of Staff, casually mentioned to Heinrichs that Germany and Finland might one day, as in 1918, find themselves fighting side by side. In that case, it would be natural for the Finns to move on Leningrad. Mannerheim says General Heinrichs "firmly rejected" the very suggestion.

A month later, in February, Colonel Buschenhagen, Chief of Staff of the German troops in northern Norway, visited Helsinki and after telling Mannerheim that Germany would not remain passive if Russia attacked Finland, asked what the Finnish operative plans were in the North.

"I absolutely declined," says Mannerheim, "to give him any information about our operative plans, and also refused to discuss an eventual German-Finnish military collaboration." [13]

In the spring of 1941, the relations between Germany and Russia began rapidly to deteriorate. The Reich was taking over the Balkans — Bulgaria, Romania and Yugoslavia — and Moscow protested. It was against this background that one of Hitler's trouble shooters, Schnurre, an economist and diplomat in the Wilhelmstrasse, arrived in Helsinki on May 20. He promptly revealed to the Finns what Molotov had demanded in Berlin the previous November: a free hand for Russia in Finland. He promised that if Russia attacked Finland Germany would come to her aid. He did not reveal, of course, that Hitler intended to attack Russia. But he did request that Finland send some *military* experts to Germany to receive from Hitler, in Mannerheim's words, "information regarding the alarming world situation."

With the full approval of the President, of Mannerheim and of the government, a Finnish *military* delegation under General Heinrichs was immediately dispatched to Germany in order — to quote Mannerheim again — "to be fully informed about the present *political* situation in the world." [14]

At Salzburg, they were received by Field Marshal Keitel, chief of the German Supreme Command, and General Jodl. We know from the German secret documents that by this time all preparations had been made for the German attack on the Soviet Union. The Nazi military chiefs naturally did not reveal this, but they did tell the Finns, we learn from Mannerheim, that armed conflict with Russia "was within the bounds of possibility." [15]

In that case, Mannerheim continues, in relating the Salzburg conversations, "it was Germany's wish that Finland should in the first place hold down the Russian troops on her frontiers. It could also be conceived that the Finns would take part in an offensive against Leningrad in combination with a strong German attack upon the city from the south. On the other hand, it was hoped that Finland would assist the operations against Murmansk and Salla which were being planned by the Germans." [16]

General Heinrichs, according to Mannerheim, replied to the Germans that he had no authority to negotiate about political and military matters. The next day the Finns went on to Berlin, where they saw General Halder. He, says Mannerheim, "went considerably further" in raising the question of Finnish-German military collaboration. But again General Heinrichs declined to make any commitment.[17]

Finland was now caught in a squeeze between the two great powers of the Continent. Mannerheim argues at great length that to have provoked Germany at this stage would have thrown Finland into the arms of a Russia which had come near to destroying his country and which, the Finns now knew, had only recently made clear it wanted to finish the job. Without German supplies, the Finnish people could not continue to exist. Russia refused to send any supplies whatsoever. "Finland," says the Finnish commander, "was no longer free to decide her own fate." [18]

Nevertheless, he maintains the official Finnish thesis that Finland continued to be neutral to the very last. The second week in June, Colonel Buschenhagen again came to Finland and asked the General Staff to work out with him joint plans for operations in the North. "I had Colonel Buschenhagen informed," Mannerheim relates, "that a guarantee for Finnish participation in the war could not be given. Finland was determined to remain neutral provided she were not exposed to aggression." [19]

At the beginning of June there was feverish military activity on both sides, but Mannerheim only mentions at first that on the Soviet side of the frontier. He thought it sufficiently alarming, he says, to order partial mobilization on June 9. On June 17, he ordered mobilization of the whole Finnish field army.

We learn from the Finnish report which Professor Wuorinen has edited that the Germans were very busy in Finland too. Between

[16] *Memoirs.*
[17] *Ibid.*
[18] *Ibid.*
[19] *Ibid.*

June 7 and 10, some 38 German ships arrived at Finnish Bothnian ports; from June 11 to 21, 36 more docked. From Northern Norway an entire German S.S. division marched south into Finland. From Finnish ports an entire German army division marched north.[20]

Did the Finns by now know the date on which Germany planned to attack Russia? Mannerheim says word came to him only on the evening of June 21, a few hours before the attack began. But on the 19th, he gave orders for manning the Åland Islands, *effective on June 22*, the day the Germans jumped off. Already on June 15, after consultation with the President, he placed — as he himself recounts — all Finnish troops in the North, which included the entire Third Army Corps, under a German Commander-in-Chief.[21] This might have been considered an act of self-defense but it was scarcely a neutral act. Nor was the deployment of such sizable German forces in northern Finland toward the Soviet frontier. They were certainly no longer "in transit" to and from Norway, though the Foreign Office in Helsinki maintained that they were — on the very day hostilities began.

We come now to the heart of the Finnish case: *that Finland only joined in the war after it was attacked by Russia following the Nazi onslaught on the Soviet Union.*

On the morning of June 22, 1941, a few hours after the German attack began, Hitler proclaimed that Finnish and German troops "stood side by side." Mannerheim protests that "Hitler had no right whatever to make such a declaration." [22] At any rate the Finnish Foreign Office hastily telegraphed that same day a statement to all legations, including those in Berlin and Moscow, maintaining that Finland intended to remain neutral, though she would defend herself if attacked by the Soviet Union.

It is the Finnish contention — and the facts themselves seem indisputable — that the Russians thereupon did attack. At first there was only sporadic shelling along the frontier and from the Hanko base, but on the twenty-fifth, Mannerheim declares, the Soviet Air Force made extensive attacks on ten Finnish towns, including Helsinki and Turku, in the course of which twenty-six Russian bombers

[20] *Finland and World War II.*
[21] *Memoirs.*
[22] *Ibid.*

were shot down.[23] It was on that day, the Finns say, that the government intended to make a statement in Parliament that Finland would stay out of the German-Russian war, unless attacked. The heavy bombing changed the government's intent. To be quite objective about this, it is difficult to understand how the Finns could expect the Russians to wait until the German army and air force attacked them from behind the Finnish frontier.

On the twenty-third, Molotov had asked Finland whether it would remain neutral. He had not mentioned any concessions if it did, and there is no record that the Finns suggested any. I heard it said in Helsinki that had the Kremlin then and there offered to restore the 1939 frontiers, Finland might well have remained out of the war, and defended itself against the Germans instead of the Russians.

However, before the Finns could reply, the Soviets cut off communications between the two countries.

On June 25, the Finnish Parliament met in secret. The government proclaimed that Finland had been attacked by Russian forces and that it was now at war. The Diet voted its unanimous approval, and that evening Mannerheim returned once more to his headquarters at Mikkeli to resume command of the military struggle against Soviet Russia.

The Finns insist to this day that it was a separate war. They have compared it to the situation of the United States in 1812 when this country fought Britain independently, during the Napoleonic wars, without considering itself an ally of Napoleon. On July 4, 1941, President Ryti told the United States Minister in Helsinki that Finland was not "allied" to Germany; it was merely a "co-belligerent."

The distinction was not appreciated in Great Britain (nor later in America). The British had welcomed Russia as an ally, well realizing that their chances of defeating Nazi Germany in a struggle which for a year they had been carrying on alone were enhanced by the addition of such a great power on their side. As British spokesmen pointed out, war was indivisible; and Russia's enemies were now Britain's enemies.

Nevertheless the British did not, despite Russian urging, immedi-

[23] *Memoirs.*

ately break diplomatic relations with Finland. It was Hitler who insisted that the Finns close down the British Legation in Helsinki, and this they did on July 28, causing a diplomatic break. Still Britain, again despite Moscow's prodding, hesitated to declare war. However, in September, after the German-Finnish forces had reached the 1939 frontiers of Finland and were obviously preparing to push beyond them, despite the Finnish protestations that their sole war aim was to regain the territory taken from them by Russia in 1940, the British government informed the Finns that unless they ceased hostilities and refrained from pushing further into the Soviet Union, Britain would feel compelled to treat Finland as a hostile power not only during the war but during the peace negotiations.

It must be remembered that at this moment Russia seemed doomed. The Finns, like almost everyone else in the West, thought that the war was as good as over and that the Soviet Union was about to collapse. What better moment to secure *strategic* frontiers from which any future Russia would find it difficult to attack Finland? What better moment to add East Karelia, which had never belonged to Finland, but which was full of Finnish-speaking people, to the motherland?

Finland rejected the British demand.

On November 28, it received a second one. This time the British simply demanded that the Finns cease all military operations before December 5. And then on November 29, Churchill wrote a personal and secret letter to Mannerheim, whom he had greatly admired in the past.

It was not necessary, the British Prime Minister suggested, "to make any public declaration, but simply leave off fighting and cease military operations, for which the severe winter affords every reason, and make a *de facto* exit from the war. . . . It would be most painful to the many friends of your country in England if Finland (after the war) found herself in the dock with the guilty and defeated Nazis."

Mannerheim, as he says in his account of this episode,[24] was on the spot. He had already given, seven weeks before, on October 6, an order to halt the advance as soon as one town, Karhumäki, before which his troops stood, was taken. But he could not, he says, tell that to Churchill. It would have been disloyal to the Germans, for

[24] *Memoirs.*

Russia then could release most of its troops from the Finnish front for service in the areas around Leningrad and Moscow, which were now being threatened by the Nazi armies. Moreover, says Mannerheim, it "would undoubtedly have resulted in countermeasures on the part of the Germans, upon whom we were already economically completely dependent."

Mannerheim therefore replied: "I am sure you will realize that it is impossible for me to halt the military operations . . . before the troops have reached the positions which in my opinion will provide us with the necessary security."

On December 4, the Finnish government replied to the British ultimatum by saying that Finnish forces would "soon" attain their strategic objectives. On December 6, Britain declared war on Finland. On the same day, which was Finland's Day of Independence, the Parliament solemnly denounced the 1940 Treaty with Russia and formally declared that the reoccupied territories had once more been joined to Finland.

On the next day came the Japanese attack on Pearl Harbor, followed on the 11th by Germany's declaration of war on the United States. Mannerheim immediately wondered if this might mark a turning point in the war, as had America's entry into the first war in 1917. But few other Finns seem to have shared such a thought. For the overwhelming majority the detested Soviet Union, the aggressor in 1939, seemed thoroughly beaten. Finland had won back what had been unjustly taken from her the year before. The days of Bolshevism in Russia were obviously numbered. Finland had contributed to the downfall of the most evil autocracy in modern times. Eventually the West, America and Britain above all, would appreciate this. The future looked bright to the Finns as they set about in the December snows to celebrate Christmas, 1941, and to reflect upon their victories.

The victories had come quickly and with relative ease. Within a couple of months the old 1939 frontier was regained, and Finland's war aims thus achieved. Or were they? There was lively debate within the Finnish government and in Parliament whether or not to take advantage of the Russian debacle and push on a little further. There was much talk of securing more "safe and secure" frontiers. Some wanted to take Eastern Karelia. A few, however, thought it would be prudent to stop at the old border. To Mannerheim, flushed with his triumphs, this last view, as he says, seemed "academic." Since Finland had been attacked, he thought it was entitled to push "beyond the frontier if it should be desirable from a military point of view." [25] He refused to give in to great German pressure to attack Leningrad from the North after the Germans reached it on the South early in September — a stand he stubbornly maintained throughout the war because of, he says, political reasons. But he wanted to advance further elsewhere and take East Karelia, and in September he did so.

Much later — when I came to Finland — Tanner would tell me that this was Finland's greatest mistake of the war, though at the time, judging by some of the speeches he made, he was not so sure. In the fall of 1941 he too was demanding "safe and secure boundaries" beyond those of 1939 and explaining that it was "necessary to render harmless, in a military sense, the areas behind the boundaries." [26] But after the disastrous outcome of the war for Finland, he, like many of his fellow countrymen, looked back and realized that had the Finns remained on their 1939 borders, they might have got much better peace terms.

By the beginning of December, 1941, the last Finnish objectives were achieved. East Karelia was conquered and the Russians had evacuated the base at Hanko. The Finnish army dug itself in for defensive warfare over the long, hard winter. A number of troops were demobilized. By the spring of 1942, some 180,000 soldiers had been sent home.

Yet Russia did not fall, as expected. The Germans were halted before Moscow in mid-December and soon were being forced to retreat. Leningrad held out. On Christmas Eve, 1941, the first Russian peace-feeler was received in Finland through the Swedish Foreign Office. In January, President Ryti visited Mannerheim at his headquarters to discuss it. The general must have shocked him.

". . . I stated that my faith in Germany's chances to win the war had been shaken . . . I did not exclude the possibility of a [German] collapse on the Eastern front." [27]

But because of their fear of German countermeasures and also because of Finland's complete dependence on Germany for food supplies,

[25] *Memoirs.*
[26] *Finland and World War II.*
[27] *Memoirs*, p. 443.

the President and his Commander in Chief — we learn from Mannerheim — decided that to resume contact with the Russians now "was
out of the question."

To the outside world, at least, Finland seemed intent on cement-
ing her close relations with Germany. On November 21, 1941, she
had joined the Berlin-Tokyo-Rome anti-Comintern Pact, thus ap-
pearing to place herself solidly in the camp of the Axis. On June 4,
1942, Hitler visited Finland to congratulate Mannerheim on his
75th birthday and on his having been made a Marshal.

"This visit astounded me," Mannerheim dryly remarks, "and gave
me food for serious thought." [28]

In Washington Secretary Cordell Hull, who had declined to break
diplomatic relations with Finland or declare war and whose principal
aim had been to bring pressure on the Finns not to help the Germans
cut the Murmansk rail-line by which American arms were reaching
Russia, publicly stated that the United States was much concerned
with Hitler's visit. On the following day the American Minister in
Helsinki was hastily assured that Hitler's visit had brought no change
in Finland's situation. And Mannerheim emphasizes that in fact he
did succeed in preventing the cutting of the Murmansk line
throughout the war by refusing to aid the Germans, despite incessant pressure, in the venture.

In the end, of course, Finland's fate depended upon the fortunes of
Germany, and when these began to decline in 1943, it dawned on the
Finns — or at least on a few leaders, for censorship long prevented the
public from realizing how badly the war was going — that the country's only hope for decent survival lay in extricating itself from the
war.

Admittedly, as the Finns fully realized, that was a difficult task.
Germany's reaction to such a step would be violent. At the very
least, she would cut off supplies to Finland. Where could the Finns
obtain enough food to stave off starvation? And what guarantee was
there that the Russians would not simply march in and take over the
country? In fact, what was to prevent the Germans from doing
that?

On February 3, 1943, the day after the German Sixth Army surrendered at Stalingrad, there was a conference at Finnish headquar-

[28] *Memoirs*, p. 450.

ters attended by the President of the Republic, the Prime Minister, the Foreign Minister and the Commander in Chief. Mannerheim says they all agreed that the war had reached a definite turning point and that Finland must use the first possible opportunity to get out.[29] Professor Wuorinen's anonymous but highly authoritative source declares that the Finnish commander said it was clear that Germany was going to lose and that therefore all agreed that an attempt to conclude peace with the Soviet Union and Britain should be made.[30]

At this juncture the United States, which still maintained diplomatic relations with Finland, offered to help. On March 20, 1943, the American Chargé d'Affaires informed the Finnish government that the United States would be glad to assist in arranging contacts with Russia for the purpose of discussing peace. This step was welcomed in Helsinki and efforts were made to obtain from Washington information as to Moscow's general terms and whether the United States was prepared to guarantee that the Soviet Union would live up to those terms. It was also decided that the honorable course would be for the Finnish Foreign Minister, August Ramsay, to go to Berlin, tell Foreign Minister Ribbentrop what was up, and ask his approval. It was certainly an honorable gesture, but it was not a very realistic one, and Mannerheim strenuously opposed it. However, Ramsay went; and as was to be expected, Ribbentrop exploded. Finland must not only reject the American offer; it must sign a formal agreement with Germany not to make a separate peace.

To back up its demands Germany cut off all food shipments to Finland and reduced oil shipments by one-half. In these circumstances Finland reluctantly declined the American offer of mediation but stubbornly refused, at the insistence of Mannerheim, to sign any agreement to refrain from making peace on its own.

Opportunities to make peace now arose. In November, Madame Kollontai, the Soviet ambassador in Stockholm, told Eric Boheman, chief of the chancellery of the Swedish Foreign Office (and in the 1950's Swedish Ambassador in Washington) that if Finland were prepared to discuss peace, her representative would be welcomed in Moscow.

Despite the difficulties and the general apprehension over what Moscow's terms might be, the Finns needed little urging. At the

[29] *Memoirs*, p. 460.
[30] *Finland and World War II*, pp. 144, 150.

end of January, 1944, the government asked Mannerheim to come to Helsinki to give it a frank appraisal of the military situation. He confirmed its worst fears. Soviet forces had just broken the German siege of Leningrad and could now throw overwhelming forces against the Finns north of the city on the Karelian Isthmus.

"Germany," Mannerheim says he told the government, "had in all probability already lost the war, and if the enemy were to concentrate sufficient forces to make a breach on our front, he would be able to do so." [31]

A fortnight later, with this information at hand, the government sent Paasikivi to Stockholm to meet Mme. Kollontai. On February 19, after several conversations with her, he returned to Helsinki with Russia's minimum terms for an Armistice.

They were such as to plunge the government and the commander in chief into deep gloom. Moscow demanded immediate acceptance, without discussion, of the restoration of the 1940 frontiers and the internment of all German troops in Finland. Russia was willing to discuss reparations and the future of Petsamo.

To give up again a tenth of her cultivated land which the Karelian refugees had, in the meantime, returned to till was bad enough. But to intern the strong German forces seemed impossible.

However, the Finns, in their reply of March 8, asked that at least they be given an opportunity to present their views of the Russian terms. This was flatly rejected by Moscow on the tenth and Finland was given to the eighteenth to accept the conditions. The day before the deadline, Finland replied that it could not accept the Soviet terms in advance without discussion and renewed its request for further talks. Moscow yielded to the extent of asking Finnish representatives to come to the capital forthwith, "to receive from the USSR an explanation of the armistice terms."

On March 27 and 29, Paasikivi and Enckell listened to the Soviet explanation from Molotov himself. It was quite an earful. Finland was to intern or expel all German troops by the end of April at the latest, and if necessary Russia would be glad to help in this. Finland was to pay the Soviet Union within five years $600,000,000 worth of reparations in the form of goods. It was to cede Petsamo. And, of course, the 1940 frontiers would have to be restored. If these condi-

[31] *Memoirs.*

tions were accepted, Russia might relinquish her lease of the Hanko base "without consideration."

The Finns decided that it was impossible for such a small nation to shoulder such a heavy reparations burden or to drive out or intern the Germans within a month. On April 18, the government, after unanimous approval of Parliament, rejected the Russian terms.

"The acceptance of these terms," said the Finnish reply, "which in part [internment of German troops] cannot be carried out for purely technical reasons, would actually weaken and destroy the possibilities for Finland to exist as an independent nation and, experts agree, would place a burden [reparations] on the Finns which is far beyond their ability to bear."

Marshal Mannerheim has described June 10, 1944, as "the black day of the war" for Finland. After an artillery barrage of "a violence unknown in the two wars" Soviet forces broke through the Finnish defense line on the Karelian Isthmus for a distance of six miles. By June 20 the Russians had captured Viipuri and were beginning to drive the Finns out of East Karelia. Mannerheim now frantically asked for more German help: more planes, more guns, more divisions.

At this point, Ribbentrop stepped in to get what he had failed to obtain a year before: a Finnish promise not to conclude a separate peace. He suddenly appeared in Helsinki on June 22. The Germans, he said, did not want their arms "to fall into the wrong hands." But if Finland were prepared to guarantee that it would not quit the war except in agreement with the Reich, more arms and planes and troops would be immediately forthcoming.

Once again Finland was caught in a squeeze. On June 23, while Ribbentrop was still in Helsinki insisting on no separate peace pact, a message was received from Moscow by way of Stockholm. It said:

> As we have several times been deceived by the Finns, we wish to receive a declaration from the Finnish Government, signed by the President and the Minister for Foreign Affairs, that Finland is prepared to surrender and approach the Soviet Government with a request for peace. If such a document is received from the Finnish Government, Moscow will be prepared to receive a Finnish delegation.[32]

[32] *Memoirs*, p. 482.

"The choice," remarks Mannerheim, "was between unconditional surrender and the signing of a treaty (with Germany) which increased the chances of creating conditions for obtaining an acceptable peace."

The Marshal, too, was looking for a way out of the war. He says he knew the war was lost. But he thought that if Finland, with German aid, could fight on a little longer, it would get better terms from Moscow. So he proposed one of the most peculiar diplomatic engagements of the war. President Ryti was to be the sacrificial goat. He was to sign a personal letter to Hitler, pledging that he would neither make a separate peace with Russia nor allow any government under him to do so without the agreement of Germany.

Mannerheim, as well as all the other political leaders except the Social-Democrats, who opposed it, considered this a justifiable "out." To them it bound only Ryti, as long as he was President. The assurance to the Germans, they considered, would not be binding for another President — who soon was to be Mannerheim himself.[33]

Ryti signed the letter — an act for which he would have to serve a long prison sentence after the war following the trial of the "war criminals," which the Soviet government forced the Finns to stage. Though this was not understood at the time — indeed in the Allied lands Ryti was denounced as a "stooge" of the Germans or, at least, as a "fool" who believed in June, 1944, that the Germans were still going to win the war — there seems no doubt now that Ryti simply sacrificed himself for what he thought was the good of his country.

"It is to the honor of President Ryti," Mannerheim comments in his *Memoirs*, "that he signed the undertaking though fully conscious of the consequences. In the trial for responsibility for the war, I stated that on that occasion President Ryti performed a meritorious civic act, and I adhere to this opinion." [34]

The Finnish President's pledge to Hitler, however, was too much for President Roosevelt and Secretary Hull. On June 16, Hjalmar Procopé, the Finnish Minister to the United States, who had been such a popular figure in Washington during Finland's heroic resistance in the Winter War, had been given his passport. On June 30, the

[33] Mannerheim explains the deal as follows: "An undertaking in the form which I proposed would not bind the people of Finland. If the President resigned from his office, Finland would be free to act as the situation demanded." (*Memoirs*, p. 482.)

[34] *Memoirs*, p. 483.

United States formally broke off diplomatic relations with Finland. It never did take the final step, however, of declaring war.

The end now rapidly approached for Finland. Actually, by the end of July Mannerheim had succeeded in stabilizing the situation at the front. The furious Russian attacks ceased, and the Soviet Command withdrew most of its armor and many of its crack troops for more important service further south where the Germans were in full retreat from the Baltic to the Black Sea. It was the German debacle which made it necessary for the Finns to immediately seek peace while they still had strong military forces of their own in being.

On August 1, as the result of a "gentleman's agreement," President Ryti resigned on account of "ill health" and on August 5, after Parliament had passed a special bill dispensing with the electoral college, the Diet elected Mannerheim President of the Republic. The Marshal was now the highest political as well as military authority in the land. He set about immediately to get Finland out of the war. Ryti's promise to Hitler, Mannerheim felt, no longer held good, and he so informed Field Marshal Keitel, who visited him at Headquarters on August 17.

A week later, on August 25, the Finns asked Mme. Kollontai in Stockholm to inform her government that Finland wished to resume negotiations for peace. The Russians replied on the twenty-ninth that they would receive a Finnish peace delegation on two conditions: first, that Finland sever all relations with Germany; second, that all German troops must withdraw from the country, or be interned, by September 15, at the latest. The Russians added that these terms were made on behalf of Great Britain also, and had been approved by the United States.

Parliament voted 108 to 45 on September 2, to accept these conditions. On the same day Finland broke off diplomatic relations with Germany and demanded that German troops evacuate Finland within a fortnight. This was a fateful day for Finland. That evening Mannerheim wrote a moving letter to Hitler.

In this hour of hard decisions I am impelled to inform you that I have arrived at the conviction that the salvation of my nation makes it my duty to find a means of ending the war. . . . When Field-Marshal Keitel recently visited me, he insisted that the people of Greater Germany could doubtless continue the war for

another ten years if necessary. I replied that even if one might
hope that this be true of a nation of ninety millions, it was equally
true that we Finns were physically incapable of continuing the
war. . . .

I wish especially to emphasize that Germany will live on even
if fate should not crown your arms with victory. Nobody could
give such an assurance regarding Finland. If that nation of barely
four millions be militarily defeated, there can be little doubt that
it will be . . . exterminated. I cannot expose my people to such a
fate.

Even though I can hardly hope that my opinions and reasons
will be accepted by you, I wish to send you these lines before
the hour of decision.

Our roads will probably soon part, but the memory of our German brothers-in-arms will live on. . . .

I regard it as my duty to lead my people out of the war. The
arms which you have generously given us I will never of my
own accord turn against Germans. I cherish the hope that, even
though you may take exception to my letter, you will share my
wish and the wish of all Finns, that the change in our relations
may not give rise to animosity.[35]

A Finno-Russian armistice was arranged for September 4 (though
the Soviet troops, possibly because of a misunderstanding or poor
communications, did not observe it until 24 hours later), and on
September 6, the Finnish delegation left Helsinki for Moscow. The
Finns were not hopeful, but at least they were beginning negotiations as the result of an armistice and not of a surrender, as the
Soviets had at first demanded.

Arriving in Moscow on September 7, the Finnish delegation, headed
by Prime Minister Antti Hackzell, was kept waiting a week before
being summoned to the Kremlin. The strain was too much for the
Prime Minister, who on the fourteenth, when the summons finally
came, suffered a stroke. On September 18, the Finnish government,
having received Russia's terms, debated whether or not to accept
them and was unable at first to come to any conclusion. That evening, however, an ultimatum was received from Moscow demanding
that the preliminary peace agreement be signed by noon of the following day. The Finnish government's hasty convening at 5 A.M.
on the nineteenth was followed by a session of Parliament at 7 A.M.,

[35] *Memoirs*, p. 494.

at which authority was given the Finnish delegation in Moscow to sign. This it did at noon on September 19, 1944.

It was a dearly purchased peace. The Finns were pushed back to the frontiers which the Soviet Union had dictated after the Winter War. Petsamo, on the Arctic, Finland's only warm-water port, was lost. In place of Hanko, the Russians demanded a military base at Porkkala, only twelve miles southwest of Helsinki.[36] Reparations were reduced by half — to three hundred million American dollars to be paid in goods over six years. All German troops were to be driven out or interned within two and a half months. Yet during that time the Finnish army was to be demobilized to a peace footing.

The Finns Fight the Germans

There now began the weirdest chapter of all in the turbulent war story of Finland. For the German troops refused to leave Finland, and the Finnish army found itself in the painful position of having to drive them out — the very comrades in arms with whom the Finns had been fighting against a common enemy for three weary years.

On September 15, the deadline the Finns had given the Germans to start their evacuation, German forces demanded the surrender of the Finnish garrison on Hogland, a strategic island which guarded Helsinki from the East. When the demand was refused, the Germans attacked the island in considerable force, backed by the fire of German warships, but were beaten back after a bitter fight in which the Finns took 700 German prisoners.

But the hardest task was to get rid of an army of 200,000 well-equipped German troops who controlled the northern third of Finland above Oulu and Kajaani. The Russians made it doubly difficult by insisting that while the Finns were ejecting such a sizable force they must rapidly demobilize the Finnish army! Also, the government was fearful that many Finnish officers, as well as troops, might mutiny before they would fire on Germans.

---

[36] Today Russian guns at Porkkala command the Finnish capital and could smash it to smithereens within an hour. It is as if Alexandria, Virginia, were a Soviet base, with guns which could level the Capitol, the White House, the Pentagon — and all the rest of the capital of the United States — in an hour or two.

The fighting between the Germans and Finns actually turned out to be hard and bitter, and to the surprise of the Finns, if not to others in the West, the Hitler forces were so ruthless in their retreat that they made a wasteland of all of Lapland and of considerable territory to the south. Not only communications were destroyed, which was expected, but every city, town, village, hamlet and farmstead through which the Germans passed. By the end of 1944, the Finns, however, had driven the Germans into a narrow pocket in the far northwest, a few miles from the Norwegian coast, where they held out until the end of the war.

The German devastation in the North cost Finland $300,000,000 in property destroyed — an economic burden which had to be added to the crippling reparations charge imposed by Russia. There were heavy casualties too, which had to be added to the 54,000 men killed in the second war against the Soviet Union.

As the New Year came in 1945, the Finns were thankful to be at peace after four war-torn years. But there were many of them who wondered whether the shattered, defeated country could survive. In the long run, they knew, that depended partly on the Soviet Union. But they were realistic and courageous enough to know that it also depended on themselves.

The Miracle of Reconstruction

The Finns accepted their hard fate with amazing fortitude. There was no whining. At the Paris Peace Conference in August, 1946, the Finnish Foreign Minister, Carl Enckell, made the shortest speech of any delegate from a defeated country. When the peace treaties with Italy, Romania, Bulgaria and Finland were signed on February 10, 1947, Finland was the only one of these countries which did not lodge a note of protest at the time of signing.

It was not that the Finns considered the peace treaty just. On the contrary, they thought it cynically violated every principle of the Atlantic Charter. Worse, it left Finland exposed to the tender mercies of the men in the Kremlin. Despite its wrongs, however, the Finns were doggedly determined not to mope about it but to look to the future, and by hard work and austere living and infinite personal sacrifice to make it as bright as possible.

They set to work immediately to solve the two main problems of reconstruction. The first was how to pay more than a half-billion dollars in reparations to Russia. The second was how to settle 477,000 refugees — more than one tenth of the nation's population — from the territories which the Soviet Union had just grabbed.

This twofold task was comparable — had the United States, with its forty times greater population, been in Finland's place — to Americans having to pay a war indemnity of 20 billion dollars and having to find farms and homes for 18 million refugees. It was a formidable burden to have to shoulder.

The armistice of September 19, 1944, had stipulated that Finland should pay Russia in goods to the value of 300,000,000 United States dollars over a period of six years. But when the details of the reparations agreement were worked out a few months later, the Russians demanded payment reckoned in 1938 prices. Since prices had in the meantime doubled, this meant that the Finns had to pay double the value in products — or $600,000,000. After lengthy discussions the Soviet government finally agreed to add 15 per cent in their calculations of prices for ships and machinery, and 10 per cent for finished goods.

Twice the Soviet government made substantial concessions which lightened the reparations burden for the Finns. At the end of 1945 it extended the delivery period from six to eight years. And in the summer of 1948, it canceled half of the deliveries due after July 1 of that year. This cut amounted to $73,500,000, or a quarter of the entire reparations, thus reducing the total to $226,500,000. And though the cancellations consisted mostly of wood products, which were easiest for Finland to pay (but which Russia, with its own vast forests, did not need) the Finns were grateful to receive such a large measure of relief.

Russia also agreed to cancel most of the fines which it had imposed on Finland for late deliveries. Because the Finns were not always able to obtain in good time all the raw materials they needed from Western markets to manufacture goods on reparation account, and also because of delays brought about by Communist-incited strikes, their deliveries of some products were occasionally late, though each year they more than made good for this by supplying other items ahead of schedule. The reparations agreement provided for fines of 5 per cent per month for late deliveries and altogether they totaled $4,-600,000. However, Russia remitted all but $800,000 of these.

One of the worst aspects of the war indemnity for the Finns was that they were required to pay so much of it not in goods which they normally exported, namely products of the forest industry, but in ships and machinery, which they had never before built for export. In order to meet the Russian demands, Finland had to build up an entirely new machine and shipbuilding industry which she did not need and which was bound to upset her economy and make it further dependent on Russia, as the sole customer for such goods. In the end, 72 per cent of the reparations bill was paid in ships and machinery, and only 28 per cent in wood products.

The way the Finns went to work to pay off the Soviet Union on schedule is astonishing. The country had been bled and devastated by four years of war; there was an acute shortage of housing for the workers — in fact, there was a shortage of everything: clothing, transportation, electric power (the Russians had taken one third of the hydroelectric capacity), machinery and raw materials. And during the first two years of peace, the Finns were forced to live on hunger rations.

Yet they labored, without complaint, like beavers. They built and delivered to the Russians, among other things, 623 vessels, 30 complete factory plants with power stations, 1000 transportable power stations, 701 steam and Diesel locomotives, 80 turbogenerators, 52,000 electric and gasoline motors.

And on September 19, 1952, a day of great relief in Finland, the Finns completed exactly on schedule their final reparations payment to the Soviet Union.

It is difficult to compute exactly what the final bill came to. The total sum, in prewar American dollar prices, amounted to $226,500,-000. Most Finnish experts agree with Professor Bruno Suviranta, of Helsinki University, who calculated the total value of goods, in prices current when they were delivered to Russia, at $570,000,000. Professor John H. Wuorinen of Columbia believes it amounted to some $900,000,000 if, as he says, "total costs were included." [37] By any calculation the sum was a heavy burden for a war-torn country of four millions to pay off in eight years.

[37] *Foreign Affairs.* July, 1954.

The second great task of reconstruction was to find land and homes for 477,000 Finns, mostly Karelians, who had become dispossessed by the Russian acquisition of 10 per cent of Finland's territory. Some 200,000 of these had earned their living from agriculture on 34,000 farms. The government considered it urgent from both an economic and social standpoint to find new farms for them at once. The problem was not only physical but psychological.

Land for the new farmers had to be taken, in large part, from those who already owned and worked it. And Finnish peasants have a fierce love for their land and do not like to part with any portion of it. Neither do owners of estates though they can better afford it. There was a further complication. The Swedish-speaking Finns opposed the settlement of the Finnish-speaking Karelians in regions where they were dominant.

However, in view of the problem and the urgency of settling it at once, the Land Acquisition Act, passed by the Diet in May, 1945, had to be — and was — quite radical.

It provided for the acquisition of land for the refugees either from state-owned tracts or from existing farms and estates. In the case of the latter, the law stipulated that as much land as possible be obtained by voluntary purchase but it authorized compulsory purchase when necessary to obtain the required amount of acreage. Actually three quarters of the land needed had to be acquired by compulsion; and though owners of some 200,000 farms, 70 per cent of all there were in Finland, had to relinquish a part of their acreage to the refugees, the Act stipulated that land must first be taken from areas owned by corporations and the Church, from neglected farms, or from estates held by persons whose principal occupation was other than farming.

Compensation was paid by the state for all land thus acquired at 1944 prices. The Karelians received approximately the same acreage which they had owned in the regions ceded to Russia, and they were given, in addition, compensation for the loss of homes, farm buildings and stock with which to pay for new homes and buildings and stock on their new farms.

Resettling a tenth of the population, half of them on farms, was a considerable undertaking, but in this, as with reparations, the Finns lost no time in putting the project through. By the end of 1951, when the program was virtually completed, the evacuees had acquired 28,000 self-supporting farms and 15,000 rural house and garden plots, the latter varying from two to ten acres and being sufficient to allow the owners to grow their own vegetables and keep a cow and a few chickens. Altogether this represented the acquisition of 675,000 acres of tillable soil, plus about the same amount of arable but uncleared land and 3,000,000 acres of forests. As in Norway and Sweden, most Finnish farms include adjacent woods sufficiently large to provide fuel and also timber for building needs.

The Land Acquisition Act provided land not only for the Karelian refugees but for some 57,000 war veterans, war widows and orphans as well as tenant farmers and agricultural workers who had been dispossessed or who had lost their jobs because of the break-up of the big estates and larger farms. About a third of these families were given self-supporting farms and the rest home and garden plots.

A great deal of building had to be done for those who were settled on the land. And while the state granted generous economic support, it insisted that the new settlers help themselves by doing their own building from timber available in the forests attached to their farms. The state paid for certain building materials, plumbing, electric wiring and roofing, but experts in Helsinki assert that by encouraging the new owners to construct their own houses out of their own timber, the government's share in the total costs came to no more than half of the expense of the new building.

I came across some remnants of estates whose owners were in a bad state, or claimed to be. They could not, they said, efficiently farm on their reduced acreage. I remember the defeated but charming atmosphere in one great manor house. The cultivated proprietor and his fashionable and beautiful wife, who had recently returned from wintering in sunny Italy, showed me through the elegantly appointed rooms of the old Russian-style house and, over champagne on the veranda that looked down a broad expanse of lawn toward a picturesque lake, lamented that they could not go on much longer on the few acres which the government Land Resettlement Act had left them. I had the sudden feeling that here was a Finnish version of Chekhov's *Cherry Orchard* being acted out in real life.

The Trial and Imprisonment of the "War Criminals"

The trial of the "war criminals" is another of those singular chapters with which the brief history of the Finnish Republic is so full. There were naturally quite a few persons in Finland, especially on the far Left, who felt that those responsible for bringing the country into the war on the side of Germany should be punished. There was even stronger feeling against those who had prevented the making of an earlier peace, whose terms might have been less disastrous. But it was only the Communists, no doubt egged on by the Soviet Government, who staged nationwide demonstrations demanding that the "war criminals" be brought to trial. Actually, Article 13 of the Armistice Agreement, which had been signed by Great Britain as well as by the Soviet Union, stipulated that the "war criminals" must be tried.

But how to do it — by due process of law? The question was warmly debated all through 1945. K. J. Ståhlberg, Finland's most eminent jurist, a former President of the Republic and venerated as an "elder statesman," was asked for a legal opinion. He held that those who had taken a lawful decision for war and peace could not, under Finnish law, be charged with a crime, however wrong they might have been. The only way they could be "tried" would be to pass a retroactive law, and this was contrary to all the precepts of Western justice. Moreover Finnish law did not provide for the establishment of a special court to pass judgment on political responsibility.

However, that was exactly what the Finns, though reluctantly, and merely to appease Russia, proceeded to set up. It was empowered to try former members of the government who had "in a decisive way contributed to Finland joining Nazi Germany in the war of 1941 against the Soviet Union and Great Britain, and who during the war had prevented the conclusion of peace."

Prime Minister Paasikivi had advised during a session of the Diet in July, 1945, that all individuals compromised by their part in the war should retire from public life. Apparently it was believed that this step might appease the Soviet government and their stooges, the Finnish Communists, sufficiently to enable the government to postpone the trial indefinitely and, in fact, forever. For a large body of public opinion by this time was deeply resentful that scapegoats were to be made of leading men, who whatever their shortcomings and mistakes, had acted legally, constitutionally and in a way which had been endorsed at the time by an overwhelming majority of the Parliament and people.

But the Russians and the Communists were not appeased by the mere withdrawal of the wartime leaders from public life. They insisted on trials for the "war criminals," as stipulated in the Armistice Agreement.

So, in the fall of 1945, eight men, prominent in public life during the Second World War, were arrested and, on November 15 brought to trial before the special Court of War Responsibility. They included Risto Ryti, who had been President of the Republic during the war, and Rangell, Ramsay, Linkomies and Tanner, who had held important cabinet positions. Tanner was the outstanding figure of the noncommunist Left.

The verdict of the court was a foregone conclusion. All eight men were found guilty and sentenced to from two to ten years in prison. Ryti received the severest sentence: ten years at hard labor. Most noncommunist Finns, I gather, regarded the sentences as merely part of the price which Finland had to pay for its defeat, and the general regard for most of the convicted leaders was not at all diminished. As one Finnish editor explained to me, the eight men had to make their sacrifices too in order to keep the Soviet Union appeased. There seems to have been little bitterness on the part of the convicted men themselves. They accepted their punishment as necessary for the good of the country. Tanner jokingly told me that his four years in prison had been among the most "rewarding" of his life. "I learned," he said, "that prison gave you a unique opportunity for study, contemplation and the writing of books." He himself composed his *Memoirs* while behind the bars. All the prisoners were eventually released before the completion of their sentences, Ryti being held the longest.

The chief counsel for the defense, incidentally, was Hj. J. Procopé, who had been Finnish minister in Washington during the war until he was asked to leave in 1944. His book on the trial was published in Sweden, but its sale is forbidden in Finland because of the fear in government circles that it might unduly offend the Russians.

The Shadow of the U.S.S.R. over Finland

Since the end of the last war one of the cornerstones of Finnish policy has been not to provoke the Russians. It is part of the price of precarious national survival. Finland must get along with the Soviet Union or perish. Hence its firm determination to stay out of Big Power politics and, specifically, though the sympathies of the vast majority of citizens are with the West, out of the Cold War between the Communist and the free world.

But will this policy of neutrality in the great struggle of the mid-twentieth century suffice to preserve this sturdy little democratic neighbor of mighty totalitarian Russia? The Finns do not know; they say only time will tell. Total security, or even a reasonable amount of security, they know, is not to be had in this century. Any day the Russians, on one pretext or another, may take them over, or threaten to.

There was, for instance, so soon after the nightmare of the two lost wars, an ominous moment in 1948 when it looked as if the hour of their liquidation as a free people had arrived, as it had that year for the free people of democratic Czechoslovakia.

Toward the end of February of that year it was announced in Moscow that Stalin had written a letter to President J. K. Paasikivi proposing that Finland and Russia sign a Treaty of Mutual Assistance and Nonaggression. The anxiety in Helsinki was great. There was reason for the Finnish government to fear that the Soviets contemplated a treaty which would go far in reducing the country's remaining independence. The Czech Communists, backed by Moscow, had just carried out their *coup d'état* in Prague, which robbed Czechoslovakia of its democracy and its sovereignty and transformed it into a satellite of the Soviet Union. Many in Helsinki, and in many another Northern and Western capital, feared that it might be Finland's turn next.

It is probable that the violent reaction in the West to the Communist *coup* in Czechoslovakia saved Finland. At least that is the opinion of many persons I talked to in Helsinki. They believe that the Kremlin at first intended to present demands that might well have added Finland to the list of Russian satellites. They say that Stalin was surprised and shocked by the sharpness and extent of Western reaction to the Czech affair — not the least by President Truman's swift action in bringing about peacetime conscription in the United States and his enunciation of the Truman Doctrine, which promised American aid to any other countries threatened by Russia.

The Finnish delegation in Moscow, drawing out the negotiations as long as possible in order to benefit from this turn of events, noticed a change in the Kremlin that augured better for Finland. As a matter of fact, the Finns believe that the draft for a treaty which the Russians produced at the beginning of April was a hastily contrived substitute for one that had been far worse.

Not that any of the noncommunist parties in Finland approved it. But the government felt it had no choice but to sign, and this it did on April 6, with the beaming Molotov making a public declaration to the effect that he hoped that Finland's neighbors would note that the U.S.S.R. had the interests of the small northern states at heart!

Finland certainly maintained her independence, but the treaty did, nevertheless, draw her more firmly into Russia's orbit. By its terms, Finland agreed to defend itself and to accept Soviet military aid in the eventuality of Finland or the U.S.S.R.'s being attacked *through Finland* by Germany or any state allied with Germany. In case of the threat of such an attack, the two countries agreed to "confer with each other."

Both countries also agreed to confirm the Finnish peace treaty which binds them "not to conclude any alliance or join any coalition directed against the other party." This pledge prevents Finland from ever joining NATO or any Western or Northern coalition, since Moscow has held that such combinations are directed against the Soviet Union. Also, as a cabinet minister in Helsinki pointed out to me, Article 2 of the Treaty, which provides for consultations in case of the "threat of an armed attack" by Germany or her allies against either Finland or Russia over Finnish territory, might well be interpreted by Moscow to take in all the Western democracies if Germany were admitted to NATO. In that case, the United States and Britain could be considered as "allies of Germany," and already the Kremlin has proclaimed that the NATO alliance is a "threat" against the Soviet Union.

Incidentally, Article 6 of the Mutual Assistance Treaty pledges both countries to "observe the principle of the mutual respect of sovereignty and integrity and that of noninterference in the internal affairs of the other state."

I could not discover any feeling in Helsinki that the Finns are counting absolutely on Russia respecting the "sovereignty and integrity" of Finland from now to eternity. As to noninterference in Finnish affairs, the policies and activities of the powerful Communist party in Finland give an ironic answer. Nor has Finland felt sufficiently independent of the U.S.S.R. to accept Marshall Plan aid, ally itself with the other northern countries or even join the peaceful Nordic Council which was recently established to further Scandinavian co-operation.

Finally, it might be noted that although Russia pledged itself in the Peace Treaty of 1947 to support Finland's application to become a member of the United Nations, the U.S.S.R., along with Poland, vetoed that application when it was made in September of the same year. The Soviets have managed to keep Finland out of the UN to this day.

In 1953 there was a startling economic development in Finland. For the first time in history, Russia replaced Great Britain as Finland's best customer. Businessmen, bankers, labor leaders and politicians in Helsinki all emphasized to me that if this drift of Finnish trade to the Soviet Union continued, there was danger of Finland becoming so economically dependent on her big neighbor that her political independence might be placed in jeopardy as well.

There were two reasons for this shifting of Finnish foreign trade. The first was that after the collapse of the Korean war boom, which had greatly benefited Finland's chief exports, wood products and especially pulp, prices for these products on the world market slumped and the West drastically curtailed its purchases of them from Finland.

The second reason was that Finland which, as we have seen, was forced to build up a much larger machine and shipbuilding industry than it needed, in order to meet Russia's reparations demands, found itself, after the indemnity had been paid off, with a great industrial plant on its hands for whose products only the Russians were customers. The Soviets had been getting them for nothing as reparations. Now they were quite willing to pay for them. The Russians were — and are — in need of Finnish machinery and ships. The West does not need them. On the other hand, the Soviet Union does not need Finland's main source of export, wood products. The West does — at least in normal times.

But the Russians, in order to make Finland as economically dependent as possible, agreed to buy *both* industrial *and* wood products from Finland. In 1950 the U.S.S.R. made a five-year trade agreement with Finland. In that year trade with Russia, exclusive of reparations, amounted to just 7 per cent of Finland's total foreign trade. The next year it more than doubled. By 1953 it came to one quarter of Finland's total foreign trade — and if the Soviet bloc of satellite countries is included, the figure was 30 per cent.[38] In fact, by 1952 Finland had become the greatest exporter in Europe to the countries behind the Iron Curtain.

For a nation trying to get back on its economic feet after two catastrophic wars, this growing trade with the Soviet bloc was at first naturally welcomed by the Finns. But soon they woke up to the fact that it was fraught with danger. Finland was putting itself in the position of being at the mercy of the Communist world. If Moscow, for political reasons, decided one day to curtail the trade or discontinue it altogether, as it had done once after the Winter War, Finland would be badly hurt or even paralyzed. The Finns therefore turned once more to the West and asked not for gifts, which so many other noncommunist countries were receiving, but for increased trade so that it could remain economically independent of Russia.

It cannot be said that the United States, which was spending billions of dollars to help other countries preserve their freedom in the face of the Soviet-Communist threat, responded very warmly to this modest and reasonable Finnish appeal.

As recently as 1950 America had ranked second after Great Britain in its share of Finland's foreign trade. The following year it dropped to fourth place, as Western Germany and Russia surpassed it. In 1953, the United States purchased but 7 per cent of Finland's total exports; the Soviet Union took 25 per cent.

[38] Until 1953, of course, a good part of Finland's exports to Russia were in the form of reparations and did not figure in the regular balance of trade. In 1951, for example, reparations accounted for nearly half the value of the $128,000,000 worth of goods sent to Russia. In 1952, the last year of the war indemnity, one-quarter of the $154,000,000 worth of goods shipped to Russia were on reparations account. In 1953 the figure dropped to $145,000,000, but all of it was in free exports.

The following figures of Finland's foreign trade for 1953 show the position:

| | (In millions of dollars) | |
	EXPORTS TO	IMPORTS FROM
Soviet Union	145.	112.9
Great Britain	125.1	83.1
Western Germany	39.8	40.3
United States	41.1	26.4
Other countries	218.7	264.6
TOTAL	569.7	527.3

That the excellently staffed American Legation in Helsinki called the attention of the United States government to the urgent necessity of increasing American trade with Finland in order to keep her out of the grasp of Russia, I have no doubt. But its appeals, and similar ones from the Finns and other sources, seem to have fallen on rather deaf ears. The Finns, understandably, could not quite see why it was apparently so easy for the United States to *give* billions of dollars to countries threatened by Soviet Russia and Communism and so difficult to arrange for the yearly purchase of an additional forty or fifty million dollars' worth of Finnish pulp and paper, which was, after all, in short supply in the United States.

Certainly the Finns were grateful to have been granted loans totaling $150,000,000 from the Export-Import Bank and the International Bank. They recognized that under the Battle Act they were not eligible for direct American aid, since they were delivering tankers, icebreakers and other strategic goods to Russia. They had, in fact, never asked for American handouts, having declined to join the Marshall program—though this was largely because of the fear of provoking Moscow. But they did want to sell us a little more so as to increase their economic independence.

By the middle of 1953, when an economic crisis brought down the Agrarian-Socialist coalition government in Finland and for a while made any government based on political parties impossible—a caretaker cabinet of experts had to take over for the remainder of the year—exports to the United States were falling off catastrophically. I remember at that time going over some figures with a Helsinki economist. Sale of pulp to America the first six months of 1953 fell to a third of that of the same period the year before—sale of paper dropped by a half — and this despite lower prices than America was paying from other sources.

In the end, it was Great Britain which came to Finland's rescue — not for political reasons but because of the recovery in the demand for timber, pulp and paper. A trade agreement between the two countries provided for British purchase of 154,000,000 dollars' worth of Finnish goods in 1954, which meant that Britain once again regained her traditional position as Finland's biggest customer.

But for how long? Moscow did not remain inactive in the face of the British bid. In July, 1954, the Soviet Union signed a new five-year trade agreement with Finland, providing for an increase in purchases of Finnish goods from $145,000,000 in 1954 to $147,500,000 in 1956 and rising progressively up to $164,000,000 in 1960. Soviet orders for ships and engineering products ensured full operation and full employment in those Finnish industries which would go bankrupt without this Russian business.

But that was not all. Finland had been exporting some $40,000,000 more a year to Russia than she imported, and she wanted the balance paid not in goods for which she had no use, but in a currency which would be convertible, which the Russian ruble wasn't. In the 1954 trade agreement the Russians surprisingly obliged the Finns by offering to pay $10,000,000 annually on the balance in gold or convertible currency and to arrange for the remaining $30,000,000 to be paid in goods from the satellite countries which Finland normally would have to pay scarce dollars for, such as oil from Romania and coal from Poland.

The trade negotiations in Moscow in 1954 also brought a lessening of political tension between Finland and Soviet Russia. On Soviet initiative, the foreign ministers of the two countries issued a joint declaration pledging themselves to work "for peace and security in accordance with the principles of the United Nations Charter." Moreover, they agreed to raise their diplomatic missions to the status of embassies. Shortly thereafter, the Finns, anxious to assure the West, announced that the government would be pleased to accept ambassadors from other countries as well.[39] This surprising manifestation of Soviet good will both in the economic and political field, coming after so many unbroken years of chicanery, hostility and aggres-

[39] The United States made this change in September, 1954.

siveness, gave the Finns a feeling of at least temporary relief and provided them with a much-needed breathing spell.

Days of Crisis

It came in good time, too.

The previous summer, when I was in Finland, there had been a severe crisis, both economic and political. Because of high labor costs, inflated domestic prices, heavy expenditures on social welfare and a falling world market, Finland had priced itself out of its principal export business: paper and pulp and other wood-processed products. Many mills were forced to operate at a loss; many others shut down for lack of sales. Foreign trade dropped disastrously; unemployment mounted. And the government's till was just about empty. The maximum legal limit of advances to the state from the Bank of Finland had been reached.

At this point the Agrarian-Socialist coalition government fell apart. The agrarian Prime Minister, Dr. Urho K. Kekkonen, proposed that wages be reduced and social welfare costs, especially to industry, be drastically cut, in order to allow Finnish exporters to be able to sell in the world market. The Social-Democrats, backed by the Trade-Union Federation which they controlled, insisted that wages continue to be tied to the cost-of-living index — in other words, that domestic prices be lowered first, and then wages. They also opposed the cuts in social welfare. To help the export industries, they proposed government subsidies. To cut wages and social welfare benefits, they argued, would play into the hands of the Communists. Dr. Kekkonen retorted that if Finland's economy collapsed, as it seemed in danger of doing, that would be an even greater boon to the Communists.

Since there was no possible combination of political parties which could agree on an economic program — especially with elections coming up in 1954 — President Paasikivi appointed a caretaker government of experts under Sakari Tuomioja, Governor of the Bank of Finland. Tuomioja promptly asked President Paasikivi to order new elections as soon as possible. They were not due until July, 1954, but Paasikivi ordered them for March.

Before the elections were held commercial developments outside of

Finland had solved the very economic problems which the Finnish politicians had been unable to come to grips with. Pulp prices in the Western markets rose by 10 per cent in the latter half of 1953 and prices for Finland's other wood-processing exports increased correspondingly. Orders began to flow into Finland from the West and with higher prices they could now be filled at a profit. To the surprise of everyone in Finland, the year 1953 actually ended with a favorable trade balance of $42,000,000.

The elections of March, 7-8, 1954, produced little change in the political lineup. A coalition government dominated by the Agrarians and Social-Democrats was formed under Ralf Toerngren, leader of the Swedish People's Party. It was succeeded in October, 1954, by a purely Agrarian-Social Democratic coalition government under Dr. Kekkonen, who thus became Prime Minister for the fifth time since the war.

The relative position of the parties in the Finnish parliament since the war is shown in the following table:

	1954	1951	1948	1945
Social-Democrats	54	53	54	50
Agrarians	53	51	56	49
People's Democratic League (Communist)	43	43	38	49
Conservatives	24	28	33	28
People's Party (until 1950 National Progressive Party)	13	10	5	9
Swedish People's Party	13	15	14	14

The make-up of the various political parties in Finland may be briefly summed up. The Social-Democrats, in their political, economic and social outlook, resemble the right wing of the British Labor party, and draw their main support from the working class. They are violently anticommunist. Their most prominent leader is Väinö Leskinen, a dynamic and popular figure, who was thirty-seven on the day of the 1954 elections. His uncompromising fight against the Communists had made him a special target for press attacks from Moscow. He is at present Minister of Interior.

The Agrarian party represents the farmers and rural villagers. It takes a middle-of-the-road position in all matters except agriculture, whose interests it naturally champions. Its leader, Dr. Urho K. Kekkonen, is a shrewd and ambitious politician and perhaps the most controversial figure in contemporary Finland. His opponents accuse him of trying to monopolize the ability to get along with the Russians. A more unpolitical and objective view might be that Dr. Kekkonen has certainly succeeded in establishing himself as a substantial non-communist party leader whom the Russians trust.

The Conservative party represents business and industry as well as the bulk of the professional and prosperous middle-class citizenry. The People's party was founded in 1950 to replace the liberal Progressive party, though it is somewhat further to the Right, and in the last election it attracted considerable support from the urban middle-classes. The Swedish People's party, of course, represents the Swedish-speaking population and its leader, Ralf Johan Gustav Toerngren, has sat in all postwar cabinets except that formed in October, 1954.

The People's Democratic League is the façade for the Communist party. Besides the Communists it includes a small faction called the Socialist Unity party, consisting of "fellow-travelers" who broke away from the Social Democratic party in 1945 when it looked as if the Soviet Union would make the Communists the wave of the future. Recently, a good many leaders of the Socialist Unity party resigned from the League and returned to the Social-Democrats after accusing the Communists of having seized "dictatorial power" over the organization.

Madame Hertta Kuusinen, who heads the Communists in Parliament, is one of the most colorful figures in Finland and probably the most prominent and powerful woman Communist leader in the world. She is the daughter of Otto Kuusinen, President of the Finno-Karelian Soviet Socialist Republic, and who may be remembered as the "president" of the farcical "Democratic People's Government of the Republic of Finland" which Stalin set up at the beginning of the Winter War.

Conceded by her bitter opponents to be personally attractive and intelligent, Madame Kuusinen is a shrewd political tactician, insofar as Moscow gives her any leeway. She is also noted for her husbands. The first one, Tuure Lehen, was an acknowledged expert in street fighting and is today a Russian citizen and a general in the Soviet Red Army. For some years after the last war he was reported to be active in training "barricade squads" in preparation for The Day in Finland, which fortunately never came.

Madame Kuusinen's next husband was Yrjö Leino, one of the top men in the Finnish Communist party although overshadowed by the powerful personality of his wife. He obtained the key post of Minister of Interior after the war, when the Communists were represented in the coalition governments, and proceeded in the traditional manner to communize the State Police. This is a customary means of gaining the physical power to take over a country, as the Communists demonstrated in Czechoslovakia at the very time that Leino was at the height of his power in Finland.

Alarmed at Leino's abuse of his office, the noncommunist parties, led by the Social-Democrats, succeeded in pushing through Parliament in 1948 an expression of no confidence in him. When he refused to resign, he was simply dismissed in accordance with Article 36 of the Constitution, which provides that members of the Council of State "must enjoy the confidence of the Diet."

There was some apprehension among the Finns that the reaction in Moscow to this act might be dangerous, but it turned out to be no more disturbing than the customary attacks in the Soviet press and on the radio against the "Finnish reactionaries," chiefly the Social-Democrats.

There have been no Communists in any Finnish government since then, and later in 1948 the Socialist Prime Minister, Karl August Fagerholm, abolished the Communist-infested State Police after a Commission of Inquiry had revealed not only what its aims were but that its practices included tapping the telephones of cabinet members. Also a good many members of the State Police turned out to have had criminal records.

As for Leino, the story does not end there. Following his dismissal from the Cabinet he took to the bottle and, as one Finnish journalist put it, generally went to pieces. Whereupon he was denounced as a traitor by the Communist party! Madame Kuusinen promptly divorced him. For her, it was unthinkable to be married to a man not in good standing in the party. Later Leino wrote his memoirs, in which he claimed to have refused — "for Titoist reasons" — to carry out a Communist plan to take over power in Finland. But nobody paid much attention to him and though his story was plausible he declined to present any documentary proof. No publisher therefore could be found for his manuscript.

In the general election of 1948, the Communists, largely because of

the Leino affair and related events, lost heavily, their representation
in Parliament being reduced from 49 to 38 seats, out of 200. In the
next election in 1951, they regained some ground, increasing their
following to 43 seats, and as we have seen, maintained that strength
in the 1954 polling, much to the surprise of the political prognostica-
tors, who had expected them to lose considerable strength.

Why are the Communists so strong in Finland? How is it that in a
free election with secret balloting some 430,000 — 21.5 per cent of
the Finnish electorate — voted for the Communist ticket in 1954?

I heard many explanations of Communist strength while I was in
Finland, and they may now be briefly summed up.

First, there is a feeling among many workers that the Soviet Union
will eventually take over Finland — in which case the Communists
will be the privileged group. The very power and prestige of Russia
since the war makes for a special kind of attraction to some Finns.
Numerous workers feel that the Social-Democrats are too mild and
compromising in their championship of the working class, as is seen in
their continual co-operation with the "bourgeois" parties.

Then, the Communists have profited from the long and bitter
memories of the Civil War. This aspect has been summed up by a
former Finnish Communist leader, Arvo Tuominen, who was secretary general of the party until 1939. "The Civil War and the subsequent reign of terror did more to open the way for Communism in
Finland than all the other factors put together. The Finns are a people with long memories. Those 200,000 odd workers who had fought
in 1918 and thereby lost their all, swore a bitter revenge. This lust
for revenge has been handed down to the second and third generation. Communism in Finland thus became almost hereditary."

Also, the 1944 armistice terms protect the Communists against
persecution by the government. As we have seen, they were outlawed in Finland from 1930 to June, 1941, and also during the second
war, and their leaders jailed. The armistice agreement stipulated
that they all be released from prison and that the party be recognized as legal. Moreover, the treaty forbade the tolerance of anti-
Communist fascist organizations.

While the Socialists and middle-class parties are free to criticize
and attack the Communists, as they continually do, this freedom is
restricted. They would not dare today, for example, openly to casti-

gate the Communists as the tool of the Kremlin and as a conspiracy serving the interests of a foreign and not very friendly power. They know that Moscow would not tolerate it.

The Communists greatly benefit from this state of affairs. Many young voters do not know the real nature and aims of the party, and the façade of the People's Democratic League has also helped to camouflage them.

Finally, due to interesting and peculiar circumstances, as they say in Finland, the Communists are easily the best financed party in the country. Though their leaders deny it, there seems no doubt that the Finnish Communists receive the bulk of the profits from the operations of the former German commercial enterprises which were taken over by the Soviet government after the war. Some of these firms, such as the Waldhof Concern in the wood-processing industry, were recently sold by the Soviets to capitalist enterprises but the Finnish Communists still benefit from various businesses dealing in engineering, fuel, shipping, movies and dressmaking. Also, the Communists operate a number of trading firms which receive preferential treatment from the state trading commissariats of the satellite countries.

The vast funds from these sources not only enable the Communists to conduct propaganda on a scale which no other party can afford but allow the party to pay its functionaries well. The manifold enterprises themselves provide lucrative employment for many a Communist. Thus, as one socialist ruefully told me, it often "pays to be a Communist in Finland these days." Not all Finns who vote Communist are members of the party, by any means. Party membership is estimated at about 45,000, or one tenth of the Communist vote in a national election.

Thus of all the northern countries Finland has by far the biggest Communist problem. In Norway, Sweden and Denmark, as we have seen, the Communists are so small as to constitute merely a nuisance. Only in Finland are they a powerful political party. But their importance should not be exaggerated. Some 78 to 79 per cent of the Finnish electorate regularly demonstrate in the national elections their opposition to Communism. And they have the governing power and have shown since 1948 that they know how to keep it.

Some hasty visitors from the West, I was told in Helsinki, make the blunder of thinking that because the Socialists and Communists, with ninety-seven seats between them in Parliament, are only four

short of an absolute majority, there is a danger of Finland going
"Marxist."

Nothing could be further from the truth. There is no possibility
of the Social-Democrats combining with the Communists to take
over the government. Indeed, as the most conservative Finns are the
first to remind you — and as we have seen — it is the Socialists who
have taken the lead in the fight against Communism. And though
they are often irked by the conservatism of their "bourgeois" allies
in government, they have consistently and courageously and loyally
worked with the middle-class parties to keep Finland anticommunist
and free.

The Trade-Unions and the Communists

The Trade-Unions of Finland have also played an effective part
in stopping the Communists. The struggle between the Social-
Democrats and the Communists for their control has been a bitter
one and for a while — in 1949 — the issue hung in the balance.

This basic conflict is not a postwar development in Finland as it is
in many countries. Toward the close of the 1920's, the Communists,
knowing that their party was likely to be banned by law — as it was,
in 1930 — succeeded in penetrating and obtaining the key posts in
the Finnish Federation of Labor, then known as SAJ, from its Finnish
name, *Suomen Ammattijärjestö*.

In 1929 the Social-Democrats withdrew from SAJ and in 1930
formed their own noncommunist Confederation of Trade-Unions,
which from its Finnish (and for a foreigner, jawbreaking) name of
Suomen Ammattiyhdistysten Keskuslitto, became known as SAK.

SAK has never fallen under Communist domination. But it has
come close.

Up to the outbreak of World War II, it remained relatively weak,
with a membership of only 70,000 out of some half a million wage
earners. Conservative laws and the hostility of business towards unions made the Finnish trade-union movement generally weak between
the wars. A number of key industries, such as wood-processing, remained unorganized and a general practice of collective bargaining
was frowned upon both by the government and the employers.

The hard experience of the war and the fact that at its end the government and the industrialists were anxious to stem the frightening growth of Communism brought a change of attitude toward unionism, and two significant developments occurred. Membership of SAK expanded rapidly, and in 1944 it was able to negotiate, after the Swedish model, a General Agreement according to which SAK and the Finnish Employers' Federation recognized each other as the exclusive bargaining agents between unions and management. By 1947, SAK boasted a total membership of 341,538.

Once again, as before the war, the Communists went to work to gain control of the trade-union movement. By 1947 they had taken over eleven of the forty affiliates of SAK, including such key unions as the Transport Workers, the Textile Workers, the Forest and Floating Workers, the Wood Industry Workers, the Construction Workers and the Bricklayers. When delegates to the Fifth Convention of SAK were elected in 1947, the strength of the Communists nearly equaled that of the Social-Democrats, so that the top jobs in the Secretariat had to be equally divided and in the Executive Committee, which runs the Labor Federation between conventions, there were six Communists to eight Socialists.

In 1949 the struggle for control of the organized labor movement in Finland reached its climax. Actually that year the Communists staged a double offensive. They tried to break the hold of the Socialists on the unions and take them over themselves; and they attempted to drive the minority Social-Democrat government under Premier Fagerholm out of office. They failed in both objectives, but in the fight for the unions they came close to victory.

The battle began in August with the Communists staging a nationwide series of wildcat strikes. In the Kemi area, which they dominated, there were riots and some workers were killed. The Communists thereupon called for a general sympathy strike. It did not come off, and thanks to the energetic resistance of the Socialist labor leaders, only the Communist-dominated unions joined in the wildcat strikes. The noncommunist key figures in SAK then ordered the Communist unions to put their men back to work. When the latter refused, SAK expelled them. They were told they could only return when they were able to run their organizations on a democratic — that is, noncommunist — basis. Eventually all but two unions did clean house and were restored to membership in the National Federation.

It cannot be said that the Communists have been entirely eliminated from the Finnish trade-union movement. But today they control only 7 of the 39 SAK-affiliated unions, the largest and most strategic being the Construction Workers, with 23,000 members. Control of the unions in the principal export industries of wood-processing as well as in transport, including the dock-workers and seamen, has been firmly wrested from Communist hands. And SAK has cleaned out the Communists from all key posts in its central offices.

Having accomplished this, the Socialists followed the example of other Western trade-union movements and withdrew SAK from the World Federation of Trade Unions (WFTU), which then became completely Communist. Because of the government's fear of Russian reaction, SAK has not joined the anticommunist International Confederation of Free Trade Unions (ICFTU), which the democratic national labor federations, led by the British, American and Scandinavian organizations, established after their withdrawal from WFTU. But SAK sends observers to its annual world congresses, as it does not do to the WFTU meetings. And most of SAK's important affiliates are members of the International Trade Secretariats which today are members of the ICFTU.

Finland, like Sweden, has a white-collared union, called the Confederation of Intellectual Workers, or HTK from its Finnish name, *Henkisen Työn Keskusliitto*. It has 26 affiliates and a total membership of 65,000, the largest single union being the Federation of Civil Servants with 21,000 members. Whereas SAK gives the bulk of its political support to the Social-Democrats, HTK backs the middle-class parties. However, as in most countries, the unions have not been able to prevent the deterioration of the salaried position of the white-collar workers relative to that of the organized manual wage-earners.

Progressive labor legislation, like collective bargaining, was fully achieved in Finland only after the last war. A Collective Agreements Act, passed by the Diet in 1946, officially sanctions collective bargaining and lays down rules and regulations which were largely agreed upon in the privately negotiated General Agreement of 1944 between the Workers and Employers' federations. The law stipulated that no worker or employer can be prevented from belonging to a union or association; but it also guarantees the freedom *not* to join any organization.

As in the other northern lands, there is a Labor Court to judge on the interpretation of collective contracts. The President of the Republic appoints the head of the Court and two assistants, of whom one must have experience in labor relations and two as judges. The President appoints three additional members of the Court on the recommendation of the Labor Federation and three on the recommendation of the Employers' Association. A system of state mediation in labor conflicts is similar to that we have seen in the other northern lands. The Ministry of Social Affairs is empowered to issue a temporary injunction against a work stoppage if it is liable to threaten the breakdown of essential public services.

A law of 1949 sets up Factory Committees composed of representatives of management, labor, supervisory personnel and engineers, which have considerable more power and scope in advising on the running of an industry than in the other countries we have considered. A committee is empowered to receive all the information it considers necessary from the management (as it is not in Sweden) and the employer has to bear the committee's costs.

Postwar legislation also provides for paid vacations for all employees. Manual workers employed by the same firm for less than five years receive a paid vacation of two weeks; after five years they get a three weeks' vacation. Employees of shops and offices fare a little better. After ten years of service they are entitled to a month's holiday with pay.

Average wages of industrial workers in Finland are 75 cents an hour, which roughly buys about twice as much as in America. But the workers regard their social welfare benefits as additional wages and so, it must be added, do the employers, who in Finland have to bear a much larger share of their cost than in any other country in the North.

How the Finns Live

For the most part, the Finns live from their forests. In order to import fertilizers and tractors for the farms, and metal and fuels for in-

dustry and transport, and thus maintain a high living standard, the
Finns must sell a good part of their forest products abroad. In the
normal years since the last war, wood products have constituted 90
per cent of Finland's exports. A good world price and a steady demand for them make Finland prosperous. Falling prices and demand
provoke, as we have seen, economic calamity.

Some 71 per cent of Finland's land is covered by forests, the highest
percentage of any country in the world. Though the Peace Treaty
deprived her of 13 per cent of her wooded area, Finland still has 53 million acres of forest, being surpassed in Europe only by Russia and Sweden. On this vast tract stands 48 billion cubic feet of timber, with an
annual growth of one and a half billion cubic feet, of which about a
billion and a quarter is cut annually. Pine predominates, providing
nearly a half of the total timber stand, with spruce furnishing about a
third, and birch one fifth.

This is Finland's chief natural resource, her main source of wealth.

Well over half of the forests (58 per cent) are owned by individual
farmers who derive a substantial part of their income (as well as ful-
filling their requirements for fuel and building material) from felling
and selling their own timber. Lumbering and logging also give winter employment to a large number of small farmers and agricultural
workers. The state owns somewhat over a third of the forests, and
wood-processing industries about 7 per cent.

The annual cuttings of timber furnish about one tenth of the national income, but this is only the beginning of this source of wealth.
The sale of pulpwood, pit props, poles and of sawn timber brings in a
sizable income. But most important of all is the output of the wood-
processing industries — pulp, cellulose, plywood, wallboard, cardboard,
prefabricated houses and newsprint — which furnish one third of the
country's total industrial production and provide employment for
one fourth of the workers.

The metal industry is second in importance. Largely through Russian
insistence on reparation payments in machines and ships, this industry
has more than doubled in capacity since before the war and employs
twice as many workers. It turns out ships, locomotives, railway cars,
motors, complete woodworking plants, power plants, electronic gear
and hundreds of different kinds of machines. Altogether the metal industry accounts for a little more than a quarter of Finland's total industrial production.

Finland, like most other countries with an expanding industry, is power-hungry. Having no coal or oil of its own, it has turned, like Norway and Sweden, to water power. The Soviet Union acquired one third of Finland's hydroelectric plants in the territory she seized under the treaty of peace. But the Finns set to work with characteristic energy to build new ones and Finland now derives some 5 billion KWH per annum from her water power stations, or 80 per cent more than before the war. At that, only one third of her potential water power has as yet been harnessed.

Many factories and some of the steam locomotives burn wood as fuel, and an immense portion of the total cuttings from the forests (38 per cent) is consumed for heating homes and buildings during long cold winters. Still, Finland imports two million tons of coal annually, three quarters of it from Poland in a three-cornered trade deal with Russia which saves the Finns from expending foreign exchange. Oil imports come to nearly three quarters of a million tons a year, of which Great Britain, Russia and France supply two thirds.

Although the state is the largest single business entrepreneur, the economic life of Finland is dominated by private enterprise, which enjoys more advantages and fewer government restrictions than in the other northern countries. This is perhaps partly due to the fact that "bourgeois" political parties have always had a majority in Parliament.

Nevertheless, the state's share in the ownership and operation of business enterprises today is surprisingly large — considering that it was largely acquired by nonsocialist governments. As we have seen, there is one overwhelming reason for this: lack of domestic private investment capital. In many fields only the state has been able to do the financing or — as is often the case — has been willing to risk capital.

An example of this is in mining. In the 1920's, the government purchased the Outokumpu copper mine when the private company operating it was unable to obtain the capital for further, and not very promising, operations. Today it is the biggest mining enterprise in the country, and makes Finland Europe's largest producer of copper. Likewise the state was the only one interested in exploiting the country's iron ore deposits. Private capital simply would not risk going into it.

As owner of so much of the country's forests, the state is heavily engaged in the wood business. In this field too the government stepped in where private capital was timid and bought up several wood-processing concerns to handle the products of its own forests. As in the other northern (and most European) lands, the railroads are owned and operated by the state, as are the telegraph and telephone service, although the major part of the network of local telephone lines still remain in private hands.

The Finnish government supplies four fifths of the marketable electricity supply from state-owned power plants. It owns and operates the dominant companies in metallurgy and shipbuilding. It runs the artificial fertilizer business and the biggest restaurant chain in Finland. It is responsible for one fifth of the building construction.

Altogether, state-owned enterprises turn out 15 per cent of the net national product. Almost without exception they are run as joint-stock companies and operate under the same laws and regulations as private undertakings. This principle of organization, the Finns say, keeps the interference of the government and Parliament of the day to a minimum, restricting it largely to deciding who shall receive the chief posts in the companies' administrations.

A Note on the Co-ops in Finland

Of all the northern peoples, the Finns have gone furthest in the development of co-operatives. Total membership in all co-ops — consumer, agricultural, productive and financial — is one million and a half in a country of four millions. In the principal field of consumer co-operatives there are a million members — a quarter of the population. Nearly every family in the country belongs to at least one co-op. Thus co-operative membership in Finland is about twice that in Sweden, Norway and Denmark.

The Finnish co-operatives' share in total retail trade is also double that in the other lands of the North, amounting to roughly one third. Moreover, the co-operative credit societies in Finland constitute one of the financial bulwarks of the nation. Deposits in them amount to nearly one fifth of all bank deposits and their loans account for one quarter of all money lent in Finland. The resettlement of the Karelian refugees and the war veterans after 1944 as well as the reconstruction of the devastated North was financed by the state largely through the co-operative credit organizations. The Central Bank for Co-operative Credit Societies, known in Finland as OKO, is one of the country's largest financial institutions.

As in the other countries we have considered, the Finnish co-ops go in for all kinds of business activity. Their own factories produce much of what they sell in the retail outlets, including processed foods, flour, hardware, cosmetics, furniture, matches, men's, women's and children's clothing and shoes, and bedding. They also go in for building construction and sell life, fire and accident insurance.

One peculiar development of the consumers' co-op movement in Finland deserves mention. Founded in Czarist times soon after the turn of the century, it split in 1916 into two groups which had become bitterly divided on ideological grounds. The division was primarily between workers and farmers.

The former were convinced that the principal aim of the co-operative movement should be the gradual transformation of the capitalist system into a co-operative society somewhat along the lines of Social Democracy, though they accepted the basic co-op tenet of neutrality in politics. The farmers had no interest in such ideological aims. They insisted that the co-ops restrict themselves to purely practical matters, namely, the securing of economic benefits for members.

The labor-dominated co-ops therefore withdrew from the General Union of Co-operative Societies (YOL) and from its great wholesale establishment, SOK, and formed their own union of societies known as KK, and their own wholesale organization, which is known by its initials OTK.

Today the two groups, labeled as the "neutral" movement and the "progressive" movement, have about the same number of members — a half a million each — and do about the same amount of business. The split brought both advantages and disadvantages. The healthy spirit of rivalry and competition between the two organizations keeps both of them on their toes and stimulates efficiency, the production of better goods and services, and the drive for membership. On the other hand, they are weakened by the splitting of their capital resources and of their mass purchasing and productive power. Both SOK and OTK belong to that unique organization, the Scandinavian Co-operative Wholesale Society, which acts as a joint purchasing body of imported goods for all the northern co-operatives.

In Finland, as elsewhere in the North, the co-operative movement is not only an important factor in the economy but a way of life for a large part of the population. Some foreign visitors to Finland have felt that one of the greatest achievements of the co-ops has been in education. J. Hampden Jackson perhaps put it best when he wrote:

> To the co-operative movement the Finnish housewife owes her education in domestic science, the farmer in modern methods of crop and stock raising and in book-keeping, the wage earner in what Quakers used to call the re-creative use of leisure, and the public as a whole in democratic principles and the elements of economics. What the Finnish people would have become without co-operation can never be known; perhaps there would have been no alternative between remaining a poverty-stricken, backward and exploited peasantry or becoming a regimented and collectivized community on the Russian model.[40]

Agriculture in Finland

The land itself and the climate are not very promising for farming. Geologists say that Finland has probably the oldest and hardest crust of earth in Europe. Granite, gneiss and crystalline slate are barely covered by the infertile gravels and clays on which Finnish farmers try to grow their crops.

Added to this is the cold, harsh and often fickle climate. Finland lies entirely between 60 and 70 degrees north latitude (as compared to the British Isles which lie between 50 and 60 degrees) and receives only a part of the warming effects of the Gulf Stream, which aid growth in Norway and Sweden. At that, Sweden raises 80 per cent of her crops in regions farther south than the southernmost part of Finland. There are definite latitudinal limits, north of which the main crops cannot be grown. Autumn wheat and sugar beets can only be sown in the southern fifth of the country, spring wheat and oats in the southern half, though rye, barley and potatoes thrive up to and beyond the Arctic Circle.

The summers are short (though the northern days are long), and early frosts and subnormal temperatures often are disastrous for the

[40] *Finland*, by J. Hampden Jackson.

harvests. In 1950, for example, one quarter of the spring wheat and one tenth of the barley crop was ruined by unseasonable weather.

No wonder the Finnish farmer, though courteous and kindly, strikes you as a dour and hardened fellow. Farming is a stern and discouraging pursuit. Since the war it has often turned out to be, even when harvests were normal, a losing business, as well. For 1950, for instance, the Ministry of Agriculture calculated that if self-and-family labor (which is 85 per cent of all labor on Finnish farms) were priced at the wages paid to hired labor, the average loss per acre on crop and livestock raising was five dollars.

The following year the Economic Planning Council found that prices obtained by farmers in southern Finland for all their products covered an average of only 75 per cent of the costs — and it is in the South where the farming is best.

How, then, do Finnish farmers keep from going bankrupt? In two ways. They receive a supplementary income from their forest land and from hiring out as laborers in cutting timber and logging. Many of the smaller farmers work in nearby factories (industry in Finland is dispersed in many rural areas). Secondly, they receive government aid in the form of annual subsidies totaling $20,000,000 to assist them in the purchase of fertilizers and farm machinery and in soil improvement. They are also granted tax reductions, reduced prices on many essential goods and cuts in interest rates on their loans. But the farmers, not unnaturally, demand prices for their commodities adequate to meet their costs of production. This the government has continually promised them, but being caught in a squeeze between its desire to lower the cost of living so that industries can export at a profit and the plight of the farmer, it has hesitated to raise farm prices.

The unprofitability of farming has brought about a radical change in the manner of gaining a livelihood in Finland. As recently as 1936, some 60 per cent of the people lived from agriculture. At the beginning of the last war, in 1940, more than half (52 per cent) still made its living on the land. But the 1950 census showed that the number living exclusively from farming had dropped to a bare third (32 per cent). And they produced but one fifth of the net national product. The trend in Finland, as in most other countries of the West, was to the towns and cities. In 1880, only 10 per cent of the population was engaged in industry, construction, transport and commerce. Today nearly half (45 per cent) are.

By American standards, farms are tiny in Finland. Nearly two fifths of them are under 12 acres of cultivable land, and a third vary from 12 to 25 acres. In other words, nearly 72 per cent of Finnish farms are not large enough adequately to support a family from the cultivable soil on them alone. Some 24 per cent with cultivated tracts of from 25 to 62 acres and some 4 per cent varying from 62 to 125 acres are. The number of farms above 125 acres is less than 1 per cent.

Since the climate makes the growing of grain for human consumption difficult and hazardous, the Finnish farmers concentrate on hay and on green and root fodder crops to feed cattle. Dairying and cattle breeding is their chief occupation and the foundation of Finnish agriculture. In milk, butter, cheese and meat, the country is now self-supporting, but from one quarter to one third of its bread grains must be imported, the principal source being Russia.

Incidentally, Finnish farmers tell you of how AIV has revolutionized cattle feeding and greatly increased their milk supply. AIV is the discovery of Professor A. I. Virtanen, who received a Nobel Prize for it. It consists simply of treating green fodder stored in underground silos with a chemical which preserves the proteins and vitamins.

The farmers, as we have seen, are the backbone of one of the two principal consumer co-operative movements in Finland. But without their producer and credit co-ops, they doubt whether they could survive.

The dairy co-ops are the most important. In Czarist times, most of the dairies in Finland were operated by the owners of large estates, who unmercifully mulcted the farmers. Later joint-stock dairies were founded but tended to make profits for everyone but the farmer. The first co-operative dairies were formed in 1903 under the auspices of *Pellervo*, which is the parent body of the original co-op movement in Finland and of the "neutral" organization today. At the present time there are 400 co-operative dairies in Finland, and they handle 70 per cent of all milk produced.

There are also, as in the other northern countries, well developed farm co-operatives for the slaughter of livestock and the processing of meat; for the marketing of cheese and eggs and butter; for the improvement of cattle breeding, for the purchase of seed and fertilizer and farm machinery, and for the establishment of farm-machinery pools. All farmers get their financing from the co-op credit societies and their insurance from similar organizations. Membership of self-supporting farmers in one or more agricultural co-ops is virtually 100 per cent.

Finland also shared with the other northern countries in the great emigration to America. The Finns started arriving in the United States and Canada shortly after the Civil War. Between 1893 and 1900, some 50,000 Finns came to the New World. The next decade saw Finnish emigration to America reach its peak with a total of 158,832. Altogether some 350,000 Finns emigrated to our shores before the movement came to a stop at the beginning of the 1930's — a number equal to one tenth of the country's population in 1932. Many took to lumbering and farming, which had occupied them at home, settling in northern Michigan and Wisconsin and the Northwest, though there was a sizable group which stopped in Massachusetts. While a good part of the Finnish immigrants sought economic opportunities that were denied them in a stagnant agriculture and in towns which were slow to industrialize, it must be remembered that there were many who sought in the new world political freedom from the oppression under the Czars. Finnish sociologists often point out the serious loss to Finland of the emigration of so many of her finest sons across the Atlantic. In this case Finland's loss was America's gain.

Social Welfare in Finland

Though Finland is generally reputed to be much less of a social welfare state than the other three lands of the North, it spends 10 per cent of its national income and 30 per cent of the national government's budget on what is called "social expenditure."

The biggest item in the country's social security bill comes under the heading of Child and Family Allowances. The main objectives of this scheme, the Finns frankly admit, are two: to increase the birth rate and augment nominal wages and salaries. That these allowances, as well as many other benefits such as marriage loans, housing subsidies and maternity care have helped increase the birth rate, there is no doubt. Between 1938 and 1948 the birth rate rose from 19.6 per thousand to 26.9, and the population of the country from 3,672,000 to 3,940,000. In 1954 the population had risen to 4,164,000 and Finnish sociologists were talking of an eventual population of fourteen millions, which they say the country could easily support.

Under the Child Allowance Act of 1948, the state pays a family, regardless of its financial status, $62 a year for each child under 16. Payments were made in the 1950's on a million and a quarter children and thus came to more than $75,000,000 a year. Temporarily — so the government says — the employers must bear half the cost, which is collected by assessing them 4 per cent of their annual wage bill. The state, aided somewhat by the municipalities, defrays the other half out of taxation. The beneficiaries pay nothing directly.

The family allowance, whose purpose also is to stimulate the bearing of more children and help defray the added expense, is paid to parents having four or more children. It amounts to $17 a year per child, beginning with the fourth, and payment is made in kind, usually in household goods, the idea being to improve the living standards of large families.

Child and family allowances account for one third of all social expenditures.

Despite the lack of a national health insurance scheme, the expenditure on health services in Finland comes next in importance, accounting for one fifth of the total cost of social welfare.

There are some 300 voluntary sickness insurance societies, mostly organized in industrial plants, but their total membership is only 200,000, and though under state supervision, they receive no government financial aid. However, in Finland, as in the other countries we have been considering, almost all the hospitals are public, maintained by the state or municipalities, and they provide medical care at a small fraction of the actual cost. Thus to stay in a Finnish hospital comes to only fifty cents to one dollar a day, including surgery. In addition, the state makes the municipalities and rural communes responsible not only for public health but for general medical care. Thus in the rural areas, which predominate in Finland, the general medical care outside of hospitals is maintained by "municipal doctors" employed by the local authorities and partly paid by the state. Their charges to individuals are nominal.

So far as I could ascertain, the Finns, at least in the country districts, where most of them live, achieve almost all the benefits of a national health insurance plan and escape some of its bureaucratic disadvantages. They get, as they say, "high class, low cost medical care." Actually 60 per cent of the country's doctors are either employed in the public hospitals or in the public health service. This leaves 40 per cent in private practice, as against 50 per cent in Norway, where there is compulsory health insurance. There is, incidentally, a shortage of doctors in Finland, which has only 47 of them per 100,000 of the population, compared to 102 in Denmark and 135 in the U.S.A.

The third most important social security benefit in Finland is that providing state pensions for the aged and the disabled. Since old age and disability insurance premiums only began to be paid after the war, the funds at hand are not yet large enough to enable payment of the full pension and have to be made up by "supplementary" pensions, the cost of which is defrayed from public taxation. When the Finnish scheme eventually comes into full operation it will differ from those in the other northern lands in that it will be based on ordinary commercial insurance principles: that is, a Finn, at the age of sixty-five, will receive roughly only what he and his employer have paid into it, plus the interest accruing. Theoretically, it will not cost the state a cent, though there are many in Helsinki who doubt whether it can succeed in providing adequate old age support without government grants. As it is, the pension is small, amounting to about one fifth of a person's income while he was self-supporting. Thus a person earning $1000 a year will receive an old-age pension of $200 — and this is the maximum. Payment of premiums is compulsory for all persons over eighteen, and every individual must contribute 2 per cent annually from his income. If he is employed, the employer must pay half.

Unemployment insurance in Finland is carried out by private societies, usually trade-unions, and is voluntary. Benefits amount to a maximum of $1.50 a day for not more than 120 days in any twelve successive months. The state reimburses the societies, of which there are only a dozen, for from one half to two thirds of the benefits paid out. Since there is little unemployment, only 15,000 persons take out the insurance.

In the other northern lands, Poor Aid has dwindled to almost nothing because of the all-embracing nature of modern social security. In Finland, however, aid to the poor is still a considerable factor.

Some 132,000 persons are "on relief," and the total cost comes to $31,000,000 annually.

The shortage of housing after the war presented Finland, as it did most countries which had been engaged in the world conflict, with a serious social-economic problem which has by no means been solved. In 1952, eight years after the end of the war for Finland, the Ministry of Social Affairs estimated the urban housing shortage alone at 75,000 dwelling units, and because of the growth of population the demand was increasing by more than 10,000 units a year. Though expenditures for public and private building run to more than half a billion dollars annually, about all the Finns have been able to do since 1950 has been to keep up with the mounting population by building 10,000 units a year. The housing shortage therefore remains.

To cope with it the government set up in 1949 a Housing Committee known as ARAVA with a four-year appropriation of nearly a hundred million dollars (22 billion marks) to help finance new building. ARAVA loans are granted as second mortgage credits up to 65 per cent of construction costs and at an interest rate of only 1 per cent. Amortization is over a period of from 27 years (for wooden houses) to 45 years (for those of stone and brick). The ARAVA program has been beset with difficulties, chiefly caused by the old bugbear of inflation and the consequent steadily rising costs of materials and labor. Houses built in 1950, for example, cost 25 per cent more than those built the year before. Each year ARAVA's appropriations buy less housing. In Finland, according to the latest census (1950) there are an average of one and a half persons per room in all household dwellings, which means that overcrowding is still a serious problem.

There are numerous other fields of social welfare in Finland — such as maternity aid and benefits; so-called Home Aid, in which Home Sisters (nurses), trained and paid at government expense, take over the running of a household when the mother is incapacitated; Home-Founding Loans, by which the government helps young married couples set up housekeeping; Accident Insurance, which is compulsory for all employees and whose premiums are paid — as are so many in Finland — by the employer; and numerous organizations to look after the blind and the lame and the vagrants and the juvenile delinquents. As in the other northern lands, there are statutory Child Welfare

Boards in each community with amazing powers to handle problems of neglectful parents and wayward children — they have the right to commit "difficult" children to reformatories, of which there are 24 in Finland, without bringing any specific legal charges.

The Finns, I found, have little patience with vagrants, whom an Act of 1936 defines as "persons capable of working who habitually shirk work." They are warned to heed their ways and find employment, failing which they are hustled off to workhouses, of which there are eight, or even to hard labor in the prisons. Women vagrants outnumber men two to one.

In Finland too there are a multitude of private voluntary Social Welfare organizations, of which the General Mannerheim Child Welfare League and the Save the Children Society are among the most prominent.

We have seen that social expenditure in Finland comes to one tenth of the national income. Who pays for it all?

The state pays the most — for some 43 per cent, which means that individuals and business firms account for nearly half out of the taxes they pay. But employers shoulder a great deal more. Their direct contribution, which before the war came to less than one fifth, is now one third, or 32 per cent, and this does not include their voluntary social welfare expenditures, which are considerable. The communities chip in 18 per cent of the cost of social services — a sum which of course comes out of local taxation. Individuals pay only 7 per cent — in premiums for various social insurance schemes.

By American standards, taxes in Finland are pretty steep. Income tax ranges from 8 per cent on an annual income of $260 to 55 per cent on one of $30,000. An unskilled worker in Helsinki making $130 a month pays income tax (national and local) of 20 per cent if single and 12 per cent if he is married and has two children. A person making double that amount pays 25 per cent and 18 per cent, respectively.

The income tax was reduced in 1952 by some 30 per cent, but this relief was largely offset by the rise in the sales, or turnover, tax from 15 to 20 per cent. Finland must have the highest national sales tax in the world. It brings in more government revenue than the income tax — $220,000,000 against $176,000,000 in 1952, to take a typical year — and is a great burden to the modest income groups, which make up 99 per cent of the population.

There is also a tax on property and fortune of from one tenth of one per cent on $2,000 to 20 per cent on $170,000. To finance the resettlement of the war refugees, the government imposed a special capital levy in 1944, payable over five years, of from one half of one per cent to 4 per cent. Large companies paid 20 per cent in shares outright.

A Note on Temperance

An official booklet on Social Welfare published by the Finnish Ministry of Social Affairs in 1953 declared that "in the development of the liquor situation in Finland five distinct phases can be noted, namely: (1) a home-brewed ale phase lasting to approximately 1700; (2) a home-distilling phase, 1700-1865; (3) a factory distillation phase, 1866-1919; (4) a Prohibition phase, 1919-1932; and (5) since 1932 a state monopoly phase."

That pretty well sums it up.

Since repeal of Prohibition in 1932, and the passage of the Alcohol Beverages Act of that year, the liquor business has been in the hands of a state monopoly known as ALKO. It has sole rights to manufacture, import, export, sell and control the serving of drinks in Finland. As in Sweden until recently, purchasers of spirits, wine and beer must have a passbook (with photograph) which is honored at one state liquor store only. Unlike Sweden, Finland has no quota system. One can buy as much as one likes, or can afford, though special "buyer controllers" are liable to question you if you buy too much. If you are observed drinking excessively or are arrested for drunkenness, your passbook is taken away. There are no restrictions on serving drinks in restaurants, if they are licensed by ALKO and are located in large towns or cities.

For some reason alcoholic drinks may not be sold in the country districts. This is also true of the other northern lands and the reasons therefor remained a mystery to me during my journey. For the country people are far from being teetotalers. I checked on this in Finland and found that the imbibing of alcoholic drinks in rural parts was nearly as great as in the large towns and cities.

Taking cognizance of this indisputable fact, a committee set up by the Finnish Parliament in 1948 recently suggested, after an exhaustive survey, that alcoholic drinks should be made more easily obtainable in the countryside.

Most of the big temperance societies continue to plump for total Prohibition, despite its fiasco after the First World War. There are many large temperance organizations in Finland, such as the Friends of Temperance, with 677 local societies and 35,000 members; the Finnish Social Democratic Temperance League with 774 local societies and 47,000 members; and the Center for Temperance Work among the People, with 455 local societies and 67,000 members.

Actually alcoholic consumption in Finland continues to be among the lowest in the world. It is still a little under two liters per year per head. Since the war, the drinking of hard liquor has been falling off and the consumption of beer rising. Arrests for drunkenness are considerably fewer than before the war, as are cases of homicide and assault due to intoxication.

In the meantime ALKO continues to be one of the most lucrative enterprises owned and operated by the state. It does an annual business of some $100,000,000. Its tidy profits, after a 7 per cent annual dividend is paid on its 60,000 shares, all but two of which are owned by the government, go to municipal and national social-welfare funds. No individual or commercial firm, the Finns like to point out, makes any money from selling liquor.

A Passion for Culture

Of what other country could it be said in our day that an artist, a composer of music, is regarded by the entire nation as its most eminent citizen?

Such is the universally acknowledged position in Finland of Jean Julius Christian Sibelius, whose seven symphonies and numerous other works including cantatas, concertos, tone poems, piano suites, chamber music, incidental music for the theater and even a piece for a brass band have earned for him a world reputation as the greatest composer of the twentieth century.

Few artists have been so honored in their lifetime, and perhaps no other achieved such immortality among his fellow countrymen while he still had many years to live. When Sibelius celebrated his eighty-eighth birthday on December 8, 1953, his fellow Finns literally spread his name across the land. Fifty towns picked that day to name streets or parks after him and that evening his works were performed at gala concerts throughout Finland.

It was a typical gesture of this hardy northern people, for whom the arts — all the arts — are a national passion, enjoyed not by the few who are well off or by a handful of "longhairs" or "eggheads," but by the mass of the people, peasants, workers and middle class, including businessmen.

This is a land where the heroes, with the exception of Marshal Mannerheim, are not soldiers but poets, musicians, novelists, painters, sculptors, architects and scholars.

For half a century the genius of Sibelius has been the bright star in Finland's cultural life, but if it has been the brightest it has not been the only one, by any means. The novelist Frans Emil Sillanpää, winner of the Nobel Prize in 1939; the architects Eliel Saarinen, who lived much of his life in America where he exercised a profound influence on the development of the skyscraper, Alvar Aalto, one-time professor of experimental architecture at the Massachusetts Institute of Technology and hailed by many as the Frank Lloyd Wright and Le Corbusier of Finland, and Erik Bryggman, the peer in many ways of Aalto; the sculptor Väinö Aaltonen, who has earned a world-wide reputation — all these and many others, scarcely less gifted, have contributed to a cultural flowering that is unique for so small a country in our century.

In the applied arts, too, especially in glass and ceramics, the Finns have proved immensely creative. "Arabia" is said to be the largest ceramics factory in Europe, turning out a quarter of a million pieces a day; but what is much more important to the Finns, "Arabia," like some other organizations and institutions in the country, has made a notable contribution to the problem of enabling artists to live from their work in a commercially dominated society. It employs fourteen noted artists, pays them a regular salary, provides each with a large studio, and gives them complete freedom to create what they will.

Finnish glass, though not so well known as Swedish, rivals it and perhaps in artistic quality exceeds it. Certainly — or so at least it seemed to my inexpert eye — Gunnel Nyman was the greatest artist in glass of recent times, an opinion I often heard echoed in the North.

Her brilliant career was cut short at the height of her creativeness by death in 1948 at the age of thirty-nine, but there are others who are carrying on in her tradition at the principal glass works at Karhula, Nuutajärvi and Riihimäki, whose products, simple but graceful and beautiful and imaginative in design, are much in demand by connoisseurs the world over.

The problem of the artist and writer making a living from his work in a highly populated country such as the United States is great enough, but in a land of four millions such as Finland it is infinitely greater. Yet the Finns, like their Scandinavian neighbors, have striven to solve it. When Sibelius was only thirty-two, the Finnish government of what was then a mere Grand Duchy under the Czars awarded him a lifetime pension so that he could give up his teaching and devote himself exclusively to composition. Since then the government has enabled many an artist, writer and scientist to concentrate on his chosen work by subsidizing him.

The Finnish Academy, founded in 1947 to promote creative work in the arts and sciences, pays its twelve distinguished members not only a regular salary but also an annual subsidy, all of which comes out of the coffers of the state. No duties or obligations are imposed on the members other than the continuance of their creative work and the offering of guidance to young scientists and artists of special promise. The state-supported theaters, of which Finland, despite its small population, has more than any other country in the world — not proportionally but actually — enable actors and directors and stage designers and technicians to earn annual salaries which spare them from the hazards so common and so heartbreaking in many other lands. The Finnish Artists' Association, aided by state grants and private endowments, administers several traveling scholarships and stipends for young artists.

But it is the culturally minded public which gives art in Finland its main sustenance. An astonishingly large number of people buy paintings, sculpture, books and the products of handicraft. Business firms, churches and various organizations are among the best customers of the artists. Aaltonen, whose reputation is enormous throughout the land, often receives a commission for a sculpture from some remote village whose farmers and tradespeople have banded together to raise the money to meet his considerable fee. Recently he was called upon to design the stage settings for Tennessee Williams's *The Rose Tattoo* at the Finnish National Theater in Helsinki.

Of all the arts, that of the theater is probably the most popular in Finland. Considering how phlegmatic the Finns appear to be, their passion for the stage and their devotion to it is surprising to a foreign visitor. Underneath their dour exterior, the Finns evidently have a temperament that is both emotional and dramatic. Unable or unwilling to express it in their daily living, they let it burst out in the theater. They not only flock to see professionally played dramas but in large numbers they contrive to do a little acting behind the footlights themselves in some three thousand amateur companies which give regular repertory performances throughout the year. In fact, the amateur dramatics movement in Finland has no equal anywhere in the world.

There are some 85 professional theaters in the country, 31 of them subsidized by the state and 7 by various municipalities. The remaining ones have a professional basis, in that the principal actors and the director are professionals, with the supporting cast made up of ambitious amateurs. The government lists its subventioned theaters as "educational institutions," though there is nothing academic about them and, like theaters the world over, their principal task is to entertain.

There is no commercial theater in Finland, as that term is understood on Broadway or in London's West End. That is, there is no profit for the management or for individual backers. A case of a play being taken off because it fails to make money is unknown in Finland. This system creates almost a paradise for producers, who freed from financial worries are able to give their customers the very best in classical and modern dramatic works.

A little over half the plays presented on the Finnish stage in an average year are translations from foreign works. French and English dramas predominate among these, though Scandinavian, nineteenth-century Russian (Chekhov above all) and American works are well represented.

Over one hundred American plays have been staged professionally in Finland in the last three decades. Those of Eugene O'Neill have been the most popular, no fewer than fourteen of them having been played. Almost any repertory includes during the year *Mourning*

Becomes Electra (a great favorite in Finland), *Anna Christie, Ah, Wilderness* and *Desire under the Elms*. Elmer Rice's *Street Scene* and Maxwell Anderson's *Winterset, Joan of Lorraine* and *Anne of the Thousand Days* have been hits both in Helsinki and the provincial towns. Of the younger American playwrights, Arthur Miller and Tennessee Williams have been the most popular. Williams's *Streetcar Named Desire* and *The Glass Menagerie* enjoyed long runs and his later play *The Rose Tattoo* was given a stellar production by Finland's first playhouse, the National Theater in Helsinki, with the country's leading actress, Ella Eronen (who had played Blanche in *Streetcar*) assuming the leading role, and Edvin Laine, one of Finland's top directors, directing. Some who saw the play first in New York and then in Helsinki thought the latter production excelled the former in many ways. Arthur Miller's *Death of a Salesman*, I was told in Helsinki, has been the most successful new foreign play performed in Finland since the war.

The state encourages not only the excellent professional theater but the 3000 amateur groups, of which 73 workers' companies are said to be among the best, as well. It finances a self-run organization which acts as a clearinghouse for the provincial dramatic societies, providing them with the scripts of both classical and new plays and suggestions as how best to stage them. In addition it employs two full-time professional producers who journey about the country holding special courses for amateur producers and advising local groups on acting, lighting and the making of scenery. The trade-unions and employers finance a similar organization to help the workers' dramatic groups.

Finland is the only country I have ever seen where the live theater more than holds its own in competition with the movies and radio. (As yet, there is no television in Finland, and because the population is largely rural and scattered over wide distances, its introduction creates a special and difficult problem.) Radio broadcasting is, as in the other northern lands, a state monopoly with the government holding 90 per cent of the stock in the company and owners of receiving sets, of which there is an average of one to every family, paying an annual license fee, which is the sole source of revenue for the national network. Over half (60 per cent) of the programs are devoted to music.

Movies are of course popular among the people, but there are fewer film houses than in Denmark, which has approximately the same population. The total number is 500, with an aggregate seating capacity of 150,000. Hollywood provides well over half the films shown — some 275 out of 400 in a typical postwar year.

Sports also play an important part in Finnish life. Ever since 1912, when Finland, though not yet an independent country and numbering only three million inhabitants, emerged second only to the United States in track and field, and first in wrestling, at the Olympic Games in Stockholm, athletics has been one of the little nation's chief pastimes. Such Olympic champions and world record setters as Paavo Nurmi in the distance runs, Matti Järvinen and Yrjö Nikkanen in the javelin and Clas Thunberg in speed-skating became national heroes and statues of them were erected by popular subscription.

Because of the bitterness left by the Civil War, the organization of sports in Finland has been split in two, the workers forming their own national body, the Workers' Sports Union, and the "bourgeois" continuing with their original organization, the Finnish Athletic and Gymnastic Federation. The former has 1000 sports clubs with 215,000 members and the latter 1500 clubs with 350,000 members. There is also a smaller Swedish-speaking national Sports Union with 160 clubs and 50,000 members. In the 1950's a strong movement set in to amalgamate the three bodies and rid Finnish sports of its class and linguistic basis.

Because of the climate, winter sports are the most popular of all in Finland. Skiing, without which Finland could probably never have been settled, is a national habit, as it is in Norway and Sweden. The most popular winter game is *bandy*, a combination of hockey and soccer played on an ice rink. There are over 500 clubs, with 90,000 members, devoted to *bandy*.

The Finns, I was surprised to learn, also have their own version of baseball which they call *pesäpallo*. It now competes with track and field and soccer-football as the most popular of summer sports. The "diamond" is smaller and more elongated than in baseball, the bases are differently placed and the pitcher, called the "server," stands at the plate opposite the batter and merely tosses the ball in the air for him to strike at, eliminating the necessity of a catcher. However, there are nine men to a team. Like cricket, the game has a time limit — one hour and fifteen minutes, and at least nine innings.

All sports in Finland except boxing are amateur and are largely financed by government-sponsored betting pools on the soccer-football games. The memorable Olympic Games in Helsinki in 1952, the very staging of which was a considerable feat for so small a country and city, was a high mark in Finland's postwar life, serving not only to stimulate interest in sports but contributing mightily to erasing the bitter memories of the recent lost wars and the difficulties of postwar life.

Somehow, the hard-working, theater-loving, sports-minded Finns find time to read too — books as well as newspapers and magazines. Helsinki has the largest bookstore in Europe — and probably in the world — in the Akateeminen Kirjakauppa, situated in the Stockman Department Store, itself one of the greatest of such establishments anywhere. I spent more than one pleasant morning browsing through A.K.'s twelve miles of bookshelves, on which could be found all the books, classic as well as last week's, published in any of the major languages of the world. Compared to many large nations, with their well-known paucity of bookshops, every large village in Finland, including many in the sparsely settled, harsh country above the Arctic Circle, has a well-patronized bookstore.

The public libraries, even in the remotest towns, are excellent, numbering 3000 and lending an average of six and a half million volumes a year — or nearly three books for every adult in Finland.

Finnish publishers issue an average of 2000 titles a year, of which one sixth are translations from foreign languages. Since only four million persons on this earth, including children, know Finnish, the sale of books is remarkable. Waltari's *The Egyptian* sold 100,000 copies in the original edition in Finland, which is equivalent to a sale of 4,000,000 in the United States.

The Finns are avid newspaper readers too. Their 62 dailies and 52 biweeklies have a combined circulation of a million and three quarters — larger proportionally than that in the United States. *Helsingin Sanomat*, owned and edited by Eljas Erkko, president of the Finnish-American society, a stanch friend of the United States and a former foreign minister, is the best daily paper in the country. It has the largest circulation (200,000) and the most news and advertising. People in the capital refer to it as "the *Times* of Helsinki." The magazines in Finland are not very attractively gotten up, by

American standards, but *Kotiliesi*, designed for housewives, has a circulation of a quarter of a million. Based on sales per capita, an American publication of that nature would have to have a circulation of nine million copies to equal it. There are some 750 periodicals published in Finland.

It is typical of the emphasis on education in Finland that the budget of the Ministry of Education is double that of the Ministry of Defense, though of course the postwar treaty limitations on the size and armament of the Finnish army keep military expenditures down.

Illiteracy has long been nonexistent in Finland. Already in the seventeenth century there was a church law which made it obligatory for everyone to learn to read and write. Those who didn't were denied civil rights; they could not even marry. As a result literacy became universal. This seems to have displeased some of the Czars, who, after Russia took over Finland at the beginning of the nineteenth century, looked with suspicion on the high standard of popular education which the Finns maintained. Indeed, when the Finnish Diet passed a compulsory School Attendance Act, the Emperor refused to sign it, and it became law only when Finland achieved its national independence.

It obliges all children to complete the eight years of the grade school, or folk school, as it is called in Finland. Actually a pupil finishes primary school in seven years and then must attend "continuation classes" for an additional year in which so-called "practical" instruction is offered. This is designed to prepare those who do not intend to go on to high school for taking a useful place in society. The girls are given courses in home economics, child nursing and sewing. The boys study agriculture, forestry, woodwork and mechanics. Courses in sociology and literature are continued.

Under the Finnish system, pupils who go to work after completing their primary education still retain close relations with their school, which offers them further educational and cultural opportunities. It places its library and reading room at their disposal and enrolls them in reading clubs, choral societies, physical training and sports clubs. Teachers receive extra pay for helping out in youth services. Free medical and dental service is provided for all school children, and

Finland was the first country in the world to pass a law — in 1943 — providing for one free substantial meal daily for all pupils.

The primary public schools are run by the communities, but two thirds of their expenses are defrayed by the state. Finnish educators think this is a desirable balance in that it provides the financial basis for first-rate schools and teachers and yet gives the municipalities a good deal of responsibility.

The position of the public school teacher in Finland is rather enviable. Salaries are relatively high and if a teacher is the father of a family, he receives extra pay. Overtime is paid for teaching periods above the normal and for extra-curricular school activities. Twenty years of service entitle a teacher to a full pension amounting to 60 per cent of his total salary. Tenure is well established. According to law, a teacher belongs to the category of so-called irremovable officials. He (or she) can only be fired on the grounds of legally substantiated crime. If a teacher's post is abolished, he must be given another without delay, and if none is immediately available he receives full salary until one is found. Though in his instruction a teacher must be impartial, he cannot be discriminated against because of his political views.

This unusually strong legal position of the teacher in Finland derives partly from the days of Czarist rule when the Finns were anxious to make their public school system as independent as possible from Russian interference.

Secondary schools, which correspond roughly to American junior high schools and high schools and lead to entrance to the universities and technological colleges, have made great progress since the last war, attendance at them having more than doubled since 1939. A pupil may enter them from any grade above the fourth in the primary schools and their courses vary therefore from four to eight years.

Curiously enough, over half the pupils are enrolled in private secondary schools. There is a historical reason for this. Until near the end of the nineteenth century most of the state-supported high schools were Swedish-speaking. Thereafter there was a great deal of Russification of them. In order to give secondary education in Finnish, the Finnish-speaking population was compelled to found its own private schools. Today, however, their main financial support comes from the state.

Finland has five universities and nine other institutions of higher learning with a total attendance of 15,000 students, some 38 per cent of whom are women — the highest percentage of any country in the North. Helsinki University has 9000 students and a faculty of 1000 teachers, making it the largest university in Scandinavia.

Mention must be made here of special facilities for Finnish students to study in the United States. Most Americans are probably aware that Finland was the only European country after the first war which insisted on paying its war debt to America in full. Perhaps not so many remember that Congress passed a law in 1949 stipulating that the remaining payments of interest and amortization on that debt, which run until 1984, be spent on grants to Finnish citizens for study and training in the United States, and also for the purchase of American books and research equipment for Finnish libraries and scientific institutions, and for grants to American citizens for scientific work in Finland. Actually, almost all of the sum, which comes to half a million dollars a year, goes to defray the expenses of Finnish students for study in the United States.

There are two other types of education in Finland that deserve to be mentioned. Vocational schools number over 40, with 35,000 pupils, and though many of them are excellent Finnish educators frankly declare that there is much room for improvement.

But it is in adult education that the Finns, like the other northern peoples, excel. In Finland too, one gets the impression of a beehive of activity in the interest of continuing the education of those whose formal education has come to an end.

From Denmark came the Folk High Schools, chiefly boarding schools for rural youth, of which there are 81 in Finland with an annual enrollment of 4000.

Workers' education is even more extensive. There are 99 so-called Workers' Academies with an attendance of 40,000 students, most of them manual workers. The vast majority are night schools, since the pupils work during the day. But some of the best are regular boarding schools.

I drove out early one Saturday morning with Olavi Lindblom, the secretary-general of the Finnish Federation of Labor, to visit one of them at Kiljava, 25 miles north of Helsinki. This is known as the Trade-Union Institute and is maintained by the Federation with the help of state funds. Of pleasant, simple, modern architecture, it was

beautifully situated in a pine forest on the banks of a lake. The halls
and rooms were tastefully done in paneled birch and a number of good
modern paintings and sculptured works added to the décor. Since
most of the pupils — for this term they happened to be largely from
the Metal Workers' Union — come straight from noisy factories, one
object of the school, Lindblom explained, was to provide a serene and
esthetic atmosphere. Also because the majority of workers were de-
voting their vacations to taking a summer-school course, there was
recreation for them in the woods and on the lake after study hours.

Primarily this school is for promising young leaders in the trade-
union movement. The principal courses are in history, literature,
writing, public speaking, economics (including cost accounting) and
union practices and background. Only a union official educated in
such matters, Lindblom argued, is really competent to bargain intelligently with an employer and to get labor's viewpoint adequately heard in Parliament and government. In fact, the emphasis
of the trade-union movement on workers' education is remarkable.

The Institute at Kiljava holds two kinds of courses. One covers a
winter term of seven months. In the summer there are four terms of
one month each. In both cases the students board and room at the
institution. I sat in for a few minutes with a class to which Lindblom
was giving an hour's lecture on Finland's economic situation, the relations of prices, profits and wages, the problems of export, and so on.
The students were brawny men, with hard, alert faces, and they
busied themselves with taking notes and, after the lecture, with
earnestly popping questions, just as any students might do in a university classroom. Theoretically politics is barred at this school,
though since the Socialists ousted the Communists from the leading
positions in the Labor Federation they see to it, I gathered, that no
propaganda from Moscow is taught.

Under a special Workers' Academies Act of 1927, the state pays
half of the expenses of the 99 workers' schools.

Finally, there are in Finland some 2000 "study circles," with 30,-
000 members, which are partially financed by the state. A quarter of
them are run by the Workers' Cultural Union, an organization which
co-ordinates the educational program of organized labor. The two
largest correspondence schools in Finland boast 27,500 pupils between
them.

Education never seems to stop in Finland.

A Finnish Paradise

One cannot take leave of this remarkable little country without making at least mention of an institution which is peculiarly Finnish — the sauna. Everywhere I went in the countryside, farmers, land-lords, people with summer cottages and directors of such institutions as the Workers' Institute at Kiljava, showed me with pride their sauna — a log cabin, usually lying along a lake, which is specially constructed as a bathhouse.

The sauna, contrary to what I had imagined, is not a steam bath. It is not a Turkish bath. The Finnish bath is dry, though at one point in the process some steam is introduced by pouring water over stones which have been heated red hot on a primitive wood-burning furnace. The steam gives a momentarily pleasant tingling feeling to the skin, but is quickly absorbed by the wooden walls and ceiling of the sauna, so that the air remains dry. That is why temperatures as high as 280 degrees may be obtained, though the ideal heat, the Finnish experts say, is between 190 and 200 degrees.

The whole purpose of the Finnish bath is to induce perspiration. That is why the air is kept dry. The Finns say that when your skin drips in a Turkish bath it is not from perspiration but from the condensing of water on the surface of the skin.

There is quite a ritual to taking a bath in a log-cabin sauna. The late H. J. Viherjuuri, who wrote a learned book on the subject, listed eight principal phases in the following order: perspiration, producing steam, beating with birch leaves, washing, rinsing, cooling off, drying, rest and refreshment. To most Finns, cooling off means jumping into the snow, or, better still, into a hole in the ice in winter, or into the cool waters of a lake in the summer. Viherjuuri says that the moment of supreme enjoyment comes when one leaves the heat of the sauna and plunges into a hole in the ice. If a man goes to a public sauna in the city, by the way, the birch-beating and the soap-scrubbing which follows is done exclusively by women — which, considering one's state of nakedness, is at first somewhat embarrassing to some foreigners.

Many a Finn talked to me at length about the sauna's being an essential part of the way of life in Finland. It is more than just a means of getting clean, more even than a physical rejuvenation. It is a boon to the mind and the nerves as well, bringing a wonderful feeling of relaxation, a relief to nervous tension and worry. As one eminent Helsinki professor wrote: "The *sauna* banishes psychological troubles. In its heat, the mind is relieved of all pressure, and recovers its true balance. A man bowed down with worries may come out of its doors in a philosophical and even humorous frame of mind." And Nobel Prize-winning novelist Sillanpää contends that the sauna "inspires in men thoughts and feelings which they could never experience elsewhere." In fact, some of my Finnish friends compared the sauna to paradise.

In all of Finland there are half a million private sauna bathhouses — or one for every other family — and when the public saunas in the cities and towns are counted, it is estimated that nearly every person in the country regularly takes a sauna bath. Saturday is the great day for a sauna in the country. To a Finn it is a means of washing away the dirt and fatigue of a week's hard work and renewing himself in body and mind for the week which lies ahead.

What of the Future?

Though the Finns are a martial race, as they have shown in their centuries of wars with the Russians, the Peace Treaty of 1947 left them largely disarmed and therefore less able to defend themselves than at any time since they won their independence in 1918. The treaty limits Finland's total defense force to 41,900 men — 34,400 in the army, 4500 in the navy and 3000 in the air force. The last named is permitted to have only 60 planes, none of which may be bombers. Finland is forbidden by the treaty even to experiment with atomic weapons, guided missiles, non-contact mines and torpedoes, and she may not possess submarines. Actually, the Finns call up by conscription each year less men than they are entitled to; when I was in Finland the defense forces were 10,000 men under the treaty limit.

But the Finns do not lose any sleep over their defenselessness, or over their other handicaps and troubles, for that matter. One hears no whining and little complaining in Finland. Many persons there pointed out to me the advantage of being largely disarmed: the country can devote its wealth and productiveness to peacetime reconstruction and the welfare of the people.

They do not worry as much as most Westerners think they ought to over the fact that the Soviet Union is in a position today to gobble them up and destroy their splended civilization, with its democratic freedoms, any time the Kremlin feels like it. The Finns have learned to live for the day and not to trouble themselves unduly about the morrow. If you ask them, they will give you plenty of reasons why they do not believe Russia will swallow them up. They will tell you that Russia's rulers, beginning with the Czars (Nicholas II excepted) and continuing with Lenin and Stalin, always had a certain respect and even regard for the Finns which made them handle the country differently from others such as Poland, Romania and the Baltic nations. They will add that Stalin and Lenin and other old Bolsheviks were always grateful for the refuge they found in Finland during the days of their persecution. They are sure the Kremlin realizes that a satellite or annexed Finland would cause it far more trouble than an independent Finland. They believe that Moscow sees distinct advantages in a free, neutral Finland ensuring a neutral Sweden. Finally, they are confident that only the aggression of the Soviet army across their frontiers can make Finland Communist and satellite, and that the Russians know such a step would bring on a new world war.

So they go on building their free nation, as if it were as permanent as anything else in the precarious twentieth century. Out of their struggle with a cruel climate and their experience of eight centuries of foreign domination and war, they have evolved an infinite capacity to endure. They call it *sisu*, and it has given them their granite character, as hard as the granite layer of rock which lies but a few feet under the soil of Finland.

To some outside it may seem a poor and forbidding and frozen land. But to the Finns it has great loveliness and color: the deep green of pine and spruce against the pure white of winter, and in the summer, as Professor Wuorinen has put it, the silvery lakes, the sparkling sea "and verdant fields ringed by forests, in the softer greens of the days when the sun stands high in the heavens and hardly sets for weeks on end. Not a land of grandeur but of quiet, clean beauty that touches the heart and elevates the mind."

That the Finns will preserve it, free and decent and democratic, as one of the four lands of Northern Europe which, as we have seen in these pages, have added more than their share to Western Christian civilization, there can be little doubt.

Appendix

Acknowledgments

A good many generous and thoughtful persons helped in the making of this book.

TOR MYKLEBOST, of the Norwegian Embassy in Washington and an author of note, is perhaps first among them. Abetted by JOHN C. METCALFE, my lecture agent, he first proposed the trip to the northern countries and then arranged it, and he was of immense help in the gathering of information about his native land. PAUL R. REYNOLDS, my literary agent, first suggested the possibility of doing the book should the journey turn up sufficient material.

LITHGOW OSBORNE, an old friend, who had been United States Ambassador to Norway and who is now the president of the American-Scandinavian Foundation, opened many doors in the Scandinavian countries and proferred much good advice. ALLAN KASTRUP, head of the New York office of the American-Swedish News Exchange, was tireless in checking my facts about Sweden and in helping with much of the research. Also of aid in respect to Sweden were SVEN AHMAN, New York correspondent of Stockholm's *Dagens Nyheter*, SVEN BACKLUND, of the Swedish Embassy in Washington, and MRS. BRITTA AMENDOLA.

HENRIK KAUFFMANN, Danish Ambassador in Washington, who played a heroic role in his country's affairs after it was overrun by the Nazi armies, arranged numerous meetings in Denmark with persons of every class and party and also helped me to obtain a great deal of new material about his country. C. H. W. HASSELRIIS, of the Danish Information Office in New York, ably supplemented his help. The AMBASSADOR OF NORWAY and the AMBASSADOR OF SWEDEN in Washington and the MINISTER OF FINLAND also gave me the benefit of their counsel, and MAX JAKOBSON, the scholarly press secretary of the Finnish legation, put his fine mind to helping me to unravel the story of modern Finland.

None of these persons, official or unofficial, nor indeed those in the four countries themselves whom I shall mention, are to be held responsible either for the opinions and judgments expressed in this book, or for its mistakes and shortcomings. For these, the author bears the sole responsibility.

I sought out hundreds of persons in the northern countries, and I collected several trunkfuls of documentary material. The listing of the latter would be of interest only to specialists; the complete listing of the former, to whom I owe a debt of gratitude for the information and understanding they gave me, would fill several pages.

Among them were, in Norway: KING HAAKON VII; HALVARD LANGE, the Foreign Minister; ERIK BROFOSS, the then Minister of Commerce and now President of the Bank of Norway; GUNNAR JAHN, his predecessor as President of the Bank of Norway; KONRAD NORDAHL, head of the Norwegian Federation of Labor; HAAKON LIE, secretary-general of the NORWEGIAN LABOR PARTY; PER MONSEN, associate editor of *Arbeiderbladet;* DR. KARL EVANG, the dynamic head of the Public Health Service; SIGURD SKANGEN and CHRISTIAN OSTBERG, both shipowners; THOMAS TORSVIK, foreign editor of the *Bergens Tidende;* DR. OTTO MOHR and DR. FREDE CASTBERG, former and present chancellors respectively of the University of Oslo; PROFESSOR SIGMUND SKARD, of the American Institute of Olso University; PHILIP BOARDMAN, an American on the university faculty and an authority on the Norwegian language dispute; FRANCES BULL, literary critic and professor of literature at the university; SIGURD HOEL, one of Norway's finest novelists; TRYGVE LIE, former Secretary-General of the United Nations; HANS OLAV, Norwegian Minister to Finland; ARNE HAUGLAND and JON EMBRETSEN of the Foreign Office; FINN MOE, editor, and head of the Foreign Relations Committee of the Storting; MRS. INGRID SEMMINGSEN, authority on Norwegian emigration to America; and MRS. CARLOTA FRAHM, the literary agent.

The then American Ambassador, CHARLES U. BAY, and several members of the Embassy staff, generously co-operated with me in my quest for material. Among them were: NORMAN NORDSTRAND, T. C. TORLAND, EUGENE C. MARTINSON, ROSS WHITMAN, GORDON MIEN, LLOYD LARSON and MARK LEISERSON.

In Sweden, I have to thank first of all MAC LINDAHL, of the Swedish-American News Exchange, who with an efficiency and drive that was truly formidable arranged for me to see scores of persons and probe into every aspect of Swedish life. TURID LINDAHL, his wife, aided him — and me.

Others in Sweden who gave me the benefit of their wisdom and who helped me to find the documentary material I needed included: PROFESSOR HERBERT TINGSTEN, editor in chief of the Stockholm *Dagens Nyheter;* ANDERS YNGVE PERS, editor in chief of one of the leading provincial dailies, *Vestmanlands Läns Tidning* of Västerås, a sort of William Allen White of Sweden; CARL-ADAM NYCOP, editor in chief of *Expressen*, who has a fabulous reputation in Sweden for successfully founding new publications; NILS THEDIN, editor in chief of the co-operative weekly *Vi*, which has the largest circulation of any publication in the country; TORE BROWALDH, a director of the Swedish Employers' Federation and head of Sweden's largest bank; PROFESSOR ERIK DAHMÉN, of the Stockholm School of Economics and the Enskilda Bank; PROFESSOR ERIK LUNDBERG, head of the Institute of Economic Research; ROLF VON HEIDENSTAM, one-time President of the International Chamber of Commerce, Chairman of the Board of the great AGA enterprise and of the *Svenska Handels-banken;* DR. HAROLD NORDENSON, President, and OLOF LEFFLER, Managing Director, of the Stockholm Chamber of Commerce; ÅKE VRETHEM, Managing Director of the vast ASEA enterprise; LARS AKSELSSON, head of the Swedish Taxpayers' Association; GÖSTA REHN and GUNNAR DAHLANDER, of the Swedish Federation of Labor.

Also: LIEUTENANT GENERAL BENGT NORDENSKIÖLD, then Commander in Chief of the Swedish Air Force; MAJOR GENERAL RICHARD ÅKERMAN, Chief of the Defense Staff; ARNE LUNDBERG, permanent Undersecretary of State at the Foreign Office; OLOF RYDBECK, Chief of the Foreign Office Press Section; STIG DAGERMAN, novelist and playwright, and his wife, ANITA BJÖRK, the actress; TELL DAHLLÖF, editor in chief of the magazine *Industria;* JACK FLEISCHER, the American journalist now residing in Stockholm; MRS. LENA GEDIN, the literary agent; and DR. HERBERT NATHORST, physician.

Among those in the American Embassy who gave me freely of their time and counsel were: WARE ADAMS, MARSHALL GREEN, MERLE M. WERNER and LLOYD WHITE.

In Denmark, MISS VIBEKE IACOBSEN and POUL LINNEBALLE, of the Foreign Office, were indefatigable in guiding me about the country. In Copenhagen I spent a most enlightening afternoon with NIELS BOHR, a Nobel Prize atomic physicist who escaped from the Nazis to help the United States develop the first atom bomb, and who is possessed of one of the most stimulating minds I have ever encountered.

THORKILD KRISTENSEN, then Minister of Finance and currently chairman of the Agrarian-Liberal party, was extremely helpful, as was OLE BJÖRN KRAFT, the then Foreign Minister and for many years President of the Conservative Party. To my great regret, Hans Hedtoft, the Labor Party leader and present Prime Minister, was ill during my stay in Denmark, but I was able to see some of his colleagues such as JENS OTTO KRAG, former Minister of Commerce and, at this writing, Minister without Portfolio.

EILER JENSEN, the genial head of the Danish Federation of Labor, was a fountain of information regarding the trade-union movement, and willing officials of the Employers' Federation gave me a picture of management's views. EDWARD TESDORPH, owner of one of the largest estates in Denmark and a conservative member of Parliament, was one of many gracious hosts and a mine of information about agricultural developments. The number of medium and small farmers I dropped in on, as well as the numerous managers of their co-operative dairies and slaughterhouses, were too numerous to list by name, but I learned much from them about the country's greatest enterprise.

JOHN DANSTRUP, a young historian, filled me in on much background, in regard to both current and past events, and JÖRGEN BUDTZ-JÖRGENSEN, a literary critic and translator, was not only a frequent and generous host but an inexhaustible source of information about the literary and cultural life of Denmark. At his suburban villa I met, among others, our own FRANCIS HACKETT, who now lives outside Copenhagen and talks and writes in as lively a way about his adopted land (which is his wife's native land) as he has in the past about so many other subjects.

Among others in Denmark who brought me much light were: THOMAS VOLLQUARTZ, secretary of the Society of Authors; HANS HENRIK KOCH, Director of the Ministry of Social Affairs; NILS SVENNINGSEN, Director of the Ministry for Foreign Affairs, CARL OTTO HENRIQUES, head of the banking firm of that name; Captain EMIL LASSEN; SVEN IRGENS HANSEN, of the Agricultural Council; and the chief editors of Copenhagen's daily newspaper *Politiken.*

American Embassy officials who were most co-operative included: JOHN O. BELL, Chargé d'Affaires, WILLIAM G. ROLL, LUCIUS D. BATTLE, MICHAEL WEYL, JAMES GANTENBEIN, WILLIAM R. DUGGAN, and ROBERT CALDWELL.

In Finland, HEIKKI LEPPO and MISS VERA SIRKEINEN, of the Foreign Office, were tireless in guiding me about, arranging interviews and helping to assemble material.

Among others in Finland who were most helpful were: URHO K. KEKKONEN, veteran leader of the Agrarian party and then Prime Minister; YRJO LESKINEN, leader of the Social-Democrats and Minister of Interior; VÄINO TANNER, former Socialist leader and Foreign Minister; ELJAS ERKKO, former Foreign Minister and editor and publisher of *Helsingin Sanomat,* Finland's greatest daily newspaper; OLAVI LINDBLOM, Secretary General of the Federation of Labor, V. KOLJONEN, of the Employers' Federation; Y. LEHTINEN, economist and presently Finnish Consul-General in New York; and MRS. V. KORTE, museum curator.

JACK McFALL, the American Minister, and several members of his excellent Legation staff were most helpful, among the latter being: BART WELLS, WILLIAM BARNES, WILLIAM H. WITT and JOHN LUND.

Bibliographical Material

Most of the material in this book derives from impressions, interviews, documents and the study of a mountain of official and nonofficial reports which I obtained in the northern lands.

For general background, a number of books were especially helpful, but there is space here to list only a few: *The United States and Scandinavia*, by Franklin D. Scott, Harvard University Press, Cambridge, Mass., 1950; *Scandinavia: Between East and West*, edited by Henning Friis, Cornell University Press, Ithaca, N. Y., 1950; *The Democratic Monarchies of Scandinavia*, by Ben A. Arneson, Van Nostrand Co., New York, N. Y., 1949; *The Northern Tangle*, by Rowland Kenney, Dent, London, Eng.; *Sweden — the Middle Way*, by Marquis Childs, Yale University Press, New Haven, Conn., 1936; *Language Feuds in Norway*, by Philip Boardman, Aschehoug, Oslo, 1952; *A History of Norway*, by Karen Larsen, Princeton University Press, Princeton, N. J., 1948; *Norwegian Migration to America, 1825-1860*, by Theo. Blegen, Norwegian-American Hist. Assn., Northfield, Minn., 1931; *Labor in Norway*, by Walter Galenson, Harvard University Press, Cambridge, Mass., 1949; *They Came as Friends*, by Tor Myklebost, Doubleday & Co., Inc., New York, N. Y., 1943; *Co-operatives in Norway*, by O. B. Grimley, the Co-operative Union and Wholesale Society, Oslo, 1950; *Introduction to Sweden*, by Ingvar Andersson and others, the Swedish Institute, Stockholm, Sweden, 1951; *The Making of Sweden*, by Allan Kastrup, the American-Swedish News Exchange, New York, 1953; *Social Sweden*, published by the Social Welfare Board, Stockholm, 1952; *Co-operative Sweden Today*, by J. W. Ames, The Co-operative Union Ltd., Manchester, England; *Industrial Relations in Sweden*, by Charles A. Myers, Massachusetts Institute of Technology, Cambridge, Mass., 1951; *Debate on the Foreign Policy of Sweden*, by Professor Herbert Tingsten, Oxford University Press, New York, N. Y., 1949.

Also: *A History of Denmark*, by John Danstrup, Wivels Forlag, Copenhagen, 1949; *Living Democracy in Denmark*, by Peter Manniche, G.E.C. Gad, Copenhagen, 1952; *The Danish System of Labor Relations*, by Walter Galenson, Harvard University Press, Cambridge, 1952; *Freedom and Welfare — Social Patterns in the Northern Countries of Europe*, edited by George R. Nelson, published by the Ministries of Social Affairs of Denmark, Finland, Iceland, Norway, Sweden, 1953; *Finland — The Adventures of a Small Power,* by Hugh Shearman, Stevens & Sons, London, 1950; *Social Denmark — A Survey of Danish Social Legislation,* Socialt Tidsskrift, Copenhagen, 1945; *Denmark During the German Occupation,* edited by Børge Outze, The Scandinavian Publishing Co., Copenhagen, 1946; *Contemporary Danish Authors,* published by Det Danske Selskab, Copenhagen, 1952; *Finland,* by J. Hampden Jackson, The Macmillan Co., New York, N. Y., 1940; *Green, Gold and Granite,* by Wendy Hall, Max Parrish, London, 1953; *The Memoirs of Marshal Mannerheim,* E. P. Dutton & Co., Inc., New York, N. Y., 1954; *Finland and World War II,* edited by John Wuorinen, New York, N. Y., 1948. The Ronald Press Company.

The governments of all four countries publish annually excellent *Statistical Yearbooks,* which I have used freely to check my facts and figures. Various semiprivate groups, such as the Danish Society, publish informative and up-to-date handbooks on many aspects of life in the northern lands.

Finally, with the aid of my wife, who reads the Scandinavian languages, I have gone through a sizable file of current newspapers and periodicals.

Index

Elsinore, Denmark, 249-250
Elverum, Norway, 37
Embassies, Finns invite establishment of, 365
Emden, 36
Emigration to United States, 12-13, 110-112, 383
Employers' and Labor Federations, Sweden, 132
Employment, full, in Sweden, problems and drawbacks of, 185-186; enjoyment of, 189
Enbom, Fritiof, 134, 136-137
Enckell, Carl, 347, 353
Engineers, Swedish, 131, 133
England, 226, 245, 281, 291. *See also* Great Britain.
Enterprise councils, Swedish labor-management, 183
"Equitable Society of Rochedale Pioneers," 81
Eric the Red, 290
Eriksen, Erik, 279, 281, 294
Erkko, Elias, 325, 395
Erlander, Tage, 137-138, 142, 190, 197
Eronen, Ella, 393
ERP, 189
Esbjerg, Denmark, 249
Espionage, Soviet, 27, 134, 196; Danish, 235; trials, in Sweden, 134, 136-138
Estonia, 299, 301, 327, 335
Ethyl alcohol, 164
Eugen, Prince, of Sweden, 201
European Payments Union, 255
Evacuation, Finnish, of Germans from Finland, 352-353
Evang, Dr. Karl, 64-65, 67; on sickness insurance, 67-68
Evening schools, Workers' Educational Movement, Denmark, 249
Exchange, engineer, labor leader, industrialist and student, 24; of goods, 25
Explorers, Norwegian, 104-105, 213; Swedish, 114
Export societies, Danish co-operative, 243
Export-Import Bank, 364
Exports, Norway's, 56; Sweden's, 121, 165; United States' to Sweden, 190; Denmark's, 220-221, 243, 245, 252-254; Finland's, 323, 362-365

FACTORY COMMITTEES, FINNISH, 375
Fagerholm, Karl August, 369
Family allowance, in Norway, 69; in Finland, 383-384; holidays, in Norway, 71; in Sweden, 149-150
Family and child welfare, in Finland, 383-384, 386-387; child and family allowances, 383-384; maternity aid, 386; home aid, 386; child welfare, 386-387; care of wayward children, 387
Family and child welfare, in Denmark, 260-261; maternity aid, 260; Child Welfare Committees, 260; illegitimate children, 260-261; Danish law and child care, 261
Family and child welfare, in Norway, 68-70; purpose of, 68-69; progress since war, 69; family allowance, 69; practical measures of, 69-72
Family and child welfare, in Sweden, 145-146, 148-151; purpose of, 148-149; marriage inducements, 149; practical measures of, 149-151
Famine, in Sweden, 112
Farm loans in Sweden, 175-176
Farm mechanization, Norwegian, 55
Farmer-consumer conflict in Sweden, 176-177
Farmers, Danish, make soil fertile, 242; ingenuity and skill of, 243; genius for co-operation, 243-247; own and run own farms, 244-245; profit from Marshall Plan aid, 245; most highly organized in world, 246-247; education of, 247-250; Finnish, 314-315, 323, 376, 381-383; intolerable condition of, 314; Land Purchase Act helps, 315; in depression of 1930's, 323; financial aid to, 381
Farmers' co-operatives, 56, 83, 167, 174-177, 221, 243-247, 382-383
Farmers' Federation, Swedish, 177
Farmers' Union, Swedish, 177
Farming, Norwegian, 55-56; Swedish, 111, 163, 166-167, 175-177; collective, 176; Danish, 220-222, 242-247, 253; co-operative, 243-247; Finnish, 380-383; discouraging business, 381
Farms, Swedish, 176; Danish, 242-247; Finnish, 314-315, 356-357; output per acre on typical, 315; Finnish, 380-383

state, 66-67; philosophy behind, 67; attitude of physicians toward, 68

Health insurance system, Swedish, 143-146; compulsory, 143; benefits, 143-144; cost to individual, 144-145; supplementary, 144; administration of, 145; attitude of physicians toward, 145; industrial accidents and occupational diseases, 147

Health services, Finnish, 384-385; expenditure for, 384; medical care, 384-385; hospitalization, 384; municipal doctors, 384; advantages of health insurance plan without some of disadvantages, 384-385

Hedin, Sven, 114
Hedlund, Gunnar, 137
Hedtoft, Hans, 287, 293-295
Heinrichs, Erik, 337-339
Helsingen Sanomat, 395
Helsinki, Finland, 8, 26, 297, 306, 317, 318, 320, 322, 325, 336-366 *passim*, 371, 385, 387; bombing of, 330, 340; Akateeminen Kirjakauppa, 395
Helsinki City Symphony Orchestra, 297
Helsinki University, Helsinki, 300, 311, 355
Hemingway, Ernest, 210
Herring, 59-60
Hiawatha, 300
High schools. See Folk High Schools. See also Danish Labor High Schools.
Highways, Norwegian, 30
Hirschfeldt, Lennart, 127
Hitler, Adolf, 17, 19, 31, 35, 37, 39, 41-44, 48, 117-118, 120, 123, 136, 202, 210, 216, 223, 227-228, 230, 235, 295, 323, 327, 329, 336, 338, 340, 349, 353; visits Mannerheim, 345; Mannerheim's moving letter to, 350-351
Hitler-Stalin Pact of August, 1939, 116
Hoel, Sigurd, 96
Høffding, Harald, 275
Hogland (Sursaari) island of, 325, 352
Holberg, Ludvig, 97, 99
Holiday Act, Danish, 268
Holidays, 71, 149-150, 268. See also Family holidays.
Holland, 226
Holmenkollen, 95
Holstein, 218

Holsti, Rudolf, 324
Home front, Norwegian, 44, 46; Guard, Norwegian, 108; Swedish, 128; for aged, in Denmark, 259; aid, Finnish, 386; Sisters (nurses) in Finland, 386
Hopper, Bruce, 119, 120
Horse breeders, Danish, 247
Horten, Norway, 36
Hospitality and friendliness, Danish, 244
Hospitalization, in Norway, 65-66; in Denmark, 258; in Finland, 384
Hospitals in Finland, 384
Housewife Relief Service, Norway, 70-71
Housewives' holidays, in Norway, 71; in Sweden, 149
Housing, Danish, 263-265; financing, 263-264; co-operatives, 263-265; role of Housing Ministry in, 263; private builders, 264; rents, 264; apartment buildings, 264-265; one-family homes, 265
Housing, Finnish, 386; postwar shortage of, 355, 386; subsidies, 383, 386
Housing, Norwegian, 76-81; problem of, 76-77; role of government in, 77-78; financing, 77-79; rent, 78; Housing Directorate, 79; co-operatives, 79-81
Housing, Swedish, 110, 149, 157-161; urban overcrowding, 157; dominant type of apartment, 158; rents, 158, 161; co-operatives, 158-161; apartment buildings, 160; financing, 160; public aid for, 160-161
Housing Directorate, Norwegian, 79
HSB (Tenants' Savings and Building Society), Swedish, 79, 158-159
HTK (Confederation of Intellectual Workers), Finnish, 374
Hull, Cordell, 230, 232-233, 291, 345, 349
Humiliation, Danish national, 218-219
Hunger rations, Finnish postwar, 355
Hvelte, Denmark, 226
Hydroelectric power, Norwegian, 29, 51, 56; Swedish, 130, 133, 162; Finnish, 355, 377
Hydrogen bomb, 213, 292
Hysteria, absence of, 27

IBSEN, HENRIK, 31, 96-97, 99